HARVESTING DEVELOPMENT

HARVESTING DEVELOPMENT
THE CONSTRUCTION OF FRESH FOOD MARKETS
IN PAPUA NEW GUINEA

Karl Benediktsson

Ann Arbor
THE UNIVERSITY OF MICHIGAN PRESS

Copyright © Karl Benediktsson 2002
All rights reserved
Published in the United States of America by
The University of Michigan Press

2005   2004   2003   2002   4 3 2 1

First published in Denmark by
Nordic Institute of Asian Studies

Printed in Singapore

No part of this publication may be reproduced, stored
in a retrieval system, or transmitted in any form or by
any means, electronic, mechanical, or otherwise,
without the written permission of the publisher.

Library of Congress Cataloging-in-Publication Data

Benediktsson, Karl.
    Harvesting development : the construction of fresh food markets in
Papua New Guinea / Karl Benediktsson.
    p.   cm.
    Revision of the author's thesis (Ph.D.)—Australian National University,
Canberra. 1997.
    Includes bibliographical references and index.
    ISBN 0-472-09800-4 (cloth : alk. paper)—ISBN 0-472-06800-8 (pbk. : alk. paper)
    1. Food supply—Papua New Guinea.   2. Farm produce—Papua New Guinea.
I. Title.

HD9018.P363 B46   2001
381'.456413'009953—dc21   2001041476

Contents

Illustrations ... vi
Tables ... viii
Vignettes ... viii
Acknowledgements ... ix
Abbreviations ... xii
1   Introduction ... 1
2   Markets, commoditization, and actors: spacious concepts ... 22
3   Faces in the crowd: Lives and networks of selected actors ... 54
4   Fresh food movements in a fragmented national economy ... 81
5   Fresh food markets, their history and operation in the Eastern Highlands Province ... 118
6   The travelling tuber: Kaukau and its commoditization ... 153
7   Economic dimensions, daily practice, and social networks in the long-distance trade ... 187
8   Locality, land, and labour: Processes of production in Lunube ... 223
9   Harvesting development through the market? Actors, theory, and practice ... 266

Glossary ... 277
List of botanical terms ... 279
References ... 281
Index ... 302

Illustrations

MAPS
1 Papua New Guinea ... 6
2 Eastern Highlands Province and the Asaro Valley ... 7
3 The territory of Lunube ... 10
4 Resource extraction projects ... 85
5 Urban centres ... 90
6 Goroka ... 93
7 Staple crops ... 106
8 Major cash crops ... 107
9 Major interregional flows of fresh food ... 113
10 Main market gardening areas in Eastern Highlands Province ... 129
11 Land types in the Lunube territory ... 225
12 Movements of Lunube groups since about 1930 ... 227
13 Main food garden of Gumineve and Kondagule ... 235
14 Main food garden of Moroho and Nesime ... 237
15 Main food garden of Moses and Soni ... 238

PLATES
1 Kasena from the air ... 12
2 Kasena from the ground ... 14
3 Carrots brought for sale at ADF, Goroka ... 135
4 From Goroka market ... 142
5 From the market at Asaro ... 143
6 Saina at the main market in Lae ... 199
7 Carriers on the way from garden to roadhead ... 201
8 Lae-bound truck loading kaukau ... 203
9 Urban market traders attempting to buy kaukau ... 218
10 Woman harvesting marketable kaukau tubers ... 233
11 *Taim bilong kopi* ... 242
12 Man handing out pork at a mortuary exchange ceremony ... 247
13 Man tending kaukau garden ... 252
14 Tractor tilling land for kaukau ... 254

FIGURES
1 Social groupings in Lunube from the perspective of the Gamizuho ... 13
2 Gumineve – household and next of kin ... 57
3 Kondagule – household and next of kin ... 58
4 Gumineve and Kondagule – social networks ... 62
5 Moroho – household and next of kin ... 64
6 Nesime – household and next of kin ... 65
7 Moroho and Nesime – social networks ... 66
8 Moses – household and next of kin ... 69
9 Soni – household and next of kin ... 70
10 Moses and Soni – social networks ... 71
11 Expenditure on food, drink, and stimulants in urban areas ... 102
12 Most important crops sold at ADF's depot in Goroka ... 128
13 Monthly shipments of kaukau from Lae to Port Moresby, and prices received by coffee growers ... 189
14 Kaukau retail prices in three urban areas, 1971–95 ... 192
15 Kaukau prices in various marketplaces, 1995 ... 195
16 Gender division of kaukau sellers in different types of markets ... 197
17 Land cover on the fan east of the main *hauslain* at Kasena ... 249

Tables

1 Selected Papua New Guinean economic indicators ... 83
2 Dominant staples and population in the agricultural systems ... 104
3 Produce sold at ADF's depot in Goroka, 8 May to 7 June 1995 ... 130
4 Examples of wholesale buying price, marketplace price, and retail price ... 133
5 Marketplaces: no. of sellers and items sold ... 141
6 Returns from sales trips from Kasena to four different markets ... 196
7 Plots managed by Gumineve and Kondagule ... 234
8 Plots managed by Moroho and Nesime ... 236
9 Plots managed by Moses and Soni ... 239
10 Population, land, and basic demographic parameters ... 258

Vignettes

1 Show *bisnis* – the commoditization of culture ... 87
2 A voice of moderation ... 97
3 Jesus in the marketplace ... 146
4 It's a truck's life ... 209
5 Nasty surprises ... 211
6 Oral accounts of the origins of the Gamizuho people ... 229
7 *'Ol i no wanbel'* ... 261

Acknowledgements

EM I NO ISI (It Is Not Easy) was the title of a song by Papua New Guinean popular musician, Basil Greg, that dominated the country's Top Ten for a long time during my fieldwork in 1994–95. It frequently emanated from my neighbour Tevi's tradestore, which may explain why it is still popping up in my head every now and then. In any case, the title of this song well sums up the task facing me when expressing my gratitude to all those who have contributed to the completion of this book: *Em i no isi*.

The book is a reincarnation of a PhD dissertation completed in 1997 at the Australian National University (ANU) in Canberra. The study was made possible by an ANU PhD Scholarship. A preliminary trip to Papua New Guinea was made under the auspices of the Land Management Project of the ANU, whereas the main part of fieldwork was financed by the Department of Human Geography. During fieldwork I was affiliated with the Department of Agriculture and Livestock (DAL) in Port Moresby. I am grateful to the director of its Research Division, Balthazar Wayi, for his assistance.

Sue Holzknecht in Canberra led me the first faltering steps into the world of Tok Pisin – a language that I soon learned to love. David and Gladys Strange in Sydney, previously long-term residents of Kasena, shared some of their extensive knowledge of the Dano language and local culture.

My thanks to the Gamizuho people of Kasena, and to the other Lunube people whose daily lives were subject to my curiosity, would not fit in a single *bilum*, even if those remarkable string bags are known for their capacity to expand. Only a few names can be mentioned. Very special thanks are due to Rex and Nellynne, who let me use their house, and who taught me so many things. So did Gumineve and Kondagule, Moroho and Nesime, Moses and Soni, Michael and Benaso, Steven and Monika, and Lulu. I likewise thank my next-door neighbours for their joviality, stories, and frequent gifts of food: Guhize, Agnes, Omau, Mikasimo. Garuhe, David, and Steven Gumulihe acted as occasional fieldwork assistants in Lunube. Hirengove and Maria, George, Megi, Gorumaru … the list is potentially endless. I have to revert to collectivities: to those of Kasena yet unnamed, as well as the people of Openga, Aladuka, Roka, Nahoma, Kenemba, Pikosa, Asaro, Kofika: *Tenkyu tru, olgeta.*

In Goroka, I was fortunate to cross paths with Michael Hughes at DAL. His willingness to talk about issues that bothered and/or puzzled me was much appreciated, as was his seemingly boundless hospitality. The same could be said about Michael Alpers and Deborah Lehmann at the PNG Institute of Medical Research. Big thanks also to Barry Combs and Anne Baird, Ranjan Deb, Gerard Stapleton, and many other temporary or permanent citizens of multicultural Goroka.

In Aiyura, assistance was gained from Mathew Kanua at DAL's Highlands Agricultural Experiment Station, and his staff. I also benefited from discussion with Roger Selby at the Coffee Research Institute. The staff of the Fresh Produce Development Company assisted me in many ways, in particular Michael Daysh in Mt. Hagen and Maxie Dominic in Port Moresby. I am also grateful to staff at the various fresh food trading firms and other institutions, who tolerated my nosiness and supplied information. A generous dose of thanks also to Diane Lloyd, and to Flip van Helden and Inger Stocking, who kindly put up with me for some time towards the end of my fieldwork in Madang and Port Moresby respectively. Margaret Aparo was another invaluable contact in the capital, as were Wasi and Moruwo Domai.

Turning to the ANU's Department of Human Geography, thanks are due to all and sundry: technicians and other general staff, fellow students, and academics. Few shall be named, certainly nobody is forgotten. Above all I thank Bryant Allen, who supervised the dissertation research. Michael Bourke provided valuable advice, as well as frequent excuses to go camping. I also benefited from the advice and editorial experience of Gerard Ward. Last but not least, I want to mention Robin Hide, who advised me at the beginning, but then fell seriously ill when on fieldwork himself in Papua New Guinea. Having returned to his usual enthusiastic self, he resumed his advisory capacity for my study, albeit informally. In the latter part of the writing period he was particularly generous with his extensive ethnographic knowledge and his keen literary sense.

During post-dissertation times I have continued to clock up debts. A grant from the Nordic Institute of Asian Studies made it possible to stay in Copenhagen for a period in 2000 to work on the manuscript. NIAS provided a congenial environment in which to work. Special thanks go to director Per Ronnås, for constructive criticism and encouragement, as well as to Gerald Jackson and Andrea Straub for seeing the project through to publication. Several anonymous reviewers of the manuscript provided valuable comments. My colleagues at the University of Iceland have also been of great help.

ACKNOWLEDGEMENTS

Finally, during years of preoccupation with things Papua New Guinean, the tolerance and patience of Gerður Sif Hauksdóttir and Sölvi Karlsson must be duly acknowledged. These years have not always been *isi*, but I hope they have also taught us a few things. And learning is *swit moa yet*.

Abbreviations

ADF	Associated Distributors Freezer
AIDAB	Australian International Development Assistance Bureau (now AusAID)
ANU	Australian National University
AVDA	Arona Valley Development Authority
AWRDC	Asaro–Watabung Rural Development Corporation
AWRDT	Asaro–Watabung Rural Development Trust
CIC	Coffee Industry Corporation
CPI	Consumer Price Index
DAL	Department of Agriculture and Livestock
DASF	Department of Agriculture, Stock and Fisheries
DPI	Development of Primary Industry
EBC	Evangelical Brothers' Church
FMC	Food Marketing Corporation
FPDC	Fresh Produce Development Company
KKD	Kuru Katope Dealers
KKF	Kuru Kesgo Farm
LGC	Local Government Council
LMC	Lowa Marketing Cooperative
LMP	Land Management Project (of ANU)
MFVP	Marketed Fruit and Vegetables Project
NSO	National Statistical Office
PMV	Public Motor Vehicle
PNG	Papua New Guinea
PNGBC	Papua New Guinea Banking Corporation
PNGRIS	Papua New Guinea Resource Information System
PTC	Post and Telecommunication Corporation
RMU	Resource Mapping Unit (in PNGRIS)
SDA	Seventh Day Adventist
UPNG	University of Papua New Guinea

1

Introduction

THIS BOOK TELLS A STORY of rural people and edible things, of networks which link these to other people and things, and of the local transformation wrought through the construction of such linkages. It is about attempts to harvest development by engaging with the phenomenon of the market, through participation in fresh food trade.

The collision between the world economy and specific places is a topic that currently occupies centre stage in social science. And for good reason: global interconnections – of economic, cultural, or other kinds – are more visible than ever before. Has the local dimension of social and economic life thereby been completely overwhelmed by global forces? Has place been subsumed by space? The 'end of geography'? Not so. An array of local trajectories of change can be observed. Places are not obliterated by globalization of economic relations and space–time convergence; rather they are transformed. Hence, the attention of social scientists is increasingly directed towards the actual links which stitch the global and the local together into a contiguous, if not coherent or uniform, spatial fabric (Gregory 1994a; Long 1996; Appadurai 1997). This is, in the broadest of terms, the issue which this study seeks to address: how the transformation of a locality, through processes of economic and social development, is embedded in worlds which extend way beyond the locality itself.

At the heart of rural transformation, especially in the context of a developing country, is the increasing involvement of agricultural producers in markets, be they local, regional, national, or international commodity markets. Through market integration, most rural societies have undergone irreversible changes in social relations, land management, and geographic organization, albeit at different points in time, and with widely varying outcomes.

The setting is Papua New Guinea: a country that certainly offers a window on to the processes of rural change – in fact many different windows. It is currently undergoing a rapid but uneven transformation, which affects both rural and urban areas. The political economy of the modern state and the contrivances of international markets have combined to draw local people into the orbit of national and global processes, as producers of marketed commodities, and as consumers of goods and services. They have long obtained income from cash crops, but in addition, new and often indirect links are now being forged with the world economy through transnational mining corporations and logging companies. Urban demand for food is increasing rapidly in tandem with the increased amounts of money which circulate through the national economy and the steady inflow of migrants into the towns. All this translates into change at the level of the rural village, in which the development of fresh food marketing plays a substantial part. Local idiosyncrasies in marketing arrangements beg questions, and seem related more to the creativity of individuals and to what happens in their face-to-face interactions with each other, than to any global dictation. In sum, rural development of Papua New Guinea is complex and uneven. The book is concerned with the way in which the country's fresh food markets have been and are being constructed, and the part this plays in reshaping its rural landscapes and rural societies.

Already an interesting contradiction is emerging in the narrative. External structures or global forces, determining people's options, are posited against free-willed and independent local people, doing their own thing. Villagers are autonomous, at the same time as they are caught up in a web of national and global relations. The challenge is to tell the story without emphasizing either the rigidity of structure at the expense of the free-willed individual, or vice versa. This is a situation faced by anyone who studies rural change (and, for that matter, anyone who studies the social world). Universalist descriptions of (or prescriptions for) rural development, so common in the development discourse of the last decades, have lost their lustre. Few consider themselves able to talk about 'modernization' any more without at least some caveats about the limitation of that concept, and neither is it possible these days to proffer 'modes of production' as a wholesale explanation of reality without blushing. At the same time, unbridled voluntarism and localism are hardly tenable: it would be absurd to suggest that the daily deeds of the celebrated individual are not

INTRODUCTION

influenced by supra-local forces and structures of state and capital in a variety of ways.

SOME GUIDING CONCEPTS

A good part of the book can be read as an attempt to play with these opposites. Three notions serve as *Leitmotifs*. The first is that most hazy and hazardous of words: *the market*. A concept of ancient origin, but out of which much mileage continues to be made by structuralists and voluntarists alike, its assumptions are usually left unexposed. Second, I enlist the concept of *commoditization*, which has indeed long been a staple of social theorists dealing with rural transformation. If universality can be detected in the world's myriad economic processes, it is perhaps best expressed by this word. The third concept is that of the *actor*, the social individual who has an uncanny knack of twisting current events so that universal processes take on novel appearances – and so cease to be universal. I shall make use of this conceptual troika throughout the text. It is appropriate at this stage to give a rudimentary summary of the main arguments.

A critical questioning of the concept of *the market* is central to the project. A word burdened with a long and colourful history, it is often used and interpreted in universalistic terms. The epitome of market universalism is found among the latter-day *laissez-faire* ideologues, with their sometimes blanket prescriptions for 'opening up the market', 'giving the market a freer rein', and similar solutions. Such theories first had their day during the reign of modernization theory some four decades ago, then temporarily lost some of their authority only to reemerge with a vengeance in many Western countries during the neo-liberal (or neo-conservative?) 1980s. Revamped, they were promptly transferred to the South in the Sisyphean quest for development, to the extent that some spoke of a 'conservative revolution' in development theory (Berthoud 1992: 70; see also Watts 1993). While there are some signs that pure-bred 'free-market' policies are giving way to more sober prescriptions in both the West and the South, they are being peddled in parts of the ex-socialist world as never before, with sometimes rather bizarre consequences.

Apart from pretensions to universality, the problem of such conceptualizations of the market is their reductionism. The market is reduced to 'pure' economic considerations. What is seldom acknowledged is that supply and demand, the essential ingredients in any conceptualization of markets, are not only and sometimes not even primarily economic: both are arrived at historically, through processes of social and spatial change. I therefore emphasize the need to look at markets as 'real' constellations of spatially and temporally specific circumstances. Fundamental to the project is the statement that there is more to the market than economics alone: the social, cultural, and economic aspects of human existence are entangled to such an extent that separating these aspects is not only difficult, but seriously misleading. Markets are best seen as embedded in society; socially constructed and continually reconstructed. This is analysed in the book with the help of the other two central concepts: *commoditization* and the *actor*.

Food (or whatever else) which is bought and sold in markets has become a commodity: its 'personality' is split into use and exchange values. Accordingly, commoditization is succinctly defined as 'the historical process by which exchange-value comes to assume an increasingly important role in economies' (Long 1986: 9). This process, which has been operating for centuries, can involve all factors of production and reproduction: land and labour as well as the actual products. Superficially viewed, it is a universal, global process. However, the point pursued here is that penetration of exchange values is markedly uneven geographically, and frequently ambiguous. No social group has ever taken commoditization to its logical extreme, fully excluding non-economic aspects from social relations. Commoditization involves culturally and socially influenced changes in the valuation of things. Communities 'domesticate money' (Alexander and Alexander 1995: 179) on their own terms. Again, close attention to historical and geographical context is necessary. Hence, I enquire about the local specifics of the process of commoditization, and its manifold links to place and space: constructing a universal model of the landscape of rural development is hardly a valid proposition.

Two prominent landmarks in social theory are the concepts of *agency* and *structure*. For the last two decades, some extensive explorations have been mounted into the treacherous terrain between them. Talk of commoditization as a universal process conjures up images of structural change and subjection to global forces. As should be clear by now, the position taken by the current author is one of scepticism toward such general assertions. This fits well with the recently renewed attention in many branches of the social sciences to the local scale of enquiry, which has entailed a definite shift to creative agency as opposed to structural constraints. An good example is the vibrant actor-oriented school which has appeared in rural development sociology (Long and Long 1992) and which has greatly influenced this study.

A critical treatment of the issue of agency assumes an important place in the book. The position taken here is that *social actors* are the key to understanding these links between global and local processes. Local agency, performed by individuals in their social environment, has the capacity radically to reshape the outcomes of a seemingly universal, global process. Of great importance here are the creation and maintenance of networks, which tie localities into a whole that is greater than the sum of its parts.

. . .

In sum, therefore, I want to put aside the concept of '*the* market' as a universal phenomenon, and instead endeavour to describe 'real markets' in Papua New Guinea in all their disorderliness. This description in turn rests on two concepts. One, commoditization, refers to supra-local influences, and the other, that of actors, emphasizes local possibilities and creativity. Grand theory is not the ultimate goal, but rather a detailed, theoretically *informed* description of a particular case. This approach, I argue, has deeply practical implications, as it makes possible a fresh look at rural development; one in which local voices have a chance of being heard over the rustle of papers (or the hum of computers) on the desks of development theorists and planners.

THE PAPUA NEW GUINEAN CASE

In some respects the choice of actual topic and place was secondary to the big and prickly questions discussed above, of conceptual and theoretical nature. Initially I was pointed towards Papua New Guinea by a geographer who has had a long academic and personal association with the country: Bryant Allen. I made my first visit to the country in March 1994, a reconnaissance trip of sorts, which lasted five weeks. I was able to travel to all highland provinces, observe and talk to rural people in their home villages, gardens, and the marketplaces frequented by them. I also got a glimpse of the towns with their rather different pace of life. It became obvious that given my general interests, the country would provide a highly interesting case. I decided to look at food marketing out of a small area in the Eastern Highlands (Maps 1 and 2), and to pay special attention to that rather humble but exceedingly important crop which is the sweet potato *(Ipomoea batatas* (L) Lam.), or kaukau.[1]

HARVESTING DEVELOPMENT

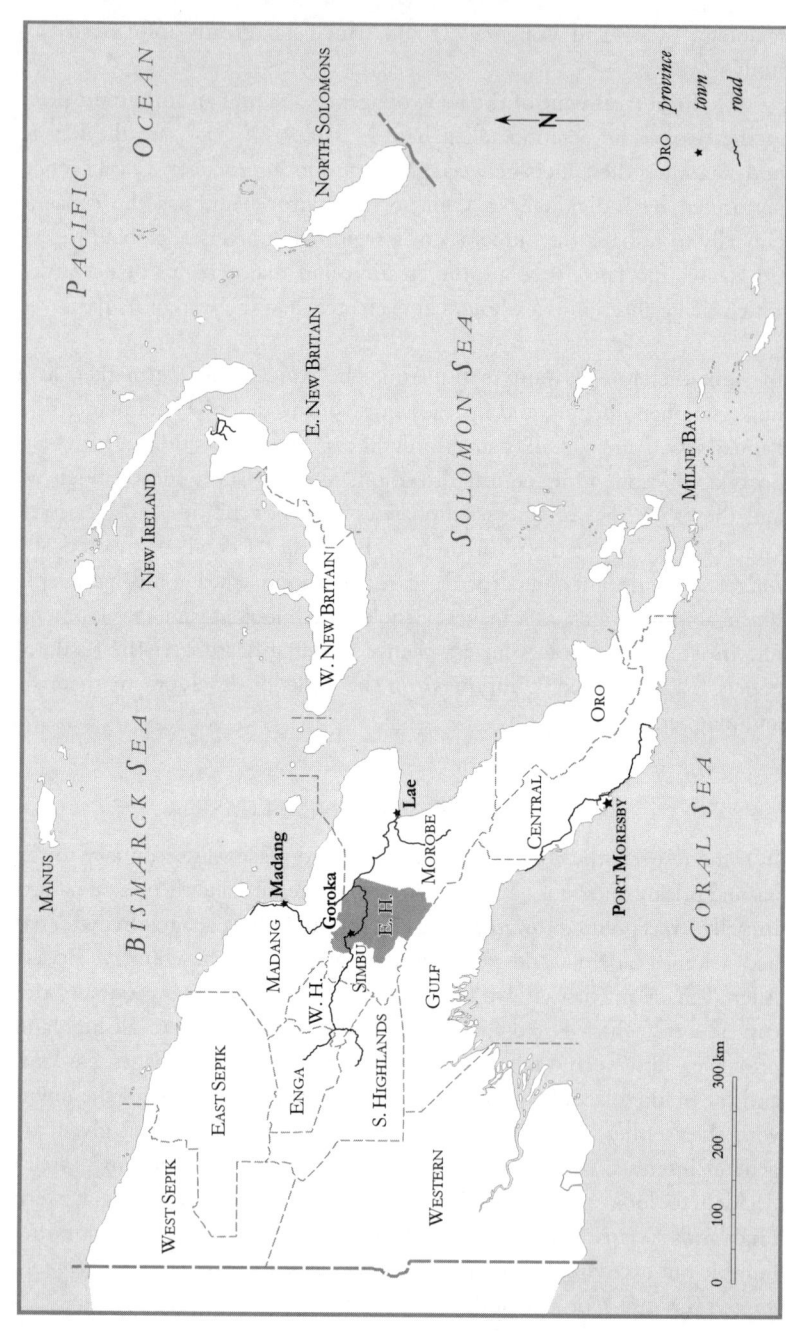

INTRODUCTION

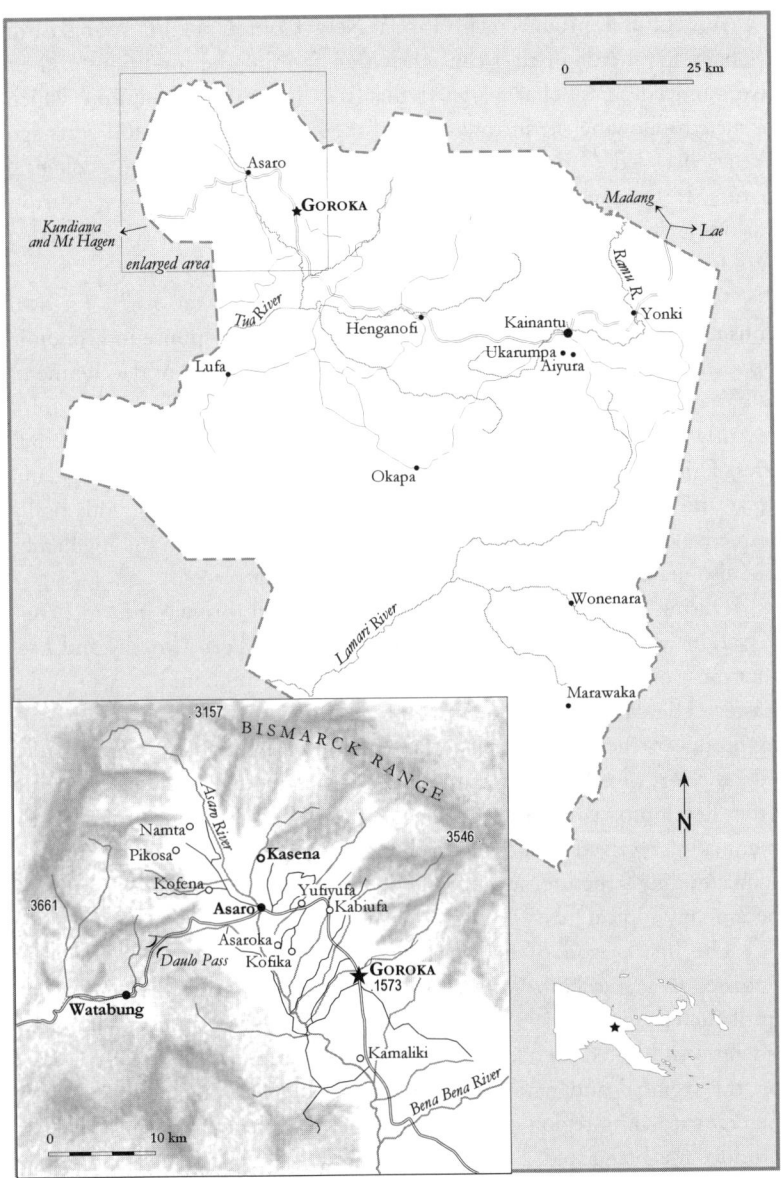

Map 1 (opposite): Papua New Guinea

Map 2 (above): Eastern Highlands Province and the Asaro Valley

Agricultural producers in Papua New Guinea are no strangers to change: they are themselves constantly transforming the conditions of their lives. Indeed, it has been argued that the 'Ipomoean revolution' which occurred following the introduction of the kaukau less than 400 years ago (Yen 1991) led to dramatic changes of economic, social, and ecological nature. In the present context, new crops such as potato, cabbage, carrot, various green vegetables, and fruit, have been and are being accommodated into local cultivation systems.

Cultivation of these 'introduced' crops is undertaken partly for own consumption and partly for sale as commodities, in response to economic opportunities that have opened up in the last few decades of development. What is just as noteworthy is that 'traditional' crops, which were until recently almost entirely grown for subsistence, have also become commodities. This is certainly the case for kaukau, now the staple of most highland areas and many lowland communities in Papua New Guinea. This bulky staple is now not only finding its way out of its core area in the highlands, but also making journeys by road and sea to distant places.

During my first fieldwork period, I discovered through informal conversations with market sellers in the biggest towns, Port Moresby and Lae, that most of the kaukau seemed to come out of a quite limited area in the Eastern Highlands: the Asaro Valley (Map 2). Moreover, it was sold mostly by producers themselves, men and women alike, but not by intermediaries of some sort or other, thus contradicting not only the experience of many other developing countries (see Kaynak 1986), but also some of the fundamentals of received economic wisdom. To understand the emergence of such a trading structure, and to describe thoroughly its day-to-day workings, became my topical foci.

The first period of fieldwork was completed in late April 1994. I returned to Papua New Guinea late in October the same year and stayed until the end of July 1995. Owing to both theoretical and practical considerations, I opted for a kind of nomadism, trying to keep one eye at least on the regional and national scales by travelling frequently between the market gardening region of the Asaro Valley and the markets in which the produce was being sold.

Even so, the emphasis on actors and corresponding hermeneutic methodology which had been adopted, called for close personal relations to be established if meaningful insights were to be gained. As the direct producer-seller marketing, which I had become particularly interested in observing, stands and falls with the grower's decisions and actions, the best place of entry seemed to be at the producer's end. Therefore a village had to be found to serve as a base.

Such a place was found soon after my arrival in the Asaro Valley. On the first reconnaissance trip, after explaining my intentions, I had in fact received a number of invitations from village people to stay with them. Rural Papua New Guineans are hospitable people indeed, and in addition there is since colonial days a lingering desire in many villages, especially in the highlands, for playing host to a *waitman* for shorter or (preferably) longer periods. The presence of a *waitman* – or to use a term which is even more pregnant with colonial meaning, a *masta*[2] – is not only seen as a potential source of wealth, but more importantly, as a tangible source of prestige for the clan and the family with which the outsider is associated. Even a bewildered student is warmly welcomed, which speaks volumes for the power which a foreign interloper is thought to possess.

Inevitably, therefore, many people wanted me to believe that precisely *their* village would be the most auspicious place to stay. Some of these invitations I summarily dismissed, on grounds of location or personal impression, but others warranted further attention. As I checked up on the most promising of these offers, I saw quickly that it had been made in earnest and was linked to a genuine interest in my research topic. So in mid-November 1994 I moved to Kasena village, home of the Gamizuho people and part of a larger area called Lunube (Map 3), into a house whose owners – a young couple with two children – were employed elsewhere in the province and did not come to their home village except on weekends. My landlady's parents, living next door,[3] accepted me wholeheartedly into the family, as did the whole village: on arrival the clan name, Gamizuho, was promptly bestowed upon me. I quickly settled down in Kasena and started scratching my head over how to inject some method into the madness which inevitably is the lot of a fieldworker.

Kasena and environs

The village of Kasena is located in the Upper Asaro Valley. A road passes through it, linking it to the western side of the valley on one hand, and more importantly, to the Okuk Highway[4] at Asaro Station on the other. This road originated in the 1950s, part of the province's extensive network of '*kiap* roads', which were built at the time by local labour under the

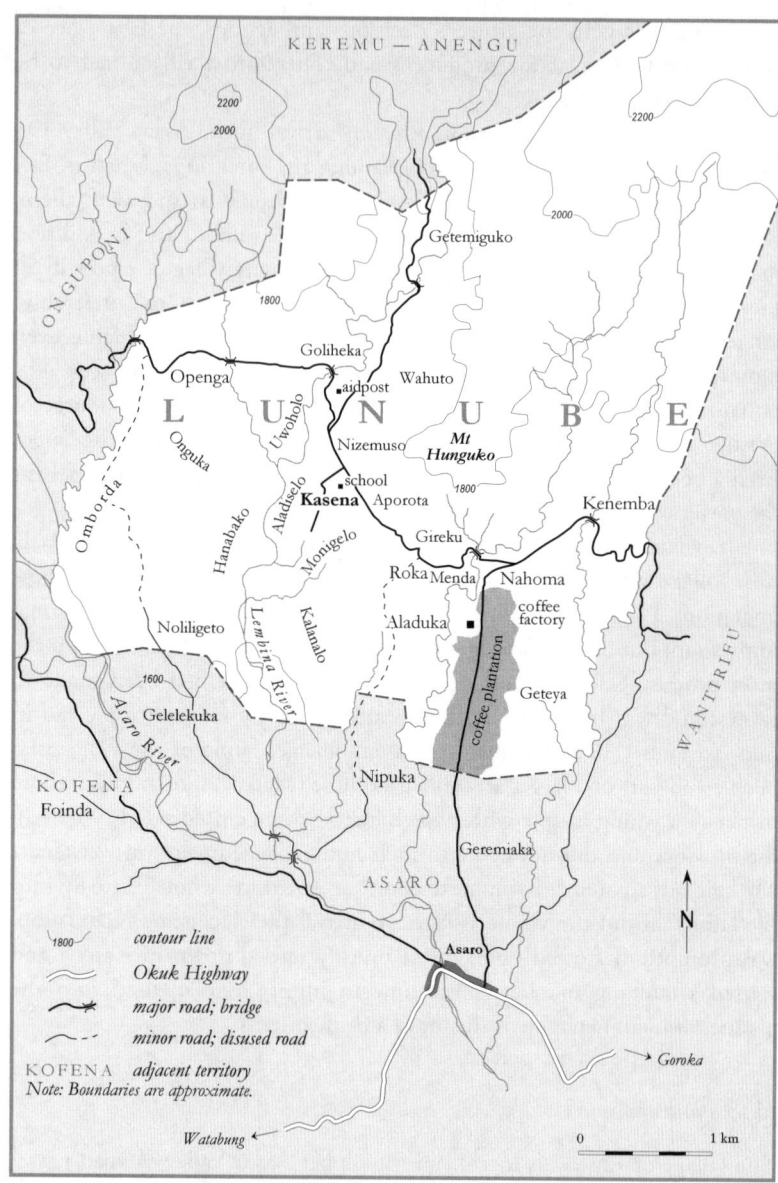

Map 3: The territory of Lunube

supervision of *kiaps* (Australian patrol officers) and their armed police.⁵ Until the 1970s, the road was maintained in the same manner it had been built, villagers compelled to work on the road for one day a week. In recent years the traffic, the rain, and the almost total lack of maintenance have taken their toll, to the extent that to describe some parts of it as a road verges on exaggeration. It is 7 kilometres of gut-wrenching, first-gear manoeuvring down to Asaro Station, and then 18 more kilometres on a magic asphalt carpet to Goroka, the commercial and administrative centre of the Eastern Highlands Province. Public Motor Vehicles (PMVs)[6] and small pick-up trucks ply the roads between Goroka and the Lunube villages.

In the Asaro Valley are found some of the most fertile soils in Papua New Guinea, and rural population densities are very high (Bleeker 1983; Bourke *et al.* 1994a, 1994b).[7] The valley's rural population was about 50,000 when the last census was taken in 1990,[8] and urban Goroka contained just over 18,000 people at that time (NSO n.d.). Two Local Government Councils (LGCs) cover the rural areas, the Asaro–Watabung LGC and the Goroka LGC. Goroka town itself is governed by the Eastern Highlands Capital Authority.

Though social organization is broadly similar throughout the Asaro Valley, any conception of regional unity is a recent phenomenon. People identify with their immediate clans and tribes, but hardly with a larger social group. The exception is when they travel to faraway places and have to explain their origin to others. The woman from Kasena selling kaukau in Gordons Market in Port Moresby thus becomes *meri Goroka*, or even *meri Asaro* if the enquirer shows some knowledge of the Eastern Highlands.

The ethnic badges used as shorthand for different subregions in the highlands were in most cases invented by the colonial authorities, missionaries or ethnographers, and based mainly on linguistic affinity, but most tribes within the valley speak closely related and mutually intelligible languages. Thus the Lutheran missionary Helbig came up with the compound name 'Gahuku–Gama' for referring collectively to the tribes of the lower Asaro Valley, who speak a similar language, but whose social and political unity was non-existent. The term later entered the academic literature through the writings of anthropologist Kenneth Read, who did extended fieldwork there around 1950 (Read 1951, 1954, 1965). The population and language which is found further to the north and west is often simply called 'Asaro' or 'Upper Asaro'. Its long-term students and analysts David and Gladys Strange[9] more appropriately refer to it as 'Dano', thereby following local convention.[10] Dano, or more accurately a dialect thereof, is the mother tongue of most Kasena people.

Making sense of social groupings, and the relations of these with particular *hauslains* (villages or hamlets), can be daunting. Early ethnographers of the Asaro Valley (K. Read 1951; Newman 1962, 1965) outlined a basic hierarchy of tribal confederations, tribes, clans, subclans, and patrilineages.[11] Newman stresses though that the groups were in a constant state of flux, with forces of fusion, fission, and segmentation at work, making strict hierarchical models difficult to sustain. When *kiaps* started traversing the highlands region regularly in the postwar years, counting and mapping its population, they put in place the nomenclature which is still used in the National Population Census. At the time, the social categories (mostly clans or subclans) may or may not have better matched with geographical units than they do now,[12] but both group structure and settlement patterns have since changed considerably (see also Chapter 8). Today many villages contain more than one clan, and vice versa, members of a particular clan often live in two or more villages.

Kasena lies in the middle of Lunube (Plate 1), which is recognized as a separate territory by other groups in the valley (Tok Pisin: *biknem Lunube*).[13] For all intents and purposes, the Gamizuho are a *clan:* an exogamous group

Plate 1: Kasena from the air. Looking southwest over the main village and fields, Lembina River, towards the Asaro River, which is seen at the top. Lutheran church and primary school in bottom right corner, EBC church left. Note clumps of Casuarina in coffee groves. (Photo: R. Michael Bourke, 1990)

INTRODUCTION

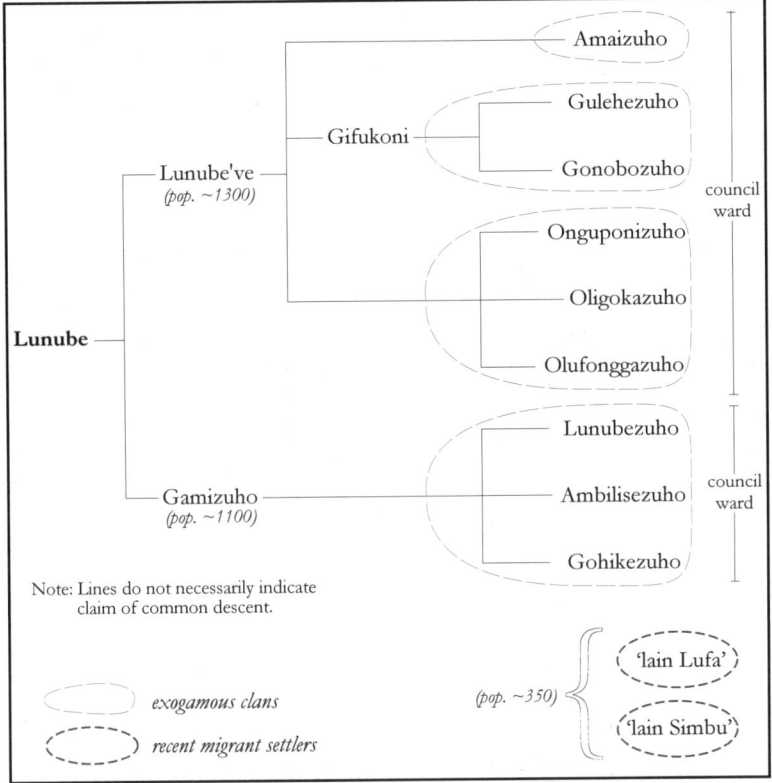

Figure 1: Social groups in Lunube from the perspective of the Gamizuho

of people claiming a common origin in the distant past. From their own point of view, the rest of the Lunube population is classified together as the Lunube've, although it in fact contains several different exogamous clans (Figure 1). That the organization is somewhat fluid is best demonstrated by the inclusion of the Amaizuho clan. Stories depict them as having moved from the western side of the Asaro River some decades ago, before 'contact'. Still partial outsiders, they remain free to marry into any of the other clans, but at the same time they have now secured land and settlement rights, by virtue of their long stay in Lunube.

Social relations between these clans, and with clans outside Lunube, are mediated by intricate exchanges of gifts (Plate 2), which are linked to various life-cycle events: births, deaths, and first and foremost marriages. As

Plate 2: Kasena from the ground. People carrying cooked pork and other food to an exchange ceremony.

a rule, residency is patrivirilocal. At marriage, the wife moves to the hamlet of the husband. 'Brideprice' is paid to the clan of the bride, consisting of money (can be several thousand kina)[14] and several large pigs. This is the first in a series of transactions between the clans involved. Usually a particular man from the bride's patrilineage assumes responsibility for 'looking after' the woman in her new surroundings, bringing frequent small gifts of food and assisting with money if needed. He and his clan can then expect a reward in some years' time, when the wife has proved her worth – worked hard in the gardens and borne children for her husband's clan. This 'delayed brideprice', which also consists of money and pigs,[15] is called in Tok Pisin *nuspes* (literally: 'noseface'), and some of the most spectacular festivities in Lunube are linked to such payments. The reputation of the giving clan hinges on the generosity displayed in such ceremonies, and substantial resources are devoted to success in this regard. Sometimes there is also a third, smaller, payment when the woman has reached old age. In Tok Pisin, this is termed *beksaitbun* (literally: the 'backbone' payment). Death is also an occasion for gifts to change hands, but especially the death of a prominent male. This calls for gifts of bananas, sugarcane, and other food from the garden, as well as money, to the kinsmen and kinswomen of the deceased. These gifts are returned some time later with cooked pork and other food.

INTRODUCTION

The sociocultural make-up is further complicated by the presence of migrants from other parts of the highlands. Their presence in the Asaro Valley dates back to the days of expatriate coffee plantations, from the 1950s through to the early 1970s. Planters often hired labourers from other districts instead of relying on local labour, as the local villagers started planting their own coffee in the 1950s and were not always keen on working for the plantation owners (see K. Read 1952: 444). The backblocks of Lufa, Okapa, and Simbu, from which most of these migrants have come, did not offer anything like the opportunities of the Asaro Valley, and these areas remain relative backwaters today.

The migrants in the Lunube area are mostly from a cluster of Gimi-speaking people from the south of Mount Michael in the Lufa district. Their existence is somewhat precarious. Most families rely on temporary or semi-permanent work for local coffee or kaukau growers, often for significantly lower remuneration than the minimum wage stipulated by the state.[16] Many have access to a small section of gardening land allocated by their patrons. Socially they keep to themselves, but some migrants who have married into the Lunube clans are considered more or less locals.

Most verbal interchange between villagers takes place in the Dano language, but with numerous in-migrants and in-married persons in the area, Tok Pisin – the *lingua franca* of most of Papua New Guinea – is frequently heard in conversations between village people. There are now children growing up in these villages, whose first language is Tok Pisin. In the extremely ethnically diverse towns, Tok Pisin is *the* language. English – the language of the state, expatriates, and big business – has a limited relevance for most villagers, even if many have an elementary grasp of it since their school days.

I had some trouble coming to terms with the very high expectations which the Gamizuho seemed to have from my stay. In a sense, I got exactly what I bargained for when I asked to be accepted into the clan. Among the Asaro people themselves, tremendous importance is put on constant reciprocity in daily life. Group solidarity is tested and asserted by constantly asking – no, commanding – fellow clansmen and friends to share food and other items which they happen to have at hand (Newman 1965: 51–52).[17] A 'wealthy' newcomer, especially a *waitman* (or in Dano, *gulehe* – red man), is subjected to similar demands, but doubled and redoubled. I was asked to buy batteries for the radio, saucepans, chicken feed, even a *kopimasin* (coffee pulper). More than one keen kaukau grower also asked me if I could

15

help them forge a new market, by getting their produce to Australia for sale. I suspect that my inability to meet such demands – bar a handful of the less extravagant ones – was more frustrating to myself than to my hosts, who perhaps never really expected much, but were simply exploring the dimensions of the relationship.

Fieldwork

> Everyday life consists of the little things one hardly notices in time and space (Braudel 1981: 29).

The formulation of the research project called upon a detailed examination of Braudel's 'little things'. I set out to explore the daily practice of individuals, aiming for an understanding of their lived experiences. A combination of observation and in-depth interviewing were the main methods used. Throughout fieldwork I used Tok Pisin in interviewing. Perhaps a more realistic description of these would be 'conversations' (Gudeman and Rivera 1990). Quite often I had prepared for a one-to-one interview, only to find myself and the supposed other half of the conversation surrounded by listeners, who inevitably became speakers themselves. Instead of going through the routines of an interview, such conversations frequently developed into the rambling, messy commentaries which are the stuff of group talk in daily life. Some might involve the interpretation of present life, others developed into storytelling about the ancestors and their exploits – the *tumbuna stori* which give meaning to many local happenings of the past and in the present. While sometimes attempting to coax the raconteurs gently into talking about things of special interest to me, such as historical changes in land use or specific marketing developments, often I simply followed wherever they would take me.

For a project which is by nature nomadic, logistics is the stuff of which nightmares are made. I was fortunate: throughout the fieldwork period I had the use of a four-wheel-drive utility owned by the Land Management Project of the Australian National University.[18] I was on the road for much of the time, travelling through most parts of the Asaro Valley and occasionally to other parts of the Eastern Highlands, as well as to Lae and Madang (see Maps 1 and 2).

And whenever a vehicle is seen moving on the roads in the highlands of Papua New Guinea, prospective co-travellers appear out of the blue. If they succeed in halting the vehicle, they fling their *bilum* (string bag) into the utility's tray and simply jump on board after it. Or – my Toyota Hilux sporting a double-cab – they get into the cab and start talking to the driver. Most often I relished being able to give people a lift. It was also greatly appreciated by the local people and facilitated many a conversation. In short, the Hilux proved itself to be an essential fieldwork tool. Yet the four-wheel-drive bliss had its uncomfortable moments. The Gamizuho of Kasena quite explicitly told me that not only did they define me as 'their' *waitman,* but that the vehicle more or less belonged to their clan. Constant attempts were made to get me to take someone or something somewhere. Frequently too I was told that this or that person standing at the roadside should not get a ride, as he or she was not a member of the clan, or even worse, belonged to an enemy clan. It is perhaps above all a measure of the individualism of my own culture that this became one of the most irksome points in the relationship with my hosts: I found their proprietary attitude towards me and the vehicle most unpleasant.

At the same time, I became acutely aware of my own power and of the difference between haves and have-nots in terms of transport. Again, the gender dimension surfaced: while many (by no means all) men are involved in vehicular *bisnis* of some sort, women are the transport have-nots. One does not proceed far along the road before encountering a woman, barefoot, sidestepping the ruts and the mud, dodging splashes from the passing vehicle, perhaps en route to market with a heavy *bilum* strung over her forehead and a toddler hanging at her arm. In spite of frequent warnings about police checks or accidents with potentially dire consequences, I could not help but end up with the trusty Toyota literally overflowing with humanity.

ORGANIZATION OF THE BOOK

The remainder of the book is organised into eight chapters. In Chapter 2, some rather abstract social theory is juggled with previous writings on Papua New Guinea. I look at general theoretical approaches to the integration of rural people into markets, and examine how commentators on the development experience in the Papua New Guinean highlands have interpreted the process. My argument is that agency in its social context has sometimes been missing from these analyses. I therefore propose an actor-oriented analysis, which pays close attention to the networks that constitute 'the market' and thus transcends the dichotomies of 'structure–agency' and 'local–global'.

Chapter 3 charts the social universe of some of my core households and the individuals of whom they are composed. These households, whose members feature prominently in later chapters, have 'networked' in different ways, and their family situation and physical resources differ. Genealogies of senior males and females are elicited, and linkages with the world beyond the village are mapped. Many, but not all, of these linkages are based on kinship.

Attention is then turned to the broad contours of the political economy of Papua New Guinea and the organization of food marketing within that space. In Chapter 4 I identify different spaces of economic life; of production and consumption. I pay special attention to the subjective characteristics of those places that feature in the lifeworld of the Lunube people. Then the major flows of fresh food commodities on a nationwide basis are mapped.

Chapter 5 traces the history and outlines the current characteristics of two contrasting types of fresh food markets in which the Lunube people participate, namely 'formal' wholesale trading and 'informal' marketplace selling. I discuss in some detail the practices of actors within these contrasting arrangements of markets. These practices differ substantially, as the two forms of markets are embedded in social relations in very different ways.

The remaining chapters are concerned more directly with the long-distance kaukau trade, its origin and current practices. Chapter 6 takes up the history of kaukau as a subsistence crop and traces its recent metamorphosis into an important commodity. While politico-economic changes since the 1970s have played an important part in bringing about the present lively kaukau market, its emergence also owes much to local cultural and political circumstances, together with the specific life trajectories of certain local personalities. In other words, it is a prime example of a socially constructed and socially embedded market.

Chapter 7 outlines the characteristics of the trade, in economic and social senses. As most households selling kaukau also grow coffee, the question of links between kaukau marketing and the state of the world coffee market is explored. Growers certainly keep a keen eye on both coffee and kaukau prices, but the relationship is not a simple one. I next present a detailed description of selling trips which the growers undertake, and the use of social networks which makes them possible. In my fieldwork, I endeavoured to follow the produce from garden to market.

Chapter 8 deals with the changes in land utilization and accompanying social processes which have occurred in the villages of the Upper Asaro in recent times, where the kaukau trade plays a large part. I draw on the information gained from the core households mentioned above, describing how each of them manages the portfolio of resources at their disposal. As in the previous chapters, the reader should bear in mind that the 'ethnographic present' is 1994–95.

I agree with those *enfants terribles* who argue that academic writing is to a large extent storytelling or rhetoric (see McCloskey 1990). Instead of hiding the storytelling aspect behind a façade of academic sobriety, I have allowed ample room for stories of the kind that are sometimes labelled, somewhat dismissively, 'anecdotal evidence'. The empirical chapters are also interspersed with 'vignettes' containing material that is in some ways tangential, but nonetheless relevant, to the main account. Some historical recollections, observations of specific events during fieldwork, and various similar snippets, are presented in these boxes. This is an attempt both to get the reader closer to the 'heart of the place', and to breathe some life into the process of fieldwork. I also feel I owe it to the people with whom I stayed – avid and skilled storytellers themselves – to get across the unsanitized, earthy humour, or the sadness, or whatever other tone their narrations took when they recounted them to me. That said, I acknowledge that the voice is mine.

Chapter 9 concludes the project, by looking at some of the theoretical and practical implications of the analysis. A focus on social agency highlights features of markets which are no less important for understanding their place in rural transformation than the traditional emphasis on economic variables, or overarching structures of state and the logic of capital. An *actor-network* approach in particular holds considerable promise for analysing the social and spatial construction of markets.

NOTES

1 In the book, I shall use the Tok Pisin term, kaukau, instead of 'sweet potato', except when discussing the crop outside the Papua New Guinean setting. Tok Pisin is the major *lingua franca* of Papua New Guinea. Words from Tok Pisin and local languages are italicized in the text, except for the term kaukau, as it is used repeatedly throughout the text. A general glossary of Tok Pisin and local words is found in Appendix 1, and Appendix 2 contains a list of crops together with their botanical names.

2 This term is used by many older people and children, but is shunned by younger adults.

3   Actually, in February 1995 they moved over the village street and into 'my' house, after their own accidentally burned down.

4   Or Highlands Highway – Papua New Guinea's major axis of transportation between the highlands and the port of Lae (see Map 1).

5   For a rather partisan but nevertheless interesting account, see Downs (1986). He was the District Officer in Goroka when many of these roads were built. See also Crotty (1970) and Hasluck (1976: 248–250).

6   PMVs are Papua New Guinea's main form of public transport. Owned and run by individuals and small businesses, these are mostly Japanese-made minibuses which take 15–25 passengers or, in regions with rougher roads, small four-wheel-drive trucks equipped with bench seats.

7   The physical environment and its relationship to settlement patterns and cultivation practices is discussed in more detail in Chapter 8.

8   The Asaro and Lowa Census Areas, within the Goroka Census District. Howlett (1962) uses the 'Goroka Valley' as her unit of reference, including the combined watersheds of the Asaro and Bena Bena rivers. The Bena Bena Census Area is excluded here, as are the Unggai and Watabung, all of which belong to the Goroka Census District. It should be noted that the 1990 census is considered somewhat unreliable, and results from the Eastern Highlands are among the most suspect of all provincial headcounts. It is likely that considerable under-reporting took place (Billy Kavanamur, pers. comm., 1995; see also Bakker 1996). A new census was taken in July 2000, but results were not available at the time of writing.

9   Linguists associated with the Summer Institute of Linguistics, who lived in Kasena from 1960 to 1991.

10 Instead of referring to only two languages in the valley, Gahuku (or Gahuku-Gama) and Asaro, local people use a threefold classification: Alekano, Tokano, and Dano. Even within each of these there are differences from one tribal area to the next.

11 The terminology varies. Read (1951) talks of political groups, district groups, clans and subclans (*dzuha*), and Newman uses the terms 'phratry' and 'sib' in his 1965 publication for what he in 1962 called tribe and clan.

12 *Kiaps*, when they took a census, simply ordered the members of each clan or subclan to gather at its meeting place, which was then put on the map as the group's 'village', and labelled with the clan name (Skeldon 1987). These are today's census units. In fact, the takers of the 1990 census in the Eastern Highlands Province still resorted to the 'line-up' method, which contributed to its inaccuracy (see note 8, this chapter).

13 Alternative spellings which are found include Lunipe, Lunumbe, Runumbe, and Runumbei. For this and most other words of the Dano language I follow an orthography developed by David and Gladys Strange. The exceptions are certain names of places and people, about which there are now some conventions, such as Asaro (instead of spelling it Asalo).

INTRODUCTION

14   The kina (divided into 100 toea) is Papua New Guinea's monetary unit. In March 1995 the exchange rate was about $A 1.1, or $US 0.8 for K1. The currency was devalued by some 12 per cent in September 1994 and subsequently floated, which resulted in a further 10 per cent devaluation (Gupta 1995).

15   In one such ceremony, which took place in June 1995, the Gamizuho received a total of approximately K10,000. This was *nuspes* for two women who had married into the Onguponizuho clan (see Figure 1). The man who had 'looked after' one of these women got K1000, but much of the money he immediately distributed among other members of the receiving clan.

16   In 1995 the weekly minimum wage was K22.96 .

17   It perhaps indicates the centrality of such reciprocity in daily life that the terms preferred by the people for the three related languages of the valley (see footnote 10, this chapter) are different forms of the phrase 'Give me!'

18   This project, which started in 1990, involves the mapping and description of agricultural systems throughout Papua New Guinea (see *The Land Management Project* 2000).

2

Markets, commoditization, and actors: spacious concepts

> *The natives of the Waterbung area* [now spelled Watabung, about 30 km west of Goroka] *are keen to extend their gardens and to place more emphasis on the growing of European vegetables with a view to finding an outside market. Consideration is being given to the possibility and economic practicability of clearing such produce through Obihaka 'drome to which the Waterbung natives would be eager to carry their wares. This would entail a carry of about 4 hours over a high mountain range but the Waterbung philosophy is "better that than nothing at all"* (Williams 1951: 6–7).

PARTICIPATION IN A *MARKET* OF SOME SORT – almost any sort, it sometimes seems – has long been seen as a prerequisite for rural advancement, or 'development', in the highlands of Papua New Guinea. Not only by colonial and postcolonial planners and powers that be, but also, as the opening quote suggests, no less by their subjects. Since the 1930s, highlanders have become avid marketeers, both at home and elsewhere in the country. The markets which they have had a hand in creating are similar to, yet different from, markets elsewhere in the world. They are products of a worldwide historical trend of *commoditization,* which has left few facets of life unchanged. Even so, these markets are also very much the products of those who attend them during the course of their daily life. As *social actors,* the makers of the markets have drawn on their own rich cultural heritage and intricate social networks in their making.

In this chapter I look at ways to theorize about a process of this kind, and attempt to situate the development experience of the Papua New Guinean highlanders within existing theoretical discourse. The aim is to distil, out of some quite abstract debates in social theory, concepts that can help shed light on the history and present characteristics of fresh food markets in Papua New Guinea.

EXCHANGE IN PAPUA NEW GUINEA, PAST AND PRESENT

It is abundantly clear from the ethnographic literature that exchange patterns in Papua New Guinea have always been complex, and bound up with social organization in myriad ways. Malinowski's (1922) description of the *kula* in the Trobriand Islands established the area's undisputed status as the *locus typicus* of reciprocity, or the 'gift economy', which has since been the subject of numerous ethnographies (e.g. A. Strathern 1971; Feil 1984; Lederman 1986) and theoretical treatments (e.g. C. A. Gregory 1982; M. Strathern 1988; Thomas 1991; Carrier 1992).

Apart from gifts, 'commodities' also existed before any sustained contact with the world economy was established. Regarding food, various local and regional barter exchange systems flourished, based on ecological specialization (Hide 1993: 2–3). Bartering of other necessities such as stone for axe-making, as well as luxuries such as salt, shells, and plumes, was also commonplace. Extensive trading networks linked the highlands, the highlands fringe, and the coastal lowlands (Hughes 1977; Healey 1990). However, bulky and ubiquitous staples – such as kaukau – were not generally traded in the highlands. Today, barter exchange is still present under certain localized conditions. For example, fish is exchanged for starchy crops on the island of Manus (Robin Hide, pers. comm., 1995).

What, then, about fully-fledged market exchange in Papua New Guinea? Is it a recent import, or did it exist in pre-contact times, like other exchange types? In fact it did, but only in certain regions. On the Gazelle Peninsula, the necessary invention of general-purpose money in the form of *tambu*, or coiled shells, created the conditions for proper market trading.[1] Here were found permanent and monetized market*places* as opposed to temporary venues of exchange where barter was conducted.

Elsewhere in the country, as well as elsewhere in Melanesia, marketplace exchange was for the most part a colonial introduction. Detailed case studies have been undertaken of some of these latter-day marketplaces, either as part of more complete ethnographies or as independent studies (see e.g. Brookfield 1969; Jackson and Kolta 1974; Jackson 1976c; von Fleckenstein 1976; Mahoney 1980; Epstein 1982; Bourke 1986; Maclean 1989; Hide 1993; FPDC 1994).

Generalizations are hazardous, but certain apparent common features led early commentators to conclude that a distinct 'Melanesian market' had emerged, which was substantially different from, say, the marketplaces of Africa or Southeast Asia. Its main features have been described by Brookfield (1969) and Epstein (1982). The market is overwhelmingly dominated by producer-sellers, with professional full-time traders playing a limited role. Women comprise the majority of sellers. Prices are set and generally not changed through the market day. Pricing is set by volume (size of heap or bundle), never by unit of weight. Usually no haggling or hard-sell techniques are practised. Frequently the market is therefore not cleared at the end of the day, but the produce is taken away for the seller's own consumption and/or distributed among kin and family.

Although these characteristics can still be identified in Papua New Guinean food markets, there are many exceptions in the present, and it is probable that the past was not free of them either. The sharp gender division of marketing has been partially altered in the urban context, and in any case, men do have a long history of selling certain crops. Some professional traders are now found in the largest towns. Changing the price is not uncommon, although it is a rather subtle operation given that produce is still priced and sold by volume. Finally, apart from the marketplaces proper, large quantities are now sold to wholesalers or institutional buyers, through more 'formal' channels. The interactions that occur at the various nodes in these different marketing networks, and the divergent meanings produced there, were some of the major issues I looked at during the fieldwork, and they will receive further attention in subsequent chapters.

Market exchange in the general sense of the term has expanded greatly in the preceding decades. The world economy gained a toehold prior to the turn of the century with the establishment of plantations, limited smallholder cash-cropping, and expatriate trading activity in coastal and island regions (Amarshi *et al.* 1979). Whole new regions, notably the highlands, were partly drawn into the commercial sphere following 'first contact' in the 1920s and 1930s, although some peripheral areas and communities were not contacted until much later.[2] The decisive moment came after World War II, under the Australian colonial administration, when large numbers of smallholder farmers in both lowland and highland areas were incorporated into global commodity markets (Thompson and MacWilliam 1992; Seib 1994).

LOCATING THE MARKET IN SOCIETY: THE 'EMBEDDEDNESS' THESIS

These initial and partial Papua New Guinean examples give a glimpse of many and varied exchange systems, some originating in precolonial times, whereas others are the creations of the last few decades of 'development'. To a differing degree, all point to an interweaving of economic exchange with social and cultural conditions in the country's rich human tapestry. There is a *moral* dimension to the economy (see Scott 1976). This aspect is not fading away as the market makes inroads. On the contrary, moral discourse has played a central role in the very attempts at developing a market economy, as convincingly shown for instance by a case study from a remote Western Highlands community (Maclean 1989). Elements of what Hydén (1980: 18–19) has called the *economy of affection* are also highly visible, with economic ties partially following lines of descent and/or common residence. The Papua New Guinean economy is also of course a *political* economy, in which the distribution of economic surplus is a deeply contested process. Political aspects of the country's economic life range from the intrigues of global commodity trade – of which forest products are an outstanding current example (Holzknecht and Kalit 1995) – to state fiscal manipulations (Garnaut 1995), to the interminable power tussles of local social groupings (Standish 1992; see also Reilly 1999).

In short: be it in Papua New Guinea or elsewhere, the market is best imagined as *embedded* in social relations: *socially constructed*. The idea of embeddedness is central to the argument of this book, and I shall seek to demonstrate its efficacy in the chapters that follow. First, a short excursion is necessary into the theoretical territory of the 'embeddedness' debate.

Karl Polanyi is the author credited with introducing the idea of social embeddedness to the study of markets, although in fact he used it rather sparingly and not too systematically in his writings (Polanyi 1944, 1957; see also Barber 1995). His project revolved around the genesis of the market principle, and the questioning of its universality as a way of economic integration and order. He proposed that market exchange rose to become a dominant mode of integration only with the 'Great Transformation' to a capitalist market system, which first took place in the countries of Western Europe and North America in the nineteenth century. During this historical process, economic life in these countries had become separated – disembedded – from the social world. Far from being a primordial principle of human nature as some other influential theorists have maintained,[3] the market is in this formulation but one of several possible modes of economic integration. Other principles, which Polanyi derived from empirical ethnographic evidence, were characterized by embeddedness in some form or other, through which the economy was subordinated to the social process. He thus identified societies where *reciprocity* or *redistribution* were the guiding principles of exchange, instead of the market. He was deeply pessimistic about possible outcomes of an unfettered market. Taken to its logical conclusion, the atomism of such a market, devoid of morality, would lead not to its sustained self-regulation, but to chaos and self-destruction. This was, Polanyi presumed, prevented only by an intervention of states and collectivities such as labour unions, through which a degree of resistance was exercised.

Importantly, Polanyi and his substantivist anthropological followers (e.g. Bohannan and Bohannan 1968; Sahlins 1972) thus presupposed a sharp break between non-market and market-based economies, confining the former to the realms of history, and to existing remnants still found in 'traditional' societies. The theory and corresponding empirical work drew rightful attention to historical and geographical specificity and diversity, but at the cost of having to assume in non-Western, 'pre-modern' societies the existence of 'multi-centric economies' containing separate 'spheres of exchange' (Bohannan and Bohannan 1968: 227–233, 250–251), where formal market laws did not apply. The metaphor of spheres carries the impression of completely self-contained entities (Ferguson 1992; Alexander and Alexander 1995: 186). Such a radical separation is rather exaggerated. It certainly becomes suspect when the realities of Papua New Guinean economic life are examined, not least because the market actors themselves blithely ignore the boundaries. Actually, Polanyi himself argued that different forms of exchange could and did coexist. However, when the market had transformed labour, land, and money into 'fictitious commodities' (Polanyi 1944: 68–76) in a given society, it had become the sole principle of economic integration. By this measure, Papua New Guinea has a long way to go to become a fully-fledged market economy.

Another influential author, whose work is even more keenly imbued with an awareness of historical and geographical contextuality, is Fernand Braudel. *Contra* Polanyi, Braudel does not equate the general category of the market with the more specific principle of the *self-regulating* market. The latter he considers a pure fiction, nowhere to be found in reality

(Braudel 1982: 227). Tracing the genesis of market exchange on a global basis, he dates the arrival of a market economy not to the relatively recent transition to capitalism, but centuries earlier. For instance, he convincingly details the intricate networks of commodity markets in pre-industrial Europe, showing that market exchange had indeed penetrated much of economic life on the continent long before the advent of the 'Great Transformation', but coexisting with other forms rather than wholly displacing them.

To an extent, Braudel's disagreement with Polanyi is a matter of definition and semantics. The 'polysemic quality' (Dilley 1992a: 20; see also Carrier 1997) of the concept of the market is indeed evident, and deserves a few comments. First, the neoclassical economic view is that of a general, *universal principle*. This is in fact consistent with Polanyi's view of the market economy, which is ironic given that his project was in part a reaction to the rather heroic generalizations of the neoclassical school.[4] Second, a view of markets as *specific constellations of commodities, regions, and economic actors* underlies many descriptive works which look beyond the economic and endeavour to portray 'real markets' in all their complexity. In a way that resonates with much of current social theory, the search for generalities takes second place to a recognition of the diverse institutions, rationalities and cultural quirks which come into play in the construction of a market. The third common usage of the market concept revolves around the market*place*, as a geographical manifestation of market exchange, but one that has long been recognized as taking on many and varied forms (Bromley *et al.* 1975; C. Smith 1976; R. T. H. Smith 1978). In fact, this was probably the original referent of the word (Dilley 1992a), from which more general usage later took off.[5] The market was, and remains, a social gathering linked to a particular location, and not merely a mechanism of exchange.

Embeddedness and agency

While Polanyi and Braudel have both made important contributions towards a discourse of the market as embedded,[6] neither deals in any detail with human agency in the market. The former, emphasizing that the economy be seen as an 'instituted process', relegates the individuals who make up the market to structural determination. Likewise, the latter is preoccupied with the broad sweep of history – the *longue durée* – instead of short-term events. Braudel positions individuals not as movers and shakers of, but as subject to, the broad social changes towards a market economy which he so eloquently describes.

Granovetter (1985) has argued that institutionalist accounts, like much of sociology during its structural-functionalist era, suffer from an 'oversocialized' conception of human beings, leaving little room for creative agency. Conversely, the account of conventional economics is predicated upon the epistemology of methodological individualism, and portrays the individual person as 'undersocialized'. He reminds us that

> Actors do not behave or decide as atoms outside a social context, nor do they adhere slavishly to a script written to them by the particular intersection of social categories that they happen to occupy. Their attempts at purposive action are instead embedded in concrete, ongoing systems of social relations (Granovetter 1985: 487).

The smooth function of the market as an institution is based on a measure of agreement about the 'rules of the game', or what constitutes proper behaviour in the market. This includes conceptions of trust and fairness, and conversely, of cheating and malfeasance (Granovetter 1985: 487–493). Such an agreement is about the form social relations should take, and is arrived at through social struggle and/or negotiation and not, as some institutional and neo-institutional economists would have it, by virtue of functional effectiveness.[7]

In order to realize the potential of the embeddedness perspective while giving social agency the needed weight, Granovetter thus advocates studying the economy through the concept of *social networks*. This allows us, he argues, to appreciate that the economy–society nexus is more subtle than either Polanyi's schema or conventional economics would have us believe. The form which the embedded market takes in a given context depends to a substantial extent on the density and other characteristics of social networks in that context. We can therefore appreciate that, once established, the structure of the market is not a stable entity – let alone a foregone conclusion – but is, on the contrary, subject to continuing social construction through the changing relations of actors with one another. Ideas about 'the rules of the game' vary tremendously from one place or region to another. Possibilities for disjuncture therefore abound, as actors come to the market with differing ideas and ideals. Examples of such disjunctures in the Papua New Guinean case will be discussed later.

MARKETS, COMMODITIZATION, AND ACTORS

A lively discussion ensued in the late 1980s and 1990s along these lines, both as a result of Granovetter's seminal intervention, and with a renewed interest in the Polanyi project in general (see e.g. Halperin 1988, 1994; Etzioni and Lawrence 1991; Granovetter 1991; Mingione 1991; Barber 1995). Particularly noteworthy here is the work of the 'Bielefeld group' of development sociologists (e.g. Schrader 1994a, 1994b, 1995, 1996; Evers 1995a, 1995b; Evers and Schlee 1995). These writers, building on fieldwork-based research undertaken mainly in South and Southeast Asia, have sought to understand the complex interplay between 'morality' and economic logic in trade. Schrader (1995), for instance, argues for a recognition of *degrees* of embeddedness, rather than assuming a 'Great Transformation' from a fully embedded to an entirely non-embedded situation. As one endpoint, he suggests the automatic teller machine – an allegedly completely desocialized form of economic interaction![8]

The concept of the 'Traders' Dilemma', which the Bielefeld group has developed, captures the tension, inevitable in their opinion in a peasant society, stemming from the trader's need for capital accumulation and socio-cultural demands for redistribution. In many Asian societies, they argue, the dilemma is sidestepped by 'outsider' groups assuming the role of the trading minorities (Evers 1994; Schiel 1994). In the Papua New Guinean fresh food trade a similar dilemma is very evident, and its solution has long proved elusive. Wholesale fruit and vegetable trading, as a specialized and sustained activity, was, and to some extent still is, the domain of Australians or other ethnic 'outsiders'. Development interventions aimed at building up indigenous traders have proved particularly difficult to implement (see Chapter 5).

Another major contribution towards the study of development from an agency viewpoint is that of the 'Wageningen group' of rural sociologists. The germination of their actor-oriented approach can be traced back several decades, but around 1990 it was given a more coherent shape by Norman Long and his collaborators (see the collections in Long 1989b; Long and Long 1992), making it one of the more prominent and compelling directions in current rural development research. Empirically, this project is based on detailed ethnographic fieldwork carried out in Africa and Latin America, but theoretically it draws on debates that have raged in social theory at a much higher level of abstraction. These relate to the fundamental concepts of *structure, agency,* and *power* in social life.

Later in the chapter I shall return to the social theory upon which the actor-oriented approach rests. The approach provides a clue for effectively describing the embeddedness of markets, the complex social and spatial contexts out of which real markets are created, and the equally complex patterns which result from the process of market integration.

. . .

The preceding discussion has shown that the basic idea of the embedded market is indeed a compelling one, which opens up a vast arena for geographic enquiry. Markets do not exist in a social vacuum, any more than they are located on the elusive isotropic plain beloved by those location theorists of previous decades who were seduced by the formal logic of physics and neoclassical economic theory. In the case of Papua New Guinea, not only is the country extremely fragmented in social and cultural terms, but so too is its physical space. Both facts profoundly influence the nature of social interaction and go some way towards explaining the limited degree of economic integration. What Braudel (1982: 229) calls 'the terrain of the market economy' is here all but uniform. Yet a certain generalization is possible: in recent decades, most if not all Papua New Guineans have found themselves on a track towards increased involvement in markets. Here as much as elsewhere the general process of *commoditization* has been at work.

COMMODITIZATION: RELATIONS AND THINGS

The concept of commoditization stems from political economic theory, but the position and fate of peasantries under a market economy have long been close to its heart. Marx's own work on petty commodity production, which mostly dealt with industrial processes, was extended to agrarian conditions by Kautsky (1988) and Lenin (1956). Chayanov provided an alternative angle, focusing on the peasant household rather than the laws of capitalism (Chayanov 1966). Up until the 1970s a stalemate of sorts characterized peasant studies. The Leninist conviction of an inevitable differentiation of peasantries into a rural proletariat and a landowning bourgeoisie was pitted against the Chayanovian perspective of a separate logic which enabled peasants to survive under capitalism (e.g. Ennew *et al.* 1977; Harrison 1977, 1979). In order to break out of this straitjacket, attention then turned in the 1970s and 1980s to specifying the exact processes through which market integration takes place in peasant societies (e.g. Mann and Dickinson 1978; Friedmann 1980, 1986; Bernstein 1981; Chevalier 1983;

Bernstein and Campbell 1985). The commoditization debate has highlighted some important questions.

The transformation of social relations

According to political economy theorists, we need to look at several different aspects of change in social relations. First, commoditization involves rural households or families increasingly having to secure their reproduction, as units of production, through the market (Bernstein 1981). Second, and related to the first, it may entail a degree of specialization, whereby, for instance, commodity producers abandon 'subsistence' to a greater or lesser extent (Friedmann 1980). Third, some writers have stressed increasing 'market mentality', as exchange-value calculations assume first place when decisions regarding production or exchange are made (Chevalier 1983).

An issue of great theoretical complexity is that of reproduction and differentiation. Bernstein (1981) has addressed this through the Marxist concepts of *extended* versus *simple reproduction*. In the former case, the producer is able to accumulate capital and redeploy it for continued profit, whereas the latter is the lot of the majority of the world's peasants. These tread water, unable to accumulate, but still capable of reproducing the organizational unit (e.g. the household or family) at a similar level from one production cycle to the next. In either case, commodity production entails that reproduction becomes dependent upon market relations. This affects both production inputs and consumption items. Bernstein (1981: 11–13) draws attention to the 'simple reproduction squeeze' which is characteristic of many rural societies undergoing commoditization. There is a tendency, he maintains, for returns to labour to decrease, compared with costs of production. This, in turn, puts pressure on labour and land, and given that producers have limited ability to change to more effective technology, intensification is the result. At worst, a downward spiral is set in motion, leading both to impoverishment and degradation of land.

Social differentiation results from the inability to achieve even simple reproduction. The Leninist prognosis of the obliteration of the peasantry has not come to pass, but Gibbon and Neocosmos (1985) make the important point that the apparent stability of smallholder farming as a sector in many developing countries may obscure a high 'turnover' if one looks at the level of individual enterprises. In their view, one can speak of a 'generalized commodity economy' whenever reproduction is linked to commodity exchange, even if commoditization has not conquered all conditions of production. For the longer term, Bernstein identifies three different trajectories of rural producers within an economy so structured (discussion in Long 1986: 16). First, a possible outcome is specialization and individualization, whereby households/families become the main units of economic decision-making. Second, a gradual deepening of social divisions within the rural sector often takes place, culminating in differentiation as discussed above. Third, farm households may follow a diversification strategy, drawing on off-farm income sources in addition to agricultural production in order to survive.

The process of commoditization in agricultural production is somewhat different from the other economic sectors such as industry, by virtue of the fact that agriculture is based on biological resources, or on the processes of nature. It has been argued that this fact sets limits to accumulation, as natural processes are not as amenable to technical tampering in order to harmonize production time with labour time, and to continually accelerate the production process (Mann and Dickinson 1978). Other views emphasize the ideological or moral constructions that show up in many peasant or family farming populations, enabling households to exploit family labour. Often such ideologies involve patriarchy and the subordination of women (Friedmann 1986).

Make no mistake: political economy theory has addressed some quite fundamental issues for understanding how market integration transforms rural communities. Nevertheless, what is striking about much of this literature is the limited space accorded to human agency, in other words the ability to shape the course rather than simply follow it blindly. Commoditization is frequently depicted as a linear, inexorable progression which culminates in the complete subjugation of the small rural producer under a global system of capitalist production. When admitted, local historical and geographical specificities to do with culture, social relations, and ecology, are usually not allowed into the analysis to the extent that the economic determination, which is built into the foundations of this theory, is jeopardized.

The social life of things

A different and altogether more flexible approach to commoditization is provided by a group of scholars who concern themselves not so much with abstracting the forms of exchange and relations of production, as with describing the actual items being exchanged and the sociocultural value constructions embodied in the 'social life' of these (material) items (see Appadurai 1986b). In a sense, these scholars take the Marxian bull by the horns, as Marx had identified 'commodity fetishism' – the tendency to divorce 'things' from the social conditions under which they were created – as one of the hallmarks of capitalism.

For Appadurai, what characterizes most things or classes of things is their ambiguity. The 'perfect commodity' does not exist. Rather, a thing may enter into a commodity *situation* during its social life, in which 'its exchangeability (past, present or future) for some other thing is its socially relevant feature' (Appadurai 1986a: 13). Only during the instant of exchange is it unambiguously a commodity. One therefore has to trace the 'biography of things' (Kopytoff 1986) in order to understand their place in economy and society. During their 'life', things/commodities travel over a contested terrain of exchange, along sometimes tortuous and twisted paths, which are formed by struggles over social meaning (Ferguson 1992: 59). Like Marxist political economy, this treatment of commoditization puts politics and power at the centre of the process, but it does so in an altogether more subtle way which also gives due recognition to culture and social organization (Kopytoff 1986).[9] Material goods become part of discourse, and then function partially as cultural statements, sometimes on a grand scale (see A. Long 1992).

In Papua New Guinea, *buai* (betel nut) provides a fascinating example. Previously an important consumption item and/or gift in certain areas only, it has been diffused into almost every corner of the country. In the process, it has been given new meaning through association with 'national culture' (Hirsch 1990). The greatly increased demand has catapulted *buai*, together with its accompaniments *daka* (betel pepper) and *kambang* (powdered lime), into the realm of commodities, creating a national market of considerable vigour. Compare this with rice. The popularity of this imported staple has much to do with convenience and economics, as has often been noted (see Bourke *et al.* 1981), but this is not the whole story. Rice has also become highly symbolically charged, and in two contradictory ways. Rice consumption has on the one hand been eagerly embraced as a sign of affluence and of participation in the modern, commercial economy. It has also however become an emblem for dependence, at least among politicians at the national level. The idea of growing rice in Papua New Guinea to satisfy the country's needs refuses to die, although economic reasoning has shown it to be a less than 'rational' undertaking (Gibson 1993, 1994).

The project of Appadurai *et al.* dovetails nicely with the general concept of embeddedness in its more recent formulation by Granovetter and others, and related social constructivist and actor-oriented approaches to rural development. It draws our attention once again to the fact that the identities of people, or indeed of things, are not fixed or immutable. On the contrary, the continual construction of such identities is part and parcel of the process of market integration. The outcomes of commoditization are to a substantial extent negotiated by local actors, yet these are tied into supra-local networks.

. . .

The concept of commoditization is a valuable heuristic device for a study of agricultural transformation in Papua New Guinea. Despite the comparatively recent arrival of the (world) market as a major influence on the lives of many of its peoples, the processes of commoditization have wrought irrevocable change. One must be careful, however, not to lapse into deterministic assumptions as to the outcomes at the local level. Rather than getting bogged down in the quagmire of structuralist exegesis when confronted with the diversity of local situations, it is more useful to pay attention to the ongoing social construction of such diversity.

PREVIOUS STUDIES OF THE PAPUA NEW GUINEA HIGHLANDS

It is now time to try and bring the somewhat disparate theoretical deliberations offered in the last two sections more clearly into the context of the highland valleys of Papua New Guinea. If we accept that the market has made inroads in virtually every rural community in the region via the process of commoditization, what part have local actors played in the transformation? And what have been the ramifications for their own everyday lives, in terms of social relations, and in terms of the land resources upon which their existence is to a large extent predicated? In surveying a selection of previous writings on market integration and rural development in the region, and attempting to situate them within the wider theoretical literature, I frame the review in terms of several interlinked issues of particular significance in the Asaro Valley. These underlie much of the empirical discussion in subsequent chapters.

Accumulation and embeddedness

According to the universal model of the market, the individual actor is a central variable in any development equation, as one of the many participants in the market, and as an entrepreneur. Several observers of rural development in the highlands have written on issues of entrepreneurship and economic rationality (Finney 1973, 1987, 1993; Moulik 1973; Jackman 1977; Crocombe *et al.* 1967; Fairbairn 1988). Considerable effort has gone into showing that rural smallholders and subsistence cultivators *are* in fact the rational beings of neoclassical economic theory, or at least quite sensitive to the messages of the market (see e.g. Shand and Straatmans 1974). This is no wonder, given that certain cultural traits appear to fit quite well with capitalist behaviour. Paramount here is the *bigman* syndrome: status and leadership in Melanesian societies is achieved rather than inherited.[10] The pressure for achievement is tremendous. When the energy is channelled into market ventures, capital accumulation and development will ensue – if the theory holds. Embeddedness of the economy is thus seen as working in favour of the market, initially at least, but this sits somewhat uneasily with the underlying universal model of a disembedded market.

The study by Finney (1973) of business development in the Eastern Highlands is especially important in the context of this study. Finney concurred with the claim made earlier by Epstein (1968) about cultural predispositions towards market participation. Having selected some ten 'business leaders' and examined their careers, he argued that 'the Gorokans already had their own analogue of the spirit of capitalism and needed only linkage with the cash economy to express it' (Finney 1973: 122). He illustrated how their entrepreneurship in a 'new economy' was rooted in an 'old society' (Finney 1973: 170), resulting in a peculiar blend of traditional and modern motives and methods. With reference to Polanyi, he speculated as to whether fully-fledged modernization must entail complete severance of those ties, but did not come up with a conclusive answer.

Those whom Finney called 'business leaders' – a term that captures well the market optimism of modernization theory – later writers, influenced by the dependency school or Marxist political economy theory have dubbed 'rich peasants' or 'big peasants' (Good and Donaldson 1977; Donaldson and Good 1978; Amarshi *et al.* 1979; Connell 1979; Gerritsen 1979, 1981; Fitzpatrick 1980; Howlett 1980). The first big peasants appeared in the 1950s, when coffee production expanded greatly in the highlands, and since then coffee has continued to be the base for economic advance for many individuals. Another cohort of big peasants seemed to be appearing in conjunction with state-sponsored cattle projects in the 1960s and 1970s (Grossman 1983). Most of the early ones had established a relationship with an Australian coffee planter (who more often than not had been an administration officer, or *kiap*, before), for example as *bosbois* (labour overseers), and had themselves established substantial coffee holdings under the aegis of their mentor. The second and no less important key to their success was a successful utilization – or manipulation – of their relations with kinsmen and fellow villagers to gain control of labour and land, much as traditional big men had done. Later many branched out into other commercial ventures, particularly trucking or tradestore operations, but both of these activities had also been an Australian affair. Some have taken their commercial activities well beyond a level that justifies any peasant connotations. They are now well and truly capitalists.

For Finney, the expectation – or hope – clearly was that the business leaders would pull the rest of the community with them on to a path of economic development. From the political economy viewpoint, a major question was the extent to which commoditization had produced permanent cleavage between this 'class' of swashbuckling individuals and their fellows of lesser means. Gerritsen (1979) declared that this had occurred as early as in the 1950s and 1960s. He used the control of land and the presence of paid labour as the main criterion for inclusion in the 'big peasant' class (1979: 36). Donaldson and Good (1978) came up with an even simpler yardstick: the ownership of coffee pulpers. The categories of 'big peasants' (or in Donaldson and Good's terms, 'rich peasants') and 'rural capitalists' are on the other hand not clearly separated. These writers saw ample evidence of the members of this new class acting in concert to further their interests, enjoying for instance a 'most-favoured' status in dealings with the agricultural extension apparatus (see McKillop 1975), and aligning generally with the bureaucratic elite of the colonial and postcolonial state. Early big peasants also entered regional and national politics, and this has become the rule rather than the exception for enterprising men of all complexions in the postcolonial period.

Other writers have warned that an application of class analysis to Papua New Guinea is fraught with hazards (Turner 1984; Standish 1992). It has been pointed out that Good's trajectory of 'rich peasants' into 'rural capitalists' does not involve any clearly identified qualitative change in social relations (Fahey 1986: 150–151). This makes his otherwise Marxian class analysis problematic.[11] Connell, although he readily acknowledged that stratification is emerging, saw 'no evidence of class action outside the towns and little within them' (1982: 513). Whether this was completely true or not when he was writing, the boundaries between the still embryonic classes are certainly fluid and frequently transgressed. Many, if not most households in Kasena village, where I did my fieldwork, utilize hired labour at some point in time. Coffee pulpers abound. If we want to stick with class analysis, we must at least invent plausible criteria to distinguish between the *a priori* theorized classes.[12]

Thus rural development in the highlands has frequently followed logics which seem to be somewhat different from the logic of capital. It is undeniable that big peasants exist in the Asaro Valley where I did my fieldwork, men who have accumulated both considerable wealth and political power. Yet there are also many examples of them being turned overnight into very small peasants indeed, through intergroup warfare or other social calamities: this is a precarious class at the best of times. The cattle projects, described by Grossman (1983) as creating intense inequalities in the 1970s, have also faded away with not much to show for all the effort that went into them. Ploeg (1985b) points to the issue of intergenerational transfer, and argues that the emergence of big peasants will not create permanent social cleavage (see Finney 1973: 177–178). Also, as the wealth amassed through commercial undertakings is not often channelled into productive investment, but rather used to support ventures into the sphere of regional and even national politics, the *bigman*'s quest for continued 'bigmanship' within and beyond his own clan often ends up siphoning too many resources from the commercial venture for the latter to prosper in the long run (see Zimmer-Tamakoshi 1997; Finch 1997).

In other words, what has developed is neither a clear-cut capitalist and class-ridden economy as Marx would have it, nor even a rudimentary Polanyian 'Great Transformation' – let alone a completed one. I cannot but concur with Long, when he generally chides 'political economists who attempt to resolve the heterogeneity of third world economies by inventing such strange sociological categories as "disguised proletarians", "potential capitalists" and "wage-labour equivalents"'(Long 1986: 13). A more fruitful way is to emphasize that the market is very much an embedded one in this context, with deep implications for entrepreneurship and accumulation. A disembedding of the economic from the social has certainly not taken place in the area in the last decades, as Finney himself acknowledged in his 1980s restudy (Finney 1987, 1993), and as I observed in the Asaro Valley in 1994–95. Traditional social mores have not only proved resilient, but have to a certain extent been buoyed by integration into the market (see C. A.

Gregory 1982; see also Lewis 1992 for a description of a similar development in the Philippines).

Sustained autonomy or a simple reproduction squeeze?
Equally complex questions arise when we look at the opposite face of this same coin, namely the processes affecting the lower end of the rural socioeconomic spectrum. At first glance, the bulk of highland households seem to fit reasonably well into the mould of simple commodity production (Thompson 1986, 1987). They, like practically all Papua New Guinean households, need some cash to survive. School fees, clothes, and bought foods link their continued reproduction to the market, and there is no turning back to 'pure subsistence' in that sense. On the production side, all households must purchase some necessary inputs, such as bushknives and axes. Other market-purchased inputs, such as fertilizer, pesticides, and seed, which have so effectively 'captured' the peasantry in many other parts of the world, are not universally utilized, but are bought by some smallholders, especially those involved in the cultivation of introduced vegetables. Most development projects, in which smallholders have been involved, deepen their reliance on market relations in this respect, either by design or default.

Howlett (1973) was the first to raise the question of 'terminal development' in a discussion of the Goroka (Asaro and Bena Bena) Valley. She argued that after two decades of modernization at breakneck speed, structural limits to economic advancement were coming into play. The bulk of the rural population were caught up in the role of small coffee growers, relying on one cash crop whose international commodity markets had proven capricious, unable to progress further as factors of production – land and skilled labour – were limited. Some years later she suggested that large-scale rural proletarianization in the formal sense was only kept at bay by the continued access of most rural Papua New Guineans to family or clan land. Even so, market integration had 'intensified regional differences' (Howlett 1980: 194) and the economic marginality of many areas within the new cash economy meant that many were now functionally landless.

Gregory suggested that 'the distinguishing feature of the PNG economy was the non-emergence of land as a commodity' and attributed it, as have many others, to the tenacity of kinship ties (C. Gregory 1979: 389). Moreover, colonial pacification 'froze' a previously fluid system of land holdings and land claims. This had the double effect of limiting the market economy while allowing the gift economy to flourish.

MacWilliam on the other hand, taking a much stronger Marxist view, sees the argument about the extent of market integration as a misplaced one. The deed is done, and the non-commoditization of land is irrelevant (MacWilliam 1988). Invoking Marx's distinction between *formal* and *real subsumption* of labour under capital, he considers the smallholder cash-cropping households as no longer peasants or simple commodity producers, but rather as units of production which are already fully subsumed, in the 'real' sense. He emphasizes the 'consumption' of state infrastructure – roads, education, health services – as an important means of incorporation (Thompson and MacWilliam 1992: 130–131). Together with commodity stabilization funds, ostensibly designed to keep the smallholding sector viable whatever the vagaries of the world market – or in his view to keep people anchored to land in a manner comparable to 'working for the dole' in industrialized countries (MacWilliam 1996) – this points, he argues, to the alliance of the state with the interests of capital in securing continued accumulation. Development projects aimed at smallholders also ultimately serve this purpose, but the failure (or unwillingness) of aid agencies and others to recognize it means that 'schemes to extend household production, of both immediately consumed items and marketed products can be treated as a part of a design to raise living standards while maintaining smallholder autonomy' (Thompson and MacWilliam 1992: 120). In this analysis, development rhetoric conveniently veils both the underlying motive of maintaining and expanding the accumulation of surplus, and the political contests which accompany subsumption.

Finally, consider the approach of geographer Grossman (1983, 1984, 1987). Although he aimed at giving due weight to agency, his analysis also portrayed the impact of market integration in somewhat deterministic hues. Having studied a village involved in both coffee growing and cattle husbandry, he argued that commoditization has gone hand in hand with a loss of autonomy (Grossman 1984, 1987). Village bigmen transformed into 'cattle bosses' had *de facto* limited the access of fellow villagers to land by fencing off large tracts (Grossman 1983). He illustrated how a sudden increase in incomes due to a coffee boom in the late 1970s led to the partial abandonment of food gardening in favour of pastimes such as gambling and drinking, the symptoms of what he called 'subsistence malaise' (Grossman 1984: 219). In populist fashion, he argued strongly for the resurrection of subsistence. In fact, the villagers he studied abandoned their cattle a little later, and Grossman acknowledged that their autonomy was still far too great to warrant the label of Bernstein's simple reproduction squeeze.

What is one to make of these generally negative assessments, coming from such different angles? Although the situation differs from area to area, highlanders in general still enjoy a substantial degree of autonomy. Household production of food for own consumption remains a strong feature of livelihood strategies even in the most economically 'advanced' areas, such as the Asaro Valley. Commodity production has not taken hold as thoroughly as MacWilliam argues, nor have its effects been as devastating as Grossman maintains. I would certainly not go as far as to argue that highland smallholders are immune from the effects of state power and market uncertainties. For example, they certainly cannot do much about the fluctuating prices their produce receives on world commodity markets. Despite a measure of price stabilization, such fluctuations quickly filter through to the local level. Yet the dependence on coffee as a cash crop has never been total among the masses of the Asaro: at least partial 'exit' from the market (Hydén 1980) remains a possibility. Growers frequently neglect their coffee gardens if what the global market has to offer does not please them. Such responses cannot be captured by locating agency in 'disembodied social categories' (N. Long 1992: 21), such as class. Coffee growing is not only about sheer economic survival, but also about recognition and prestige. Cultural and social influences on production decisions also remain strong. Not least, ultimate rights to land are vested in clans or patrilineages.

This is not to say that all is well with the 'peasantry' in the highlands. As Howlett initially pointed out, the most vulnerable in the current political economy are those whose land is locationally and physically marginal. Many of those have ended up in a highly precarious position as migrant labourers for the more auspiciously situated commodity growers. Yet most of these continue to hold rights to land in their home villages, and can (and sometimes do) move back if they so choose.

Compared with the overwhelming interest in the social processes surrounding coffee production, fresh food marketing has received little attention. It is often treated as a byproduct of subsistence cultivation, with little impact on the structure of rural society. Although this is true in some areas and for some crops, the significance of marketing and market gardening for rural differentiation in a locality such as the Asaro Valley warrants a closer look, given the scope of these activities there.

Patriarchy and intra-household relations

Recent researchers (especially Overfield 1995) have drawn attention to the fact that differentiation along the lines of gender may well be a more important feature of market integration in Papua New Guinea than any class- or quasi-class-based differentiation. Gender roles and their changes following commoditization are indeed well documented in the wider literature on smallholder farming. Although exceptions do exist (e.g. Benton 1987), the tone of this literature is generally gloomy: it shows women bearing the costs of market integration, while men reap the benefits (e.g. McCall 1987; Spiro 1987; Trenchard 1987; Harriss 1989).

The highlands of Papua New Guinea have long been recognized as profoundly patriarchal societies (Gelber 1986). Traditional subsistence cultivation of kaukau and pigs was based largely on women's labour. Through virilocal residency, women's access to the fundamental productive resource of land was, and remains, vested in their husbands' patrilineages. Miscellaneous ideological constructions, often alleging women's unclean nature or inclinations to sorcery, were utilized for reinforcing women's subordinate status and legitimating their sometimes brutal suppression by the men. Hence, when it arrived with the Australian *mastas*, the modern market economy interacted with a complex pre-contact pattern of gender inequality. With many of the flag-bearers of modernity coming out of a 'blokey' rural Australia – a society not especially noted for its gender sensitivities – it comes as no surprise that the colonial period did little in the way of achieving a more equitable balance. The 'smallholder' of postwar development policy and practice was decidedly male. The coffee trees – and the money that grows on them, to paraphrase Brookfield (1968) – ended up in the hands of men. Nor have postcolonial politics and development efforts managed to change markedly the rules of the game, although addressing the gender issue has been a stated aim of the development policies of the state (Avalos 1995).

That notwithstanding, while the world of coffee sales (although not necessarily coffee *production*) is a man's world for the most part, the fresh food market is a different story altogether. Women are much more numerous than men in the small-scale urban and rural marketplace trade (Hide 1993: 4–13). The long-distance kaukau trade has, in the Asaro Valley at least, attracted the attention of most men big and small – and women. Two conjectures have been aired to explain women's prominence in the marketplaces. One is that this is a logical extension of their role as subsistence gardeners (Christie 1980). It is pointed out that the 'gendering' of certain food crops as male or female has to some extent been carried over to the marketplace (Maclean 1989), although such classifications are not rigid. The other interpretation is that this is a response to women's marginalization in other cash-earning activities (Jackson and Kolta 1974; Overfield 1995). Significantly, men are much more prominent wherever high-value, 'introduced' vegetables are sold to institutional buyers or wholesalers, as well as in the long-distance kaukau trade, where much larger quantities are sold by each individual than in the local, hinterland-based markets of the highlands.

On the positive side, the fresh food markets have provided women with cash-earning opportunities, which although often small (Hide 1993: 13–20), may be crucial for the reproduction of the household (Sexton 1993: 129). On the other hand, Overfield has shown that returns to labour are substantially lower in market gardening than in coffee production, and consequently sees women's involvement in the former as evidence of their marginalization. Attempting to explain what he terms 'market failure' in the highlands, he makes much of those intra-household contradictions based on gender. The 'optimal' strategy of concentrating scarce land and household labour on the higher-returning coffee is not followed, he argues largely because of women's precarious position (Overfield 1995).

It should be noted that in spite of women's generally subordinate status, true 'big women' in the economic sense are found in the highlands, although they are few and far between (Kuman 1987; Rumint 1987; Zimmer-Tamakoshi 1997). A fresh food development project running for some years has attempted to redress the gender balance in commercial gardening, by strengthening the entrepreneurial capacity of a handful of individual women (Maxie Dominic, pers. comm., 1995). Sporadic attempts at collective action, in the form of women's development corporations, have suffered from similar political frictions, as have many male commercial ventures (Dickerson-Putman 1986: 340–364).

Sexton (1986, 1993) described an especially intriguing development based on wholly local agency; the so-called *Wok Meri* movement. In this case, women set up a separate savings and exchange system parallel to the 'men's economy'. Sexton interpreted this as a kind of protest against the economic dominance of men and what women saw as their improvident use of household funds. It was an effort to enhance women's status and rights to property and prestige, and seemed to have diffused rapidly from its origins in the 1960s in Simbu over to the Eastern Highlands. Although my own fieldwork location was quite close to the Daulo area where Sexton worked in the late 1970s, I found scant evidence of similarly organised women's movements in Lunube.

MARKETS, COMMODITIZATION, AND ACTORS

At this stage I do not want to draw strong conclusions from previous highlands literature regarding the impact of market integration on women, but merely reiterate that markets are amongst those arenas of social life in which the identities of women, men, and 'things' are negotiated. Gender inequalities and struggles enter into their social construction in an important way, and yet again blanket declarations are best avoided in favour of a careful description of socially embedded markets in their local context. The fresh food market makes an especially interesting case.

Sustainability and land degradation

Finally, we come to the issue of the land resource itself, and the oft-discussed connections between population growth, commodity production, agricultural intensification, and environmental deterioration. Papua New Guinean rural communities were the subject of numerous village-based studies of 'cultural ecology' in the 1960s and 1970s (e.g. Rappaport 1968; Clarke 1971), based on the premises of systems analysis. These studies clearly revealed ecological relations and resource management under subsistence regimes as being anything but simple. However, concerned as they were largely with remote communities, which were only tenuously integrated into markets, they shed little light on the pressures and processes set in motion by commoditization. The subsequent emergence of 'political ecology' as an important method of analysis in human geography and development studies (Blaikie 1985; Blaikie and Brookfield 1987; Bryant 1992; M. Lewis 1992) has specifically addressed the interrelations between societal processes at the macro level and local environmental change. It is the 'land manager' who stands at the juncture. Ample evidence exists to show that land degradation is by no means restricted to societies under pressure from the capitalist market. In fact, parts of the Papua New Guinean highlands provide a prime example, as social and economic pressures for prestige exchanges in the old social order led to intensification and the advance of grasslands in place of forest (Allen and Crittenden 1987).

The Papua New Guinean evidence of the effects of market integration is equivocal. While Grossman (1984) saw portentous signs of a breakdown in land management accompanying the cattle projects of the Eastern Highlands, others have pointed to the fact that land managers here have much more control over their actions than in many other countries. The simple reproduction squeeze is not forcing them to intensify, by insidious indebtedness or other means. On the other hand, the combined effects of subsistence, commodity, and 'social' production (for prestation, which is still very important) with a high rate of population increase is a concern in places (Allen 1993, 1996). Parts of the highlands are very densely settled, the Asaro Valley in fact being close to the top of the table (Bourke *et al.* 1994a). These tend also to be the areas where market integration through cash crop production has become most pervasive, adding to the pressure on land. More than two decades ago Ward *et al.* (1974a: 23) spoke of frequent land disputes as evidence of 'cultural if not absolute land shortage' in the Eastern Highlands, although they did not specify what 'cultural' entailed in this context. Certainly there is no shortage of land disputes in the Asaro Valley at present. The Asaro case raises the specific question whether the relatively recent development of large-scale cultivation of kaukau for marketing may have added to existing pressures.

. . .

I have identified several major (and overlapping) themes in the literature on rural development in the Papua New Guinea highlands, which are acutely relevant to the case of the Asaro Valley. All these themes are linked to the wider questions discussed earlier, of the embedded market and the processes of commoditization. I contend that previous works have at times paid little attention to highlanders as *social actors,* within their own national, regional, and local economic space. By framing the discussion in this way, these writers are implicitly denying local rural people their creativity and agency and, in terms of development practice, pointing the way to paralysis rather than empowerment. This is precisely what the actor-oriented approaches, which I introduced earlier, aim to rectify, but without falling into the voluntarist trap. It is now time to return to some hunting and gathering in the foothills of social theory, in order to clarify my use of the actor concept.

DEALING WITH DIVERSITY:
AN ACTOR-ORIENTED APPROACH

The tension between the voluntaristic and structural views of rural transformation is nothing new. It is a truism that action – not only the action of rural people under increasing market integration, but in society at large – is at once voluntary and patterned. Attempts at reconciling these facts reverberate throughout the history of social theory.[13]

Dissolving structure and agency

Social theorists attempting to deal with the problem have at times resorted to inserting somewhere between structure and agency something that serves to mediate between these opposites (Thrift 1983). The intervention of Giddens (1979, 1984) has been particularly prominent in human geography (D. Gregory 1982; Pred 1983, 1984; Thrift 1983; Duncan 1985; Storper 1985; Gregson 1987; Rose 1987; Simonsen 1991), as well as in recent actor-oriented research into rural development (N. Long 1989a, 1992; van Donge 1992; Long and van der Ploeg 1994). Giddens starts off from the premise that people possess considerable *knowledge* about the social system of which they are a part, a system that consists of social interaction. He defines 'structures' as the sets of rules and resources upon which actors draw (Giddens 1984: 16–25). By definition, structures are durable and exist independently of individuals, but are nevertheless reproduced – and modified in the process – through social interaction of knowledgeable agents. Apart from purposeful action, much of everyday action is based on practical knowledge, embedded in routines (Giddens 1979). Action is based in part on unacknowledged conditions, and it inevitably has some unintended consequences. The crucial point is that 'structural properties of social systems are both medium and outcome of the practices they recursively organize' (Giddens 1984: 25). This is the process of *structuration*.

In the early 1990s, Giddens was increasingly criticized for his *de facto* emphasis on the structural side of the scheme, or on the recursivity of social life which stems from spatial and temporal routines, rather than on inventiveness and intentionality (Simonsen 1991; Thrift 1993; D. Wilson 1995). The debate about structuration has not been resolved in a fully convincing manner. It is now widely acknowledged that structure and agency must be seen as inseparable. We certainly need to look at agency as socially anchored, and we need to recognize that it can be either *structurally reproductive* or *transformative* (Hays 1994). Above all, we need a clearer picture of actors as human subjects, who as social beings transcend the dualism of structure and agency. Splitting the social with the help of these opposed concepts is not particularly helpful (Pile 1993). If we dissolve the structure–agency dualism, what are we left with?

Agency and rationality

It is essential to explore further the notions of agency (or action) and the actor. Several models of action have been offered (Hindess 1988). The simplest model takes it to be no different from decision-making. While incomplete in that decision-making on its own is not a sufficient conceptualization of agency, the model draws attention to other actors than individual persons. Not only individuals, but all entities capable of making decisions can be seen as actors: firms, agencies of the state, religious organizations, and so on. The action of the latter, however, cannot be reduced to the sum of individual acts. And the decision-making model reminds us that the capacity to act cannot be ascribed to amorphous categories like 'class' or 'society', which do not have the means collectively to decide on the course of action. Many of the Marxist-inspired writings on rural development in Papua New Guinea seem to make precisely this mistake, for example by portraying 'big peasants' as a rather too homogeneous and self-conscious class.

A more complex model is what Hindess (1988) terms the 'portfolio' model of action. Here the actor carries along a permanent portfolio of beliefs and desires, which are called upon as relevant in a given situation. Add the assumption of a stable ranking of these beliefs and desires, and we have the basics of the rational actor model. This is not the place to review the debate on instrumental rationality and rational action (but see Barnes 1988; Barnes and Sheppard 1992; Miller 1992), except to note that the rational actor model runs aground on the underlying sweeping assumption of the nature of humans as incessant maximizers, whose actions are always egotistic. On the other hand, the portfolio model, without the additional assumptions of the rational choice formulation, gives room for action that draws on more diverse rationalities and motives: it is not assumed that in each and every case only those actions that are instrumentally rational are chosen from the portfolio (Barnes and Sheppard 1992). Action can thus be based on diverse, fragmented rationalities. Methodological individualism is avoided, as actors can be social groups as well as individuals. Hence, Hindess's formulation injects a certain relativity into the concept of action, which accords better with the diverse contexts of space and time.

Hindess uses the term 'social action' to cover action by supra-individual actors. The term is not altogether appropriate, as it implies that action of individuals is something other than social. Of course, every act of individual actors is inscribed in their sociality. Even if it does not impinge directly on their fellow members of society – which it most often does – it is given meaning through the socialization of the acting person. During fieldwork in Papua New Guinea, I paid most attention to *individuals* as actors. In this particular context, and given my concern with the creation of a market which is characterized not by firms but by numerous small individual sellers, it proved the most meaningful entity for locating action. Individuals, even within a family, take decisions about what to sell, where and when. That said, these are unequivocally social individuals, enmeshed in family and descent-group relationships as well as social networks beyond this immediate sphere. In the next chapter I show the composition of such linkages for selected individuals, men and women, in the households I observed most closely in Lunube.

A different facet of action is brought into focus in Habermas's (1985a, 1985b) well-known theory of communicative action. Although his project is about establishing a supposedly universal theory of the rationalities of action, it does take due notice of intersubjectivity and social construction. Habermas visualizes social life as composed of two spheres: the *system*, which concerns material production and reproduction, and the *lifeworld*, in which the objective and subjective aspects of existence are tied together with the creation of symbols and meaning. It is in the system that we find action in the functional, goal-oriented, or instrumentally/strategically rational sense. In the lifeworld, however, a different form of rationality reigns: communicative rationality. Action here (what Habermas terms 'communicative action') is directed towards reaching an understanding between the individuals or parties involved. This adds a whole new dimension to the concept of action: at its core is social *inter*action, through which the actor defines him or herself in relation to others and the world (Miller 1992). The aim is to achieve understanding, to be able mutually to exchange knowledge. Action in this sense is just as much about what people say – the statements they are making (verbally or otherwise) about themselves and others – as what they do.

Carried over into a study of the market, both these conceptualizations are potentially useful. Hindess's emphasis on the portfolio does away with maximization as the essential characteristic of the market actor. The embeddedness of the economic in the social in its many forms can thus come into play in a much more decisive manner. But this does not address the issue of how the values and rationalities, which make up the portfolio, are themselves constructed. The concept of communicative action goes some way here, by inviting us to look at the symbolic values and value constructions occurring in the market. Apart from the market process itself, the things/goods/commodities exchanged are enveloped in symbolic meaning, which is constantly being redefined. Habermas talks of the 'colonization of the lifeworld' by the system as one of the most pervasive processes of modernity, evidenced by the hegemony of instrumental rationality in commoditized market economies. But we should be careful here not to assume a complete powerlessness of the actor as the inevitable outcome of such a process. Power is indeed a central, but slippery concept.

Power

A classic definition of power is that it is 'the ability to affect the actions or ideas of others, despite resistance' (Olsen and Marger 1993: 1). This is an objectivist view which looks at power as a measurable quantity: some have more while others have less or nothing at all. Established patterns of power become embedded in the structures of domination. In actor-oriented research, power has a somewhat more subtle meaning, which avoids the polar opposites of 'powerful' and 'powerless'. All people are considered to have some space for manoeuvre, enabling them to exercise some degree of power, but its distribution and the forms it takes 'always implies struggle, negotiation and compromise' (Long and Villarreal 1993: 159).

The view of power as diffuse – as something that percolates through society at large – has come to the fore in much recent social theory. I find the formulation of Crespi (1992) particularly helpful. He argues that 'objective' or structural power has received a disproportionately large share of the attention. We should look more closely at what he calls subjective power.[14] This is defined as the capacity of individuals and groups to cope with the contradictions thrown at them in everyday life, relating to their definition of themselves, their social situations, and intersubjective relations. It thus becomes the intersecting point where the agency–structure dilemma is played out.

Subjective power then relates, first, to the 'inner power' which individuals use to reconcile the contradiction between their own 'inner world' or lifeworld, and the 'outer world' made up of relations with things and other persons. The contradiction centres on identity: I have to define myself simultaneously as part of society, in order to be accepted by others, and as different enough not to become 'flattened to [my] social image' (Crespi 1992: 102). Power in this sense is not imposing one's will on others, but asserting a space of one's own, through resistance if need be. Second, there is 'outer power', which develops in the mutual relations between subjects, as these tie into material conditions and institutional structures. Finally, power is objective only when its possession becomes dependent upon specific places or roles in the social system. In this form power becomes a structural controlling device.

A conceptualization like that of Crespi allows us to get beyond the tendency to look at power as a matter of haves and have-nots, and instead look at it as 'a social relation diffused throughout all spaces' (Nederveen Pieterse 1995: 184), omnipresent and constantly negotiated.[15] Even those who are seemingly powerless frequently find ways of resisting (Scott 1985), of creating their own spaces for action, enrolling others in their own projects and in turn becoming enrolled in theirs (Villarreal 1992). Power ceases to be simply a possession, or a measurable quantity. It follows that we should listen carefully to the 'muffled voices of opposition and mobilisation' (Long and Villarreal 1993: 159) which many analysts of development concerned with macro-structures of political economy – of power as a device for control – have simply not heard.

Geography and actors: the market as a network

When making the shift down from the overarching concepts I have been discussing, the actor-oriented approach becomes clearly spatial. Its affinities with structuration theory and ideas of the embedded market are evident. In his work, Giddens made explicit references to space (as well as time) as a quite basic ingredient in the piquant stew that is social life.[16] Likewise, Granovetter's formulation of the market as a network is inherently spatial. The geography of the actor-oriented approach as formulated by Norman Long *et al.* emerges out of their Giddensian conception of actors as knowledgeable and capable:

> [A]gency (and power) depend crucially upon the emergence of a network of actors who become partially, though hardly ever completely, enrolled in the 'project' of some other person or persons. Effective agency then requires the strategic generation/manipulation of a network of social relations and the channelling of specific items (such as claims, orders, goods, instruments and information) through certain 'nodal points' of interaction (N. Long 1992: 23–24).

For the individual actor, place or locale is at once enabling and constraining, and his/her manipulation of networks of interaction is one of the keys to realizing the various strategies, or 'projects':

> Assuming that society is made up of networks with specific spatial configurations, it [is] crucial to understand space as a socially constructed, multi-dimensional structure in part based upon actors' livelihood strategies (Verschoor 1992: 185–186).

The metaphor thus gives substance to the other heuristic notions used in this approach. The *interfaces* (N. Long 1989b; Long and Villarreal 1993), where the various actors in the development process confront one another, are local nodes in a network of power and knowledge, sometimes ephemeral, but at other times becoming durable parts of the social structure. Individual actors create their own space for manoeuvre through a local encounter within a wider network of relations (Villarreal 1992). While the 'global' trends of commoditization and institutional incorporation (bureaucratization) shift the basis of power relations, they do not eliminate power at the local level. Instead, new 'points of leverage' and spaces for manoeuvre are created.

The network metaphor has indeed assumed centre stage in studies of agriculture and food, with growing attention paid to *actor-network theory* (Arce and Marsden 1993; Marsden and Arce 1995; Busch and Juska 1997; Goodman 1999; Lockie and Kitto 2000). The originators of this theory (Callon 1986; Latour 1993, 1997; Law 1994, 1997) envisage networks as radically hybrid constructions, woven together by *translation*, both between people, and between people and other entities or things. Actors assume power by putting into circulation various intermediaries – for instance money, regulations, police batons, or books about rural development – thus enrolling and mobilizing other entities in the network. Even non-human entities in this way become 'actors' or 'actants' (Latour 1997) in a constantly evolving network. Seen in this way, the 'Leviathan' of the market becomes no more, no less, than 'a skein of somewhat longer networks that rather inadequately embrace a world on the basis of points that become centres of profit and calculation' (Latour 1993: 121).

While the move towards a 'radical symmetry' between humans and non-humans made by the actor-network theorists is open to debate (see Marsden 2000), this has certainly opened up new ways of accounting for diverse realities. It allows a more nuanced tale to be told about markets than is provided by the dualisms of the global–local and structure–agency.

CONCLUSION

Can theory get a hold on the patterned desperation in which most people live their lives? (Inglis 1993: 160)

The concept of the market is truly a many-faced one. Both Polanyi and Braudel took us, in different ways, beyond the simple model of the universal market, based on the 'market principle'. Subsequent writers have emphasized the need to look at human agency in the everyday practice of markets. While the market *principle* has a geography – the geometric landscape of central place theory – market *practice* has multiple, sometimes strange and always socially constructed geographies.

We have seen that rural Papua New Guineans are at least as difficult as any other people to shoehorn into pre-fabricated theoretical boxes, however sophisticated these boxes may be. Sharp criticism has been launched in recent years at development theories of various complexions, for their proclivities to generalize without regard to local specificities and practice. Not that theory is irrelevant. Naïve empiricism is hardly a feasible option if one wants to understand the workings of markets in Papua New Guinea. On the contrary, I also hope to have demonstrated that concepts from social theory which give human agency its rightful space are invaluable when it comes to understanding the diverse outcomes that result from the integration of rural communities, such as those that form the subject of this study, with the market economy through commodity production and exchange.

The projects and strategies that are shaping food markets in Papua New Guinea, with their intended and unintended consequences, involve individuals who act within a specific social and spatial universe. Looking at these real markets not simply as a happy meeting of supply and demand as if nothing were more straightforward, but rather as continually changing products of *social* interaction, negotiation, and networking, in a fractured national economic space, involves travelling into the lifeworld of their creators.

NOTES

1. Whether such trade, even among the Tolai of the Gazelle, was as impersonal as the ideal type of the market would have it, is another point. It has been argued that, in contrast with African markets, barter and other impersonal market-like exchange in pre-contact Melanesia had in fact not been conducted according to the 'market principle', but was instead a form of reciprocity in disguise (Keil 1977), involving dyadic relations rather than multiple groups. Keil attributes this to a lack of security; the institution of the 'peace of the market' did not exist until post-contact times.
2. However, innovations like steel axes (albeit in limited numbers) and certain new crops had come into the central highlands earlier through the traditional trading networks (Hughes 1971).
3. Notably Adam Smith, the founding figure of classical political economy and neo-classical economics, who famously declared that there exists a 'certain propensity

in human nature ... to truck, barter and exchange one thing for another' (Smith 1900: 12).

4   Important though it is, I do not wish to embark on a review of neoclassical economics, but refer the reader to recent discussion and criticism of its theoretical premises and implications for development practice (through 'modernization') by Vandergeest (1988), Banuri (1990a, 1990b), Lubasz (1992), and Brohman (1995a, 1995b). The concept of the (economically) rational actor is an especially suspect generalization (see Barnes 1988; Barnes and Sheppard 1992; Miller 1992).

5   Walker (1988: 388) states that the universal market model, which came to dominate neoclassical economics from Walras onwards, was 'nothing more than an idealization of a French village square.'

6   It should be noted that Braudel does not even use the term, although his study can justifiably be situated within the 'embeddedness' position.

7   The new (or neo-) institutional approach emphasizes the variability of collective, institutional arrangements in economic systems, and interprets them as rational solutions to economic problems. For example, the evolution of non-market institutions is seen as a response to lower transaction costs in cases where markets fail. Granovetter (1992: 25) accuses the institutionalists of succumbing 'to the ruinously high temptation in social science to tell functionalist stories', but this does not apply to all these theorists (see Eggertsson 1990). While the new institutionalism has drawn rightful attention to problems of transaction costs and property rights, it relies on a similar rational-actor model and methodological individualism as neoclassical economics. For an extensive discussion of the approach in relation to development studies, see recent volumes edited by Harriss *et al.* (1995) and Acheson (1994).

8   I beg to differ here. True, the ATM which I commonly use may appear detached and free from moral complications, but on the other hand it has a genealogy: it is of course a thoroughly socially constructed machine. Moreover, it is perfectly capable of calling forth an emotional response from myself, and sometimes it appears grumpy and non-cooperative when I try dealing with it.

9   One of Kopytoff's examples is the automobile. A 'biography' of an African car would tell a very different story from that of a middle-class American car, or a French peasant car (Kopytoff 1986). Indeed, tracing the short, but eventful life of a Papua New Guinean village *trak* (truck or utility) would reveal an interesting social, cultural, and spatial history, and perhaps unexpected valuations (Thomas 1991: 29).

10 Actually, the picture is considerably more complicated (see Feil 1987: Ch. 5), but at least for the Asaro Valley, the *bigman* model has considerable merit.

11 Standish (1984: 276) also accuses Donaldson and Good in particular of 'highly selective use of material ... lack of explicit theory, and negligible fieldwork'. It is indeed striking that much of their discussion (see Donaldson and Good 1978, 1988) is built around the same few entrepreneurs Finney had identified

MARKETS, COMMODITIZATION, AND ACTORS

in the Eastern Highlands. Finney's 'ten apostles of capitalism' (Standish 1984: 278) also feature prominently in Gerritsen's work (1979).

12 This is in no way meant to devalue the importance of asking questions about class and social differentiation. On the contrary: a recent account of the ways in which members of an emergent urban elite in Papua New Guinea increasingly try to create distance between themselves and the ordinary rural villagers (Gewertz and Errington 1999) gives ample reason to ponder the creation of new injustices and new forms of exploitation.

13 See what could justly be termed the Mother of all Quotes, at least for the social scientist – Marx's famous remark from the *Eighteenth Brumaire* about people as makers of their own history: 'Die Menschen machen ihre eigene Geschichte, aber die machen sie nicht aus freien Stücken, nicht unter selbstgewählten, sondern unter unmittelbar vorgefundenen, gegebenen und überlieferten Umständen' (Marx 1960: 271).

14 A somewhat similar distinction is made by Slater (1992: 299), who separates power *over* from power *to act, to resist*.

15 To bring this (temporarily) back to earth, I offer the following illustrative example from the Papua New Guinea highlands literature, of a power struggle in an emerging market: In the 1970s, coffee sellers in the Okapa region adamantly refused having their beans tested for dryness by biting them. The itinerant coffee buyers bought for very low prices, having no guarantees of the quality of the drying. Those who wanted to pay a higher price, but insisted on testing the beans, risked violent reaction (von Fleckenstein 1975). Here, the exertion of power obviously led to an outcome somewhat less than optimal – for all participants!

16 Considerable cross-fertilization has occurred between structuration theory and time-geography (cf. Pred 1977, 1982, 1984; Giddens 1979, 1984; Thrift 1983; Hägerstrand 1984).

3

Faces in the crowd: lives and networks of selected actors

> *Although we think of the market as a disembodied principle, without location and without people (with only "buyers" and "sellers"), the markets that exist are located in real places, with real people trading in them (Davis 1996: 55–56).*

WE NOW COMMENCE A JOURNEY into a world thick with 'real' places and people. In this chapter the life histories and sociospatial networks of the members of several of the households, with whom I had closest contact during fieldwork, are traced. Their biographies are presented in a condensed verbal form, and the structure of their kinship links and social networks is graphed. Some of the people discussed feature prominently in the kaukau marketing story told in later chapters, and all participate in local fresh food markets. These sketches serve as illustrations of the complexity of the social world of the Lunube people, but the households and individuals discussed should not be taken as necessarily typical of the diversity of situations. 'The typical actor' is almost a contradiction in terms anyway.

To understand the actions of growers in the fresh food markets at the present time, we must situate them both in time and within a network of social relations. The 'situated life story' (Simonsen 1991: 429), concerned as it is with an intermediate spatial and temporal scale, provides important clues here. On the one hand, it locates the person within the processes of the *longue durée*; of the relatively slow changes in the world political economy and cultural mores. This is the temporal dimension in which institutions are created and recreated, among them the institution of the market itself. On the other hand, life history is crucial for understanding the day-to-day conduct of individuals, which largely consists of routinized actions, but which also is marked by a degree of spontaneity. Likewise, places or 'locales' in the parlance of Giddens, form the connective tissue between the wider spatial scale of the international and national context of action, and the more circumscribed space of daily practice. They provide the 'settings of interaction' (Giddens 1984: 118), which constrain and enable at the same time. As Simonsen suggests,

> In the heart of the mediation between individual and collectivity stands individuals' biographies or life stories in time and space. It is here that human practice and consciousness are connected with the temporal-spatial context ... through the notions of generation and locality (Simonsen 1991: 429).

PORTRAITS OF SELECTED HOUSEHOLDS

I have agonized over whether or not to use people's real names in these accounts, as they contain personal and family details. In the end I decided not to use pseudonyms, as not only would the distancing and 'disembodiment' this entailed go against the whole philosophy of my project, but it would also be less than sincere towards the people, who themselves very much wanted me to tell their stories. For those with knowledge of local personalities it would be possible anyway to see through any disguise. While on fieldwork, I made it clear to those concerned that I was going to write about their personal circumstances.

Gumineve and Kondagule

It is no happenstance that I start with this couple: for the best part of my fieldwork period I shared a house with them, ate with them, and argued with them (see Chapter 1). I therefore had closer access to their social world than to that of any others. The house I rented in Kasena was that of their daughter and son-in-law, who lived elsewhere, but were in fact very much a part of the household dynamics. Apart from all this, Gumineve and Kondagule are an interesting couple for various reasons, as the following life histories show.

In his early fifties, Gumineve belongs to the Ambilisezuho subclan, and can claim distinguished ancestry (Figure 2). His father Gimbe – a frail old man during my stay in Kasena – was one of the most respected *bigmen* and fight leaders of the whole Gamizuho clan in the old order of things.[1] So were Gimbe's own father and grandfather. For example, it was stated that

Dende, Gumineve's great-grandfather, had first claimed much of the land which his now numerous descendants call their own.

Gumineve's youth coincided with the tumultuous postwar period of social and economic change. He is of a generation which glimpsed both worlds. His was among the last cohorts of young men to go through full initiation ceremonies associated with the *namo* cult (see Newman 1965: 66–68). He also went to school for a short period of time: the Asaroka Bible School, where Lutheran evangelists taught the basics of the new religion. He was about 14 years of age at the time, but his parents had already found him a wife. Tormented by the taunts of his fellow students, who called him 'the married one', he left school, never to return. At least he had learned the bare essentials of reading and writing – albeit neither in English nor Tok Pisin, but in the language of the catechists: Kâte.[2]

The prospective wife turned out to be compatible neither with Gumineve nor with his parents, and was sent packing after a short period. Eventually, or in his own words, when he had *mausgras* (beard), he courted and subsequently married Kondagule from the village of Ovia on the western side of the valley (Figure 3). They settled down in Kasena and were allocated substantial portions of Gimbe's large landholdings, for food gardening and coffee. Gimbe had in the 1950s planted coffee, together with other men of Kasena, and some of this was handed over to Gumineve. They had two children early in their relationship, and the third much later.[3] They did well. For some time they participated in a vehicle *bisnis* with others of Gumineve's patrilineage, later with his own brother Gihiro. Also they ran a small tradestore for a while. Both are common strategies of aspiring highland villagers.

Their older daughter Nellynne was sent to Asaroka Lutheran High School, where she met Rex, her husband-to-be, who is of Simbu origin but with settler parents and relatives at Asaro. The young couple continued on through National High School,[4] while keeping a strong presence at home in Kasena where they, for example, built a *haus kapa* (house with a roof of corrugated iron). Gumineve and Kondagule made them partners in their own coffee and gardening enterprise, which was at this time (just before 1990) taking on an added dimension: commercial kaukau growing. The household was among the first to sell kaukau in Port Moresby. Gradually, Rex and Nellynne became the driving forces on the commercial side, despite living in Aiyura (see Map 2), where the *saveman* (educated) Rex had a job at the Highlands Agricultural Experiment Station, and Nellynne had a clerical job in Kainantu. They were seen by Gumineve and Kondagule as a

FACES IN THE CROWD

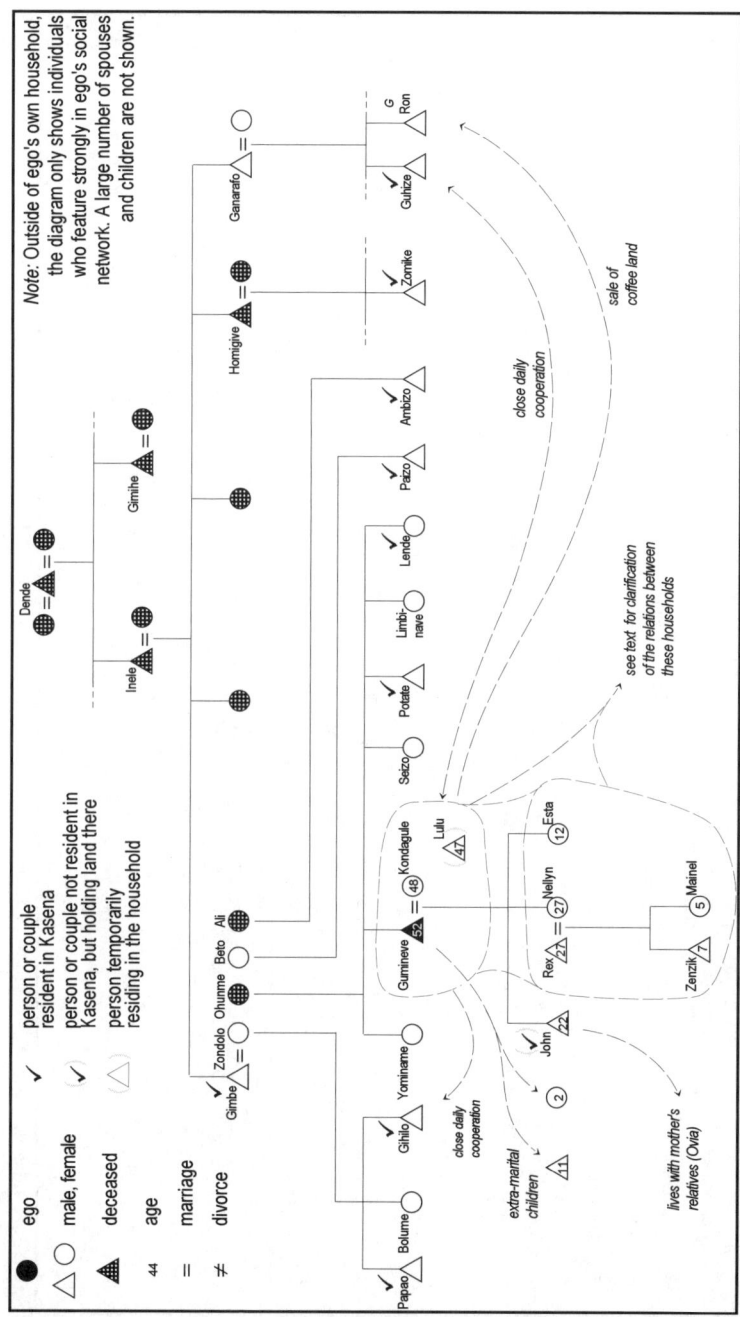

Figure 2: Gumineve – household and next of kin

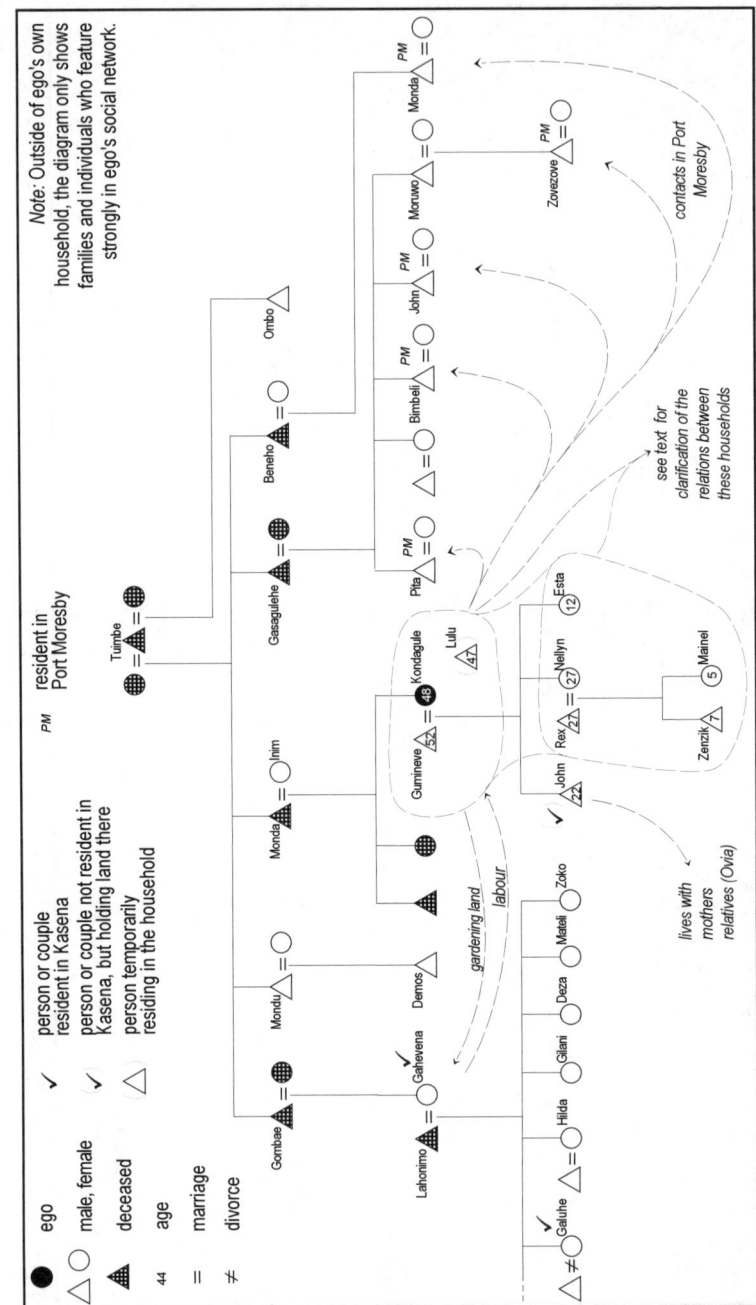

Figure 3: Kondagule – household and next of kin

link to the 'other' Papua New Guinea; to the brave new world of education, commerce, and Western knowledge. They would elevate the name of the parents and the whole Gamizuho clan. They would also look after the older couple in financial terms in years to come.

The search for security and/or prestige took other forms. During the late 1980s and early 1990s coffee prices were low, but the shipments of kaukau from Lunube to Port Moresby had started, and Gumineve and Kondagule were putting more energies into market gardening than ever before. They sold their main coffee garden to an educated relative who was at the time making a name for himself in the coffee business.[5] The price was very low, but the expectation was clearly that this was not a one-off transaction, but would lead to ongoing financial and other benefits from the wealthy, town-dwelling buyer. In fact, this did not happen. Although he continued to contribute to brideprices and other outlays of his kinsmen and kinswomen, he did not become a stable source of funds for Gumineve and Kondagule personally. Their monetary income is now largely predicated upon market gardening – and no less importantly, contributions from Rex and Nellyn.

Politics must not be forgotten. Gumineve stood for election as the representative of the Gamizuho in the Local Government Council in 1992, following in the footsteps of his younger brother Gihiro, who had been *kaunsil* (councillor) some years before. The office of *kaunsil* is fiercely contested in the Asaro–Watabung area. Five other candidates came forward but, in his own interpretation, he charmed enough voters with his short campaign speech to be elected, much to his own surprise – and delight. During my stay in 1995 he was convincingly re-elected. Although the council had been severely restricted financially for some years, Gumineve had managed to get some money for the building of a new community school in Kasena,[6] and for the upkeep of some local churches.

His own monetary reward from politics is slight. At the time of my fieldwork (which coincided with an acute crisis in state finances), councillors were not being paid their rightful remuneration of K40 per month. Disillusioned, Gumineve once stated that *kaunsil* work was '*rabis wok*' (rubbish work), but still he clearly relished his political role and the prestige it brought, and spent much time at Asaro in discussions with his fellow councillors.[7] Rex, Nellynne, and Kondagule, on the other hand, were not happy with the inevitably reduced attention he could pay to the family's own many and varied projects. In his defence, he stated that he had previously often used some of his wages to hire labour for gardening.

The couple's only son, John, was at the time of fieldwork living in his mother's village, although he retained some access to garden land in Kasena. He had been embroiled in controversy in Kasena, and had therefore been more or less thrown out, or at least told to stay in Ovia and keep a low profile for a while.

Kondagule also had her own share of controversy. An avid gambler, she spent long hours playing cards with other villagers, men and women. During her frequent sales trips to Lae and Port Moresby she found new and exciting cardplaying partners, and Gumineve, Rex, and Nellynne suspected her of squandering some of the money from marketing – which she steadfastly denied. This was the source of considerable friction in the family. It underscores the complex constellations of interests and power relations which characterize 'the household': it is not necessarily, or even usually, the unproblematic, harmonious unit which appears in the assumptions of many economic theories (Hart 1992).

Gumineve and Kondagule's household was indeed complex. When I moved to Kasena, it counted no less than eight other persons. There was Gahevena, Kondagule's 'big sister' (see Figure 3), with five of her daughters. For reasons explained in Chapter 8, they left the household early in 1995. There was also a young man from Gulf Province, who had been living in Port Moresby. There he had got acquainted with Kondagule in 1994, when she was selling kaukau in Gordons Market. He had talked her into buying a plane ticket for him up to Goroka, as he wanted to see the highlands. He had lived and worked with the household for a while, but had become restless and wanted to get back to Port Moresby. He left in the new year. Finally, there was Lulu, or 'Lembinave' as he was called by the Lunube people. He was a relative from Kondagule's natal village of Ovia, who had stayed with the couple for a long time and taken part in most of its daily tasks. He had to leave in April 1995 when warfare in the tribal area of Kofena on the western side of the valley threatened to spill over to Ovia.

In fact, it is common in many highland societies for outstanding leaders to attract protégés to their households for longer or shorter periods. It was, however, clear that Rex and Nellynne had doubts about the value of this for Nellyn's parents, and their opposition played at least a part in the departure of the *manki Kerema* (the young Gulf man). They also insisted that Lembinave should return to Ovia, arguing that his presence brought danger upon the Gamizuho, as the Ovia people had taken sides in the Kofena war even if they were not directly involved in the fighting.

A generational gap may therefore be in the making, with a 'nuclear-family' individualism of the younger, educated generation clashing with the somewhat different preoccupations of the older. An incident which occurred shortly after my arrival indicates the differing conceptions of the preferred societal order. Just before Christmas 1994, a large post-funeral exchange ceremony was held in Kasena, following the untimely death of an educated and wealthy clan member. The various patrilineages which make up the three subclans of the Gamizuho contributed pigs, chicken or other food, which was then distributed to other clans from far and wide in the Upper Asaro. Rex and Nellynne also came home to Kasena to spend the Christmas holidays there, bringing with them a large pig they had bought at a piggery not far from Lae, as well as ten live chickens. Along with the 70-odd other pigs and countless fowl, these were killed, and cooked in *mumus* (earth ovens) during a day of much commotion in Kasena. Yet all the food that Rex and Nellynne brought was not destined for the clan distribution ceremony held on the following day, but for a much closer circle of their own relatives and helpers; among them girls who had minded their two young children at Aiyura. As he handed out the portions, Rex stressed in his short speech that this was *fri kaikai* (free food) – the *mumu* had not been made to sort out any troubles, but simply to have a good time. He told me later that he disapproved of the large communal redistribution ceremonies and had therefore chosen to put on a true family feast.

Being so immersed in village and council politics, Gumineve is well connected within the Upper Asaro Valley. The household's connections beyond the region are however mostly through Kondagule, as many of her 'brothers' have left their natal village to settle in Lae and Port Moresby (Figures 3 and 4). The Port Moresby cluster is especially large and close-knit. With little education, some of the migrants have found work there as drivers of company trucks or PMVs; others work as security guards, while others still subsist on petty trading of *buai* (betel nut). They live in the various settlements of the capital (e.g. Morata, Badili, Moitaka), where together with other migrants from their area they form small *wantok* groups. When Kondagule and Gumineve venture to Port Moresby, which they have done several times during the last decade, these are the people with whom they stay, and who provide them with transport, and in many other ways assist them in navigating the city.

Moroho and Nesime

On the Sunday afternoon when I first drove through the Lunube territory – before deciding to stay there – I stopped to give lift to a group of people

HARVESTING DEVELOPMENT

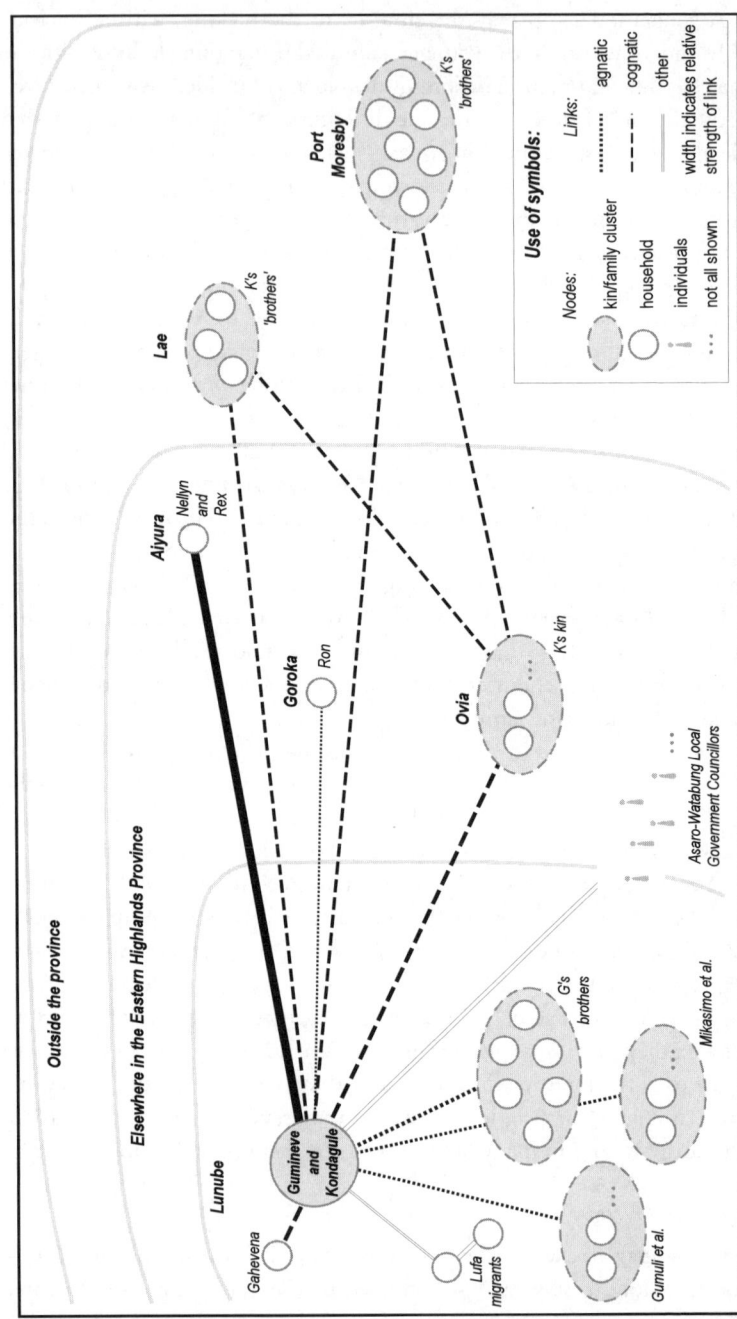

Figure 4: Gumineve and Kondagule – social networks

from Kasena coming from church on the other side of the valley. A middle-aged, muscular, softly-spoken man got in the front seat beside me and started asking me what business I was doing there. Having told him, he immediately made me an offer to enter into a partnership with him: he had ample land, he said, and together we could do big things in the fresh food market. This was Moroho Kukuwo, who became one of my key informants as well as a personal friend (although I never did become his business partner) after I had settled in Kasena a little later. In a way the incident encapsulates his own and his wife Nesime's life story. Always on the lookout for new opportunities, Moroho was for instance among the first, and possibly the very first, to send kaukau directly out of the highlands for sale in the markets of Port Moresby.

In fact, Moroho's father Kukuwo had as a young man moved from Manto (near Asaro) to Kasena, which was his mother's natal village, as a result of fighting. Although many Kasena people knew this, Moroho himself did not like to talk much about it, perhaps knowing that such 'foreign' origins could be turned against him if quarrels over land arose. Not that it seemed to me that he needed to worry; he is a respected member of the Lunubezuho subclan (Figure 5) and very much involved in exchanges and other matters of the group.

In his youth, Moroho received little or no formal education; he can neither read nor write. He did, however, spend a year working on a Department of Primary Industry (DPI) station in Wewak. He also attended an agricultural training course for a short while in the early 1970s. This will be discussed further in Chapter 6, as it played a considerable role in the rise of long-distance kaukau marketing. To pre-empt the story, in the 1970s Moroho attempted to become a commercial farmer, together with other young and ambitious Lunube men. Although this did not turn out as expected, Moroho has never ceased searching for other possibilities to profit from what he is undeniably good at: vegetable growing.

Nesime comes from Namta on the western side of the valley. As with Kondagule, a large number of her kinsmen and kinswomen have migrated out of their home village to the bright lights of Port Moresby and Lae. These feature strongly in the couple's social network beyond Lunube (Figures 6 and 7). Also, the couple have an important Port Moresby contact in a young, educated Lunubean relative, Kiff, whom they looked after when he was young. These households are linked by flows of gifts and money. When Moroho and Nesime first sent kaukau to Port Moresby, they enlisted

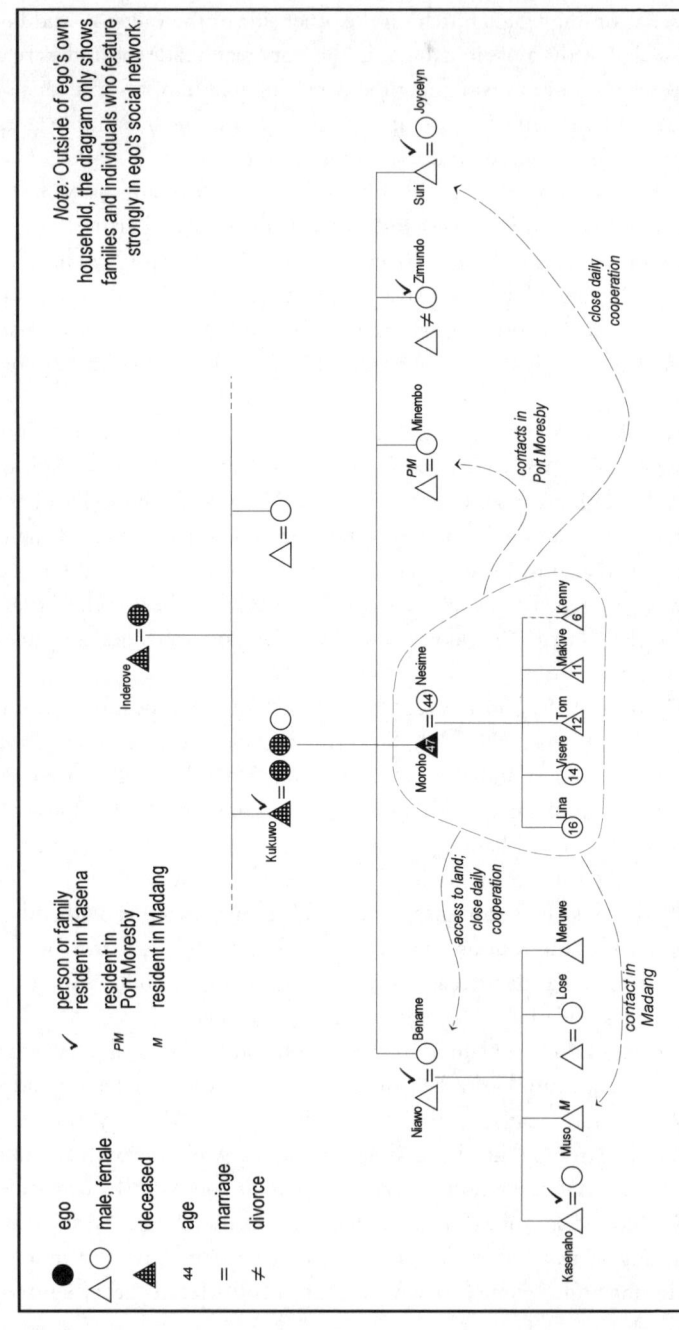

Figure 5: Moroho – household and next of kin

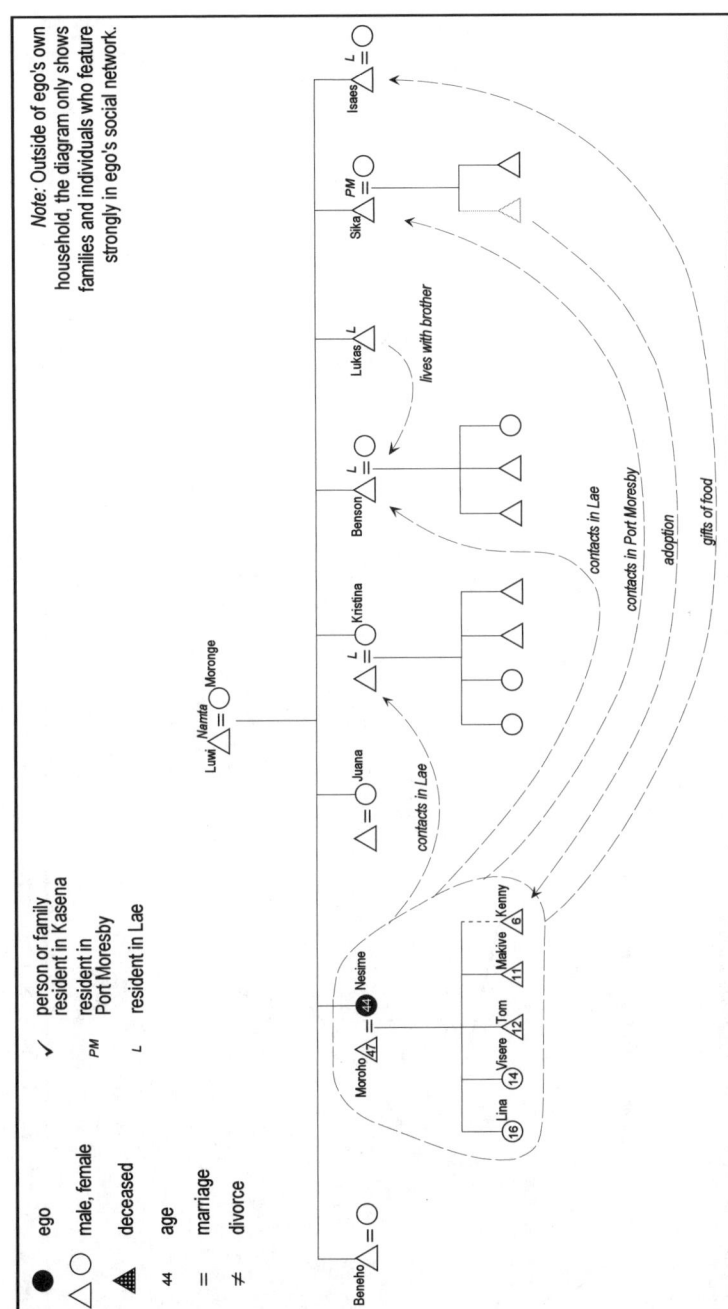

Figure 6: Nesime – household and next of kin

HARVESTING DEVELOPMENT

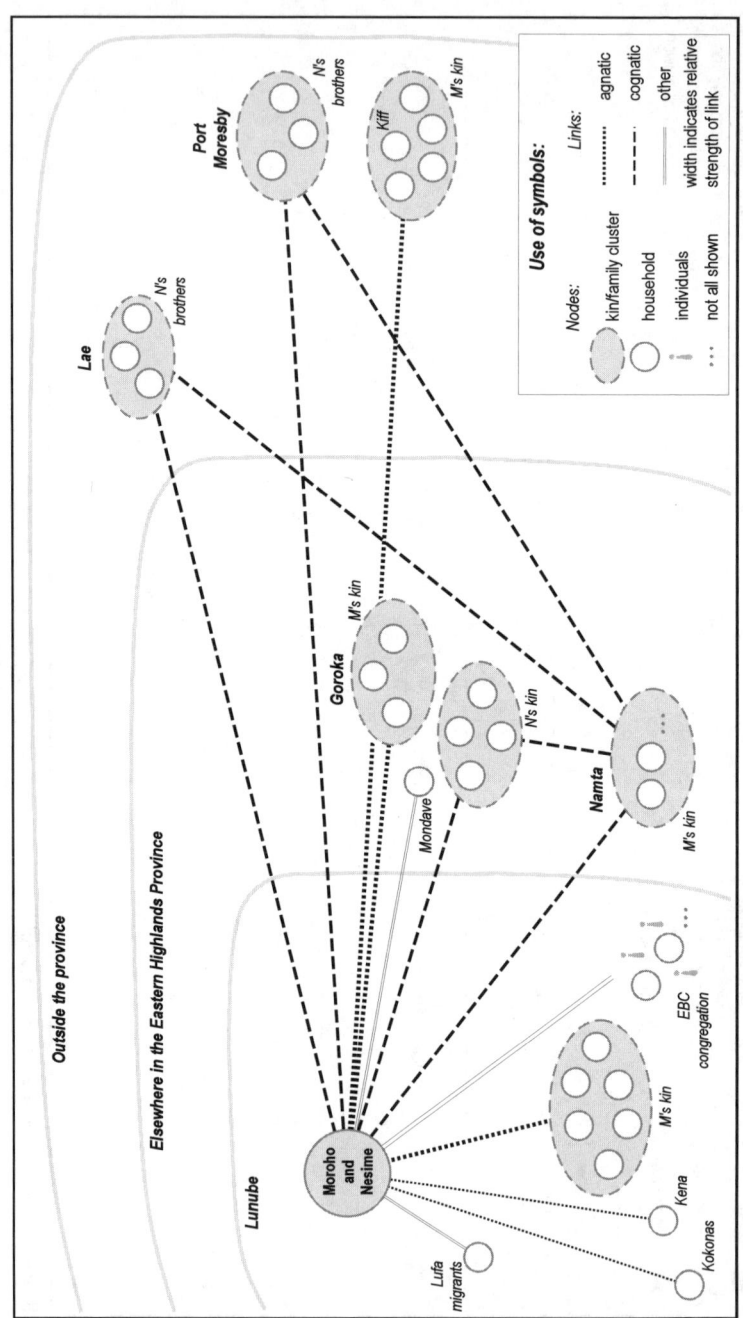

Figure 7: Moroho and Nesime – social networks

him and his family to sell it, but this did not turn out as planned. That story will also be told later.

Moroho and Nesime also spend considerable time in the affairs of their church – the Evangelical Brothers' Church (EBC), which has won over many Eastern Highlanders from the longer-established denominations. The couple were originally Lutherans, but stated that they disliked the moral laxity of the Lutheran church. EBC required its followers to give up the pleasures of alcohol, *buai*, and gambling, and thus prevented them from wasting their money – as they said they had tended to do in the past. EBC has a large and immaculately maintained church building in Lunube, and boasts the membership of its most notable businessman, Mondave Wobo. Mondave, now living in Goroka, is a significant node in their social networks. Moroho's relative in Goroka, who is an EBC pastor, is another very important link. The couple maintain strong ties to kinsmen and women from both Moroho's and Nesime's side both in Goroka and Port Moresby, but in Lae they rely on Nesime's brothers from Namta (Figure 7). They cultivate these social links with frequent visits and gifts of food and sometimes money, which, it may be added, sometimes flows the other way. This is very much a 'traditional' way of networking.

The household has relatively large coffee and vegetable gardens. They sometimes buy coffee from other villagers and process it, and they have even on occasions provided 'seed money' for Nesime's relations to do the same. They are also shareholders in Hunguko Coffee Ltd, which runs a coffee plantation and processing factory. The company was formed by the Lunube people to take over an expatriate-owned plantation which was established on their lands in the 1950s. The dividends paid to shareholders are not large, but this tells us that it would be simplistic to locate Moroho and Nesime unequivocally as 'peasants' or 'simple commodity producers'. Their livelihood strategies are rather more complex than that.

Moses and Soni

This household is interesting for several reasons. First, it provides an example of uxorilocal residence, instead of the virilocal norm. The land which is their main physical resource is claimed and held through the female head of the household, but this land is rather limited in extent. Second, because of the family's composition and the couple's emphasis on educating their children, the demand for income is high. Both these characteristics can and do influence their actions in market gardening and in markets.

Moses is around 40 years old, the daughter of a respected village leader (Figure 8). Her father Gumuli had not only been a strong fighter in the old days, but in his youth aligned himself strongly with the Lutheran church soon after it started its work in the area. Moreover, he became a pioneering smallholder coffee planter during the 1950s and was a forerunner in various other economic enterprises which greatly furthered his reputation, but which have since become commonplace. Gumuli is still considered one of the leading elders of the clan. He has all the hallmarks of a successful *bigman*, being a forceful personality who has drawn upon various sources of spiritual and worldly authority throughout his life – although his success is far from obvious in material terms nowadays, judging from his very Spartan surroundings in old age.[8]

Moses has to some extent followed in her father's footsteps and is now one of the village's most respected and influential persons in religious matters, although being a woman she does not carry any marked political clout. She finished schooling to Grade 9, making her one of the best-educated women in the village. Her religious activities, apart from regular church attendance, range from work with Lutheran women's groups throughout the area, to leading frequent evening prayer meetings in Kasena. For such meetings, the couple has built a separate house beside their own dwelling.

Soni, on the other hand, is a migrant. He hails from the Gimi-speaking area around Agotu in the Lufa District – from where several families have migrated to the somewhat brighter lights of Kasena (see Chapter 1). At home he finished Grade 5 of primary school. In his bachelor days he spent several years working as a labourer at a brewery in Port Moresby. When back in his home area, he married his first wife, a Lufa woman, with whom he had two children. Moses entered the scene later, but Soni's kinsmen were not willing to fork out a second brideprice for her. Moreover, Moses insisted on monogamy in accordance with her strict Christian principles. Hence Soni divorced his first wife and moved to Kasena. The couple have five children together (one born in 1995) and have also raised the son of Moses' divorced sister as their own. The eldest son is at the Asaroka High School, and the boy they have fostered is hoping to proceed beyond his Grade 9. Not far behind are the other children.

In Kasena, Moses lays claim to some of her father's considerable land. Admittedly, the old Gumuli now has a veritable army of descendants (see Figure 8), among whom the land has been carefully distributed. Moses'

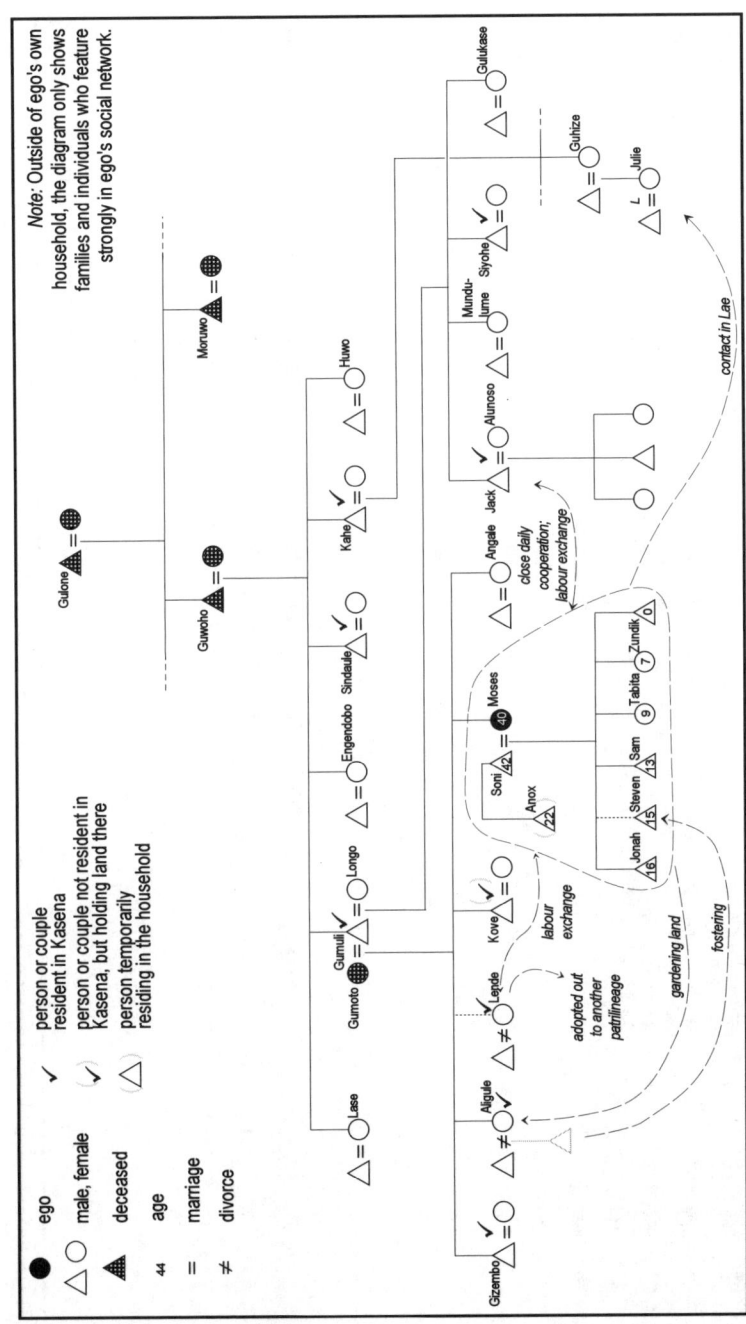

Figure 8: Moses – household and next of kin

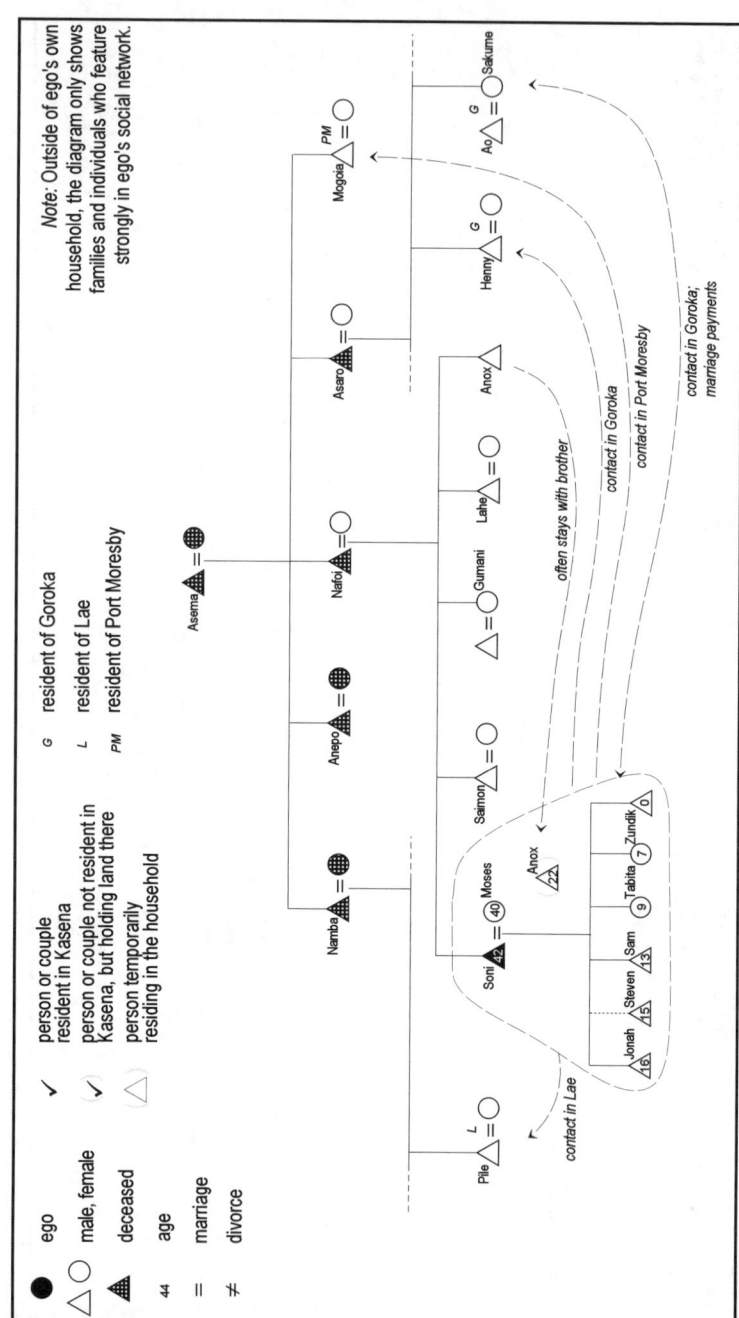

Figure 9: Soni – household and next of kin

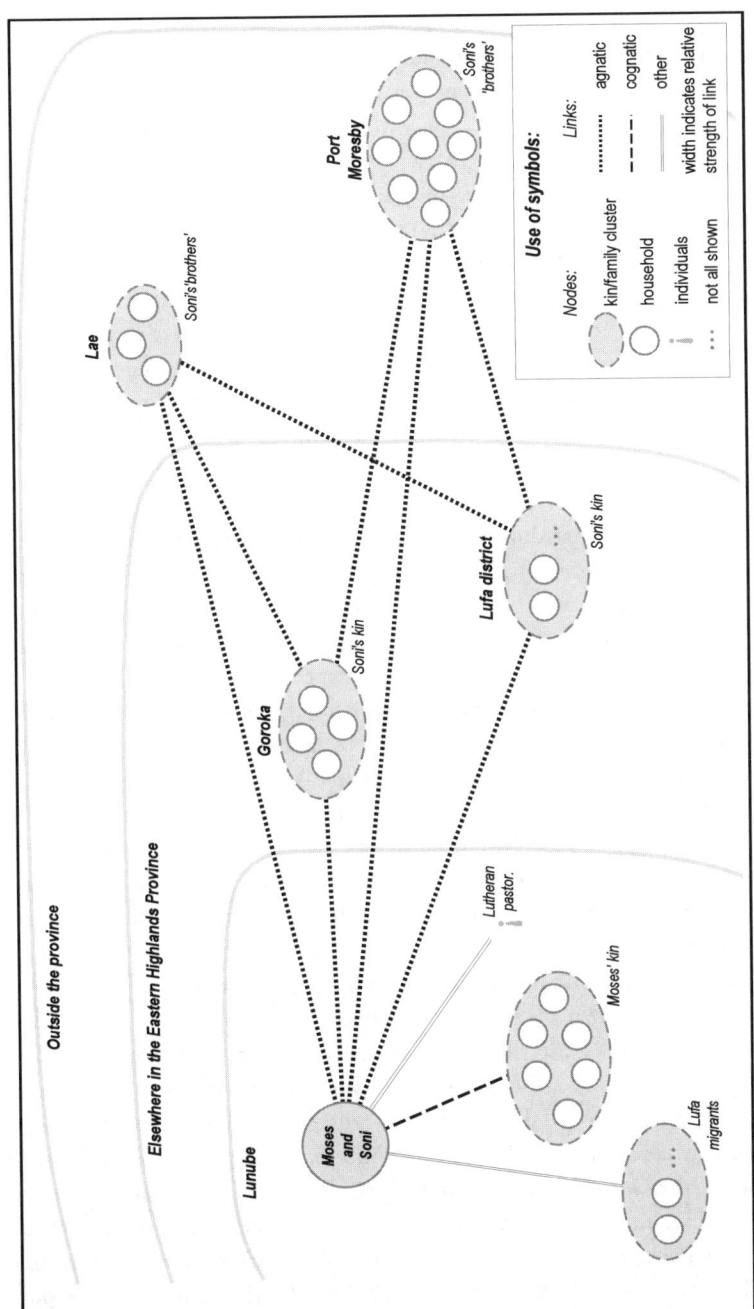

Figure 10: Moses and Soni – social networks

holdings are not particularly extensive, but the household livelihood strategy is made up of many strands. Gumuli's old coffee grove – amongst the very first plantings in Kasena – is now theirs. Gumuli had also bought the first coffee pulper in the village, which his children now use, and Soni and Moses sporadically buy 'cherry' coffee and process it to parchment for sale. Food crop gardening for the market is also pursued, with kaukau, potato, and carrot among their cash crops. Soni especially is regarded in the village as a *man bilong wokim gaden* – a keen and clever gardener. They have only once, in 1992, sent kaukau to Port Moresby. Soni found that prices were good, but the selling trip had been rather too costly. Since that sale they have stuck to the Lae market. Sometimes they go together on a sales trip to Lae, spreading their sales efforts between different marketplaces. Then Moses sells at the large main market, whereas Soni takes produce for sale to the smaller markets around the city.

They even had a tradestore at one stage, but gave it up in 1993, when Soni was hit by a car during a trip to Goroka to get cargo for the store. Finally, as many other women do, Moses frequently sells *buai*, scones, cooked meat or vegetables at the *hauslain*. Any substantial amounts of money are deposited into their passbook account in the bank in Goroka, although some are tucked away in the house in case of unexpected day-to-day expenses.

And they have need for money: this is a large family and they are keen on education for their children. For those families whose children reach high school, fees become a major economic issue. In 1995 the fees for a student at Asaroka High School were close to K500. At the beginning of the year, Soni and Moses had to muster all their resources in order to cover this. A little coffee was being harvested in the village in December and January, and Soni bought some and processed it. They also harvested whatever vegetables they could from their gardens for sale. This was an almost Chayanovian situation of working towards a target income.[9]

Moses states that she usually hands over to her husband the bulk of the money from a sales trip, this being in her reckoning the proper Christian thing for a wife to do. On the whole this is a rather harmonious relationship, but on occasions I did witness some disagreements. For instance, once when Moses had harvested a small quantity of kaukau which she intended to sell at the Goroka market, Soni insisted that she put her religious duties first – a church meeting in a distant village, which the Lutheran pastors had organised and wanted her to address. *'Wok bilong Bikpela, em nambawan. Wok mani – maski!'* (God's work comes first. Work for money does not matter!) stated her husband – and he had the last word. The incident is intriguing, because some years ago Soni had hopes of getting a 'proper' vegetable *bisnis* going in their main food garden. He had been assured of a K1,000 loan from a Goroka bank, but Moses then called a halt, as the prospect of repaying K50 a month for a lengthy period did not appeal to her. In any case, given their somewhat limited landholdings, a commercial vegetable enterprise would probably have meant the end of food self-provision for the household.

Their social network beyond the local arena is most notable for the extent to which it includes Soni's *wantoks* (Figures 9 and 10). Rural-to-urban migration has been more marked from remoter and more rugged areas, such as the one where he comes from, than from the central Asaro Valley, and his kinsmen now form close clusters in Goroka, Lae, and Port Moresby. In Lae, Moses also has relatives whom they can stay with.

OTHER HOUSEHOLDS: VARIATIONS ON A THEME

While these were some of the people with whom I had closest interaction during fieldwork, I also encountered households of quite different composition, and which had followed other strategies of livelihood. A brief introduction to three of these helps to demonstrate the diversity of solutions.

Saina and Dinamo

When I first came upon Saina and Dinamo, I was walking through the garden lands of the Amaizuho clan, just east of Kasena. They were working in a large, recently planted, and particularly well-maintained commercial *kaukau* garden assisted by an army of relatives. They told me they had their sights on Port Moresby. I included them in my core group with the view of following the progress of the garden and its produce from its beginning to the Port Moresby market in the end, which I did. In addition, Saina and Dinamo seemed able and willing informants and/or discussants, which proved correct.

Again, here is a household whose claims to land are anchored in the happenings of the immediate post-contact era. Saina's grandfather had assumed ownership over a large tract of land in Aladuka (see Map 3), just about all of which the large third generation has taken into cultivation. They also maintain claims to land in Wahuto, where the other half of the clan lives, but this is steeper and less suited to intensive cultivation. Land scarcity is becoming an issue. One of Saina's brothers reasoned that if only his father Hungule had been content with one wife instead of two, there would have been ample land for all his sons. In any case, the crunch will probably come with the next generation.

When Saina was in his teens, his older neighbour Mondave Wobo had made a big garden. He hired a group of youths, which included Saina, for the task of planting kaukau. This was the start of the trade to Lae, as will be traced in Chapter 6, and Saina resolved to try a similar approach later. In the meantime he got around a bit, working for example as a security guard in Port Moresby for a short time.

Saina and Dinamo were married in 1985, and have one child. They took over some 500 coffee trees from old Hungule and a plot of good gardening land. An additional plot of land was 'bought' shortly after their marriage, for K100 and a pig, although Saina maintained in fact that his grandfather had long ago used the plot. This is sufficient to furnish them with a modest cash income and most of their food. The extended family is close-knit, and the sharing of food and other necessities is common.

Although both are easygoing and convivial personalities, there was some evidence of diverging interests and opinions. Apart from coffee and vegetable sales, Dinamo sometimes cooked rice and greens and sold around the *hauslain,* for example at the *disko,* which was a common form of entertainment in Aladuka. Such selling of store-bought rice or meat (not to mention peanuts, *buai,* and cigarettes) is a very common practice in Lunube, and a measure of the pervasiveness of the cash economy. Earnings from this, and from her small-scale market sales at Asaro or Goroka, were her own, she maintained. She bought daily necessities with the money and contributed in her own right to events and needs within the extended family. She indicated that many men did not share the proceeds from coffee sales with their wives but spent the money on their own pleasures. Although Saina did in fact send money when he went to sell kaukau in Port Moresby in April 1995, much of this went to pay the village *wantoks* from whom he had borrowed in order to get the kaukau to the city in the first place. Dinamo expected him back home with the rest of the money in time for the coffee season. When he stayed on in Port Moresby for some weeks, and as a result had little or none of the money left when he finally returned, she was definitely not amused.

Their social network is not particularly extensive. When in Lae, they sometimes stay with relatives, but more often they choose to stay in paid accommodation. In Port Moresby, however, Saina can tap into the network of city-dwelling people from Lunube. They usually stay with Saina's 'brother' and *poroman* (friend or age cohort) Robert, who is a most important contact for them. At the time of my fieldwork, Robert worked at a tradestore in East Boroko, owned by a Lunube businessman. And what a remarkable node this unassuming store had become, not only in the network of Saina and Dinamo, but for numerous other Lunube visitors to the capital. Its owner, Mande Sirifave, was a central figure at the start of the Port Moresby kaukau trade, and had continued to provide support to his *wantoks* ever since.[10]

Meson and Mariana

This couple lives in Pikosa at the northwestern end of the valley, about an hour's drive from Kasena. Owing both to the location and to repeated bouts of intergroup warfare in the valley west of the Asaro River, I was unable to observe them as closely as the other households presented here. However, I certainly saw that their economic strategy is a very active one, to say the least, and ties in with Meson's search for local political prominence. They are in their late thirties. Meson is the son of a local *luluai* and later councillor; Mariana is from nearby Kofena. They have three children. Economically well off, they live in a house made of corrugated iron, they own a petrol-driven coffee pulper and a truck – although a lack of spare parts had rendered it immobile when I stayed with them.

The base for their prosperity is coffee, but Meson is the head of a 'business group' he has organised with six of his 'brothers', which commands about nine hectares of coffee. He talks of all this coffee as his own, however. They occasionally plant kaukau and other food crops for sale, usually on a large scale, hiring tractors and gangs of labourers for planting and harvesting. They planted a large kaukau garden for the Port Moresby market during my stay, spending K800 on tractors and labour. This was however not a great money-earner for them, as when the garden was harvested, the 'sister' whose land they had 'borrowed' for the venture claimed half the produce as her own. During my stay they also entered into a partnership with a landowner in the Markham Valley, with whom Meson had been acquainted for some years. The plan was to plant a large garden with watermelons for sale in Port Moresby. They had just started that venture when I left.

Apart from agricultural pursuits, they operate a tradestore in one end of their house. The sign above the store's door reads 'Upper Asaro Komuniti

Youth Group', but that is in fact yet another and unrelated project. Meson has organised a youth group which had been contracted by the nearby coffee plantation at Nomba to guard against theft of coffee. He also has plans to have the youth group do some maintenance of the dilapidated bridges in the area, and of charging passing vehicles a road toll in return. Such impromptu privatization has become common practice in the region following the breakdown in the capacity of the state to maintain this vital infrastructure. Finally, to complete the listing of the household's staggering array of economic ventures, Mariana also has a foot-operated sewing machine, which forms the centrepiece of a small-scale dressmaking operation. She buys cloth in Goroka and sells her products occasionally in the village and in the Goroka market.

All this activity is linked to religious convictions; they are fervent Baptists, who believe in a heavenly reward for demonstrated diligence on earth. But perhaps more important is the linkage to political ambitions. Meson has twice stood for the Provincial Assembly, and once even for the national Parliament. He had thought it would further his name to *pilai politiks* (play politics) as he put it, but as he had not matched the cash handouts of the numerous other candidates during the campaigns, he was not elected. Nevertheless, the list of candidates for the seat of Daulo Open in the 1992 national elections remains pinned to the wall of their house. Meson's photo among those of other notables of the Asaro–Watabung region serves as a reminder to visitors that here is a man to be reckoned with.

Michael and Benaso

Finally, I return to Kasena. Michael and Benaso are a couple in somewhat different economic circumstances from most of the others. They are in their forties and have fostered four children from other Kasena families, whom they raise as their own. In contrast with most other households, coffee plays a negligible role in their portfolio of activities. Michael is the second youngest son of his parents, who had four sons and two daughters altogether. He maintains that his father had already allocated his coffee to the older two brothers when Michael had reached his teens. Michael was left with a piece of land which, although of good quality, was not large enough to sustain both a coffee garden of any size and a suitable food garden.

Even so, as a young man Michael did make his mark in the village. He quit school at Grade 5 and started working for one of the first villagers to set up a tradestore in the 1970s. He then ran a tradestore of his own for a number of years. Soon after he married Benaso he secured a driver's licence and managed to buy a pickup truck, with some help from his brothers and relatives. During this time, in the late 1980s, he and his wife also started selling kaukau to Lae, and indeed to Port Moresby, becoming one of the first to do so. On their first trip they shipped a total of 52 bags from Lae to Port Moresby and made about K4,000. With the bulk of this money he bought a used bus in Port Moresby and had it shipped over to Lae. A bank loan made it possible to add a small truck to the operation. Michael had made a name for himself as a *man bilong bisnis*. And then he took another wife.

Yet this state of affairs did not last very long. Michael got into arguments with his 'brothers' regarding his management of the vehicles and wives. In the end he sold both vehicles, having defaulted on a bank loan. His second wife was unceremoniously driven out by his irate kinsmen, who argued that she was a spendthrift and was subverting the good developmental intentions of their brother. Whether from this trying experience or not, Michael and Benaso became devout Christians and joined the fundamentalist Foursquare church, which has remained central to their daily lives ever since.

Lacking coffee, they have to rely on other means of earning income. Benaso now plants kaukau and sells in Lae on a regular basis. Like most other women, she also frequently sells small quantities of vegetables in Asaro or Goroka, and cooked rice at the *hauslain*, in the old tradestore which her oldest foster son has taken over and which is now one of the main hubs of leisure activity in Kasena. Michael, on the other hand, makes good use of his driver's licence and his social networks. Early in 1995 he got a job, through an acquaintance in Lae, as a driver for a company there. He stayed in Lae for the next months, sending money home and occasionally coming for a brief visit. He told me he liked it that way; when he was tired of working in the garden at home he would go and find a job, then return home after a while when he tired of city life.

CONCLUSION

There is no shortage of interesting individuals and complicated households in the Asaro Valley. At the beginning of this chapter it was stated that we should not necessarily expect the 'typical actor' to emerge out of these descriptions. Even so, the households just introduced show many similarities. These are all nuclear families of sorts, albeit with strong kinship links and cooperation at the village level. The 'household' is indeed a flexible unit in the Asaro Valley. Households may include non-kin members temporarily. Informal adoption of relatives' children is very common. Patron–client relationships often mean temporary or long-term presence of distant relatives or even unrelated persons in the households of politically and/or economically important men. Because of such flexibility, households seem to shrink or expand quite frequently.

Also examples abound of differing agendas and interests of household members. While situated within households, men and women retain their individuality, and negotiate for themselves some room to manoeuvre.

Commoditization of the rural production process has affected all these households in a broadly similar way. They are involved in a mix of coffee and vegetable production for markets, in addition to producing a large part of their own food. This furnishes a yearly income which for this area is well above that of most other rural Papua New Guineans. I estimated from the frequency and size of food crop and coffee sales that the income of Kasena households was commonly in the range of K2,000–3,000 in 1995, but this varies of course considerably from one household to the next, and from year to year with fluctuating coffee prices.

If we were inclined to map the location of these households on that controversial terrain which is 'the peasantry', they would probably end up somewhere in the fuzzy, indeterminate middle. Certainly, these are not 'proletarians'. When Michael repeatedly leaves his village and wife behind to pursue wage work in town, this is of his own free will rather than economic compulsion, even if he has no coffee. Only Meson and Mariana come close to being 'big' or 'rich peasants'; yet there is something quite precarious about their position.

Generalizing about the form of social networks is likewise a hazardous undertaking. Networks differ from one person or household to the next, and they are constantly being recast. However, the mappings reveal that for many people in the Upper Asaro, the expansion of social networks which has happened in the last decades has not been so much through the establishment of qualitatively different links as through the spatial widening of the old village networks. Rather than a disembedding of the economic from the social, with impersonal ties becoming more important than kinship links, we could say that the village has been extended to the settlements of Lae and Port Moresby.

An interesting feature which emerges out of these portraits is that, for linking the Asaro villages to Lae and Port Moresby, the social networks to the relatives (brothers real or classificatory) of the women are no less important than those of men. It would not be prudent to assume that they are generally *more* important, as this is by no means a 'representative' sample, but it is obvious that the construction of the networks of each household in many instances leaves women in a relatively strong position when it comes to arranging a stay in town.

It is clear, however, given that these are still overwhelmingly kinship-based ties to often marginally placed town-dwellers, that the links between 'urban' and 'rural' Papua New Guinea are somewhat tenuous. The networks of knowledge and power upon which the Asaro people have drawn in the construction of their markets do not interface strongly with the 'formal' urban economy. Market information travels along 'segmented knowledge networks' (Box 1986); a process far removed from the costless and effortless distribution of information in the universal market model. This of course affects the form taken by the markets constructed with the aid of these linkages. An appreciation of the discontinuous nature of economic space in Papua New Guinea will help us see how households and individuals deal with the political economy in their attempts to harvest development through the market.

NOTES

1 Gimbe, or '*lapun* Handene' as he was also affectionately called, died in 1996. He was born in 1912 if the old Village Book is to be believed, and was thus in his early twenties when the Australians arrived in the upper Asaro.

2 Kâte is spoken in the area inland from Finschhafen, Morobe Province. The station at Asaroka was established in 1937 by German Lutherans of the Neuendettelsau mission, who had been operating in the Finschhafen area and Markham Valley for some decades. They had chosen Kâte as their *lingua franca* when working among speakers of non-Austronesian languages, such as those of the Asaro Valley. Its use in the highlands was discontinued in the early 1960s (Neuendorf and Taylor 1977).

3 Gumineve also had children with two other women, living elsewhere. Towards the end of my stay, one of these women, from the Lufa district, appeared in Kasena with her child. Her relatives had settled in Kasena earlier. She and her young daughter moved into our house. Kondagule, although intensely jealous at first, accepted this addition.

4   The state-run National High Schools take their students through Grade 11 and 12 and provide entrance to University education. The much more numerous Provincial High Schools, many of which are run by missions, offer Grades 7–10.

5   Transfers of land and individualization of land tenure are discussed further in Chapter 8.

6   The previous school in Lunube, run by the Salvation Army at Omborda on the western edge of the tribal territory, had been razed to the ground during fighting with the Onguponi tribe in 1990. Afterwards, the Lutheran church allowed the building of a new community school on its land in Kasena. It was still far from complete during my fieldwork, but new classrooms and houses for teachers were being built by parents, using the money provided by the Council and the Education Department.

7   Gumineve was also one of 18 leaders who formed a Peace Committee during the 1995 war at Kofena, which took up virtually all his time for a while. But this indicates his stature in the Upper Asaro in general.

8   In his heyday, Gumuli was the driving force behind the first vehicle purchase in Lunube, in the 1960s. He also built the first 'permanent' house in Kasena in 1974; a fibro-sheet cottage located some 200 m away from the main *hauslain*. His daughter Aligule lives there now.

9   School fees for children of poorer households are often paid by village leaders, or by better-off villagers who have taken on the role of 'godfathers' and look after (*lukautim*) the welfare of the child with gifts of food or money. The flow of gifts is usually reversed when these children form their own households and become economically independent.

10 Mande's own biography and his part in creating the kaukau trade in its present form is told in Chapter 6.

4

Fresh food movements in a fragmented national economy

> *I worked as a security guard for Burns Philp. Started in Goroka, but they sent me to Tabubil. I stayed there for a while, and then they transferred me to Moresby. I was about two years in Moresby. But the company got the profit from my work. I only got a small part. When I work in my garden, all the profit goes to myself (John, interview 5 February 1995).*

VILLAGERS OF THE ASARO VALLEY are acutely aware of the disjunctures in the economic space of their country, and they have their own ideas about the flows of wealth in the political economy. As we have seen, their social networks extend beyond their rural home into other spaces that are quite distinct – economically, socially, and culturally. They take in the space of the urban economy, be it in the neighbouring highland town of Goroka or the coastal cities of Lae and Port Moresby, where they sometimes go to sell their produce. More indirectly, their living conditions also relate to that peculiarly frenetic space which has emerged around various projects of resource extraction. Such projects have increasingly become Papua New Guinea's economic dynamos.

There are several interlinked 'big pictures' here which must be clarified, as they are basic to an understanding of the demand to which the fresh food growers-cum-sellers have responded. We need an outline of the national economy and its spatial dimensions. We also need to consider patterns of consumption, which are in part shaped by local cultural histories and ecologies, and in part by relatively recent global influences. Linked to both of these are uneven landscapes of power and identity of people and places, which have implications for the practices which have come to characterize the markets. These patterns are produced, reproduced, and changed through time by the interlocking of global commodity markets, state power, and local agency.

MAIN CHARACTERISTICS OF THE NATIONAL ECONOMY

The economy of Papua New Guinea has been summarily described as 'young, small, mixed, open, resource-based, high-cost, and aid-dependent' (Millett 1990: 1). While one might want to dispute the first adjective – after all, human habitation and thus economic activity of one kind or another dates back more than 40,000 years (Groube *et al.* 1986) – the others seem not far off the mark. It is small, both in absolute and per capita terms, when measured by the blunt instrument of national accounting (see Table 1). It contains a mixture of subsistence and market-based activities. Commodity trade with other countries is extremely important, and the bulk of exports derives in one way or another from the rich resource base. In comparison with its Asian neighbours at least, factors of production in the formal economy are expensive (Economic Insights Pty Ltd 1994: 43–44). Finally, the amount of external aid is equal to or higher than 10 per cent of Papua New Guinea's Gross Domestic Product. Aid brings in more money than all agricultural export commodities (South Pacific Economic and Social Database 1995). Australia, the former colonial power, furnishes more than half.

Another (and not incompatible) summary description has been offered by geographer Richard Jackson, using a somewhat different language which draws attention to the spatial dimensions of the political economy. In his terms it is 'dependent, inequitable and fragmented' (Jackson 1979: 3). The most basic contrast is that between the rural and the urban economic spaces, but first we shall look at a third kind of economic space, where the connections with the global economy are most obvious, and from where much of the money circulating through all parts of the national economy comes. This fragmented space consists of the locales of resource extraction.

RESOURCE EXTRACTION: MINING AND LOGGING

Extraction and export of unprocessed natural resources are not new to Papua New Guinea, or to Melanesia in general. The region possesses considerable natural wealth in the form of mineral and biological resources. The history of their exploitation, through this century at least, bears witness to the globalizing tendencies of the world economy.

Table 1: Selected Papua New Guinean economic indicators

Gross Domestic Product, 1992 (million K)*	4,140
Gross Domestic Product per capita, 1992 (K)	1,227
Proportion of GDP from:	
Primary activities (includes fishing and forestry)	27%
Secondary activities (includes mineral resource exploitation)	44%
Tertiary activities	29%

Value of commodity exports, 1995	Value (million K)	% Share
Agricultural products:	498	14.6%
Cocoa	48	1.4%
Coffee	215	6.3%
Tea	5	0.1%
Copra	27	0.8%
Copra oil	30	0.9%
Palm oil	142	4.2%
Rubber	4	0.1%
Other agricultural	27	0.8%
Forest products	450	13.2%
Marine products	17	0.5%
Mineral products:	2,435	71.7%
Crude oil	828	24.4%
Gold	840	24.7%
Copper	755	22.2%
Silver	13	0.4%
Total	3,400	100.0%

* *Note*: In 1992 the Papua New Guinean kina was approximately on a par with the US dollar.
Source: South Pacific Economic and Social Database 1995; Bank of Papua New Guinea 1996

Minerals and petroleum

Following the discovery of gold in the late nineteenth and early twentieth centuries, several Papua New Guinean societies played host to local versions of the extravaganzas which usually accompany the extraction of that precious metal (Nelson 1976). Drastic while it lasted, the local impact was nevertheless often somewhat ephemeral: it involved the temporary presence of a truly mixed bag of (mostly Australian) prospectors rather than a fundamental and long-lasting economic transformation of the indigenous societies towards a market economy. In the highlands, however, the prospecting journeys of the early 1930s blazed a trail for irreversible and radical change,[1] even if the gold itself proved rather elusive until much later. It is in the postcolonial period, with numerous projects on a much larger scale than before, that the economic spaces of resource extraction have come into their own (Map 4).

In the central highlands, the large goldmine at Porgera, Enga Province, is the most conspicuous manifestation and illustrates some of the common features of these projects and the contests surrounding most of them.[2] Owned jointly by several multinational mining companies and the Papua New Guinea government, it contributes substantially to the national accounts. The local economy is boosted not only through landowner royalties, but also via numerous 'community development' projects, among which is a market gardening project for supplying the employees at the mine site. The environmental impact of both the open-pit mining and disposal of tailings is large, albeit mostly quite local, and lasting damage is not necessarily as extensive as is sometimes assumed. Economically and socially, the impact of a mine such as Porgera in its home province is enormous: it has taken over the functions of a moribund local and national state. Direct effects are also felt in other provinces. Located literally at the end of the road, the mine contributes to a steady stream of *haiwes* (large articulated trucks) and PMVs up and down the Okuk Highway, to and from the port of Lae.

Similar features characterize other large mining and petroleum projects, such as the Kutubu oil project of the Southern Highlands Province, although there the physical impact is much more limited than that of Porgera. Smaller gold prospects are found in the highlands as well, notably in the Kainantu District of the Eastern Highlands, where small-scale alluvial mining has long been a feature.[3] Other mineral resource projects, large and small, are scattered throughout the mainland and the islands.

The total impact of resource rents derived from the mining and petroleum sector on the national economy at present can be judged by the fact that in the early 1990s it alone accounted for a quarter of the Gross Domestic Product (Duncan and Temu 1995: 44), and contributed close to 80 per cent of all export revenues (Economic Insights Pty Ltd 1994: 180). The closing of the Panguna mine on Bougainville in 1989, and the ensuing

FRESH FOOD MOVEMENTS IN A FRAGMENTED NATIONAL ECONOMY

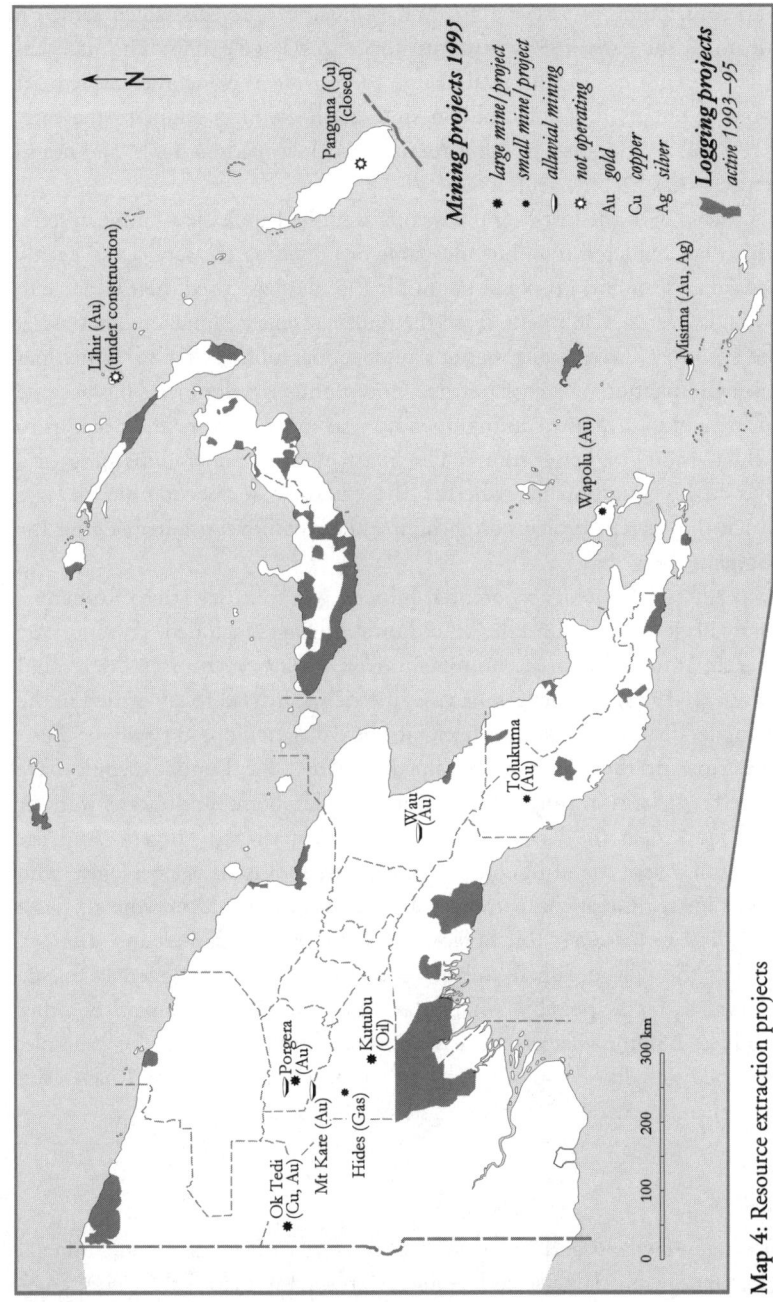

Map 4: Resource extraction projects

war, contributed to a severe fiscal crisis, but new projects which came on stream in the early 1990s made up for it to a large extent. The state has relied heavily on the mineral sector to provide the income needed for carrying out its functions, but in spite of the mining boom in the early 1990s the deterioration in infrastructure – such as roads, schools, and health centres – has become acute.

Faced with the institutional weakness of the Papua New Guinean state, which has rendered it all but incapable of providing the services so keenly desired and sought, people in the mining locales have used their leverage to try and wrest 'development' from the multinational companies. They assert their power through negotiations and cooperation, but also sometimes through litigation or even sabotage. 'Community development' has become an integral part of any mining operation, as much to keep the peace as to fulfil a vision of a better future. The lifetime of these operations varies and it is highly questionable whether the extensive socioeconomic changes which the current projects are bringing about will be sustainable after the companies have left.

Others, too, look to potential mineral wealth as salvation: in many a rural village – Kasena and the other Lunube villages included – rumours are floating around about the imminent arrival of a *kampani* (see Dwyer and Minnegal 1998). In the Kasena case, the riches are said to lay buried in the Hunguko Mountain at the back of the village. Eldorado will be here, tomorrow or the day after. In the meantime, the Lunube people have gained a toehold in some of the mining locales. Some Lunubeans work or have worked at the large mining sites in Tabubil and Porgera. And the owner of one of the most conspicuous houses in Kasena is a geologist, who works for a mineral company in a distant mining town, but who retains a close link to his *asples* (birthplace). Such successful relatives and *wantoks*, linking the village directly albeit tenuously to the mining enclaves, are utilized as far as possible when it comes to marketing kaukau or other produce. Lunube villagers with relatives working in Tabubil, for example, have occasionally sent produce by air to the mining town, and have even been there themselves (see also Vignette 1 opposite).

Logging

For many lowland and island people, the order of the day is not mineral exploitation, but large-scale logging (Map 4). International logging com-

> **Vignette 1**: Show *bisnis* – the commoditization of culture
>
> The mining company, Ok Tedi Mining Ltd, sponsored a cultural show in 1995 in Tabubil, Western Province. *Singsing* groups from the country's various provinces were flown to the mining town for the occasion. For the Eastern Highlands, a group from Kasena was chosen. Their act was not strictly local in origin, however. The 'intellectual property rights' to this package of songs, lyrics, dances and costumes had been acquired some 20 years earlier by the Gamizuho from a group near Usino in the Ramu Valley, with a payment of cash and pigs. This had proved to be a sound investment. For instance, it once earned the Gamizuho a prize at the Goroka Show.
>
> Another successful cultural innovation is the Nokondi *singsing*, which tells the story of the legendary one-footed, one-armed and one-eyed spirit, Nokondi, which has a large place in the mythologies of the Asaro Valley peoples. I was told that this *singsing* was the creation of Gumuli (see Chapter 3) and another Kasena man and had also won prizes at shows.
>
> On the Tabubil trip, the members of the Gamizuho *singsing* group took with them some 'mudman' masks made for the occasion by one of the group members, but the 'Asaro mudmen' have become the best-known cultural export of the Asaro Valley. Strictly speaking, however, the mudman act is the (jealously guarded) 'intellectual property' of Komunive village near Asaro!
>
> (See Boyd [1985] for examples of cultural commoditization from elsewhere in the Eastern Highlands.)

panies, mainly Malaysian in origin, have moved into Papua New Guinea's rich tropical rainforests in a big way. In the late 1990s between 10 and 20 per cent of export earnings came from logs, the bulk exported to Japan. While timber is of course in theory a flow resource, renewable and sustainable in perpetuity if properly managed, it is treated as a stock resource by most of the current operators. In that sense its impacts in terms of economic development are more akin to those of the mineral projects: concentrated economic energy released in a flash, but of limited duration if the current logging rates in some parts of the country continue (Thompson 1993).

Apart from concern over the environmental impacts of logging, it is persistently alleged that neither local villagers nor the state are getting their rightful dividends from the log exports (Levantis and Livernois 1998). There are accusations of underreporting, transfer pricing and other nefarious business practices, depriving the state of its fair share (Papua New Guinea 1989). Locally, little in the way of community development has been undertaken by logging companies. Road construction, the promises of which are often used as an effective lure for local communities to enter into logging agreements, is geared to the needs of the logging operations and maintenance becomes all but impossible once the logging phase terminates. Much of the resource rent flowing into local communities seems to be used for conspicuous consumption, often by a few select individuals who form the nexus between communities and logging companies through 'landowner' companies (Holzknecht and Kalit 1995: 96). This is a *Raubwirtschaft* if there ever was one, although it should be noted that in many cases local people have been just as eager to enter into logging agreements as the loggers themselves.

Implications for food marketing

In general terms therefore, the political economy of resource extraction dominates the macroeconomic picture of Papua New Guinea by providing the bulk of foreign exchange. In addition, it impacts greatly on environmental, social, and cultural processes in the localities and provinces where these enclaves of globalization are located.

The resource boom also has direct implications for fresh food growing and marketing, as the locales where mining takes place, and to a lesser extent logging, are substantial markets (see *Fresh Produce News* 1992; Morgan 1992). The demand is of two rather different kinds. First, resource extraction usually means a concentration of expatriates and well-paid Papua New Guineans, which translates into demand for introduced vegetables of many kinds. Second, the presence of labourers, mostly male and without access to gardening land locally, means that a market for staple crops also exists.

These needs are met in part by local market gardening – which is often part of the community development efforts of the company concerned – but many of the projects are located in remote, rugged, and high-rainfall areas, where large-scale food production is difficult. Part of the produce is therefore sourced from wholesalers elsewhere in Papua New Guinea, and here the food traders of Goroka and vicinity play an important role. Finally, some produce is imported from Australia. The combination of these three methods of procurement varies considerably from one project to the next.

URBAN SPACES: CHARACTER AND CONSUMPTION PATTERNS

The discussion of food markets in developing countries has often been linked to the debate on urbanization and urban–rural relations (Rondinelli and

Ruddle 1978; Epstein 1982; Rondinelli and Evans 1983; Unwin 1989). In general terms, the economic hegemony of the urban space has been seen by modernization and Marxist theorists alike as one of the hallmarks of development. Towns and cities are seen as engines of industrial production, economic growth, and social change. Dissident voices have been raised, though, drawing attention to structural asymmetries within the political economy of developing countries. Accompanying the commoditization of rural production is a net transfer of surplus from rural to urban areas: urbanism may be 'parasitic' as well as 'generative' (Lipton 1977; Harriss 1989).

The nature of Papua New Guinean urbanization

Many observers have pondered over the links between the extent and form of urbanization and structural changes in Papua New Guinea's economy (e.g. Ward and Ward 1980; Skeldon 1982; King 1993). Not only is urbanization comparatively low,[4] but the towns have an air of uncertainty about them, economically, socially, and culturally. In terms of industry, their performance is unspectacular. As service centres for rural hinterlands, their roles are limited by the incomplete commoditization of the rural economies and, in many areas, bad or non-existent rural roads. The weakness of transportation linkages has moreover meant that (with the exception of the highlands–Morobe–Madang region), no interconnected urban system is in place (Ward and Ward 1980). Instead, there is a sprinkling of mostly very small 'urban' settlements or townships with primarily administrative and mercantile functions, together with a handful of larger towns (Map 5).

Primacy in the urban hierarchy has increased in the preceding decades, in spite of official commitment, at the rhetorical level at least, to 'decentralization' (King 1993). Finally, as was touched on in the preceding chapter, many urban dwellers are recent migrants whose life is closely bound up with their area of origin, and who have less than a total commitment to the urban space: somewhat 'ambivalent townsmen' and townswomen (Levine and Levine 1979).

Yet, this is where deals are done, social contacts are established, political manoeuvres are made, and markets are constructed. In short, towns are locales of considerable national and regional power and influence. Here are found the offices (and in the case of Port Moresby, the Papua New Guinean headquarters) of big *bisnis,* be it mercantile or resource-exploitative, expatriate managers often warming the top chairs. The national and regional state

HARVESTING DEVELOPMENT

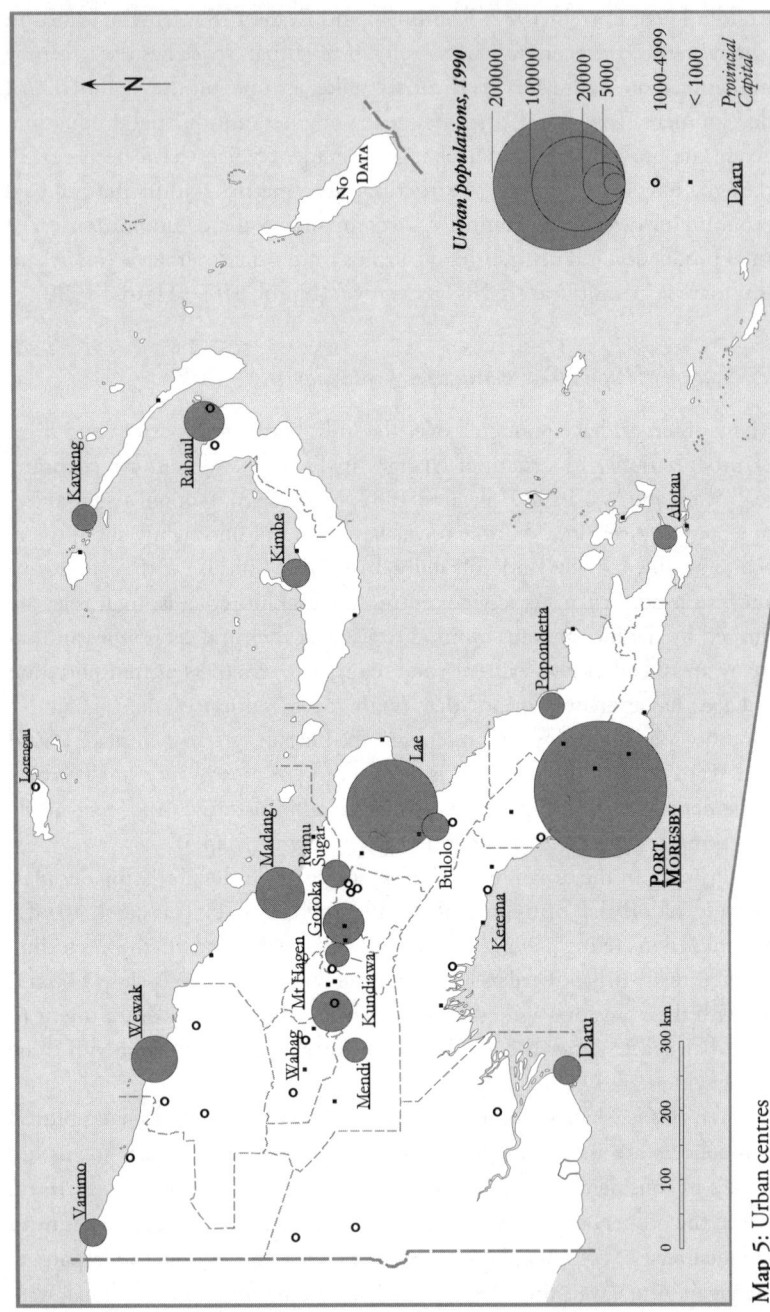

Map 5: Urban centres

resides in the towns and its functionaries often do not venture far out of them at all. An educated town elite holds the reins of government, although still most of its members were born and raised in rural areas. On a level more directly related to the issue of fresh food marketing, town dwellers are important consumers.

The roots of urbanization can be traced back to the late nineteenth century, but initially the towns were little more than 'seedy and dusty outliers of largely uninterested colonial powers' (Connell and Lea 1994: 269). Until as recently as 1960, the settlement of indigenous Papua New Guineans in urban areas was severely restricted (Jackson 1977: 22). Since then an influx of migrants has transformed them into vibrant, sometimes violent, but above all ethnically diverse places. Urban planning is all but absent, and the formal housing market is beyond the reach of many migrants. Informal shanty settlements have proliferated, often organised along ethnic or tribal lines. Constant strife is evident between the powers that be and migrants from distant provinces, the former often blaming the latter for all things evil happening in the town. Suspicion, if not animosity, is also palpable from the official side towards informal economic activities:

> The informal sector is inconspicuous, a victim of retained colonial legislation (e.g., against food vendors who compete with established interests), lack of skills, small markets, and the often more-than-comparable earnings in the rural sector. The hustle and bustle of Asian and African cities is absent, especially on Sundays, because Christianity and trading legislation combine to impose peace. Occasions where crowds gather, such as urban festivals, political rallies, or strikes, are few (Connell and Lea 1994: 271).

While this description is somewhat overdrawn – for instance, street hawkers, newspaper vendors, and beggars are an integral part of today's Port Moresby, and political struggles do in fact often bring crowds on to the streets – it would be fair to say that informal strategies of livelihood have generally not been encouraged. The most notable demonstration that such activities do exist is the lively trade in *buai*. Its growers, sellers, and consumers have defied the repeated attempts of town officials at keeping them out of sight.

The town of Goroka featured prominently in my fieldwork, and it occupies a central place in the lifeworlds of the rural people in the region. They also frequently visit the city of Lae, and most people have had some experiences in the national capital. The spatial characteristics of these three urban centres and the messages projected by their outward appearances warrant a description in some detail, as they are the venues for much of the marketing action discussed later. Goroka will receive most attention.

Goroka

These days, Goroka is a town of some 20,000 people – 17,800 called it home according to the 1990 census (NSO n.d.) – and considerable commercial activity. Although not that old, it most certainly has a history (Munster 1985, 1986). As most urban nodes, it owes its existence to Australian colonial rule, but the first outsider to settle was in fact a New Guinean missionary from the Lutheran church, in 1935. A makeshift airstrip was constructed in 1938. In 1941, just before the start of the Pacific War, the headquarters of the Australian administration in the highlands were moved from Hapatoka (Bena Bena) to present-day North Goroka, where a better airstrip had been built. With the war came the decisive feature which secured the future of the town, namely a third and much larger airstrip, which is the one still used. To this day, Goroka is built around this runway, and hence falls into the category of 'airstrip towns', examples of which abound in Papua New Guinea (Map 6).

After the war, socioeconomic change began in earnest in the region, with Goroka playing a crucial role. An important step into the money economy was taken in 1947, when the Administration started to pay wages in cash rather than the previously coveted shells (Finney 1970: 123). Mercantile interests quickly followed the first formal land purchase for the town in 1948, when the Australian Jim Leahy set up shop (Munster 1985: 24). The local villagers were quickly relieved of their newfound wealth from the land sale, but this first business was sustained by the rapid economic changes in the following years. Today, Collins & Leahy is a business empire in the highlands, with headquarters in the town where it all started.

Since the early postwar years, Goroka has never looked back. Well into the 1960s, or until the Western Highlands town of Mount Hagen started to grow, it was the main urban node of the whole highland region, in terms of population, administration, and commerce. The establishment of a hospital and a teachers' college added new dimensions.[5] But a problem of land shortage is looming. Surrounding villagers have been unwilling to part with more of their land for the town. The original town land is now almost fully built-up. An influx of population over the years has created numerous peri-urban settlements, often under the auspices of traditional landowners, outside the town land proper.

The present urban landscape of Goroka is dominated by the 1600 m long airstrip. At the northern end is the administrative and commercial heart of the town, where the major concentrations of economic power (trading banks, offices of Collins & Leahy and other companies, retail stores, and the *Bird of Paradise* hotel) and state power (provincial and local government, police and courts, post office) are located. A short way to the

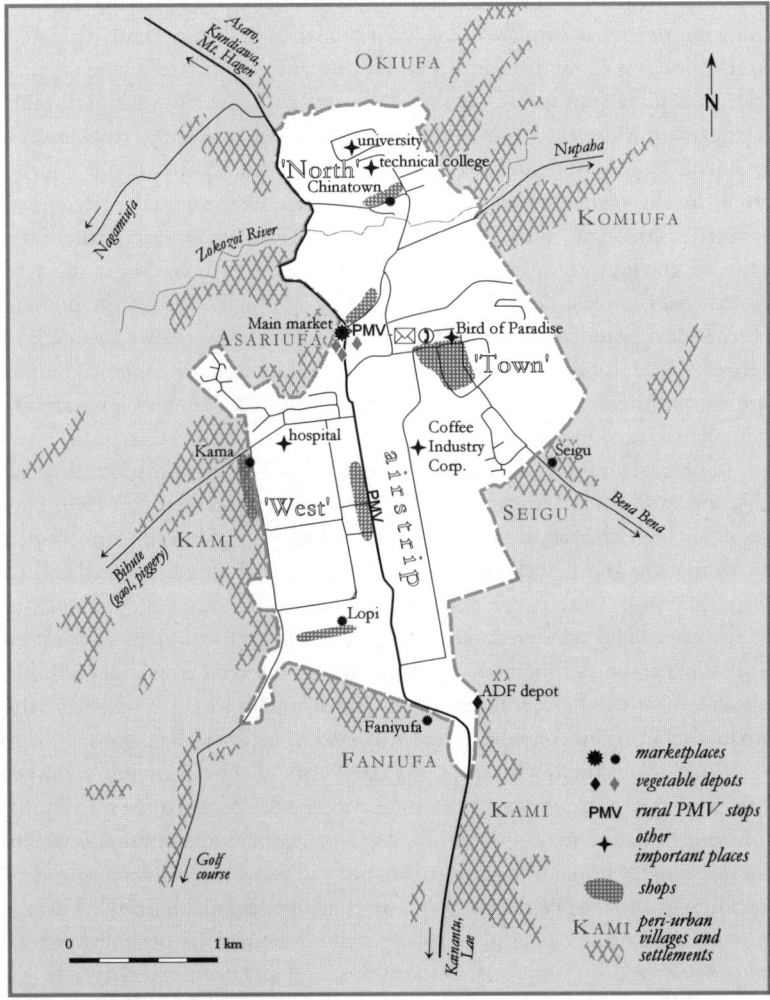

Map 6: Goroka

south, beside the airstrip, are the imposing headquarters of the Coffee Industry Corporation, an important site in the power geometry of the whole highlands region and frequent setting for political tussles.

A walk through the general stores, in the town centre and elsewhere, reveals discontinuities in the social landscape of the town. There is a gradation of supermarkets and food stores, some owned by Papua New Guinean entrepreneurs, others by Asian families, others still by large trading companies of Australian complexion. The rather unpretentious but well-stocked *Best Buy* and the somewhat similar *Steamships* both offer fresh meat and vegetables and various fancy items in addition to more ubiquitous fare. These are now run as a joint venture of Collins & Leahy with the Steamships trading company in Moresby. Various smaller supermarkets and shops stock meat – mainly frozen, from Australia and New Zealand – and canned goods. Finally, small locally owned stores carry only the barest of essentials: rice, *tinpis* (tinned fish), sugar, tobacco, *loliwara* (soft drinks), and soap. Expatriates tend to gravitate towards the larger supermarkets (which also, it must be noted, cater to local needs),[6] but the smaller stores are squarely the domain of the local populace, rural and urban. A few stores in town also carry a range of Asian food, but Filipinos, Koreans, Indonesians, and ethnic Chinese are among those who call Goroka home. Most of the Asian Gorokans are actually engaged in running stores, restaurants, and other businesses.

The organization of residential space is another clear marker of social discontinuities (see King and Diala 1988). At one end of the spectrum are spacious highset houses, two automobiles tucked underneath, surrounded by neat lawns and flowerbeds, enclosed by 2-metre high fences with barbed wire on top. At the other end are the makeshift houses of the squatter settlements, tightly clustered, often clinging somewhat precariously to the steep gullies which border the main built-up area. In between is a variety of other abodes, mostly the rather humble fibro-sheet-walled cottages, which are the major architectural contribution of Australia to its erstwhile colony.

Apart from the town centre, scattered around the urban area are other nuclei of great importance to the rural people who come to town (Map 6). These include the main market, the hub for regional PMV traffic opposite it, the congregations of coffee buyers not far away, a secondary cluster of retailing to the west of the runway, and the large regional hospital. There is now an urban PMV fleet plying the paved but somewhat potholed streets, plus trucks and utilities of all descriptions, and an occasional *dakglaska* – a Toyota Landcruiser or Nissan Patrol sporting the tinted windows that are the mark of VIPdom in Papua New Guinea.

But for most, Goroka is a walker's town. An endless stream of pedestrians continually drift between the centres of urban activity along the dusty or muddy footpaths. This is never more obvious than during a *gavman fotnait* (fortnightly public-service pay Friday), when rural people flock to town. Some have come to claim a portion of the wages paid to children and relatives who are in formal employment. Others come to sell their produce in the crowded market. Some simply *laik lukim taun* (want to check out the town) or *raun nating* (wander for the sake of it). On such Fridays, masses of these fleeting visitors make their way around town on foot.

In addition, the airstrip and the highway impart to Goroka a sense of movement and restlessness: the deafening thunder of the F28 jets as they take off, bound for the capital; the drawn-out announcing of the *boskru* (driver's assistant) of the PMV bus bound for somewhere else: '*Haaaagen HagenHagenHagen-HagenHagen ...*' The rural buses and trucks carry inscriptions, such as *Kam raun tasol* (Just visiting) or *4re Bush Rider*,[7] reminding onlookers that their home turf is not here, but elsewhere. To some extent it is precisely this perpetual motion and connections to other spaces and places which are the town's defining properties. For the rural masses it is an interface to those distant galaxies of the global market, where coffee prices get decided, and the somewhat closer spatial system of political and administrative power which centres on Port Moresby – or simply a place to catch the PMV to Lae.

Lae

> Lae – the highlanders control it. People from the highlands provinces have control of Lae (Bruce, interview 2 January 1995).

The above statement by a Lunube man points to the fact that not only have people from all highland provinces migrated to Lae in large numbers, but that for many of those living in the highlands, the city is now squarely a part of their action space. This is especially true for Eastern Highlanders, most of whom can get there in three to five hours on a good road.

Located at the coastal end of the Okuk Highway, Lae is a city of riotously luxuriant vegetation, a diverse population of nearly 100,000, and a vibrant economy. Its origins as a town date back to the Wau gold rush in the late 1920s, when it became an air transport hub for the goldfields (Jackson 1976b). The 1937 eruption at Rabaul forced the colonial authorities to move their New Guinea headquarters to Lae, although the transfer did not materialize until 1941, on the eve of the Japanese occupation of Rabaul. But the major growth spurt came with the postwar roads.

Today Lae is a quintessential entrepôt city, the strategic location providing access to and from a hinterland more extensive and populous than that of any other town in Papua New Guinea. Not only is the connection with the central highlands significant here, but also the good road link to the 'lesser highlands' around Wau and Bulolo in its home province of Morobe. It is the break-of-bulk point for a substantial slice of Papua New Guinea's imports and exports. Out goes the coffee, in comes the Australian rice and New Zealand lamb flaps. Supplies to Porgera and Kutubu pass through the wharf to be whisked up the highway.[8] Lae is also Papua New Guinea's premier industrial town, where food and other consumer-oriented manufacturing industries have been located. As an example, such global icons of modernity as *Coke* are produced here, as is the somewhat more local – but equally symbolically potent liquid – *South Pacific Lager*. Both are a part of everyday life in urban as well as in much of rural Papua New Guinea, not least in the highly commoditized highlands.

Yet, while the fortunes of the highlands and the city are thus closely intertwined, the sentiment expressed in Bruce's remark contains a strong dose of wishful thinking. After all, the city of Lae is probably the most contested urban space in Papua New Guinea. The animosity between *ol Hailans* (highlanders) and *ol Nambis* (coastals, including migrants from Madang and the Sepik provinces) is a complex phenomenon which will not be analysed here, beyond noting that it is fuelled in part by the highly visible presence of highlanders in the city's economy, including tradestore businesses, PMVs, and the food markets. More importantly though, the all-too-real experience of urban crime and violence is readily translated into ethnic or regional stereotypes in this context (see Vignette 2 below). As a result, migrants from the highlands frequently find themselves on the receiving end when local authorities wield their power.

Consider the lot of Nesime's younger brother Isaes (see Chapter 3) and his family, who reside in a settlement at '9-mile', close to the Okuk Highway as it leaves the city. In April 1995 the Morobe Provincial Government, which had long threatened to evict 'unemployed' squatters, started –'aided by local youths' (Dowa 1995: 1) – torching and bulldozing houses in some of the settlements in order to intimidate the people into leaving. Isaes, his wife, and five children not only lost their house, but also the chicken shed

> **Vignette 2**: A voice of moderation
>
> Dear Editor,
>
> I want to oppose the letter from Yanding Arong of Parakris village, Mumeng, in which he has made two important points.
>
>   Yanding, you have really got at the Highlanders with your talk of expelling the Highlands men who make trouble in the city of Lae. But I am not happy with your letter, because the name 'Highlands' is too big. There are a lot of people in the Highlands. And when you make such blanket judgements, some good Highlanders feel hurt because you include them in your complaint ... Your complaint makes it look as if you hide like a sorcerer.
>
>   You also complain about all the food which the Highlanders bring to sell at the Lae market.
>
>   I want to say that the Highlanders have plenty of good food, which Morobe Province itself does not have. So you should be happy about that and buy it.
>
> Fixie Karosa, Lae
>
> (Letter to the Editor, *Wantok,* 22 December 1994: 24)

which had been their main source of livelihood: they raised chicken for sale in the city.

In spite of these tribulations they did not leave the city, but intended to rebuild at their old place, claiming they were in fact not squatters: they had always had an agreement with the local landowner which enabled them to stay (see Kaitilla 1999). They had access to a plot of garden land which had not all been lost, although parts of it had been destroyed. Isaes had work in town. Their own social networks, including the local congregation, were also intact. When I visited the family in July, their living space consisted of a makeshift shack of corrugated iron salvaged from the wreck of their former home, and a tent where the larger children slept. The sleeping areas were enclosed in nets in an attempt to keep at bay the malaria-carrying mosquitoes which the settlement harbours in abundance. The place was muddy and unhygienic. Because of these conditions, Nesime and Moroho were no longer staying there when they visited Lae, but these had been their key contacts in the city. Instead, they looked to another brother of hers, Benson, who had until then at least escaped the wrath of the authorities. He lived in the Kamkumung settlement closer to the centre of the city, amidst a cluster of other Eastern Highlands migrants.

Port Moresby

The capital of Papua New Guinea is an enigmatic place – at once central to the political and cultural life of the nation, and yet somewhat peripheral to its economic life. Established in the late nineteenth century as the administrative headquarters of the then British Protectorate of Papua (Oram 1976), it has maintained its political centrality in spite of proposals around the time of independence to move the capital to a site that would be more central in the spatial sense.[9] Port Moresby is today a supremely important node in the power geometry of the whole country, and counts over 200,000 inhabitants.

The city is not a compact urban whole, but a collection of distinct centres, suburbs, and settlements spread over a large area and separated by steep hills. The distances and the motor-vehicle-oriented planning of this sprawling city do not make life easier for the walking poor, but a network of PMV routes serves most areas. As in Lae, many of the PMVs are owned and run by highland migrants, some of them from the Asaro Valley.

From the old colonial town at Fairfax Harbour, the built-up urban area has expanded eastwards and northwards, engulfing several pre-existing villages in the process. 'Town' remains the focus of finance and big business, exemplified by new and thoroughly international-looking mirror-glass office towers facing the harbour. Much retail trading has moved to the suburb of Boroko, which is more centrally located. Housing patterns exhibit similar sociospatial discontinuities as already described for Lae and Goroka, but accentuated in Port Moresby by marked 'altitudinal differentiation' (Connell and Lea 1994: 276), as expatriates and wealthy Papua New Guineans have retreated into tower apartment blocks perched on Tuaguba Hill.

The administrative-political centre of Waigani bears the stamp of planners far removed from Papua New Guinean conditions. Scattered high-rise office blocks desperately attempt to impress the citizens with their stern 1970s concrete modernism. The multi-lane avenues and roundabouts are reminiscent of the profligate use of space which characterizes another capital – that of Australia. Not far from this somewhat contrived splendour is Gordons Market, which for many visitors from the Asaro Valley has become a far more tangible interface with the capital and its opportunities. Of course, the political machinations in *Mosbi* do have a direct bearing on their life, not least through the administration of 'Electoral Development Funds' by local Members of Parliament. Alas, while the scheme serves to distribute some of the money that the nation earns from its resource boom (as well as from other sources, such as Australian budgetary aid) to rural areas, grave doubts exist about its personalized nature and corresponding cronyism.[10]

Concentrations of Eastern Highlanders exist in many settlements and other low-cost areas of the city. Those few with better education and jobs enjoy a much better standard of housing,[11] and a better standard of life in general. Margaret Aparo, from Kasena, is one of these. Her life interfaces palpably with all the three distinct spaces of the country's political economy. A bank clerk, she spends her working day handling money which in large part comes out of the scattered resource projects on which Port Moresby thrives, being the linking node with the global economy. Margaret's is a thoroughly urban lifestyle. She lives in East Boroko with her two teenage children and the occasional visiting *wantok*, in a flat owned by her employer, the Papua New Guinea Banking Corporation (PNGBC).[12] She is divorced from her Motuan husband, but retains some connections to his relatives in the capital, and in the village of Lea Lea an hour's drive to the north. In her social life she mixes with people from virtually all of Papua New Guinea. She has travelled to Australia, visiting her former workmate who now lives in Wollongong. In short, her social networks extend well beyond kinship links, and are altogether broader spatially and socially than those of most of her rural-dwelling Gamizuho brothers and sisters.

Even so, she places strong emphasis on maintaining the ties to her rural home village. She tries to go and stay in Kasena over the Christmas and New Year holidays, and makes the occasional trip at other times during the year (see King 1992: 11–12). She also contributes money to events within her clan, such as marriage and mortuary payments. Also, travellers from Kasena are frequent guests in her flat during their sojourns to the capital. While she acknowledges that this is something of a drain on her finances, she is happy with the close contact. She also has on occasions acted as a trader for a female friend of hers in Kasena, using her social networks in Port Moresby to sell the latter's consignment of carrots directly to restaurants in the city.

At the other end of the social scale are the far more numerous Asaro Valley migrants who live in the settlements. Their livelihood strategies span a wide range of activities. Many, especially women, do not hold jobs in the formal sense of the word, but make a living by selling *buai* around the town. Some collect empty soft drink bottles for recycling. Many men have found employment as drivers, manual labourers, and especially security guards.[13] Private security business is a fast-growing sector of the economy in this city, as in fact elsewhere in Papua New Guinea, employing a large number of mostly highlander[14] guards and almost as many ferocious-looking dogs.

For many migrants, however, even if they have made the city their home, their social networks and lifestyles can perhaps best be described as part-village, part-urban. The contradictions are recognized by the village *wantoks* and relatives who occasionally visit them, as evidenced by Gumineve's comments about life in the Badili settlement:

> In this block, they live just like they do in the village. They play cards and drink beer and roam around drunk. They do not think like they live in town. They do not think about work. They do not live well (Gumineve, interview 31 December 1994).

Urban food consumption

The three urban areas just described are the most important markets for fresh food grown by the people of the Upper Asaro. We now look closer at the patterns of food consumption in the towns and how the demand for highlands-grown food crops fits therein. An Urban Household Survey conducted by the National Statistical Office in the late 1980s provides a good overall picture (Figure 11). Goroka and Port Moresby were both surveyed in 1985–86, with a sample drawn from all socioeconomic strata, whereas Lae was somewhat incompletely covered in 1989 (Gibson 1995: 29). That notwithstanding, the results are broadly comparable between towns, and while prices have gone up considerably since the late 1980s, the relative expenditures should still be similar.

According to the survey results, Port Moresby is indeed an expensive place to live. This partly reflects its location in an agriculturally marginal location with limited road connections to regions better suited for food crop production, but partly also the more 'moneyed' nature of the urban economy in Port Moresby, which is home to a large section of the country's formally employed. This aspect of the capital frequently elicits comments like this one from Asaro villagers:

> Moresby is good, but – it's not *that* good. Living in the village is quite all right. It is better than life in Moresby. Moresby is a city, and they live off money. And we have gardens, we live off our gardens, and – the people of Moresby, it's like money is their garden (Esta, interview 15 April 1995).

Expenditures are lower in Lae, although the difference is not overwhelming. In Goroka on the other hand, they are much lower. Even so, while the expenditures of people in the capital for food, drink, and stimulants are nearly twice those of Goroka residents, the proportional allocation of the expenditure to the different food groups is relatively similar. Over a fifth of the food expenses are to buy cereals, namely rice and wheat, both of course imported. Other popular items of consumption in all the urban areas include the animal protein foods which are recent additions to the country's diet: poultry, other fresh, frozen or tinned meat, and tinned fish.

The largest contrasts are in those foods where the ecological and cultural setting differs most. Fresh fish is thus a common consumption item in Port Moresby, whereas it is (not surprisingly) hardly ever eaten in Goroka. The opposite is true for kaukau, which is not an item of great prominence in Port Moresby, whereas close to 10 per cent of the value of all food purchased in Goroka is kaukau.

Given what was said above about the ethnic and social diversity of the cities and towns, it is obvious that their food markets are quite segmented. The figure obscures this. It is probable, for instance, that the diet of the migrants from the highlands in Port Moresby includes much more kaukau than that of those of Central Province origin. What this means for the hopeful kaukau sellers who come to Port Moresby is that, despite the size of its population, it does not comprise a particularly large market for their esteemed tubers. Lae, by contrast, while much smaller, has a higher proportion of 'acculturated' kaukau consumers.

Be that as it may, neither kaukau nor vegetables account for much in the budgets of Lae and Port Moresby households. For kaukau at least, this is not only the result of different tastes, but also of the convenience of rice, and of economics. For a long time kaukau has not been competitive with rice in terms of cost per unit of energy (Spencer and Heywood 1983; Joughin and Kalit 1986; Fereday 1993). Around 1990 an urban dweller could buy about twice as many calories in rice as in kaukau for the same amount of money (Fereday 1993: 15). Costly internal transportation and marketing has undoubtedly played a part in that situation.

Food preferences are of course neither cast in stone as culturally defined 'tastes', nor are they simple derivations of economic logics. The meanings attached to food are subjected to unceasing cultural revaluation. Gibson (1995) has argued against the commonly held belief that 'traditional' root crops are considered inferior to the imported cereals. This contradicts much received economic wisdom about the inevitability of a transition to cereals. There may be hope for kaukau in the towns after all.

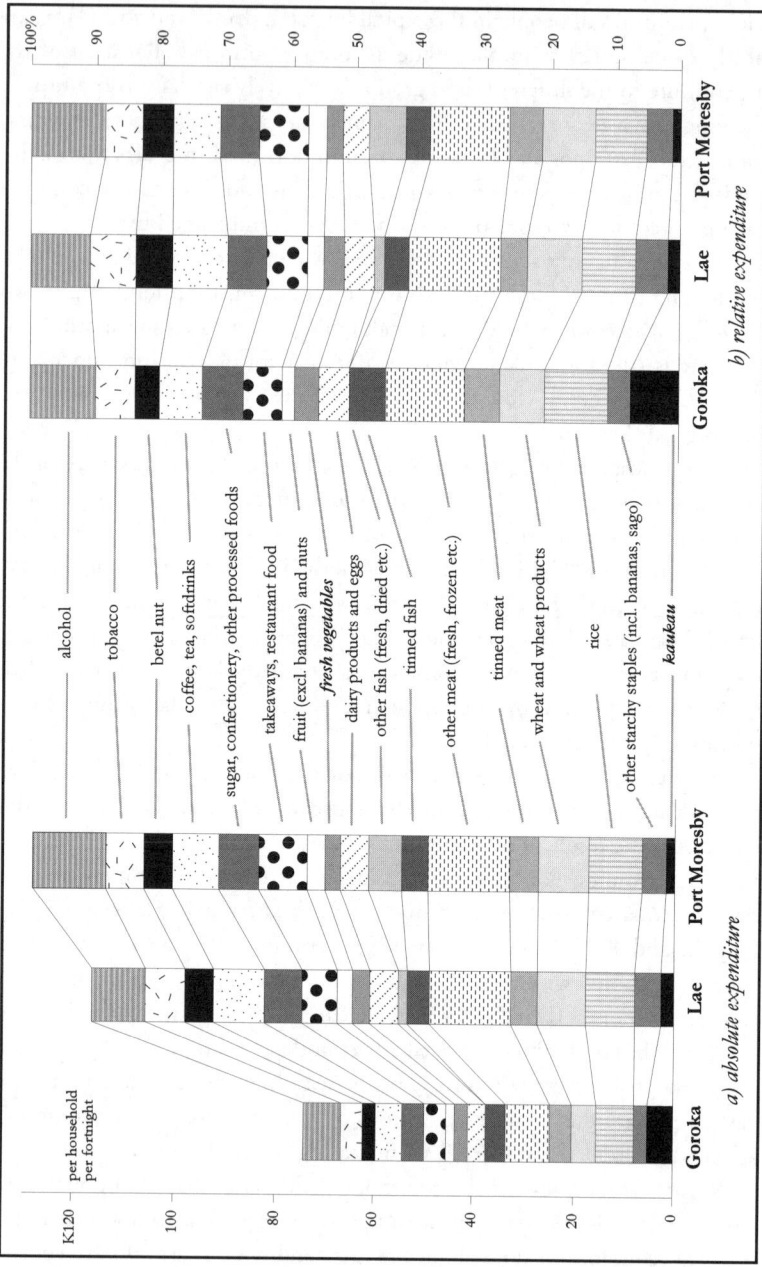

Figure 11: Expenditure on food, drink, and stimulants in urban areas

FRESH FOOD MOVEMENTS IN A FRAGMENTED NATIONAL ECONOMY

THE DISJOINTED RURAL ECONOMY

Finally, we come to the rural economy, which is the economic space in which the everyday life of most Papua New Guineans is lived: according to the 1990 census, about 85 per cent are rural dwellers (NSO 1994b). Although methods of formal national accounting are notoriously prone to underestimating subsistence agriculture – the main pursuit of these people – there can be no doubt about its economic importance. In addition, agricultural products make up close to 15 per cent of the value of all export commodities (see Table 1). This may not seem all that much in comparison with the exports of minerals, oil or logs, but for most rural people cash cropping has far more meaning. Apart from those relatively few who have suddenly found a mine just outside their garden fence or become drawn into the maelstrom of logging, the boom in resource exploitation is virtual reality rather than real.

It is, of course, nonsense to talk about a single rural economic space. On the contrary it is highly uneven. It is not my intention to describe it in any detail, but instead to look briefly at three sources of variability which are most relevant to understanding the structures of food demand and supply. First, the agricultural systems on which the rural settlement rests to a large extent, have evolved around different sets of *staple crops*, for ecological and other reasons. This relates again to the regional differences in consumption and food preferences, and which rural migrants have to some extent taken with them as they have moved to towns. Second, the recent advent of commodity production has involved new sets of (mainly export) *cash crops* which have quite specific distribution. Third, *accessibility* has become an important aspect of determining the way in which different locations interface with the global economic system of which all of them are a part.

Subsistence cultivation and staple crops

Apart from the regionally important sago and bananas, various root crops or combinations of them dominate the map of subsistence agriculture in Papua New Guinea (Map 7). Of all the root crops, kaukau has by far the largest spread, and its primary place is reinforced when we look at the numbers of people for whom it is the dominant staple crop (see Table 2).[15] Almost two-thirds of rural Papua New Guineans rely on it, either on its own or together with other crops. Sago, which comes in as a distant second, is concentrated in the Sepik provinces and in the Papuan lowlands, where it

Table 2: Dominant staples and population in the agricultural systems

Dominant staple	Co-dominant staples	Population 1995 no.	%
Kaukau (sweet potato - *Ipomoea batatas*)	none	2,213,000	56
	taro	123,000	3
	banana	104,000	3
	X. taro	50,000	1
	yam	30,000	1
	cassava	21,500	1
	sago	12,500	<1
all systems based on kaukau		2,554,000	64
Sago *(Metroxylon sagu)*	none	436,000	11
	taro	500	<1
all systems based on sago		436,500	11
Banana *(Musa spp.)*	none	252,500	6
	yam	34,000	1
	sago	7,000	<1
	X. taro	6,500	<1
	cassava	4,000	<1
all systems based on banana		304,000	8
Yam *(Dioscorea spp.)*	none	157,500	4
	taro	76,000	2
all systems based on yam		233,500	6
Xanthosoma taro *(Xanthosoma sagittifolium)*	none	54,500	1
	taro	17,000	<1
all systems based on Xanthosoma taro		71,500	2
Taro *(Colocasia esculenta)*	none	31,500	1
Cassava *(Manihot esculenta)*	none	10,000	<1
	X. taro	6,500	<1
all systems based on cassava		16,500	<1
Coconut *(Cocos nucifera)*	none	1,500	<1
No crops dominant (more than three main crops cultivated)		315,000	8
Estimated total rural population in 1995		*3,964,000*	*100*

Notes:

(1) Data for North Solomons Province not included in table.

(2) Population for 1995 is calculated from the 1980 census figures (which are used in the Land Management Project database), assuming a uniform growth rate of 2.3 per cent per annum. This was the countrywide growth rate in the 1980–90 intercensal period. Population growth in rural areas was slightly lower than the national average during that period. Figures are rounded to the nearest 500.

(3) Percentage of the total rural population in 1995 calculated according to the method outlined above.

Source: ANU Land Management Project.

supports populations at very low densities.[16] Banana is the single staple crop which is found in agricultural systems throughout the country, although it has not become the primary staple in its own right except in a few regions.

What is noticeable from the point of view of exchange, and of food provisioning in general, is that all the staples are quite bulky and, with the partial exception of sago, not easily stored or transported. This has played a part in the limited precolonial trade in staples, and continues to affect present-day interregional trading. As the people of the highlands rely almost exclusively on kaukau, fluctuations in kaukau cultivation can, and sometimes do, adversely affect their food security. This is, however, alleviated in part by the fact that climatic conditions over much of the highlands permit continuous planting, and it is also possible to store kaukau in the ground for some time after the tubers have matured (Bourke 1988: 14–21). The recent addition of store-bought food has further improved food security and nutrition, as we shall look at later.

Cash crops

Deposited on to the layer of subsistence cultivation is another one of cash crop production (Map 8). For our purposes, coffee deserves most attention. It is far and away the most important export cash crop in terms of employment – approximately 40 per cent of all Papua New Guinean households are to some extent involved in its growing (Grey 1993: 96) – as well as in terms of export earnings. Although there are coffee plantings elsewhere, the bulk of the coffee is located in the central highlands. Arabica coffee grows up to about 2,100 m above sea level and there are populated areas in the highlands above this altitude.[17] In the lowlands, the lower-priced Robusta variety is important in East Sepik Province. About 80 per cent of all coffee is grown by smallholders, and 20 per cent on plantations (Stapleton 1997: 1).

Although some coffee is picked and processed at any time during the year, the bulk of the crop is harvested in the period from May to August. This seasonality sets up something of a 'feast and famine' cycle in many highland rural economies. During the *taim bilong kopi* (coffee season), large sums of money are spent on food, alcohol, and other consumption goods, both on an individual and household basis as well as sometimes extravagant communal reciprocal gift exchange and feasting.

The economic environment of coffee growing and processing is circumscribed by state-devised regulations and institutions, and is highly politicized.

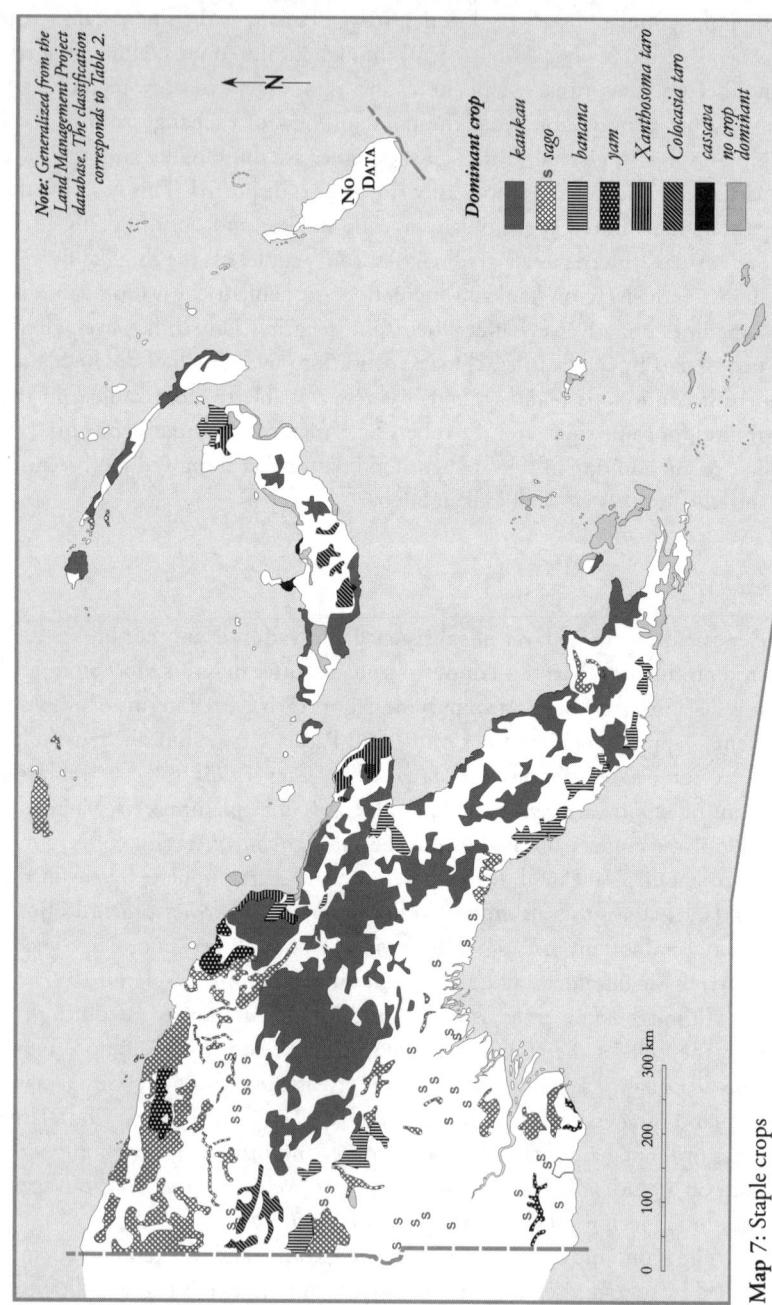

Map 7: Staple crops

FRESH FOOD MOVEMENTS IN A FRAGMENTED NATIONAL ECONOMY

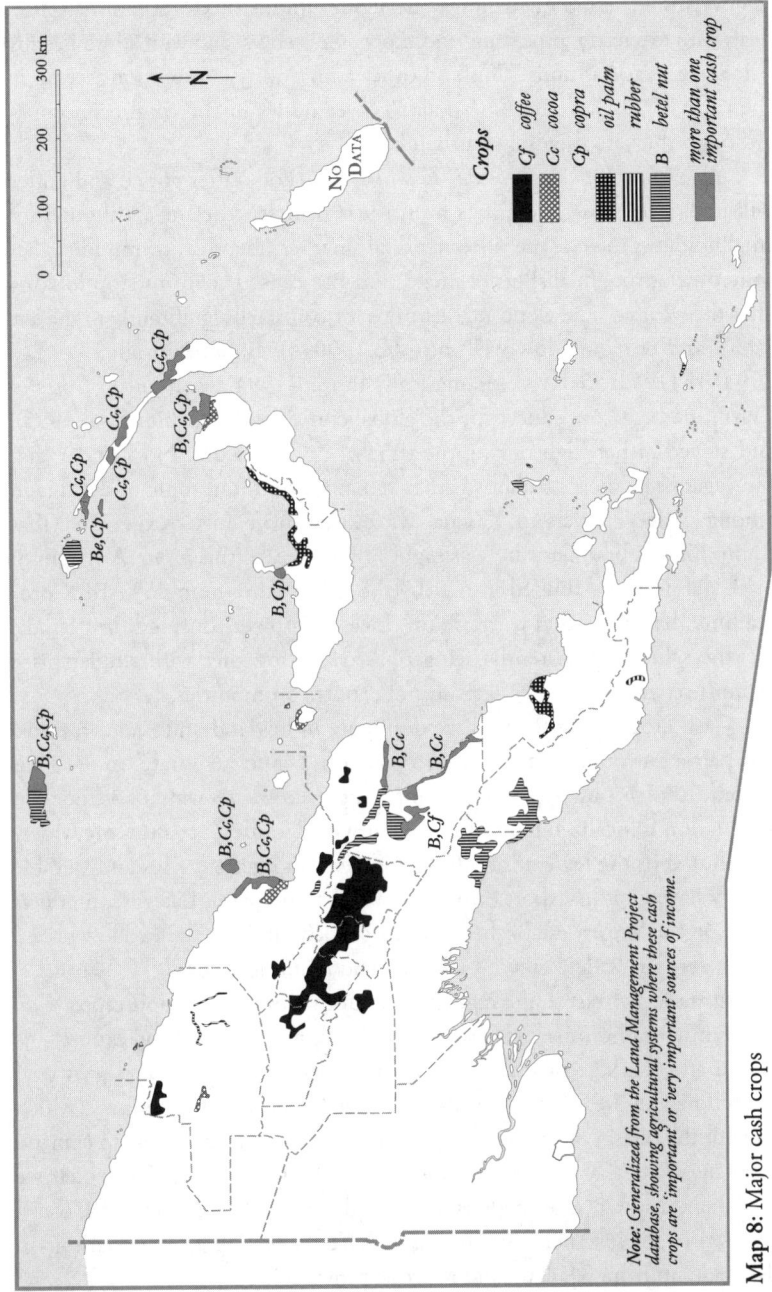

Map 8: Major cash crops

A government-established body, the Coffee Industry Corporation (CIC), deals with extension, processing and exporting licences, and with administering price stabilization funds. This and other commodity corporations set up in the early 1990s have become major power nodes in the rural economy – although they are themselves urban based.

'*Lukautim kopi na kopi bai lukautim yu*' (Look after coffee and coffee will look after you), the CIC's motto reassuringly proclaims, although for smallholder growers the international market for this commodity has sometimes brought disillusionment, and has caused them to stop looking after their coffee. The world market price for coffee fell significantly in the late 1980s and remained low well into the 1990s (Economic Insights Pty Ltd 1994: 181).[18] It then rose dramatically in mid-1994 as a result of frosts in Brazil, the biggest producer for the global coffee market (Kuimbakul 1995), and stayed rather high during the time of my fieldwork. No wonder that the vagaries of the Brazilian weather remain a common topic of discussion among coffee growers in Kasena, who know from bitter experience that slump follows boom as surely as night follows day in this *bisnis*. A system of price stabilization, funded in part by the European Union's STABEX programme, has been used to shore up prices to growers during lean periods, but the scheme is currently being phased out together with similar price support schemes for other agricultural export commodities.

Cash crops other than coffee dominate in lowland and island regions. Oil palm, introduced in the late 1960s on a 'nucleus estate' model, has become the second most important export crop in terms of value, but production is localized in parts of two provinces only. Cocoa is more widely distributed in the lowlands, although low world market prices and variable quality have kept its export earnings lower than oil palm. Likewise, products based on the longest-established cash crop, coconut, have suffered low prices, but the crop is widely grown in coastal and island locations.

In stark contrast to the regulated environment of the export crops, *buai* (betel nut) – the most important cash crop not destined for export – is grown and marketed without any involvement of the state. It is grown in many lowland areas[19] and consumed virtually all over the country, which was not the case in pre-contact times. It is transported from supply to demand areas by road, sea, or even air, and unlike the trade in kaukau which we shall look at later, intermediary traders play a large role. Around Goroka and Asaro, for instance, Simbu settlers have come to play a crucial role in the trade up from Madang and Morobe provinces.

FRESH FOOD MOVEMENTS IN A FRAGMENTED NATIONAL ECONOMY

Accessibility

The landscape of cash cropping is closely related to that of accessibility. Economic change in the country – not least in the highlands – following its recent incorporation into the world economy, has been closely tied to changes in transportation routes and technology. The Okuk Highway (see Map 1) and the rural feeder roads, which were mostly built during colonial rule, have already been mentioned. In fact this road system, primitive as it was, completely altered the ordering of space in the highlands in a few years. Old trade routes linking the highlands with the lowlands generally had a north–south direction. Certain locations which had benefited from the traffic were left in a highly marginal position in the new spatial order (Ward 1974).

Even if I indicated earlier on my frustration with the state of the road which I travelled up and down so often from Kasena, the Lunube villages do in fact enjoy better accessibility than many other rural settlements in the country. This is of course one of the premises for their participation in coffee growing, and even more so, market gardening. Still, the road system centred on the highway is only one of several discrete road networks. The lack of spatial integration nationwide, through roads linking these partial networks, is frequently held up as a reason for the limited supply and high prices of nationally grown food. Plans for new roads, such as one linking the Lae–highlands system with Central Province via Wau, have not been put into action, due primarily to the difficulty of the terrain, but perhaps also in part to a worries one hears in Port Moresby that the capital would then been completely swamped by highlanders. Not that they are not there already in large numbers.

Driving along the highway, one clearly appreciates the economic power which emanates from this winding strip of asphalt. The electricity line from the power station at Yonki broadly follows the same route, sprouting offshoots into adjacent rural stores and even homes. The highway has thus truly become the 'backbone' of economic development in the highlands in the postwar era, to use a somewhat trite metaphor. The 'road' has itself become a metaphor for Papua New Guineans, who frequently speak of the necessity of *painim rot* (finding a road) to wealth, well-being, and development.

Despite intentions to the contrary, interregional inequalities did not become any less marked after independence. It is indeed difficult to see how that could happen, given the embeddedness of the economic system within a global capitalism, and the lack of state resources to undertake any major redistribution. It seems likely that those areas where the commodity economy has already taken hold thoroughly – such as the Asaro Valley – will continue to 'develop', while inaccessible and rugged regions are left to their own devices. It is doubtful whether the inhabitants of the highlands fringe, for instance the people who live in Wesan on the northern slopes of the Bismarck Range – a day's walk from Kasena – will ever find their road, literally or metaphorically.

Consumption patterns in rural areas

The geography of rural food consumption is no less interesting than that of the urban. The National Nutrition Survey undertaken in 1982–83 provides the best available clues to the overall pattern of rural food consumption. Grau and Smith (1992) provide maps of these data, which show that consumption strongly reflects both the local agricultural system and access to cash-earning possibilities. Regarding 'traditional' food crops, there is a close correspondence with agricultural systems (see Map 7). Throughout its area of cultivation, the kaukau reigns supreme in people's diets.

This has long been noted. Summarizing the results of many dietary studies, Bourke (1985) asserts that it supplies generally over half – and up to 94 per cent in parts of the kaukau heartland in the highlands – of all food energy, and from 19 per cent to 73 per cent of protein.[20] *'Em i bun bilong mipela – em i strongpela kaikai'* (it is our strength – it is powerful food) is a common response in Kasena when people are asked about its importance. At least on the rhetorical level, they are quick to assert its superiority over such *kaikai malomalo* ('weak' food) as imported rice. Esta, a young woman with reasonably good access to money, put it this way:

> When our evening meal consists of rice, it is not... like, it is not as filling. So we are soon hungry again. When we eat kaukau, we are not hungry so soon. We are strong for a long time, and we can go about with strength (Esta, interview 15 April 1995).

This is not to say, however, that the taste of rice or other imported foodstuffs is not savoured. It certainly is. Much of the money earned from coffee or fresh food sales is used to provide variety in the diet (Ploeg 1985a: 314), but wholesale change to imported and processed foods, as in some other Pacific cultures (with often dire nutritional consequences, see Kahn and Sexton 1988; Lewis Jr 1988), has not taken place by any means. On the contrary, the impact of new food has been generally positive in rural areas, especially regarding child nutrition, and an increase in degenerative adult diseases has so far been largely avoided (Heywood and Hide 1994). Urban elites, however, are starting to experience the negative consequences of dietary change.

The relative importance of store-bought food varies greatly with the degree of commoditization of the rural economy which, as we have seen, in turn relates to accessibility and cash-crop development. In fact, rice and tinned foods first entered the diet of Papua New Guineans through the early plantations, where these imported staples were used to feed the indigenous labour force.[21]

As the Asaro Valley was among the first areas in the highland region to be incorporated into the wider market economy, the incorporation of such food into the local diet has a history of at least 40 years. Almost 30 years ago a patrol officer could thus remark:

> Canned meats are popular but expensive to the people and on the average a family would purchase one tin a week. Tinned fish is repugnant to the elder part of the community with the younger group it is very popular [sic] (Vandenberg 1969: 5).[22]

This vividly illustrates the fluid nature of taste and its inseparability from the social and cultural constructions of what it means to be 'modern'. Neither youngsters nor elders in the Asaro Valley today find tinned fish repugnant. In fact, judging from the maps of Grau and Smith (1992: 232), in 1982–83 the consumption of tinned fish and meat was higher in the rural villages of the Goroka district than anywhere else in the country (except parts of Central and Gulf Provinces): around half the population had consumed such food the day before the survey was taken. Significantly, this proportion was much lower in other, less commoditized parts of the same province.

In accordance with what has already been said about the seasonality of coffee income, consumption of bought food varies considerably through the year (see Grossman 1984; Bourke 1988). This applies even more strongly to alcohol. During the mid-year coffee season, public drinking becomes noticeable in the villages. The concentration of ceremonial feasting at this time accentuates the seasonality. Carcasses of frozen mutton and sides of beef are used to augment the traditional pork and garden crops at most feasts. Numerous chickens now also find their ways into the *mumus* of Kasena, as small-scale chicken projects are a popular village enterprise.[23]

Movements of fresh food

It is now appropriate to add a map of the very activity which is central to this study: the interregional trade in fresh food (Map 9). The movement of fresh food within the country is a reflection of the basic configurations of economic space we have looked at. Resource projects and major urban centres are the destinations for produce, which is largely sourced from high-altitude regions.

The map does not show specifically the local supply zones of the town markets. For example, at the large market in Lae, sellers come from much of the Markham Valley, Mumeng to the southwest, and Bukaua on the coast to the east. As it falls outside the scope of this study, I have not attempted to map the flow of *buai*, which is in fact by far the most important cash crop destined for the domestic market.

For Port Moresby, the Sogeri Plateau is only an hour's drive away, and has long been an important source of fresh produce. People from the plateau frequent the markets in the capital, and there are also some large-scale firms which specialize in tomatoes and pineapples, among other things. The high-altitude Goilala territory to the north has long been seen as a potential vegetable supplier, with climatic conditions very similar to those of the central highlands, but this is extremely rough country, and an unreliable road connection has been a hindrance.

The centrality of the highlands as a supply area is therefore unchallenged. There is, however, a much smaller countermovement of coconuts and tropical fruit (mainly mangoes when in season) from the Morobe and Madang provinces up to the highlands. This is undertaken largely by individual traders, from both highlands and lowlands, who sell in highland town markets. Trading in the opposite direction is undertaken by both individuals and companies. Some perishable produce is airlifted out from Goroka and Mount Hagen, mainly by wholesale firms. Much more is trucked down the highway to Lae, both by grower-sellers and wholesale firms. A small trickle reaches Madang by road.

Some areal specialization has occurred in the highlands. Tambul is now an important potato-growing area, and some high-altitude pockets in the Eastern Highlands have also specialized in potato, which is sold largely through wholesalers. Gembogl growers have made a virtue of their cool location by growing crops such as carrot, cauliflower and broccoli for the wholesaler trade. In the main valleys of the Western and Eastern Highlands

FRESH FOOD MOVEMENTS IN A FRAGMENTED NATIONAL ECONOMY

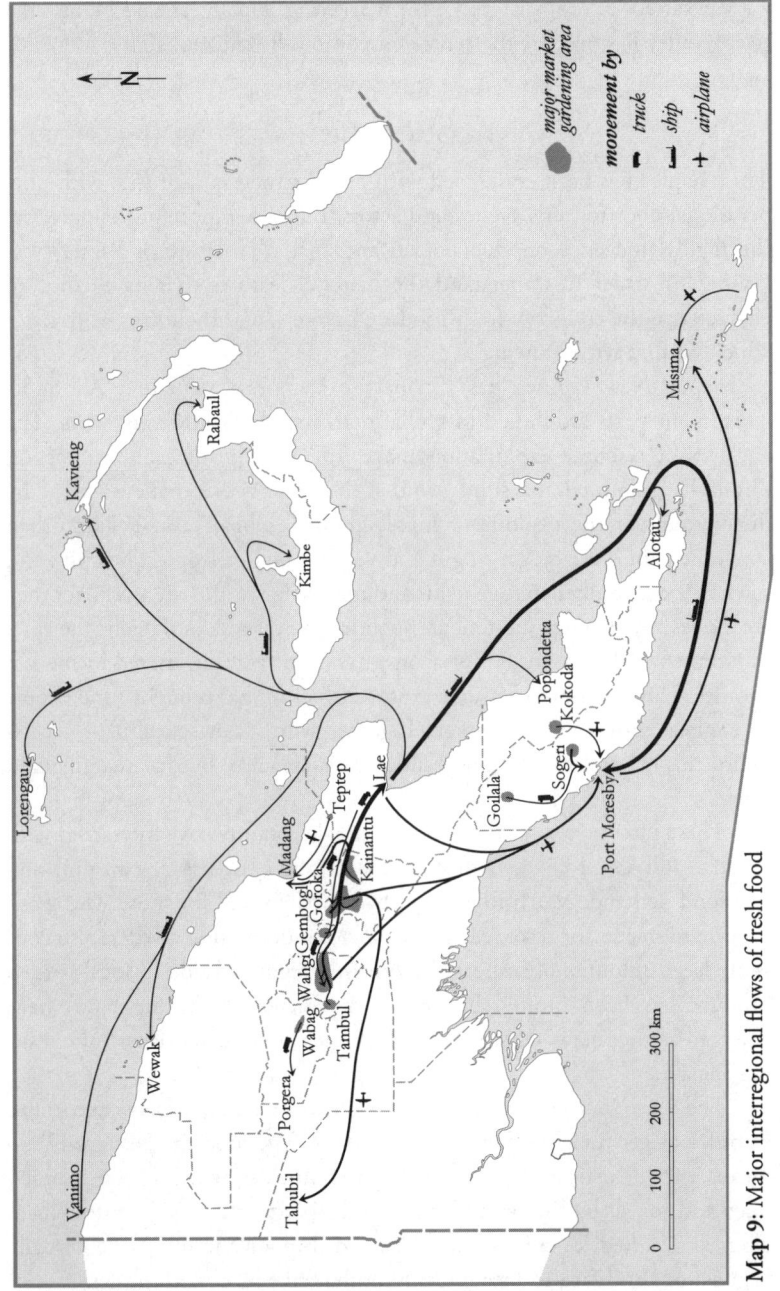

Map 9: Major interregional flows of fresh food

a great variety of crops is grown for marketing. Finally, as said before, the Asaro Valley has become the centre for commoditized kaukau.

CONCLUSION

This chapter has been concerned with broad structural features, with only occasional nods towards agency and actors. But it is important to appreciate the highly uneven economic, social, and spatial structure of Papua New Guinea, in order to understand the material features that have come to characterize the country's fresh produce markets, and the forms of practice which we find within them.

Papua New Guinea has a tripartite economic structure. All of its constituent parts are linked to global markets, but in different ways. The enclaves of resource exploitation make up one type of economic space, physically disjointed, but similar in that the projects that make it up are the direct result of the exploits of highly mobile, global capital. The urban economy is of quite recent origin and very limited in scope. The cities and towns are ethnically heterogeneous and material divisions are stark. Yet they are locales where much cultural and political power resides. Finally, the rural economy, which has existed for aeons, has been radically altered in the last decades. The adoption of various export cash crops has brought rural people in contact with a world market. Together with a new pattern of accessibility, this has created new possibilities for some areas, but has marginalized others.

These interlocking layers of the national economy have interacted with cultural and social changes to create a specific structure of consumption and food demand. Much food for urban dwellers and for those who work in the resource sector is sourced from abroad. Indeed, rural dwellers also consume large amounts of imported food. Interregional trade in local garden produce has been limited but is on the increase. The highlands have emerged as the major region of supply to urban populations and the mining enclaves.

The Asaro Valley growers have to juggle these different spaces and places in order to get their produce to the markets. The food markets are by no means 'frozen' institutional structures, the features of which are determined once and for all by the broad-brush spatial patterns I have just described. They are created, re-created, and changed through the innumerable daily transactions and face-to-face interaction that take place within them.

NOTES

1. It should be noted that the search for gold was only one of two major catalysts for the opening up of the central highlands to outside influences. The other force was the equally strong evangelistic drive of Christian missionaries, who actually were the first 'foreigners' to enter the main highland valleys, some years ahead of the gold prospectors (Radford 1987).

2. I made a brief visit to Porgera during fieldwork, and have also gained from discussions with Glenn Banks, who has studied the project in detail.

3. A large gold deposit has been explored at Crater Mountain, in the sparsely populated southwestern corner of the same province. The project is now on hold (MACMIN 2000), but if it goes ahead, economic space in the Eastern Highlands will certainly be radically transformed.

4. Only about 15 per cent of Papua New Guineans live in urban areas according to the 1990 census (NSO 1994b), compared with 62 per cent in other lower-middle-income countries (where World Bank statistics locate Papua New Guinea), and 27 per cent in low-income countries (World Bank 1994: 222). This is so even if the definition for urban is rather generous in Papua New Guinea, covering all settlements with more than 500 inhabitants and general 'urban characteristics' (NSO 1994b: 33).

5. By the late 1960s, Goroka had acquired other trappings of a 'real' town, as the following comment from a patrol report illustrates:

   Prostitutes are reported to be living in nearby squatter settlements around the Goroka township and with the recent outbreaks of syphilis especially in the Goroka area the problem of prostitution is enlarged. However the trade of the prostitute is a tenacious one which throughout history has survived all manner of suppression (Brown 1970: 5, original emphasis).

6. I was told by expatriate friends of a very upmarket retail operation, run by a large helicopter company – a firm that employs many expatriates – in a nondescript house at their airport premises. It was said to be for staff nominally, but in practice others (read: expatriates) were welcome, and some very rare culinary items were apparently available. Sticking to simple peasant fare myself, I did not check this option.

7. Reference to the Fore area, near Okapa.

8. However, the gold is airlifted out of Porgera, and the Kutubu oil is transported via a pipeline to the Papuan coast.

9. The Arona Valley, at the eastern edge of the Eastern Highlands, was proposed for the postcolonial capital of Papua New Guinea. The idea is not quite dead yet – it is mooted now and again by highland politicians (cf. *National*, 10 March 1995) – but it must be considered highly unlikely in the current economic and social climate that such a move will ever be made.

10   Members of Parliament were, in the mid-1990s, allocated K300,000 yearly to spend on development in their electorates as they see fit.

11   In a survey carried out in 1987, it was found that 'The single largest group of highlanders was from the Eastern Highlands, predominantly living in Self Help areas', in contrast with 'successful groups like those from Manus, New Ireland, Milne Bay and Kairuku who are highly concentrated in the High Cost areas' (King 1992: 7).

12   An interesting twist to rural–urban relations is provided by the fact that some of the rental residential property in Port Moresby is in fact owned by wealthy Asaro 'rural capitalists'. It has been a common strategy for moneyed Papua New Guineans to invest in residential property in the capital or in Lae, or even in Cairns or other Australian cities.

13   Also, one should mention urban gardening, which is an important component in the livelihood strategies of many migrants, both male and female (cf. von Fleckenstein 1978; Levett 1992; Levett and Ulvano 1992). This is practised both in backyard gardens in the built-up areas, as well as the open spaces between them. Highlanders (especially Simbu migrants) are largely responsible for the transformation of the steep hillsides of Port Moresby from their usual dusty brown colour into green and well-kept gardens during the rainy season. These urban gardeners grow food partly for their own consumption, but they also provide peanuts and other produce for sale at the city markets.

14   This statement is based on impression but not on research.

15   In the work of the ANU Land Management Project (see note 18, Chapter 1), upon which the map and the table are based, a 'dominant staple' is defined as a staple food crop which is estimated to cover more than one-third of staple garden area in the agricultural system concerned. If more than one dominant staple is present, the database does not rank them in terms of importance. In most such mixed systems, however, one staple crop is significantly more important than the other or others in terms of its contribution to nutrition. For instance, in virtually all agricultural systems where kaukau is amongst dominant staples, it is the most important crop nutritionally (R. Michael Bourke, pers. comm., 1995). Table 2 and Map 7 are based on such ranking.

16   The sago palm occurs naturally in these swampy environments and is exploited as such. It is also cultivated.

17   In the relatively warm Chimbu valley, coffee is grown at altitudes up to 2,400 m above sea level.

18   The possibility that the price drop may explain the development of the Port Moresby kaukau trade, which occurred in the same period, is examined in Chapter 6.

19   A related species (*kavivi*, or *Areca macrocalyx*) occurs in the highlands, but is considered inferior to the lowlands *buai* (*Areca catechu*) and not much traded.

20 It should be noted that many of the studies listed by Bourke were conducted in the 1960s and earlier, when commoditization of food following cash cropping and monetization in the highlands had not markedly altered the 'pre-contact' picture. Tinned fish and meat have certainly changed the protein intake for many highlanders – for the better.

21 German-owned plantations on the Gazelle Peninsula and Manus had initially attempted to rely on locally traded staples such as taro, yam, and sago, but rice and tinned food gradually took over (Robin Hide, pers. comm., 1997). Early mining projects, where many Papua New Guineans worked as labourers, were another point of introduction.

22 It is worth mentioning in passing that Vandenberg also remarks that '[b]etel nut is chewed by many of the elders and has a disastrous effect on teething decay.' At this time *buai* was traded up to Asaro and Goroka by villagers in Wesan (or Waitsan) on the northern highland fringe, with whom the Asaro villages proper had traditional trade links. It had also started to travel up the highlands highway, which was being upgraded from a rough track to a proper road at this time.

23 Batches of young chickens are bought, through the agricultural supply stores in Goroka, from large intensive poultry farms near Lae. In the village, the birds are reared to broiler size, using imported food which is bought at these same supply stores. A bird sells for K6–10 in the village.

5

Fresh food markets, their history, and operation in the Eastern Highlands Province

> *[E]xchange is always, in the first instance, a political process, one in which wider relationships are expressed and negotiated in a personal encounter (Thomas 1991: 7).*

PAPUA NEW GUINEANS WHO SELL FRESH PRODUCE are involved in two contrasting kinds of markets, which articulate the various spaces of the political economy in quite different ways. We can tag these as the 'formal' and the 'informal' market, knowing full well that these tags are rather awkward and carry a heavy burden of debate and argument in development studies. A fledgling *formal* marketing structure exists, where producers sell to wholesalers, who in turn supply both retail establishments in the larger towns and the many mining and logging enclaves scattered throughout the country. The *informal* market here means the open marketplaces found in every city, town, and even village, as well as along the major roads. There is also a third market arrangement which does not fit neatly into either category, where retailers, restaurateurs, and similar agents buy at the door directly from producers. I term this *direct bulk selling*.

The reason for making such distinctions in this context is that it enables us to highlight the very different ways in which social embeddedness is manifested in the current operation of these market orders, by looking at their history and how the actors in question construct them through day-to-day dealings. To a large extent, the commodities traded in the formal market are different from those sold through the informal market. The sets of actors involved are not the same either. Apart from the food growers themselves, the state (national and local) has entered into the construction of markets in various ways, through direct and indirect policy measures, regulation, and specific development efforts. Private entrepreneurs have also tried their hand at trading in fresh food, but this has not created any stability.

FRUIT AND VEGETABLE WHOLESALE FIRMS

> One problem area which at this time defies solution is the marketing of vegetables. Central food markets have not been successful. Direct purchase of vegetables by retailers tends to create monopolistic situations which exclude the small scale producer, and the direct selling of vegetables in council markets by growers is time consuming and tends to perpetuate an excessive pricing system which is not in the interests of the consumer. Clearly a better marketing system is a key requirement to an orderly local fruit and vegetable industry (Bai 1992: 12).

Various governments and governmental agencies, colonial as well as post-colonial, have attempted to establish 'formal' marketing structures for fresh food in Papua New Guinea. Not surprisingly, these attempts have been informed by a model of the market as a universal principle; an orderly and unproblematic meeting of supply and demand. The linchpin of an orderly market arrangement, according to the visions of planners and politicians alike, is the wholesale firm. Substantial development effort has been expended in getting wholesale businesses going. Of course, to a large extent the outcome depends on the producers who are supposed to supply these firms. In the development initiatives designed to address this, due emphasis has been put on such issues as regularity of supply, quality, and correct methods of transport and packaging. However, economically and socially sustainable successes have been few and far between. At present, wholesale businesses can perhaps best be seen as places at the 'interface', where different worlds intersect. The development of an organised production–wholesale–retail chain has become a perpetual and frustrating task, where market practices have sometimes made a mockery of the market principle.

A short history of development efforts

The apparent official enthusiasm for getting market gardening going has several roots. The demand for introduced or 'European' vegetables arose from the presence of Australian colonial administrators and their dependants. In addition, prior to independence in 1975, expatriates came to dominate the formal economy throughout the country. In some towns up to a third of the population consisted of expatriates (Skeldon 1982). While their numbers have dwindled considerably in the postcolonial era, expatriates continue to be a sizeable part of some urban communities, especially that of Port Moresby. Moreover, the market for introduced vegetables has continued to grow through the creation of an indigenous urban middle class, as well as through the (limited) incorporation of these foods into the diet of other Papua New Guineans.

Anxiety about the meagre supplies of fresh food to towns, and Port Moresby in particular, goes back a long way (Spate *et al.* 1953; Harris 1978). This was not without grounds: Port Moresby was unconnected to other parts of the country, and its seasonally dry environs were rather inauspicious for cultivation. The problem was solved by importing rice, tinned fish and meat, which became urban staples.

In postcolonial times the problem of supplying the towns has taken on an ideological dimension. Food imports are a particularly potent symbol of continued dependence. The import of (Australian) rice especially, but also of (Australian) vegetables and fruit, has taken on a symbolic meaning, which may explain much of the rhetoric of 'independence' and 'security' which permeates Papua New Guinean discussion of these issues (see Kepui 1986). Self-reliance became one of the central planks in government policy in Papua New Guinea, right from the Eight Aims on which the Constitution is built, through national food and nutrition policies (Heywood 1982), and down to provincial levels. (For the Eastern Highlands Province, see e.g. Department of the Eastern Highlands 1980; Eastern Highlands Provincial Government 1994.) Import substitution by locally produced fruit and vegetables fitted well into such a policy framework.

Finally, lest I be accused of cynicism, it should be stressed that there has undoubtedly been a genuine desire on the part of the Papua New Guinean authorities and development aid donors alike to enable highland cultivators – because it is in the highlands where the large-scale cultivation of these food crops is possible – to tap into a potentially profitable market, and escape the dependence on coffee as the sole cash crop.[1] The large fluctuations of coffee prices on world commodity markets have added salience to this argument. Moreover, for those parts of the highlands which are too cold to grow coffee, vegetable growing has offered a chance for economic development.

FRESH FOOD MARKETS, THEIR HISTORY, AND OPERATION

Initially, most attempts to develop the formal market were rather piecemeal, concentrating on the local or regional scale. In Port Moresby, the Government Fresh Food Project was started in 1973–74, 'as a result of pressure by urban consumers' (Fintrac Consultants Asia n.d.: 43). Its suppliers were mostly Central District growers, but some produce was sourced from the highlands and freighted by air directly, or by sea via Lae, sometimes with losses of 50 per cent or more (Gorogo 1976: 288). The appearance of highland produce on the Port Moresby scene seems to have created some anxiety on the Papuan side. Intriguingly, a city councillor even alleged that such interregional air travel of fresh produce was 'un-Melanesian' (Forbes 1975: 21). Be that as it may, growers within the Central District proved unwilling to supply the project themselves, its staff 'told with some hostility that the Government was robbing the people' (Gorogo 1976: 290). Given all this adversity, it is not surprising that the Fresh Food Project did not survive very long: it ceased buying in 1975 (Fintrac Consultants Asia n.d.: 43).

The early years of independence were a time of grand and, with the wisdom of hindsight, over-optimistic schemes. The Food Marketing Corporation (FMC) was set up in 1976 with New Zealand funding, to deal with fresh food marketing on a countrywide basis. It absorbed the remnants of the Fresh Food Project, established cool stores in highland towns and coastal cities, and provided refrigerated vehicles. Yet problems appeared, caused by inappropriate staffing as well as low volumes, high wastage, and high costs – all this 'compounded by some confusion as to whether FMC was simply a commercial operation intended to trade profitably or whether it had a development function' (Fintrac Consultants Asia n.d.: 44).

Following chronic and heavy operational losses, the project was forced to close in 1981 (Atkinson and Lewis 1992). Its facilities in Port Moresby and Lae were leased out to the governments of Central and Morobe Provinces respectively, which attempted to continue at a more local scale. In the highlands no concerted efforts took its place. Hence, in the early 1980s the tenuous marketing link between the highlands and the coastal cities was broken, although a handful of commercial private farmers maintained some contact with coastal buyers. Getting fruits and vegetables from Australia continued to be a far more reliable option for city-based wholesalers. For all intents and purposes, the development of an internal integrated marketing system was back to square one.

The next major government initiative was the introduction of import quotas in 1983 (Baulch 1987). Wholesalers were supposed to buy locally a set minimum proportion of their total sales. At first the import:local ratio was set at 3:1, but in 1986 this was raised to 2:1, and beefed up by bans on the importing of certain lines of produce. Moreover in 1987 the import tariff on fruit and vegetables was raised from 7.5 per cent to 50 per cent, although Baulch suggests that this may have been done primarily for revenue-raising purposes.

When these mechanisms had been in place for some years, an assessment of their effectiveness concluded that they had been partially successful. Volumes of locally grown vegetables did increase, although selectively. Importers could fulfil their obligations by sourcing locally only those crops that were relatively easy in terms of growing and handling (and in fact already grown in some quantities) such as potato and carrot, while continuing to procure from Australia vegetables and fruit which required more complicated production or transport procedures. Hence, the import bans did not lead to the development of a diversified local industry in the way hoped for. And the 50 per cent tariff alone proved too low to render local produce competitive (Baulch 1987). A more complete restriction on imports from 1991 led to further increases in quantity, but prices did not come down, and the quality of produce and regularity of supply to urban areas still posed problems (Grey 1993).

At the time of the introduction of import restrictions, Australian-funded research was initiated to find solutions to one of the most formidable obstacles to establishing a formal market: transportation (Scott and Atkinson 1989). Airfreighting perishable produce out of the highlands is expensive. The use of refrigerated containers was tested, with promising results. It was shown that vegetables could be transported by road and sea to Port Moresby, and arrive in good condition. Since the completion of the project, some wholesalers (notably Alele Pty Ltd in Mount Hagen) have used this method, but heavy losses during transport continue to be a problem due to mechanical breakdowns as well as other hazards inherent in trucking on the Okuk Highway (Graham Ross, pers. comm., 29 March 1994).

Currently only one development project, funded by New Zealand government aid, deals specifically with food marketing on a national basis. This is the Marketed Fruit and Vegetables Project (MFVP), now in its second phase. Arguably its most important and successful aspect is the Fresh Produce Development Company Pty Ltd (FPDC), the headquarters of which are located in Mount Hagen. Its mandate is simply to 'assist the development of a sustainable fruit and vegetable industry' (Lincoln International 1994: 3).

Goals have been more realistic than those set for the Food Marketing Corporation, and being a relatively small project, the FPDC has been restricted to operating in a few key areas: the highlands and Port Moresby mainly. To differing degrees, it has attempted to address the various problems facing growers, wholesale buyers, and retailers. An imminent reversal of the protectionist policy of the 1980s – to some extent the result of pressure from the World Bank – has added a sense of urgency to the whole issue.

The FPDC is strongly oriented towards assisting the formal market.[2] Given the constraints of its funding and personnel, and the underlying working model of innovation diffusion, the company has not attempted to spread its message directly to the rural populace at large. In practice, its staff members have tried, first, to pick out promising individual growers or traders and to work with these, and second, to assist anyone who has been bold enough to come to one of the company's offices and ask for help with a specific problem (Michael Daysh, pers. comm., 24 March 1994). The aim is to build up a pool of specialized and dedicated market garden entrepreneurs who have a long-term commitment to their business. As it would be virtually impossible to reach the tens of thousands of potential and actual market gardeners in the highlands effectively, this strategy is sensible. There is a potential danger here, however, of losing sight of social realities and the embeddedness of economic processes within them, by adhering to categories such as 'innovators' or 'entrepreneurs'. In the Papua New Guinean context, market gardening projects or wholesale trading enterprises are often only a small part of a portfolio of activities for such individuals, and their ultimate goals may have more to do with achieving prestige within their social group than with building up a sustainable and profitable long-term business. This will be illustrated further in a discussion of Goroka wholesalers below.

Even so, while somewhat limited in spatial reach, the cautious approach of the FPDC has resulted in some tangible successes in my judgement. Most noticeable are successes related to the dissemination of information and improvement of quality. Growers, wholesalers, transporters, and retailers are constantly exhorted to do better, and awareness among wholesalers and growers of the quality desired by urban consumers has increased. One of the most successful initiatives has been the publication of a series of colourful posters, each addressing quality and handling requirements of a particular crop through photographs and simple text in Tok Pisin. These posters hang in every wholesale depot and many a rural home as well, and are well-recognized and appreciated by rural people. A fortnightly newsletter in

English, with an abridged version in Tok Pisin, endeavours to provide the 'missing link' of marketing information, or as often said, 'market intelligence'. This newsletter is widely read by those involved in business and government circles (as well as by academics in such faraway places as Canberra, Australia), although it seems to have a somewhat limited rural distribution.

Another aspect of the MFVP has been the building of wholesale depots in Goroka and Mount Hagen. Drawing on the lessons from the FMC, the idea was to foster small local businesses which would be subject to the disciplining force of competition and thus stand or fall on their own merit, rather than creating a centralized institutional monolith. The local councils provided land adjacent to the municipal market in both towns, and the administration of the project has been through the Department of Agriculture and Livestock (DAL). Each building contains two separate depot facilities: space for grading and packing, and coolrooms. These were leased to local entrepreneurs upon completion. But in spite of good ideas and intentions, there have been problems with the practice. In Mount Hagen, only one company remains. The Goroka case is even bleaker.

Wholesaling in Goroka, past and present

Seen from the villages of the Asaro Valley, the combined (but not always coordinated) efforts of the state, various development agencies, and private business operators, to get formal food marketing on a firm footing have led to rather meagre results. If the people of the valley, Kasena included, sell fresh produce to wholesalers or middlemen, the transaction most often takes place in the town of Goroka. With few exceptions, very little is permanent about the fruit and vegetable business in Goroka. To understand why this is so we have to look to both the continuities of history, where partial commoditization has led to a mixed and complex rural economy, and the discontinuities of power and communication which become evident when observing the daily practice of actors in the formal market.

Barter exchange of food crops for shells, axes, and other valuables was practised with the very first patrols through the highlands in the 1930s. Government and missions (Lutherans, Catholics, Seventh-Day Adventists) quickly established themselves in the Goroka area following the first patrols, but economic change was limited until the Pacific War, apart from the hyperinflation caused by the increased supply of valuable shells and their corresponding devaluation (Finney *et al.* 1974). During the war, large gardens were established by the Australian administration in the vicinity of Goroka and in Bena Bena to feed the 40,000 or so US and Australian soldiers stationed in the Markham Valley (Bowman 1946).[3] To a large extent, this was a kind of 'forced' market gardening, and involved more than a hint of paternalism and colonial power, even acknowledging the extraordinary circumstances of war:

> The natives were given to understand that they must pay attention to the gardens at all times ... and not to allow them to fall into neglect and that when gardens are ready for harvesting they must notify the District Officer ... and then reasonable prices will be paid for their produce. They were also told that when the gardens were in full production ... and supplies overplentiful and not required that permission would probably be given them to consume some. They seemed to be quite taken with the scheme ... but for the time being I would suggest that a Native Constable be forwarded ... say once every two weeks or so ... to inspect the gardens to see if the natives are paying attention to them (Ewing 1951: 3).

It is doubtful whether these projects had any lasting consequences, although it is likely that they had an exemplary effect upon those who lived in their vicinity. Certainly the Lunube people were outside the sphere of influence of the army farms.

Conditions for more permanent commoditization of the rural economy were created with the building of numerous rural roads, which took place in the immediate postwar period and continued throughout the 1950s (Crotty 1970). The development of plantation agriculture that got under way in the 1950s also played a large role, as will be discussed in the next chapter in the case of kaukau. Traders – Australians at first, but later also including local entrepreneurs[4] – soon started to ply the new roads in search of produce, both kaukau and various introduced vegetables and fruit, which they sold to plantations and to the Administration in Goroka. The enterprise was geographically stabilized by establishing so-called *road centres*. The road centre was in a sense a kind of a proto-marketplace, although differing from the present marketplaces in that the trade was strictly 'wholesale' (Sinake Giregire, pers. comm., 26 March 1995). In fact, the Lunube people got in on the act quite quickly:

> The Road Centres are the marketing points for crops of peanuts, potatoes, garden produce, passionfruit, and kaukau, the total output of each crop being purchased either by the Administration or by European companies ... The main centres of output are at Asaro and Lunupi [sic] where the Road Centres have been established longest (Healy 1954: 5).

Passion fruit became a serious smallholder cash crop for a period in the 1950s and 1960s, although it gave way eventually to coffee. Competition with Australian farmers growing the fruit led to the imposition of tariffs in Australia to keep imports at bay (Howlett 1962: 97–98); during colonial times the rural economy of Papua New Guinea was supposed to complement rather than compete with that of Australia. The operation of the road centres as general trading points depended to some extent on the passion fruit trade. When the mobility of the village population increased with the advent of indigenous-owned and operated PMVs, these centres ceased operating. Goroka became the magnet to which the rural populace was drawn to buy and sell, mix and mingle.

Quite early on, outsiders realized the potential of the highland valleys for producing quality vegetables to supply coastal towns. Thus it was stated in 1952 that 'The Irish potato trade around Kainantu is extensive and at times all the available aircraft are required to transport the produce to the coast' (Schindler 1952: 307). The crop was likewise grown at the Lutheran mission at Asaroka in the 1950s and flown to Madang. Many Kasenans still remember an aircraft loaded with potato crashing in the mountains to the north of Lunube. Also the idea of selling vegetables to Port Moresby was mooted in the 1960s (e.g. by Donne 1965).[5]

However, the trading of vegetables from the Asaro Valley out of the Eastern Highlands did not occur on a large scale until the late 1970s, by the ambitious but abortive experiment with the Food Marketing Corporation. Growers in the area then became important suppliers of the national market, yet the infrastructure created in Goroka was not retained after the FMC closed in 1981. This interrupted the development of wholesale trading, but when the new depot facilities built by DAL as part of the MFVP came into use in 1992, one would have presumed that the road had finally been cleared. Alas, there was intense politicking over who would get to lease these new facilities, and it was suggested to me that the two successful entrepreneurs had been selected less on business merit than on some other criteria.

At the end of 1994, when I started my observations in Goroka, both these operators (Itovo and Maniga) seemed to be on their last legs. Quantity coming in was minimal and the quality varied considerably. A third wholesaler (Kuru Katope Dealers, or KKD), dealing mostly in potato, occupied a small building not far away, which also was owned by the council. Financial problems also dogged this business. At the same time, a new operator started up in Goroka, in an old shed at the southern end of town. This was

Pacific Fruits, an outgrowth of Hoveku Farms, which is a successful commercial citrus-growing enterprise based in a village some 20 km to the south of town. Pacific Fruits had been trading in vegetables from a rather primitive base in Lae for some time, but moved their operation to Goroka as most of their suppliers were highlanders (James Watson, pers. comm., 22 March 1995). Cooperation between Pacific Fruits and Associated Distributors Freezer (ADF) – a Port Moresby-based part of the Steamships consortium – led to ADF taking over the whole operation in January 1995.

Elsewhere in the Eastern Highlands Province, only two wholesalers were active at the time of my arrival. One was Kabiufa Adventist High School (see Map 2), whose wholesale operation is a part of a large vegetable growing business dating back to 1965 (Dever and Voigt 1976). Kabiufa has a reputation as a supplier of high-quality introduced vegetables and sells to a variety of clients. The other wholesaler, Anasi, was based in Kainantu and was a very small-scale operation. Finally, a Lae-based wholesaler, Morobe Produce Marketing, was the outlet for some producers from the Eastern Highlands.

Early in 1995 it became clear that the new ADF depot was set to take over virtually all formal wholesaling of fruit and vegetables in Goroka.[6] In fact, Itovo and Maniga both disappeared from the buying scene during the first half of 1995. KKD metamorphosed into KKF, but eventually this wholesaler was also forced to close its Goroka depot. The same people continued with some bulk buying in the potato-growing villages on Kuru Mountain to the southeast of Goroka, their place of origin. The Goroka wholesalers tried to invoke anti-colonial sentiments against ADF on the grounds that, being part of the Steamships consortium, it ultimately served Australian interests, but as some of them were at the same time besieged by irate growers to whom they owed money, these protests petered out. As for Anasi, the Kainantu-based buyers, their efforts seemed to wax and wane according to the various other things with which the business was involved.

Soon ADF was trading in much larger volumes than any of the other buyers had been. It was backed financially and organizationally by the largest wholesale-retail conglomerate in Port Moresby, providing a virtually guaranteed market in their many supermarkets there. The ADF buying prices were somewhat higher than at the well-equipped depots at the marketplace. Control of quantity and quality was stringent from the outset. Direct access to sales and stock information in Port Moresby made market coordination easier. By March a daily air charter service had been organised in order to get perishable produce speedily to Port Moresby. The rest, about

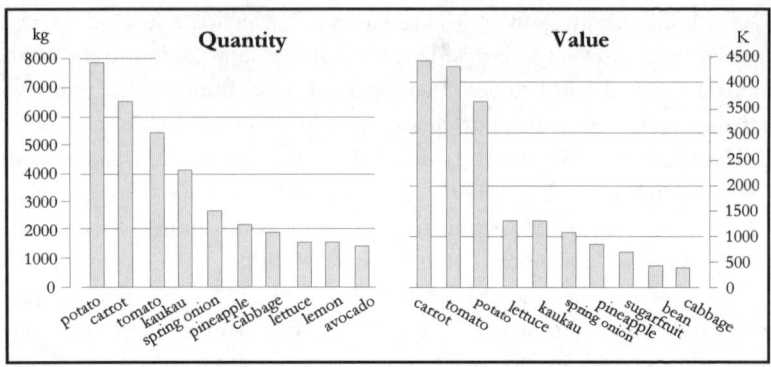

Figure 12: Most important crops sold at ADF's depot in Goroka

two-thirds of the total quantity, was sent to Lae and onwards in refrigerated containers. Table 3 and Figure 12 show the operation's main parameters at mid-year 1995.

Given the nature of the market towards which the wholesale firms are oriented – that of middle- and upper-class urbanites, expatriate and Papua New Guinean – it comes as no surprise that the 'introduced' vegetables together with potato and fruit make up 85 per cent of all produce bought. An astonishing variety of produce is in fact brought into the depot, but only a few types sold in any quantities. The three largest items – potato, carrot, and tomato – all come from rather localized clusters of producers (Map 10). Most of the potato is cultivated and sold in relatively large quantities by a few dedicated farmers, in a high-altitude area on the Goroka–Okapa road. Carrot had become very popular in Lunube while I stayed there, and commercial carrot plantings were common. Most such plantings were quite small, but the largest carrot gardens were half a hectare or more in area. Tomato came largely from the lower Bena Bena area.

Traditional Papua New Guinean food crops are also bought by the wholesalers. During my fieldwork in Goroka, increasing quantities of kaukau, together with various indigenous greens, were finding their way into the depot and thence to the nation's supermarkets. This had not been the case before the advent of ADF, at least not to any extent.

Daily practice of actors in the Goroka depots

When I left Goroka in July 1995, the ADF vegetable depot seemed to have the potential to become the first enduring business of this sort in the

FRESH FOOD MARKETS, THEIR HISTORY, AND OPERATION

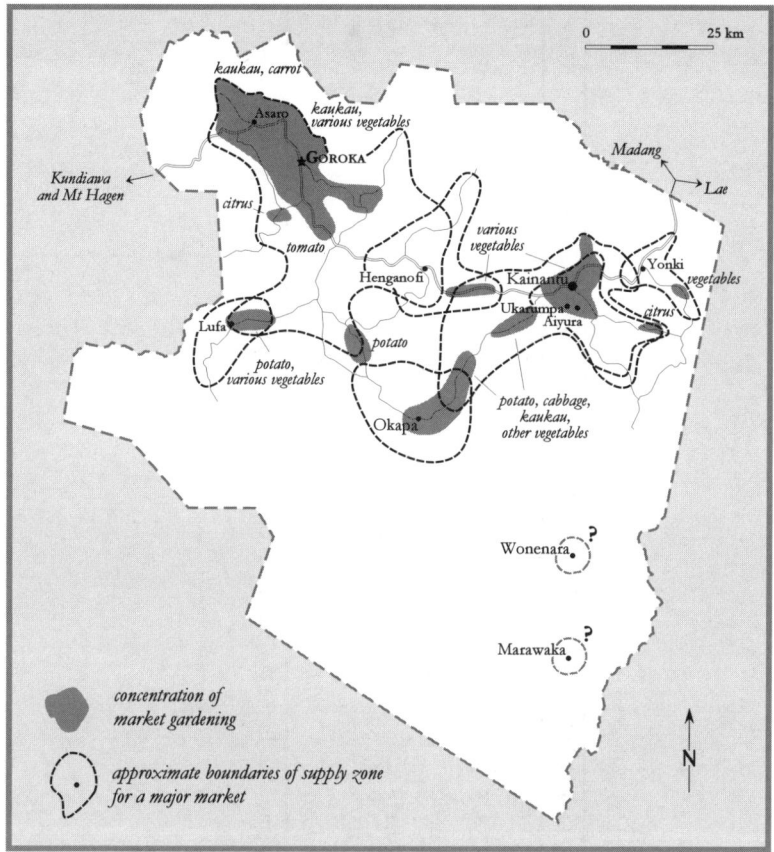

Map 10: Major market gardening areas in the Eastern Highlands Province

Eastern Highlands. But half a year is not a long time, and there were numerous possibilities for mutual misunderstanding between growers and the wholesale company. During fieldwork I spent considerable time at this depot, talking with growers and staff. The discussion below builds to a large extent on these conversations. I look at the successes as well as the points of contention in the interaction between sellers and the buyer. The story also serves to illustrate what went wrong at the other depots.

✥ Commitment of growers

The most common complaint of the wholesalers concerns the lack of any long-term commitment and consistency by the smallholder growers. There are

Table 3: Produce sold at ADF's depot in Goroka, 8 May–7 June 1995

Type of produce	Quantity (kg)		Value (K)		No. of sales*		K/sale
Traditional starchy staples	4,767	11%	1,479.30	7%	34	6%	43.51
Introduced starchy staples**	7,875	19%	3,644.41	17%	34	6%	107.19
Traditional vegetables and greens	1,640	4%	811.80	4%	50	9%	16.24
Introduced vegetables and greens	20,458	48%	12,994.90	61%	299	54%	43.46
Fruit	7,463	18%	2,461.75	12%	133	24%	18.51
Monthly total	42,203	100%	21,392.16	100%	550	100%	

Notes: (*) Some sellers bring more than one type of produce. In the buying records each type is listed separately.
(#) Potato only.

Source: Company records.

indeed few producers who have become dedicated and specialized gardeners for the formal market, and although they do exist in other regions of the highlands, they are absent from Kasena. Even the large carrot gardens mentioned above are usually one-off ventures. Households in Lunube are sporadic suppliers. It is next to impossible to put an 'average' figure on the frequency of the sales of each household, especially as the scene was rapidly changing during the time of my fieldwork. Most of my core households, however, brought produce to the depots some three or four times during the first half of 1995.

Sporadic sellers or not, approximately three out of every four are male. Most of those who do sell reasonably large quantities are men, and these often lose interest in commercial vegetable growing after a while. To some degree the lack of 'commitment' reflects the numerous other preoccupations competing with market gardening, such as the never-ending demands of customary social obligations, but also small tradestore or PMV business. A large part of the reason, however, is the access of males to another source of income, namely coffee, which (seasonally) brings in larger amounts of money. It is telling that the most determined male commercial growers are found in high-altitude areas where the cultivation of coffee is not an option.

Women make up only a quarter of the group of sellers, even if their primary role as growers of food is well documented. Most women also sell sporadically and in small quantities. However, the commercial growing of food (sold through the informal rather than the formal market) is proportionally more important to women, reflecting their marginal status in the coffee economy (see Overfield 1995).

An important factor in the apparent lack of dedication to market gardening is the fact that subsistence needs are still met to a large extent by the household's own production on its own land. What in this regard constitutes a substantial space to manoeuvre for the growers, becomes an exasperating opportunism for wholesalers, as the remarks of an expatriate involved in vegetable buying in Enga Province indicate:

> We need vegetable businesses [i.e. farms] run by the owners themselves and if they fail then there will be no income for these people. Essentially the growers **need to need income** (Hayfield 1992: 9, original emphasis).[7]

In other words, here is an 'uncaptured peasantry' (Hydén 1980), successfully resisting formal and full integration into commodity markets, and in the process subverting the received notions of rational behaviour in the market economy.

While the wholesalers bemoan what they see as opportunism, the charge could easily be levelled at some of the operators who were in business at the time of my fieldwork. They also had mixed and sometimes conflicting interests: trading in coconuts from the coast; running a food bar and a tyre shop; and importantly, they were commercial farmers in their own right. Judging from my conversations, some had very limited interest in cultivating relationships with the growers beyond getting from them what they could not supply themselves at a particular time.

❧ Prices

The sellers are acutely aware of their lack of clout in the formal wholesale market. There is no question that they are willing to bring in produce for sale in the depots rather than selling it in the marketplace, if the price is judged to be fair and payment is prompt. For example, during my stay in Kasena a marked shift into carrot growing took place, with ADF paying good prices for top-quality carrot. Nevertheless, being numerous, small-scale and disorganized, the growers are naturally price-takers in this market. They are aware of the large markups occurring elsewhere in the marketing chain, and that the prices of fresh food in the supermarkets of Lae and Port Moresby are very high (Table 4). Even if wholesalers stress that they have to deal with high transport costs and wastage, a persistent feeling exists among many growers that they are being cheated. The idea of an interest group has been floated among the most commercialized growers of introduced vegetables, but these are numerically a small minority of all sellers.

As for the ADF depot, when the operation had established itself and was getting increased quantities offered for sale, prices for many items came down a bit. Even if many growers had a sense of the relationship between supply and demand: '*Kerot i mas pulap long Mosbi nau ...*' ('there must be a lot of carrot in Moresby now ...'), most shook their heads in exasperation and saw the fluctuations as yet another confirmation of their own precarious position within the formal marketing structure.

Buying prices are not always properly displayed at the depots, but even so sellers do not generally ask for the price before they bring the produce in. They accept what is offered. This contrasts markedly with the behaviour in the coffee market, where a number of buyers compete for the smallholders' coffee. There it is common for sellers to ask about prices before weighing in the coffee, and some even have it weighed by several buyers in order to get the best reading possible. Part of the problem is the fact that potential vegetable buyers are scattered throughout the urban area. Checking prices

Table 4: Examples of wholesale buying price, marketplace price, and retail price* of vegetables commonly sold by Lunube growers, June 1995

Produce	Wholesale buyers		Restaurants		Marketplaces			Retail
	ADF	Kabiufa	Ize Napa	Bird of Paradise	Asaro	Goroka	Port Moresby	Port Moresby
Potato	47	45	35	45	62	71	114	49–159
Carrot	80/60#	40	30	–	45	73	252	199–325
Spring onion	40	50	35	50	109	84	355	30–399
Kaukau	35	15	25	45	26	34	65	120

Notes:
(*) All prices are in toea per kilogram. Apart from Port Moresby retail prices, the figures represent the gross return to a grower, transport costs not taken into account.
(#) Two grades bought.

Source: Fieldwork data; *Fresh Produce News* 1995, no. 103: 22–23 and no. 104: 21.

beforehand is hardly possible unless the grower has access to motor vehicle transport, or is prepared to spend the day walking.

◈ *Quality*

Quality is also a bone of contention. While the state-owned FMC was in operation, it was required to buy all produce offered for sale. It goes without saying that this arrangement did not encourage strict quality control among the sellers. Together with transport bottlenecks, this translated into high losses and played a part in the decision to scrap the project. FPDC, in contrast, has placed great emphasis on improving quality, working with growers, wholesalers, and retailers. Some noteworthy success has been achieved, but many wholesalers are still accepting substandard produce and trying to pass it on to their town clients. Under such circumstances it is understandable that retailers in Port Moresby have long found it more satisfactory to source their produce from Australia.

When the ADF depot started in Goroka, a much tougher stand was taken. All produce was sorted and graded on the spot, before weighing. The growers were put to work sifting through their own produce, together with the depot's staff (Plate 3). Frequently, a sizeable portion of what the grower had brought in was put aside, deemed unfit for purchase. This created great distress and a degree of shame amongst many growers. I once transported a woman with two bags of potato down to the depot, but when she realized that her produce would be tipped out on the floor, sorted, and graded, she changed her mind abruptly and decided to seek out another possibility of which she had heard. I had seen her potatoes the day before, as they were being put in the bags, and knew she had nothing to fear as they were of good quality. Eventually she sold to a restaurant for a slightly lower price, but without suffering the indignity of inspection. This was a small rebellion, which may seem self-defeating unless we look at it as an assertion of subjective power and space to manoeuvre; as a small part of a more general struggle occurring at the 'interface' between the formal economy and the rural villager.

It often takes a very long time under this practice for a seller to have the produce graded and weighed. People do not queue, but instead simply bring in their bags or *bilums* and wait somewhere close until finally a member of the staff pays attention. Some growers become a little frustrated by the long wait, but most are remarkably patient and very few try to speed up the proceedings or get their own produce dealt with ahead of that of others.

Plate 3: Carrots brought for sale at ADF, Goroka. To the left, a depot worker inspecting the quality of the produce and repacking it into netbags.

This is consistent with the often-noted absence of haggling and hard-sell behaviour in marketplaces in Melanesia in general (see Brookfield 1969).

As the depot is located at the end of the town, far from the centre where the market, shops, and restaurants are clustered, people have difficulty transporting the rejects back for sale somewhere else,[8] or back to their village if the worst comes to worst. Another Kasena woman, selling three bags of carrots on a very busy day at the depot, eventually had to throw away a third of her produce. By the time they were graded, it was too late to take them back to the village or anywhere else. She came back rather demoralized: *'Ol i bin sekim sekim sekim ... mi les tru!'* ('They checked and checked ... I am really frustrated!').

Eventually, however, the growers seem to be accepting and adjusting to the imposition of quality standards. By mid-1995 many carrot growers in Kasena, for instance, were grading their own harvest before taking it into town for sale. In that sense the approach of ADF towards quality improvement has been vindicated.

❧ *Payments*

Even more damaging for the grower–wholesaler relationship than low and/or fluctuating prices, have been the business practices of some of the Goroka wholesalers. It was common, for example, for Goroka depots to pay out only once or twice a week: all the grower got in the pocket after weighing in the produce was a small ticket with the name and the amount scribbled on it, and instructions to come back on Monday, or similar. For a villager, having to make an extra trip to town in order to collect some 10 or 20 kina is indeed a nuisance. The reason for this cumbersome arrangement was not only fear of robbery – which is present, and not unjustifiably so, in most Papua New Guinean businesses – but more significantly, a combination of bad management, undercapitalization, and chronic cashflow problems. Perhaps most importantly though, the arrangement signified indifference if not contempt for growers by the traders. One of the reasons for the popularity of the new wholesaler, ADF, was that growers were paid in cash on the spot – even if it meant that the manager had to make two or three trips to the bank in one day, so that cash actually held at the premises was kept at a minimum – or by cheque which could be cashed at the bank immediately.

. . .

To summarize, the 'formal' market is *in practice* a shifting and unstable space; an 'interface' between actors who come to this market with widely varying expectations and knowledge. Participation in it is viewed by the growers as a desirable but somewhat difficult undertaking. They perceive a big gap in power between themselves and the depot operators or buyers. The latter are seen as dictating the terms of trade, putting the growers in a subordinate position which they detest. The rationale for quality standards is not always comprehended, although this seems to be changing. On the other hand, wholesalers see the growers as unpredictable and lacking commitment. They have a point there, although many growers appear eager to enter into 'partnerships' of some sort. In any case, there have been few sustained attempts at building lasting relationships between growers and buyers. The formal market remains an interface, a space where the growers do not quite see themselves as belonging. This is evident in the small contests of power which take place in the day-to-day operation of this market.

DIRECT BULK SELLING

Potential vegetable bulk buyers in Goroka other than the wholesale depots are of three kinds: institutions, retailers, and many kinds of food bars and restaurants. Of institutions, the hospital and various educational establishments are most important. During my fieldwork in 1994–95 the hospital had been especially hard hit by the cash crisis of the Papua New Guinean state. The delivery of government services virtually ground to a halt. Purchases for the hospital had become very erratic and payments insecure. Kasena people sometimes check out the options there when in town, but this is not an outlet to be relied upon. Similarly, the Goroka Technical College and the Goroka High School both buy some produce, but rice, tinned fish, and white bread seems to be firmly entrenched in these institutions as the preferred foodstuffs for innocent young minds.[9] The local produce which is bought is limited to a few 'extras' in limited quantities, either bought at the door or at the market.[10]

As discussed earlier, only a few retailers in Goroka actually sell fresh vegetables, so a reliable outlet is not found there either. A Korean restaurant and the Bird of Paradise Hotel are the sole upmarket purveyors of gastronomic delights, and both buy some produce. Much more numerous are the *haus kaikai* (food bars or restaurants) which cater to the masses. These are scattered throughout the urban area, but many are located in the retail concentrations (see Map 6). The typical *haus kaikai* uses a great deal of imported rice and meat in its culinary creations, but miscellaneous vegetables also find their way into the various stews, and deep-fried potato chips are ubiquitous. The restaurant operators buy what they need at the door from whoever happens to come along. The main items of sale are potato, kaukau, carrot, cabbage, and a few other types of introduced vegetables. Quantities are not great; most food bars for example require perhaps two 60 kg bags of kaukau per week. What is not brought to the door is bought in the marketplace. Quality demands vary widely. Often it is possible for growers to sell to food bars produce that has been rejected by the wholesale buyers because of its looks:[11] many a crooked carrot thus gets consumed without a hiccup. Prices vary also, but on many occasions they are slightly lower than at the wholesale depots. Again, growers are squarely price takers in such a situation. They are eager to sell, but wary of attempts at cheating. Often they are not paid on the spot, but must come back to collect the payment.

It is therefore apparent that direct sales to institutions, retailers, or food bars are even more of a treasure hunt than sales to the wholesale trading firms. This is a haphazard, uncertain market. Very few of these businesses have sustained relationships with particular growers. An air of suspicion prevails: a woman whom I accompanied one day gave a false name when the buyer asked what he should write on the receipt. She put on a conspiratorial grin when she saw that I had noticed. Another small example of an almost whimsical act of subversion.

INFORMAL FOOD TRADE: THE MARKETPLACES

In contrast to the formal market, informal marketplace selling has received little official assistance. This is surprising, given that its importance for rural and urban people alike is obvious to anyone who ventures out of doors. To be fair, DAL has recognized this and attempted to collect some basic data about the larger urban markets (DAL 1990–92). By contrast, marketplace trade gets hardly a mention in many economic assessments and policy recommendations by outside experts (see e.g. Fallon 1992; Economic Insights Pty Ltd 1994), except perhaps to point out its inefficiencies (see Grey 1993: 91). Development assistance remains preoccupied with export crops such as coffee or cocoa, and on the more formal wholesale trading chain. Projects with specific emphasis on marketplace selling are these days conspicuous by their absence.[12]

This has not always been so. In the postwar period, when development efforts began in earnest in Papua New Guinea, the establishment of marketplaces was seen by both the colonial authorities and their subjects as one of the clearest and most auspicious manifestations of development.

The marketplace as an instrument for development

In the monetized economy of the Gazelle Peninsula, the marketplace has long been of considerable importance, and nowhere more so than in the town of Rabaul. Its market was in part an extension of traditional commodity exchange, and the country's first modern urban marketplace was established there in the 1920s (Epstein 1982: 14). Until the volcanic eruption of 1994, which devastated the town, it was one of the largest markets in the country.

In other urban areas the marketplace of today is more directly an innovation of colonial authorities, its intended functions and underlying blueprints strongly linked to the hazy ideal of 'development'. In Port Moresby, the marketplace at Koki boasts the longest history. An old Papuan trading site, it assumed some importance as a marketplace during World War II (Epstein 1982: 24), and a municipal market was established there in 1952 (Forbes 1975: 17). Other council markets of Port Moresby, of which

FRESH FOOD MARKETS, THEIR HISTORY, AND OPERATION

Gordons is by far the most important (now much larger than Koki), did not come into being until the 1960s. In addition, small marketplaces have developed spontaneously in all residential areas of the spread-out city, often in connection with local clusters of shops. The story is similar for other towns. Lae and Goroka both got their municipal markets in 1957 (Epstein 1982: 19, 23).[13] Both towns now have several smaller markets in addition to the large main ones. Throughout the country there are numerous roadside and village markets, which have grown up more or less spontaneously, without official intervention. Some are held on set days only, whereas others operate on any day of the week.

Apart from the general motive of provisioning the growing urban populations, there were other official rationales for the initial establishment of municipal markets. First, that the unsupervised hawking of foodstuffs around the towns was seen as a potential health hazard (Jackson 1976c: 175), although descriptions of Koki market in the 1960s, for example, suggest that even the long arm of the colonial state was somewhat ineffectual in rectifying that situation (see Epstein 1982). Second, marketplaces were seen as potential 'contact points' with the rural population, enabling the diffusion of innovations related to cash cropping and other basics which were to form the stuff of development. Free seeds of 'European' vegetables were for instance handed out in the Goroka and Mount Hagen markets by the Department of Agriculture, until the local councils took over their administration (Epstein 1982).

In some markets, notably Goroka and Mount Hagen, attempts were made to regulate prices by administrative fiat, but stiff opposition from sellers eventually led to the discontinuation of price control (Epstein 1982: 22). Why such paternal 'guidance' was attempted in the first place is not clear, but perhaps the alternative was simply seen as too chaotic.

In a sense, then, these marketplaces started out as far from 'informal'; on the contrary the original idea was to 'regularise and formalise an emerging reality' (Jackson 1976c: 175). Politics and power relations were involved from the very start. One of the best discussions of this side of the market equation is offered by Maclean (1989), who describes a small weekly market in the remote Jimi Valley. Initiated by the local councillor in the mid-1970s, that market became an expression of a general aspiration for development. Maclean goes so far as to argue that 'the fundamental rationality of this institutionalised context of exchange is a political/ideological rather than economic one' (1989: 74).

An interesting, albeit stillborn idea promoted in the 1970s was that of the *maket raun* (mobile market). It was put forward by geographers, influenced by central place and regional development theories, but deeply conscious of the peculiar problems of Papua New Guinea – in particular its lack of small rural service centres. They devised a pilot scheme for the Eastern Highlands, whereby public services (health, agricultural extension, postal services, etc.) and commercial activities (buying and retailing, entertainment, etc.) would be provided at set locations and on set days (Ward *et al.* 1974a, 1974b). Unfortunately, when the pilot scheme came to be implemented, it was not in the Eastern but the Western Highlands, with some of the careful planning invalidated. Two or three of the sites chosen for the *maket raun* were successful, with large crowds attending, whereas others were too close to the town of Mount Hagen to acquire any significance as central places in their own right. Moreover, lawlessness and fighting were problems in the province at this time, and some sites turned out to be on borders between hostile groups, with the result that few people turned up (R. Gerard Ward, pers. comm., 1996). It would be fair to say that the rural markets of today are largely home-grown, rather than the result of official development planning.

Although the urban marketplaces did go some way in meeting growing demand for fresh food in the towns, they soon evolved in a direction that did not conform to the original ideas. They became just as important as arenas for social interaction as for economic transactions, being a neutral ground for socializing in a suspicious world.[14] Hence, they quickly acquired a great significance in the daily 'space-time routines' of both the rural and urban dwellers, who have shaped their current characteristics. Most markets are now just about as 'informal' as they could possibly be, although local authorities constantly try to assert control over what happens in those marketplaces which come under their jurisdiction.

Actors in the marketplace

If the small grower feels a bit out of place in the wholesale depot, the open markets are very much a space created by the growers. Their demeanour is more confident, there is not the same suspicion of being cheated all the time, or of being an actor in a play that gives little scope for creative interpretation. Nevertheless, small battles of authority and power are constantly played out in the marketplace.

∽ Town

As noted in the preceding chapter, Goroka has a large, centrally located municipal market, which has long functioned as a true focal point for indigenous townsfolk and rural daytrippers alike. A wide variety of locally grown fruit and vegetables is sold, plus coconuts (and mango, when in season) from the lowlands, tobacco, eggs, cordials, and clothes (see Table 5). Almost the single item of merchandise that is absent is *buai*, long the bane of urban councils because of the large amount of red liquid with which its aficionados part as a result of its consumption.[15]

The facilities are maintained by the Goroka Local Government Council. This is a clearly defined space, enclosed by a 2-metre high wire fence. Three shelters are there, equipped with tables for produce, but no seats. However,

Table 5: Marketplaces: no. of sellers and items sold

	Goroka (15/3/95)		Asaro (10/2/95)		Kasena (1/5/95)	
	no.	%	no.	%	no.	%
Total no. of sellers at time of survey	354	100	112	100	26	100
of which female	336	95	103	92	24	92
of which male		18	5	9	2	8
Number of sellers offering:						
Traditional starchy staples	131	37	42	37	8	31
Introduced starchy staples*	20	6	2	2	1	4
Traditional vegetables and greens	140	40	30	26	5	19
Introduced vegetables and greens	245	69	63	56	3	12
Fruit	169	48	24	21	5	19
Narcotics#	16	5	18	16	5	19
Cooked food†	0	0	4	4	3	12
Other goods	13	4	4	4	0	0

Notes: (*) Potato only.
  (#) Leaf tobacco, cigarettes, and (except in Goroka) *buai* and its accompaniments.
  (†) Fried flour, cooked mutton or pork. Sale of cooked food is not allowed in Goroka Market.
Source: Fieldwork surveys.

sellers prefer to sit on the ground in the open area between the gates and the shelters (Plate 4). Here they have defined their own space, so to speak, even if it is hot and dusty when the sun is shining, and muddy when it rains. There is a simple but valid reason for this: the closer to the gates, the closer to the stream of potential buyers pouring in through these gates. An exception is the sellers of various indigenous leafy greens, who tend to congregate in one of the sheds, as their produce is quickly damaged by the hot sun. The shelters have been poorly maintained, although two years ago the thatched roofs were replaced with corrugated iron, courtesy of PEPSI™, which now in fact dominates the outward appearance of many Papua New Guineans town markets. Global advertising is here, for sure (see Foster 1999).

Sellers come to the market on PMVs, except for those who live in the nearby peri-urban villages. They come from as far as 90 minutes' drive away; from Daulo Pass to the west, Unggai and Henganofi to the south and southeast, but most come from not far away in the Lower Asaro and Bena Bena areas. Each day some Lunube women are amongst them, although their participation varies widely. There are those who hardly ever go to Goroka to sell, preferring markets closer to home and Asaro, or in Kasena. Others come once in a fortnight with a *bilum* or two.

Plate 4: From Goroka market. Male traders selling coconuts from Madang, women selling local produce. Note bundles/heaps, no scales are used. Market shelters are visible at the top of the photograph.

FRESH FOOD MARKETS, THEIR HISTORY, AND OPERATION

Plate 5: From the market at Asaro. Okuk Highway to the left. Several varieties of kaukau can be seen.

The Council employs gatekeepers, who collect a fee from the sellers. It varies, according to the estimated value of their produce, from 30t to K1. This is accepted but of course not particularly popular among sellers, who are almost all women. Sellers take any opportunity of sneaking in without paying the 'correct' fee. Moreover, the gatekeepers' attempts to show their authority and personal importance by bossing the sellers around, checking their tickets, and so on, are resented.[16] The market is supposed to close at half past five, but it takes a long time to get sellers and buyers to obey orders to move out.

The market has become a source of a rather more serious power struggle amongst other actors – the authorities of Goroka. From 1965–89 the Goroka Local Government Council covered both the town and the populous rural areas around it.[17] In 1989 the Eastern Highlands Capital Authority was created, in order to administer the town itself. But the market had been a handsome moneyspinner for the Council for a long time, and it refused to let go of it. The Capital Authority argues that, in its current state, the marketplace is a potential health hazard, as there are no toilets and hygiene is somewhat lacking. This is a stalemate, and in the meantime the Council collects a small treasure of K200–300 from the market sellers on a typical day, making this one of its chief sources of income. While the official justification for charging gate fees is to enable the market to be serviced and improved, there is little evidence of any money actually finding its way back, beyond paying for the gatekeepers themselves and garbage collection at the end of the day.

The Capital Authority has in the meantime made its presence felt in two markets which have developed spontaneously on roadsides elsewhere in the town, namely Chinatown and Lopi (see Map 6), by collecting a small fee from sellers. As such selling is in fact technically illegal, the ticket given out to sellers in these markets bears an inscription which symbolically asserts that these sellers – almost all women, it might be noted – are there at the mercy of the 'town fathers':

MARKET FINE
20t
For Illegal Street Vending

Three other such markets (at Kama, Seigu, and Faniyufa, see Map 6) are located just outside the town boundary, under the auspices of the landowners in each of these peri-urban villages. Following some pressure from the Capital Authority, these markets are now held within enclosed yards, but were initially perched on the roadsides.

Towards the end of my fieldwork, the minimum selling price in all Goroka markets was abruptly changed from 10t to 20t per bunch or heap of produce.[18] It turned out that this had been decided by the market authorities, not by growers. Signs were put up at some markets, proclaiming that it was now *tambu* (forbidden) to sell for less than 20t. Some confusion ensued, but the change went through in a week or so. As many commodities, such as kaukau, were sold mostly in K1 lots anyway, this did not greatly affect some sellers. Others, in so far as I could tell, adjusted their lot sizes somewhat, effectively softening the price hike. Council officials maintained that they had made the decision in response to the drastic price changes of tradestore goods, resulting from devaluation of the currency which had taken place in earlier months. I saw however in Council records that such a change had been contemplated some years ago, following a similar change in Port Moresby markets, where prices are generally much higher. One councillor is recorded as saying in 1993, when this was discussed, that it would make it possible for the Council to charge higher gate fees. Yet although the power over pricing is subject to occasional struggles in this manner, it is in the last instance very much up to the sellers to determine their price.

✤ Roadside

Located some 17 km up the Okuk Highway to the west of Goroka, Asaro Station also has a market. Here large quantities of kaukau are sold, but also a variety of other food crops, plus *buai* and tobacco (see Table 5). This is now very much a roadside affair (see Plate 5), but in the late 1960s the then young and ambitious Asaro–Watabung Local Government Council created a space for a market of the Goroka kind: fences, shelters, gate fees. But here again the space of the market has been redefined, if not subverted. Due to resentment about having to pay gate fees, or so I was told, the sellers moved a few hundred metres to the east and now occupy a corner where a busy side road joins the Okuk Highway.[19] In addition to highway travellers, many of whom suspend their journey at Asaro to buy staple foods, the station is the home of a few public servants, and there is a community of settlers – labourers and petty traders from other parts of the highlands, most notably from Simbu Province.

The Asaro market is held every day of the week,[20] Friday being the busiest day, Sunday the quietest. Lunube people frequent the market, many women selling there at least once a fortnight. Like the Goroka market, its function as a meeting place is no less important than its economic role. For example, it is a venue for much political discussion (mostly among the men) relating to the Asaro–Watabung Local Government Council. Sometimes domestic dramas are played out, and cards are played every day by women and men alike. Occasionally the market also becomes a platform for other kinds of social action and interaction – the consumption of alcohol during the coffee season for instance, or fundamentalist Christian preaching (see Vignette 3 below).

The sellers at this market come from a fairly wide area in and around Asaro. Their takings vary, but are often between K5 and K10 per selling trip. When I had been in Kasena for only a short time, new roadside markets suddenly appeared in a few other places down the highway (in the direction of Goroka). I was told that there had been a scuffle amongst the sellers at Asaro, and a group of women from the next tribal area to the east, Yufiyufa, had been told in no uncertain terms to go and make their own market. This they promptly did: not one, but three new markets sprang up. Their location

> **Vignette 3**: Jesus in the marketplace
>
> Just after three o'clock, a seller of a different kind emerged. This was a Pentecostal evangelist, who started blaring out his message through a megaphone, holding the Bible aloft and pointing a finger at the sellers and buyers, momentarily distracting them from their business and turning them into spectators. His message (in Tok Pisin) was an angry one: 'You people may have a lot of kaikai now, but beware: Jesus may come back, and very soon, and he will figure out who is worthy of his mercy and who is not. The world is about to come to an end. So you better get Jesus into your hearts right now.' His preaching went on for half an hour, business slowing down a little in the meantime. But then, I was told that this preacher comes here every week, so this is limited novelty for most of those attending the market ...
>
> (Fieldnotes – Asaro Market, 10 February 1995)

was rather unfortunate from the view of road safety, but business was brisk. But this goes to show that territoriality, the assertion of power over space, is never far away from the marketplace.

Instead of the council, the current patron of the Asaro market is a local politician-cum-businessman whose tradestore forms the backdrop to the market. In addition there is another tradestore close by, as well as an agricultural supply store. There is thus ample opportunity for the sellers to spend their money as they earn it. Many of them do just that at the end of their selling day. Almost all are women and their earnings are mostly used to support the day-to-day reproduction of their households: a bar of *Klina* soap for clothes and kids, a tin of fish, *Cheezpops* for the young set, perhaps some greens purchased from other women at the market.

Another roadside market, that at Yonki in the eastern end of the province (see Map 2), illustrates the crucial importance of location, as well as the limitations of well-meaning, but top-down, development projects which fail to consult local actors. The Yonki Power Project involved the building of a large dam for hydro-electric power and flooding of a substantial piece of land, which led to some strife between locals and authorities in the 1980s (*Times of Papua New Guinea* 1990). In conjunction with the end phase of the construction process, the Arona Valley Development Authority (AVDA) was formed in 1990. One of the ideas for the development of the area was to strengthen the local food market. AVDA therefore embarked on the building of a brand new marketplace, with all the appropriate facilities:

fence, shelters, and stalls. There was, however, a small hitch: the market was on the western side of the new dam, well away from Yonki town and adjacent settlements, which are on the eastern side. To this day the new marketplace remains empty, but sellers continue to occupy a somewhat precarious corner on the highway, about 3 kilometres to the east. This location suits buyers, who are partly highway travellers and partly employees of the power company, but is also a lot more central for the majority of sellers, coming as they do from the more densely settled areas to the east of the town and the new lake. A large market with up to 200 sellers is held at this corner on Wednesdays and Fridays and a smaller number of sellers comes there on other days as well.

❦ *Village markets*

The most local of all are the village marketplaces, where traditional root crops, indigenous greens and narcotics are the main items for sale (see Table 5). Commoditization of food has now reached virtually every highland village to some extent. Even the most important of highland preoccupations, pig rearing, has been partially affected by this process, as small and broken kaukau is frequently sold within villages as pig feed. Prices are significantly lower than in the other markets. The women who sell get only a couple of kina in hand at the end of their selling session, or not even that, but there are of course no fees to be paid, nor are any (monetary) transport costs involved.

The Lunube villages have a market of this nature, located at the main Lunube road where it runs through the large settlements at Kasena. Mercantile activity is not a novelty in this place, as Collins & Leahy operated one of their general stores here in the 1960s and early 1970s. As village entrepreneurs started to erect their own small tradestores,[21] the retail chain withdrew from the rural areas to Goroka. But in the late 1970s the local Member of Parliament – in a frantic pre-election search for a visible proof of his generosity – had a market shelter built by the roadside in front of the dilapidated store. A splendid tin roof, supported by wooden frame, on a robust concrete foundation. Stalls were put in. No more squatting in the mud during the *taim bilong ren* (rainy season).

Again, this was a short-lived innovation, as a group of *spakman* (drunkards) vandalized the setup. Opinions differed as to whether there had been any 'higher motive', but some said that it had been built on a piece of land which someone had a claim to, without proper consultation. In any case, the stalls are nowhere to be seen, but the frame and the roof are still standing, albeit leaning a bit. But the market women do not sit there any more. They prefer the bare ground just outside. The numerous card-players and the even more numerous children have taken over the market shelter. Far be it from me to condemn such an arrangement, but once I could not help asking a male friend of mine, 'Why not fix it up?' His prompt answer: *'Em i no ples bilong mipela. Memba ya i putim!'* ('It is not our place. The MP put it there!')

. . .

In contrast to the unsettled atmosphere that surrounds the wholesale depots, the marketplaces are well established and vibrant. Apart from the councils having initially established the large urban markets, official assistance of any kind to this important side of the fruit and vegetable trade is notable only by its absence. Now and then ideas on the possible improvement of the marketplaces crop up, for example relating to cool storage within markets, or improved transport (see e.g. Atkinson and Lewis 1992), but neither the national Department of Agriculture and Livestock nor the Local Government Councils have seen it feasible to try and put some of these innovations into practice. Meanwhile it is *bisnis* as usual.

CONCLUSION

We have now traced the local social construction of different kinds of fresh food markets in which the people of Lunube are implicated. Without wanting to propagate yet another dualism, I used 'formal' and 'informal' as a convenient shorthand to describe their characteristics. It would be a gross oversimplification to say that one works while the other does not, but it cannot be denied that the open, informal marketplaces have come to play a much more significant economic and social role for a much greater number of people, rural and urban, than have the wholesale vegetable depots which are part of the formal economy.

Most of those supplying the wholesale depots, with the vegetables and fruit demanded by the urban supermarkets, are not dedicated market gardeners. They are subsistence farmers and coffee growers, for whom vegetable selling is a subsidiary activity. Notable exceptions do exist, for example some 'big peasants' who specialize in growing vegetables rather than or alongside with coffee. Specialized vegetable growers are also found in smaller areas which are at altitudes too high for coffee; these are people with a long-term commitment to market gardening as their only possible cash-earning activity. Others, and these are the majority of the suppliers, bring in small quantities when and if they happen to have something worth selling. While they sometimes specifically plant a plot with crops destined for sale rather than consumption at home, they do not commit their resources thereby permanently to market production. It is more a question of *'mipela traim tasol'* ('we are just trying it out'; see Allen 1976: 310). Frequently the results are out of step with the expectations. The differences between growers and the traders, regarding power in this market and knowledge about its workings, are also acutely felt by the growers.

By contrast, in the marketplaces we see rural producer-sellers, mainly women, who rely on these markets for cash in order to meet immediate daily needs. The sellers *do* have a certain power, and 'space to manoeuvre'. They constantly use their power to redefine the space of the market, whether in the town, at the roadside, or in the village. This has happened in defiance of authorities, colonial or postcolonial, which in most parts of the highlands introduced the market as a novel form of economic transaction in the first place, and have sought to retain their power to control and regulate what happens there. To understand the nature of such struggles requires an approach which gives human agency the attention it deserves. The outcomes are certainly not necessarily beneficial or straightforward in the eyes of a market modeller equipped with the blinkers of instrumental rationality. Neither is it quite feasible, I think, to attribute the result to the iron grip of capitalism, and a heroic struggle of an oppressed class against its vicissitudes. At a more mundane level, these markets have become part and parcel of the daily lived space for most Lunube people.

NOTES

1   There are signs that some of the initial enthusiasm for establishing fruits and vegetables as cash crops was linked to the rise of coffee growing as an enterprise of *expatriate* planters in the 1950s. Witness the musings of a patrol officer at this time, regarding citrus and stone fruits: 'Such an industry is a golden opportunity to enter into a field of cash cropping in which [the highlander] would not be in direct competition with the European' (Kent 1957: 19).

2   The company has also attempted to assist informal market actors, mainly by disseminating information, but on also on occasion by more direct initiatives. These have been, for example, in the matter of sea transport from Lae to Port Moresby, where FPDC has helped streamline the procedures of consignment and handling of the cargo. Other proposals, such as making coolers available to

sellers in the large urban markets, have not so far been implemented (Michael Daysh, pers. comm., 24 March 1994).

3   Similar schemes were started in other parts of the highlands, the Markham and Ramu Valleys, and at Laloki close to Port Moresby (Bowman 1946).

4   As an aside, among these itinerant bulk buyers were Daniel Leahy Jr, now at the helm of Collins & Leahy, and Sinake Giregire, Asaro *bigman*-cum-entrepreneur and later government minister (Sinake Giregire, pers. comm., 26 March 1995).

5   As early as 1954 there are reports of a company 'exporting native grown potatoes' (Healy 1954: 5) from Goroka. Presumably these potatoes were 'exported' only out of the highlands but not to a different country, although I have not been able to find out to which market. A short-lived initiative in the late 1950s was the cultivation of potatoes by the Fore people, near Okapa, supposedly for export to the then-Dutch West New Guinea. This was organized through an expatriate trader (Sorensen and Gajdusek 1969: 328). The Fore are far from auspiciously located in relation to transport, and this brief episode is one of the more intriguing examples of the complicated spatial history of commoditization.

6   A new depot was under construction at Yufiyufa (see Map 2) during my fieldwork. This was a joint venture between Alele – an expatriate-run wholesale firm in Mt Hagen – and a local large-scale grower and entrepreneur. It had not started trading when I left in 1995.

7   *Déjà vu?* The following was written in 1969 about the people of the lower Asaro Valley:

> The people of the Lowa Census Division have the potential to be some of the richest in the Territory, and certainly this District … Yet the standard of living is stagnant … and a persuasive lethargy is widespread. … Fundamentally any lasting stimulus for economic advancement arises out of a set of felt needs. The felt needs of these people are modest to say the least (Alder 1969: 1–2).

8   For example at the other wholesale depots, when they were still in business, as these did not take quality quite as seriously. Also, unemployed Goroka settlers sometimes come to the depot to collect rejected produce, or buy it for a low price from the growers, and then resell it at the marketplace.

9   As well as for less innocent minds: the high consumption of imported food by inmates of the local gaol was 'noted with alarm' in the 1980s (Calcinai and Bourke 1982: 184).

10 The Goroka Campus of UPNG (formerly Goroka Teachers' College) has a canteen, which during fieldwork was run by a global operator, viz. the French hotel and catering chain SHRM. They bought from the ADF depot. A factor in the canteen business being entrusted to SHRM was that the former operator had been accused of misappropriating money which had been earmarked for buying produce.

11 The exception is the Bird of Paradise, which requires top-quality produce and pays well for it.

12 I have already mentioned that the FPDC includes the improvement of market place trade in its activities, but the main emphasis of the project is on the wholesale trade.

13 A patrol officer succinctly sums up the situation in Goroka at the time, and hints at a prototype in the Rabaul market:

> It is a source of wonderment to the writer that in an area such as the Goroka Sub-District where such excellent native and European foodstuffs are grown that the residents of Goroka township have to depend upon a few itinerant native vendors and the local stores as a source of supply for European vegetable foodstuffs; the supply I might add is extremely spasmodic. Not only would the establishment of a native market similar to the Rabaul 'boong' be a great boom to the European community and to the native community living within the precincts of the township many of whom are 'foreign' natives and therefore are denied the op-portunity to grow the little extras which they desire but it would be an immediate source of extra income to the native population (Kent 1957: 18–19).

14 See the following remark about Koki market:

> During one week in 1968 we counted about 50,000 individuals visiting the market of whom approximately 25 percent actually purchased something from the 2,500 vendors who had turned up to sell their produce (Epstein 1982: 25).

15 *Buai* has been in and out of the Goroka market through the years. When I arrived in 1994 a separate *buai* market was operating at Zokozoi Creek in North Goroka (see Map 6). In 1995 a new and much larger space was made available in Gahuku territory, several kilometres out of town towards Asaro, and sellers were forcibly evicted from Zokozoi. Individuals still sell *buai* within the town.

16 Similar (gendered) contests of power were noted in the 1970s, although since then the enthusiasm for keeping the market clean seems to have dampened somewhat:

> [C]hewing [of *buai*] is forbidden in the market, as is the dropping of litter of any kind. The market masters keep a vigilant eye on possible offenders… and in their anxiety to ensure the success and cleanliness of the market rap the knuckles of those lax enough to be spotted defiling the fence by leaning upon it; those taken to task are nearly always women (Jackson and Kolta 1974: 3–4).

17 Before 1965, a separate Town Advisory Council had existed (Mollok 1989).

18 Ten toea had been the base unit of price since 1957, albeit initially as one *shilling*, and then as 10 *cents* from the switch to decimal currency in 1966 until independence (Robin Hide, pers. comm., 1997).

19 Incidentally, this is the road which runs through Lunube. In addition, people from the tribal areas of Wantirifu and Keremu-Anengu come this way to get to the main highway.

20 During my stay there was only one short period during which there was no trading at Asaro, following the death of a local *bigman* and father of the market patron.

21 The operation of one of the very first locally owned tradestores in Kasena has been described by Ganarafo (1974).

6

The travelling tuber: kaukau and its commoditization

Sweet Potato is the staple. I had never thought it possible before for a people to live so exclusively on so monotonous a diet. But my respect for this vegetable has greatly increased since my patrol to the mountains. According to articles by dieticians I have read that Bread is the Staff of Life but to these people the humble Sweet Potato is their tower of hope and seems to symbolize life itself (Corrigan 1949: 3).

FRESH FOOD MARKETING IN PAPUA NEW GUINEA is an important and dynamic activity in which a large proportion of the population takes part. While considerable difference exists between the formal and the informal segments of the trading system, neither can be construed as a perfect or even a particularly good example of 'the market' which we encounter in economics textbooks. The byways of history and the complex map of power and personal motivations have led us to a different destination. Recalling Michael Mann's perspicacious remark about 'societies', real markets are likewise 'messier than our theories of them'. The people who through their actions create such markets, behave economically rationally at times, and at other times not.

The kaukau market as it is currently organised is no exception. In few instances can the importance of the actor be more visible. Growers literally go to great lengths to sell the crop. Usually they take the harvest themselves to the point of sale, squatting behind the heaps of tubers in the marketplace until all are sold, before returning to their home villages. Traders do not feature to a marked degree, in contrast to the organizationally more complex – and seemingly more economically rational – markets in many other countries. The market certainly could look very different and more efficient in economic terms, but this is how past and present actors have constructed it, for better or worse. The history of that social construction is the subject of this chapter.

Metaphorically speaking, the kaukau itself is something of a vagabond, having travelled a long way from its original home to where we find it on offer at a marketplace in Papua New Guinea. As any other commodity, it has a 'cultural biography' (Kopytoff 1986), which is intimately tied to the biographies of those who have grown it, exchanged it, and consumed it. I shall now trace this biography through space and time, starting the journey half a millennium ago and half a world away, before moving to Papua New Guinea and recent happenings in the Asaro Valley.

As the present approaches, it becomes possible to animate the kaukau history through the life stories of some key actors, situated as they are in the Goroka–Asaro context. To varying degrees, these actors have become involved with the numerous but often futile development schemes of the area, and participated in its perpetual political theatre. I pay particular attention to the turn of events since the early 1970s.

EARLY VOYAGES OF AN IMPORTANT CROP

One of the many food crops that started to circumnavigate the globe at the end of the fifteenth century, *Ipomoea batatas* was originally domesticated in the American tropics. When Europeans started documenting its biography it was widely cultivated from present-day Mexico south to the Andes. It had also been taken from America into the Pacific Ocean, becoming an important crop in the corners of the Polynesian triangle, namely Aotearoa/ New Zealand, Hawaii and Easter Island. A pre-fifteenth century diffusion into Melanesia and Southeast Asia has, however, been ruled out (Yen 1991).

The plant first arrived in Europe when Columbus returned from the West Indies in 1492 (Yen 1982: 21). Subsequently, Portuguese voyagers took it to Africa, India, and the Indonesian archipelago. Moreover, in the sixteenth century Spanish ships carried it in the opposite direction, across the Pacific from Mexico to the Philippines.

In mainland Asia, sweet potato became a supplementary crop in agricultural systems that were based on grain cultivation. In quantitative terms, China has long been the largest producer by far. Yet in Asia the crop has had to contend with a rather lowly social status, being emergency food rather than a staple on its own terms, although various ways of processing were pioneered by the Chinese. In the Philippines it took on altogether more importance, becoming a staple on a par with rice in the subsistence cultivation systems in some regions (Yen 1982: 26). Today it also features strongly as a commodity in Philippine fresh food trade, where a 'two- to three-tiered intermediation between farmers and consumers' (Roa *et al.* 1991: 330) suggests a marketing system of some complexity.

Moving into the highlands: the 'Ipomoean revolution'

From the Southeast Asian archipelagos, the new root crop diffused quickly to the island of New Guinea, where it soon achieved an extraordinary dominance in certain highland cultivation systems. The exact timing of the arrival is subject to debate, although a consensus seems to be emerging that it is indeed quite recent. The first highland cultivators to adopt the kaukau probably did so about 300 years ago.[1] To this day it continues its march, in many places displacing the old Melanesian staple root crops; taro (*Colocasia esculenta*) and various yam species (*Dioscorea* spp). Some of the most recent changes have occurred on the islands of Bougainville, New Ireland, and parts of New Britain (see Map 7), where kaukau has been gradually replacing taro since the 1940s.

The reason for the overwhelming success of *Ipomoea batatas* in New Guinea is found in a mixture of comparative agronomic advantage and social processes. Its agronomic superiority has several aspects. Plantings and planting materials are easier to manage than those of bananas, taro, or yams. Compared to *Colocasia* taro, kaukau is less vulnerable to disease. This has played a part in recent changes in coastal and island regions, where taro blight (the fungus *Phytophthora colocasiae*) has been a problem (R. Michael Bourke, pers. comm., 1997). Kaukau is also a substantially less demanding plant in terms of soil fertility (Clarke 1977). Whereas taro is primarily grown either in new clearings – where nutrients are quickly released out of the forest biomass – or in elaborately husbanded irrigated plots, kaukau can yield reasonably well on grassland soils such as those found in the central highland valleys. Yields of 15 to over 30 tonnes per hectare are common in the area (see summary of previous research findings in Bourke 1985: 99).

While taro can be grown up to similar altitudes as kaukau in Papua New Guinea, or about 2700 m above sea level (Bayliss-Smith 1996: 513), kaukau yields at elevations over 2000 m are substantially higher. Evidence from Enga Province in particular suggests that following the arrival of kaukau, an expansion of settlement took place into such higher valleys and plateaux some 200 years ago (Wohlt 1978; Allen 1982: 111). However, the plant is susceptible to frosts, which occur at these higher altitudes, as is taro.

A proliferation of cultivars, coupled with numerous technical innovations, has increased the scope for adjusting the crop to micro-environmental conditions. The plant is vegetatively propagated by cultivators, but its botanical properties and the practice of planting a mix of varieties in a single garden has ensured constant interbreeding (Yen 1991: 21). Papua New Guinea has emerged as a major centre of genetic diversity – Bourke (1985: 94) has estimated that as many as 5,000 cultivars exist in the country. Recent commoditization has led to some reduction in the varieties planted in any quantity, but the varietal profusion is still formidable.

Papua New Guinean growers have come up with numerous innovations in the methods used to cultivate the crop and maintain soil fertility and stability. The fallacy of portraying subsistence cultivation as inherently slow-moving and resistant to change is demonstrated by the continuing spread of those innovations which have proved their agronomic worth. The method of making large composted mounds is a case in point. This innovation was probably first adopted by kaukau growers in the Enga area,[2] but is now seen in much of the southern and western parts of the central highlands as well. The practice not only increases the availability of nutrients to crops, but also counteracts the risk of frost at high altitudes (Waddell 1972: 152–156), although its effectiveness in this regard has been questioned by Bourke *et al.* (1991). The planting of fallows with trees of the nitrogen-fixing *Casuarina* species is another important technique. Archaeological evidence suggests that as early as 1,400 years ago such agroforestry systems were being developed in some highland locations (Haberle 1994). The planting of *Casuarina* then became much more widespread 300–400 years ago, which coincides with the supposed arrival of kaukau.

The social side of the coin is no less intriguing, although a long-standing debate about the exact nature and scale of the social impact of kaukau has yielded few definite answers. Watson (1965, 1977) argued that the crop would have well and truly revolutionized the pre-Ipomoean highland societies. Being better suited to feeding livestock than taro, kaukau made large-scale pig husbandry possible, and with it the development of the intricate ceremonial exchange systems which still thrive. Central to this thesis is culturally driven positive feedback, or 'the Jones effect' (Watson 1977); the need to keep up with the neighbours, which ensured quick adoption of the new production regime over wide areas of the highlands, and led to considerable intensification of land use. By greatly increasing the labour burden of women, as cultivators and carers for pigs, it also contributed in Watson's view to extreme antagonism between men and women, as well as to the more or less continuous state of warfare between the social groups, which was only suppressed in the twentieth century by the Australian colonial administration.

Brookfield and White (1968) argued that the intensification associated with the advent of kaukau may simply have accentuated social developments that were already incipient, and that the crop did therefore not bring about fundamental social changes on its own. Its efficiency in terms of labour and land use, over that of taro and other older staples, would have offered a solution to societies already under demographic pressure resulting from slow growth over a long period of time. Brookfield's later discussion of 'social surplus' highlighted that the *primus motor* of intensification may well have been different from either a simple Boserup-inspired scenario of demographically induced change or a relentless logic of agro- and economic efficiency (Brookfield 1972, 1984; see also Modjeska 1977). Whatever the relative explanatory weight we put on the properties of the plant itself, population pressures, or sociocultural demands, it hardly seems an exaggeration to label the process and the resulting hegemony of kaukau in highlands agriculture an 'Ipomoean revolution'.

A humble crop?

I have already touched on how attitudes towards differing types of food and the meanings ascribed to them are subject to continuous cultural valuation. We have seen that a relatively low status is accorded to root crops in general in Southeast Asia. Many observers have noted that, during its worldwide travels, such has generally been the lot of the sweet potato in those places where it has entered into local diets. Bereft of gustatory glamour, it has 'provided for the unheralded masses' (Yen 1991: 23).

This in itself is not an indicator of any inherent inferiority of sweet potato as food. In fact, it scores quite well when stacked up against other staples, be they grains or root crops. The energy content per unit of weight of cooked tubers is substantially higher than that of boiled rice[3] – its main competitor as a starchy staple in the urban diet of Papua New Guinea. It is rich in vitamins (particularly vitamin C) and minerals, and is a good source of dietary fibre. The main nutritional disadvantage is a low protein content, although this varies considerably between cultivars. It cannot be denied however that regardless of its nutritional qualities, the bulkiness of kaukau and the difficulty of long-term storage[4] put it at a disadvantage when compared to rice and wheat, for example.

Against the general lack of Asian enthusiasm for eating kaukau, its overwhelming dominance in the diet of Papua New Guinean highlanders (see Chapter 4) is all the more remarkable.[5] Still, while highland people appear to appreciate its nutritional value both in word and in deed, the crop is culturally rather 'down to earth' in Papua New Guinea. In this regard it contrasts with some of the crops that predate it, namely taro, yam, sugarcane, and banana. In Lunube the cultivation of such crops – especially taro – was until recently steeped in ritual and magic (Kiff 1976). No such lore seems to have surrounded the cultivation of kaukau.

Neither does it enter into ceremonial gift exchange in its own right, although indirectly it plays no small part of the gift economy when transmuted into pork. Some other foods, such as banana and sugarcane, are on the other hand culturally valued as gifts. When a person dies, for example, others bring bundles of these to the grieving relatives. A presentation of mere kaukau on such an occasion would convey an emotional message of altogether less weight.

It is perhaps not unexpected that a relatively recently introduced crop such as kaukau does not carry the same cultural clout as food items which have millennia of history behind them in Papua New Guinea (Watson 1967). But this is reflected in an interesting way in the gendering of produce. Those more prestigious types of crops are generally classified as 'male', having male characteristics and belonging to the domain of men, whereas kaukau and various kinds of *kumu* (green leafy vegetables) belong primarily to women. In the highlands, men have traditionally taken care of taro gardens, and planted bananas and sugarcane, whereas women have done virtually all the work involved in kaukau cultivation, except for tree felling and fencing when a new garden is made out of fallowed land. Only in recent decades and years, it seems, has this been altered, and then only partially. It is important to keep the gendering of the crop in mind when looking at its trajectories through various kinds of markets.

BEGINNINGS OF THE LOCAL COMMODITIZATION OF KAUKAU

The history of kaukau as a commodity, in the period immediately following contact in the Asaro Valley and elsewhere in the Eastern Highlands, closely parallels the general history of the region's economic transformation and food marketing, which has already been outlined. The ubiquitous staple was not among those items which changed hands in formal contexts in the pre-contact highlands economy through gift or barter exchange, although it did feature in the sharing of food on a daily basis among neighbours and kin. Much in the same way as Polanyi (1944) proposed for the origin of market trade in general, its emergence as an item of commerce resulted out of contact between distant groups, although in the case of kaukau the distance was social rather than spatial.

It was bartered or sold for shell to explorers, missionaries, and administrative personnel right from the first patrols through the valley in the early 1930s, although this was on a limited scale. The mission station at Asaroka, established in 1937 (Wagner and Reiner 1987: 197), needed some kaukau for its workers. The establishment of Goroka as an administrative post during the Pacific War added another marketing possibility, which was to expand markedly when the base of a large labour recruitment operation, the Highlands Labour Scheme, was set up there in 1950 (Ward 1990). Throughout the 1950s and 1960s, some two to four thousand men passed through this base every year, where they would stay for a period at the beginning of their indenture, undergoing medical checks and awaiting consignment to a coastal plantation, and again following the end of their contract.

The modest postwar growth of Goroka and the presence of the labour recruitment base made kaukau the single most important item to be traded in the Asaro Valley, until smallholder coffee became productive on a large scale in the late 1950s. Not only was it supplied directly by small-scale village growers, but also by expatriate coffee planters, who entered into contracts with the Administration to supply it with kaukau while they were developing their plantations (Sinclair 1995: 194–195). It even gave rise to hitherto new forms of indigenous entrepreneurship:

> Many men spoke with admiration of a native from a village near Goroka who has nine 'wives', to whom he gives periodic large gifts for working a market garden. He sells produce to the Government hospital and barracks, and at one point in 1953 had cornered so much of the supply of sweet potatoes that the Administration had to send out trucks to buy his produce instead of waiting for him to bring it in for sale ... He is said to be *'man olosem masta'* – 'a native who is like a European' (Salisbury 1962: 158).

But such large-scale undertakings were the exception. For most rural people, the marketing of kaukau meant a long hard walk to Goroka and back. The practice of carrying kaukau into Goroka for sale from villages up to a day's walk away eventually ceased in the 1950s. Gerritsen (1979: 18) has presented the story as if kaukau had thus disappeared from the realm of commodities, not resurfacing until in the mid-1970s, when 'big peasants' seized it as a possible way out of 'terminal development'. The history of its commoditization is far more continuous than he suggested, but his emphasis on the male, large-scale, and politically vocal producers obscures what happened in the meantime. For a long while, kaukau selling was primarily women's *bisnis*. They sold directly to plantations (where some was used to feed the indigenous labour force and some resold to the Administration), to itinerant traders, and at the Goroka market.

In the meantime, there was no shortage of altogether grander visions, in which kaukau had its place. Echoing the development ideals of the time, the future for the highlands was seen as lying in a wholesale modernization of the agricultural systems, which would

> open up immense possibilities for the development of market gardening whereby efficient farmers, through mechanization, can produce traditional staple foods much more efficiently leading to the eventual elimination of subsistence gardening as we know it to-day (McKillop 1966: 54).

Reality was to be less dramatic.

The plantations: powerful agents of change

The coffee plantations warrant further description, although the story of their origin has been told a number of times (e.g. Finney 1970; Donaldson and Good 1988; Sinclair 1995). Although the first planters had started before 1950,[6] most of them acquired their land and developed it in the 1950s. In the short period from 1952 to 1954 a 'land rush' resulted in the alienation to the Administration of numerous blocks of land, which were then leased out to expatriate planters. Finney (1970) suggests that the prospect of a market for village-grown produce was one of the strongest incentives for the local groups to offer their lands up for expatriate-owned coffee estates. Worried about the complications that might result from a large-scale white settlement in the highlands, the Administration put the brakes on land alienation (Hasluck 1976: 120–127), but most plantations remained in expatriate ownership into the 1970s.

The relationship between planters and local villagers varied widely, but the idea of 'partnership' featured prominently in the first decade. As Finney

(1970) has pointed out, this did not by any means translate into a co-operative relationship where the partners were on an equal footing – nor was it ever necessarily intended to – but the term nevertheless bears witness to well-meaning, if paternalistic, sentiment. Planters and locals realized that they depended on one another. As a reliable road link to Lae was not established until 1965 (Crotty 1970), it was easier for plantation operators to buy kaukau locally to feed the workforce, instead of relying on expensive air-freighted rice.[7]

In the highlands, therefore, planters became key players in the continuing commoditization of kaukau at the local scale in the 1950s and 1960s. Their role was accentuated by the scarcity of transport. Until returns from smallholder coffee growing had made it possible for individuals and clan groups to invest in vehicles of their own, for prestige and/or profit, plantations provided the only motorized transport.[8] Many planters thus became middlemen, buying kaukau from villagers in their immediate vicinity, and selling to government institutions and other customers in Goroka.

However, it soon became obvious to observers that this state of affairs would not be sustained: 'The amount purchased by the plantations will no doubt reduce in the future and could not be regarded as a profitable or continuous outlet for native produce' (D. Read 1969: 8). This prediction was vindicated in the following years. Improved road connections with the coast brought transport costs down, making it more feasible to rely on store-bought provisions. Labour conditions at the plantations were also changed in the early 1970s, providing for higher wages, but relieving the plantation owners of the responsibility of housing and feeding the labour force. This meant that plantations were no longer in their own right important bulk buyers of kaukau. Finally, the plantations themselves changed hands. Instead of small virtual fiefdoms, where a white settler acted out the role of a benign patron over numerous indigenous clients, came local ownership in some form or other – and local political machinations. In the meantime, the planters were immensely influential figures; none more so in the Upper Asaro than Fred Leahy, whose life history will now be traced.

Foinda, Fred, and his followers

Fred Leahy came to Papua New Guinea for the first time in 1954, joining his brother Dan[9] in Goroka. He tried his hand at various jobs in the Highlands and elsewhere, for the next couple of years, including gold mining in the Bulolo area. For three years he farmed in the Markham Valley, before returning to the Eastern Highlands around 1960, working in a sawmill and then negotiating the rough-and-ready roads around Goroka in his truck. At this time the road connection to Lae was still somewhat hazardous. Not only was the road down through Kassam Pass merely a roughly-cut track, but the rivers in the Markham Valley below had to be forded.

In 1963 Fred assumed ownership of a plantation in the Kofena area in the Upper Asaro Valley. This was Foinda, a holding of some 50 acres (20 ha) of coffee, which had been established in 1955 by Graham Gilmore, an Australian planter. The new owner soon became interested and practically involved in the whole problem of rural development in the valley:

> I used to watch what was going on around me ... in all them little villages ... The government had one of these [vocational] colleges ... , out at Bena Bena. Some of the young lads from my... from our area, the Asaro, they went out there, and they did their course ... Of course when they came back, they had done all this training, and they had no means to ... they told them to, you know, go and dig their gardens and anything else ...
>
> And they sent these blokes back, then I had a tractor there, Ford tractor. So I started to send that out to give them a hand. And we were very appreciated ... The other lot didn't appreciate it ... the Ag department, they ... the government officials, they came out and said, 'You can't do this any more. You are a ... spoiling them'. And I said, 'Well you blokes [have taught them the] skills and everything else, what, do you expect them to dig 10 acres of kaukau, or 5 acres of kaukau, with a shovel? So I said, 'I'll do what I like' (Fred Leahy, interview 20 June 1995, Banz).

In the early 1970s Fred assisted several individuals and groups in this manner, by making his tractors and trucks available to them, and sometimes helping out with fencing materials. The farmer hopefuls wanted to grow kaukau and peanuts, for example. Coffee did not feature in these small projects to any substantial extent.[10] But from those beginnings evolved a small core of ambitious young men, who aspired to economic and political prominence. Some of them were to take the highlands kaukau into new realms a few years later.

A detour: wok fama

Before continuing with the biography of kaukau, it is necessary to discuss further the training initiative mentioned by Fred Leahy in the quote above. In the late 1950s the Department of Agriculture, Stock and Fisheries

(DASF, now DAL) set about strengthening its extension programme, by establishing Agricultural Stations in each province where agricultural training was to be provided (McKillop 1976). One station was set up at Korofeigu, in the Bena Bena area south of Goroka. Moreover, not far away at Kamaliki a vocational training centre of wider scope was established in the late 1960s, providing 'appropriate' education in agriculture, mechanics, and building construction. Teenagers – boys only – most of whom had finished a few years at primary school, but were not considered material for further formal educational advance, received 12–15 months of practical training (Zinkel 1970).

The agriculture component proved popular, not least because it allowed the trainees to keep some of the fruits (or vegetables?) of their labour. They were allocated 2 acres of land to cultivate under close supervision of agricultural officers from Korofeigu. The crops grown were mainly kaukau and peanuts. After paying their expenses, the boys could collect up to $150 at the end of their stay, which was no small sum in 1970. In addition, the young men received hands-on training in the arts of intensive pig husbandry, use of fertilizers and pesticides. The course also gave them an insight into the intricacies of modern commerce, with its bookkeeping, banking, and borrowing. The programme was explicitly commercial in focus: the trainees were taught how to negotiate their ways through the jungle of the market to arrive at the promised land of profit. Plainly the idea was to produce Western-minded 'family farmers'; a kind of yeomanry, who would be able to lead their fellow villagers on to the path of development through a commoditization of local agriculture beyond coffee.

There is a stark irony here, regarding the gender orientation of the project. Girls were excluded, even if the cultivation of crops such as kaukau was almost entirely the responsibility of women in the subsistence economy. Recognizing this, but drawing a conclusion which perhaps reflects the thinking of the times, an observer noted:

> The young men must be willing to accept a role that is traditionally reserved for the woman. However, the hope is that when the lads receive financial dividends for their efforts and purchase equipment for their land, other lads may decide to become farmers too (Zinkel 1970: 66).

The same skewness regarding gender applied to the more formal agricultural colleges also run by DASF, where export cash crops were the main game. In fact, female students did not graduate from these colleges until 1977 (Bannister 1982).

From Lunube, several boys took up the challenge offered by the Kamaliki Vocational Training Centre. One of them, Moroho Kukuwo from Kasena (see Chapter 3), recounts:

> They sent a message to us which said: 'Those of you who are young and would like to train at Kamaliki, you put your names down. Both those who have been to school and the others who have not ... You can come and work like ... do farmer training work. And you go to the village and start up such work there.' That is what he said, and we went for training (Moroho, interview 8 January 1995, Kasena).

Eventually they returned to their villages, naturally keen to put their knowledge into practice; to start their own *wok fama* (farmers' work). In Lunube a scheme for peanut growing was set up in 1970. A contract with a Port Moresby business was secured. In line with the ideals promoted through the farmer training, a *masta mak* (surveyor) came from Goroka and surveyed their landholdings. Concrete pegs at the corners of the plots, together with a piece of paper duly signed by the relevant authorities, took over from the *tanget* (*Cordyline fructicosa*, a tall plant) which had served the same purpose through the ages:

> We told our parents: 'Show us our land.' We said that, and then the government people came from Goroka and put in concrete pegs in the places that we marked. Someone could then not come there and make a garden, or take us to court ... *Tanget* is something of the ancestors ... and the government said 'this is something strong/powerful!' and they meant the concrete. And the government itself came and put the concrete markers here (Moroho, interview 8 January 1995, Kasena).

The visible paraphernalia of private landownership had arrived – the form of property rights which so many outside observers have seen and continue to see as essential for mobilizing land for agricultural development. DASF officers were to provide continuing support to the project for a while. Fred Leahy provided a tractor and lent a vehicle when needed. For these young men, the road to farmerhood seemed to be clear. Alas, the momentum did not last. One of them crashed the vehicle that Fred had lent to the group. The planter at Foinda withdrew his support, took back the tractor, and the group was in disarray.

Moroho Kukuwo, now in his late forties, a married man with five children, still cultivates that same plot of his dreams. He is philosophical about the outcome:

THE TRAVELLING TUBER: KAUKAU AND ITS COMMODITIZATION

We ourselves destroyed this, and we abandoned it. And now we do not have a business. Like our fathers and mothers wandered around/lived, we now wander around/live (Moroho, interview 8 January 1995, Kasena).

The surveyor's pegs are still in place, although the physical endurance of the *simen* (concrete) has not lent it any potency to produce a Western-style tenure system, as the government supposed it would do. The paper is forever lost. In any case, it does not matter the least. The *tanget* is there and Moroho can do with the land whatever he chooses. He and his wife Nesime have in fact pursued their ends in a remarkably shrewd manner, as we shall see in the kaukau story later.

The farmer-training programme came under heavy criticism from within DASF. It was for example suggested that extension should be carried out in the villages rather than moving the trainees to the stations. The scheme was discontinued shortly after 1970 (McKillop 1976: 26–29).

About 1980, the Highlands Agricultural Experiment Station at Aiyura was running short training programmes (two days) for 'commercial' kaukau growers from all highlands provinces. Although building on agronomic techniques of subsistence growers, the emphasis was on large-scale, partially mechanized production, and the participants were invariably men (R. Michael Bourke, pers. comm., 1996; see also Bourke 1982a). It is hard to trace the effect of these courses, although it is likely that they had some bearing on the increased scope of commercial production in the 1980s.

LARGE-SCALE FANTASIES AND FAILURES

Lowa Marketing Cooperative (LMC)

By the early 1970s efforts were afoot to create an organization of commercial kaukau growers, in order to increase and stabilize the supply to the town of Goroka. In 1971 the Lowa Marketing Cooperative Ltd (LMC) was formed, with the assistance of DASF, by farmers around Goroka (Nicholls 1973). Through the connection with DASF, the members of the group had access to credit, advice on quality and growing methods, and transportation for their produce, to a guaranteed market in the town's institutions. In turn, growers guaranteed good quality of their produce even if the discipline of face-to-face sale to the end consumers was removed, and they had to contend with a farmgate price which was only two-thirds of the price received in town. Regarding the latter, the precedent had been set when large quantities of sweet potato had been purchased at 1 cent per lb by patrol officers for use in a large *singsing* arranged for the Duke and Duchess of Kent. A number of group members sold sweet potato to the Administration on that occasion (Nicholls 1975: 179).

Despite such blue-blooded beginnings, the LMC was never able to achieve its aims of building up a pool of stable and well-behaved kaukau suppliers. The quantity bought varied widely, admittedly sometimes because the cooperative was deprived of storage space and therefore had to refuse to purchase produce which had been offered (von Fleckenstein 1976: 361–363). Still, it enjoyed a 'most-favoured status' in its relationship with the Administration for some years. When competitors such as the state-operated Food Marketing Corporation (see Chapter 5) and the neighbouring Asaro–Watabung Rural Development Corporation (AWRDC; see below) threatened its monopoly on kaukau supplies to institutions, intense and more or less successful lobbying ensued. From late 1974 the FMC thus bought surplus kaukau from LMC and sent to Port Moresby and Lae. Gerritsen (1979: 68–71) traced the manipulation of political connections which surrounded the cooperative and saw the whole episode as a straight-forward class action of the 'big peasants', and a significant milestone on the road toward rural differentiation.

Eventually, however, the LMC went the way of so many other development efforts: it turned up its toes. To some extent, the FMC contributed to the demise of the LMC by continuing to compete with it, despite official assurances that this would not happen. FMC also ceased to transport fresh food out of Goroka to coastal cities. In 1976 the cooperative was wound up, to be later resurrected by the most commercially-oriented of the group as an investment corporation. The kaukau market had again become an atomistic affair with little coordination.

The Asaro–Watabung Rural Development Corporation[11]

> I came up with the best rural development programme this country has ever seen (Fred Leahy, interview 20 June 1995, Banz).

I have mentioned the beginnings of Fred Leahy's involvement in rural development in the Upper Asaro. In 1974, following continuing criticism from authorities that his assistance to a select few would stir up jealousy and animosities, he tried a new approach. In cooperation with locals he formed the Asaro–Watabung Rural Development Corporation (AWRDC) and a corresponding Trust (AWRDT), of which himself and his wife were the trustees. Several 'development corporations' were being set up elsewhere in the Eastern Highlands at the time, but along somewhat different lines. Here the profits from the plantation and factory at Foinda, and the related extensive coffee-buying operation, were to be channelled into a trust fund, which then allocated financial support to rural development projects under the auspices of the corporation. Fred himself took on the role of paid manager of the corporation. The conditions of the Trust, stipulating the kinds of projects on which the money were to be spent, were also laid down by himself. The area of activity for the AWRDC was defined as that covered by the Asaro–Watabung Local Government Council, and the council had three representatives on the board of directors.[12]

By opting for a trust form and not a fully-fledged corporate structure with shareholders, Fred hoped to avoid tussles over shares and expectations of personal money handouts. He also wanted some leeway to give assistance to whomever he deemed worthy of it at any one time; not only to those who might have happened to get their hands on some shares in the first place.

Gerritsen (1979: 44) has described the AWRDC as simply a 'rural capitalist' corporation, much like other development corporations, such as Bena and Gouna. He saw it as being designed to maintain and advance the interests of an expatriate elite in alliance with an incipient rural elite of big peasants. Donaldson and Good (1988: 124) offer a similar assessment but, importantly, draw attention to the underlying populist philosophy which was mixed up with such capitalist motives. There is no reason to doubt that the enterprise was based on a well-meaning vision of – quite literally – harvesting development for the broad masses. In that sense, Fred Leahy was trying to retrace the steps of men like Jim Taylor and Ian Downs, who had earlier seen their own role as 'aiding Gorokans to enter the money economy' (Finney 1973: 49) through 'partnership'. The difference was much more direct local participation, a wider range of activities, and a spatially broader influence. Partly this was simply a reflection of the times. The early 1970s were years of much political ferment and growing nationalistic sentiment, and the writing was on the wall for expatriate planters of the old order.

Various development schemes and infrastructure projects soon got going, financed largely by coffee buying and processing. Foinda had a *de facto* monopoly, or almost so, on coffee buying in the area at the time. The corporation bought no less than 14 tractors, which were made available to those growers who were thinking big. Fencing materials were also provided.

The village of Roka saw a tobacco-drying shed erected, which still towers over the *hauslain*. The AWRDC supplied an ambulance to the populous area. A power line was constructed from the Foinda factory to a Salvation Army school at Omborda on the eastern side of the Asaro River, where a large vegetable-growing project was under way as part of a rehabilitation programme for young offenders. Bulldozers and trucks from Foinda also assisted in the building of a new road from Asaro, through fertile flats where many new gardens were being made, northwards to Omborda.[13] Commercial ventures which had nothing to do with agriculture, such as tradestores or PMVs, did not receive assistance.

A list of those who worked with Fred in the AWRDC, and who were amongst the chief beneficiaries of this novel initiative, includes many of the individuals who still dominate economic and political life in the Asaro Valley today, more han 25 years later.[14] They were all young men at the time, and most were already involved in small projects with Fred's help or working for him as coffee buyers. Some set about growing kaukau commercially on a large scale. This put them into conflict with the Lowa Marketing Cooperative, and the AWRDC unsuccessfully attempted to take its place in the Goroka institutional market. But hopes were also high at the time for the processing of kaukau. Officials of the Food Marketing Corporation assured the growers that, once a processing facility was established at Goroka, there would be a market for whatever quantity of kaukau they might produce. This did not eventuate, however.

The AWRDC was viewed with interest by many Papua New Guineans as a possible model for post-independence rural development. High-level political dignitaries such as Michael Somare, Iambakey Okuk, and Julius Chan all came to look. But things took a different turn to that originally envisaged. Subsequent events relating to Foinda Plantation and the AWRDC bear witness to a complicated struggle for power, and a corresponding and altogether sorry process of disintegration, which is by no means exceptional in the Asaro Valley, or elsewhere in Papua New Guinea for that matter.

In 1984, a group of landowners from the Kofena and Kanosa tribes claimed compensation for the land on which the plantation had been established 30 years earlier (*Post-Courier* 1984a). Simultaneously, suspicions arose that the Local Government Council, which had representatives on the board of AWRDC, had been taken for a ride. It was thought that Fred Leahy had used its good name to help him line his own pockets, something which he vigorously denies and which Council officials later dismissed as a malicious rumour. In any case, the Council pressured Fred into selling the plantation to a landowner group, headed by Paul Bayango, one of the directors of AWRDC (*Post-Courier* 1984b). The AWRDC kept the factory, but the corporation was turned into a 'conventional' private company of shareholders. The factory was then leased to the landowner group.[15]

Storm clouds soon gathered, for two main reasons. First, intense rivalries surfaced between those individuals who had been at the forefront of the AWRDC, as many of them sought to achieve political fame. Second, Paul's claim to landowner status was contested by other local groups. His father had been a *luluai*, whose name appeared on the original documents relating to the land sale. But old Bayango was of the Gambianggwi clan (Kofena tribe), whereas the land he was selling had long been subject to a claim by the Kanosa tribe.[16] Although the Kofena and the Kanosa had joined in buying the plantation, the latter became extremely unhappy with what they saw as Paul's subsequent appropriation of the whole business.

The situation gradually deteriorated into sporadic warfare in the late 1980s. In 1995–96 an all-out war ensued between Kanosa and Lindima tribes on the one hand and Kofena tribes on the other. Numerous vehicles, plantation buildings, and whole *hauslains* were burnt to the ground and the plantation and factory were severely damaged. More than 100 people were said to have been killed during these violent years. In 1996 fighting was quelled, but soon flared up again, with Paul Bayango himself killed in the year 2000. The situation at the time of writing is one of an uneasy truce, but a lasting peace seems as far off as ever (Thomas Strong, pers. comm, 2001).

Needless to say, the Asaro–Watabung Rural Development Corporation has long ceased to function. The remains of its tractors grace the roadsides around Foinda, and the iron gates of the large kaukau gardens on the flats at Gelelekuka are no longer imposing – merely depressing. The material symbols of 'modern' farming have become grotesque reminders of what Giddens (1984) calls 'the unintended consequences of action'. One member of the AWRDC group, however, contributed to a new chapter in the biography of the kaukau. The contribution of Mondave Wobo will be discussed later. First we shall look at the attempts at processing kaukau, which were mentioned above.

Turning roots into 'rice': attempts at kaukau processing

One of the most notable features of 'traditional' agricultural or food supply systems in Papua New Guinea is the absence of storage and long-distance trading of staples.[17] Traditional root crops are heavy and bulky to transport and store, and do not keep well in the tropical climate. This has long been seen as working against the development of an integrated food marketing system nationwide. It has also contributed to the entrenchment of imported rice as the urban staple and its inroads into the rural diet.

It comes as no surprise, therefore, that ideas about the processing of kaukau and other traditional staples have repeatedly been aired. In the mid-1970s the Food Marketing Corporation made some serious attempts in this regard. Dehydration of diced kaukau was tried experimentally in 1975. The product was dubbed 'kaukau rice', which somewhat ironically reveals the supremacy of the grain staple in the minds of those who designed the project. While technically feasible, kaukau rice was shown to be far from competitive economically with the imported grain. Nevertheless, a factory was set up in Goroka in 1976, partly because of a large surplus of kaukau in that year (G. S. Thomas 1982: 411). It is reasonable to assume that the activities of the AWRDC and the LMC had something to do with the increased quantity offered for sale at the time.

By the time the plant had been set up, however, the glut had turned to scarcity. Coffee prices were high in 1976, which may have led many commercial growers to put business ventures other than coffee aside and not replant their kaukau gardens. When opened in 1977, the factory had to operate well below capacity. This, in addition to high retail prices, turned an economically dubious venture into sheer folly. Other problems contributed to the inability of the product to win the hearts and minds of Papua New Guinea consumers. Standardization of the raw material is one of the commandments of modern food processing, but one that does not match well with the varietal exuberance so evident in highland kaukau gardens. And importantly, the marketing strategy left much to be desired. The end product was seen neither as proper kaukau nor as proper rice, and was left to languish on the supermarket shelves. The project did not even run for one year. Yet another grand scheme had come unstuck.

Many growers still entertain some hopes that their precious crop will eventually find its way into some sort of factory processing. At the Food Preservation and Processing Unit[18] in Lae, researchers have shown that various products, such as dried chips and flour, are technically viable. But there is a long way from that point to the bliss of a successful and sustained commercial food processing operation.

. . .

Up until the mid-1970s therefore, Asaro Valley kaukau was a crop with a fairly restricted 'social life'. While it had been a valuable commodity locally for more than three decades, demand was still limited to the rather small urban population in the area, and state institutions such as hospital and schools. Attempts at organizing commercial growers and creating a stable market had largely failed, as had attempts at breaking out of the local arena by means of processing. Continued expeditions into uncharted territories in the world of commodities seemed doubtful.

OUT OF THE HIGHLANDS: THE RISE OF LONG-DISTANCE TRADING

The 1970s saw traditional staple crops becoming increasingly expensive in comparison to falling prices for cereals (rice and wheat), when measured in relation to the energy values (Spencer and Heywood 1983; Joughin and Kalit 1988). No wonder, therefore, that in the early 1980s, Atkinson and Lewis (1992) were pessimistic about the possibility that kaukau or other root crops could ever seriously compete with rice as an urban staple. They attributed this to two factors: the low returns to labour for growers, and the (almost) non-existence of professional trading as opposed to producer-selling. Similarly, as late as 1988 the World Bank stated that

> the potential for marketing traditional rootcrops in urban areas is limited by their high weight-to-value ratio and perishability, relative to alternative staples such as imported rice. Because of high transport costs, production of these crops must be fairly close to the point of consumption (World Bank 1988: 4).

One can also detect a sort of 'alimentary essentialism' in these and some other writings on development in Papua New Guinea. With reference to the historical trajectories of Africa and mainland Asia, it is often assumed that root crops will always and everywhere give way to cereals in the process of 'development' (see Abarientos and Flores 1992). The label of under-development, of backwardness, has remained firmly attached to the poor kaukau.

Beyond the Kassam Pass: First we take Lae ...

It is thus fair to say that, in the late 1970s and 1980s, development agencies and agricultural officials gave scant encouragement to interregional trade in staples, whether through formal marketing channels or the informal open markets. Such trade did nevertheless develop during precisely that period. Although still more expensive than rice in terms of energy (Fereday 1993: 15),[19] highlands kaukau is now readily available in the markets of Port Moresby, Lae, and Madang. The move into the large urban market of Lae was made in the 1970s. A large part of that story has to do with Mondave Wobo.

❧ Mondave the trailblazer

Mondave is now in his forties, a wealthy man and well respected in the Upper Asaro. He belongs to the Oligokazuho clan, which is one of the Lunube've clans, but was fostered by a female relative married into the neighbouring Onguponizuho group at Roka (see Figure 1, Map 3). Having dropped out of primary school at Grade 3, he found himself living with relatives at Kamaliki, south of Goroka, near the site of the vocational training centre discussed earlier.

Mondave's biography, as told by himself, is a rags-to-riches story of classic proportions. It very much resembles the 'entrepreneur' stories which so excited Finney (1973, 1987, see Chapter 2). Mondave was admitted to the farmer training programme at Kamaliki in 1970 after approaching an expatriate teacher, who not only pitied his torn shorts and gave him a pair of new ones, but also realized his intelligence and drive to succeed. With other farmer-trainees, he got involved in growing kaukau for sale. He then worked as a *hausboi* (domestic helper) for another expatriate at the agricultural station at Korofeigu not far away.

At the end of 1972 he moved back to Roka, and set out to apply his newly acquired knowledge to his home turf. He acquired a piece of land through his adopted parents and bought fencing wire for $60, having amassed a 'fortune' of $100 at Korofeigu. Then he went to see Fred Leahy at Foinda, in order to hire a tractor. In Mondave's own illustrious words:

> I went. I went on Monday, and I stood there. I saw Fred. He was a stern, tall man, and gosh, was I scared of him! I turned back and went home. I went again on Tuesday ... intending to talk to him, but I was still scared and turned back. On Wednesday I went again. And he sat there, and I watched. Also the manner in which he walked, it was really different, and I turned back again.
>
> And on Thursday I went. And ... he came to the house and I stood at the gate. 'Whaddaya want?' he asked, like that. I wet my pants! And I slowly came closer, I thought he wanted to hit me. He took me inside – he was my teacher, Fred (Mondave, interview 18 June 1995, Goroka).

He then got the tractor to plough his garden and planted kaukau, co-operating with three other young men in his village. They mobilized a youth group to work for them, for a payment. In due course they harvested no less than 129 bags, each probably weighing at least 50–60 kg, and hence a total quantity in the order of 6–7 tonnes. Again, the plantation owner at Foinda helped out, this time with transport to Lae. The lot was sold there in a couple of hours, according to Mondave, as this was a complete novelty in the coastal town at the time. The story is backed up by others who went on the selling trip. This sale, in 1974, marked a watershed in the biography of the kaukau.

Mondave continued in his entrepreneurial efforts, growing and selling kaukau locally as well as buying coffee around the village. Having accumulated more money, he bought an old utility truck, and eventually in 1975, a 6-ton truck from Fred at Foinda. He entered the lucrative coffee-buying business, buying for the Foinda factory, and got quite involved with the operations of the AWRDC. Meanwhile, he continued with his kaukau growing. When coffee prices took a dramatic jump in 1976–77, the supply of kaukau to Goroka decreased as many smallholders concentrated on their coffee. Mondave however sold for exceptional prices.

After marrying a woman from another Lunube clan in 1976, he started establishing his own sizeable coffee garden at Roka and built a 'permanent' house there. He also established a large coffee block on land belonging to his true parents, to the north of Hunguko Mountain. As the coffee matured, he gradually wound up the kaukau business. In the early 1980s he was appointed as the manager of Hunguko Coffee – a company the Lunube people had set up when taking over a coffee plantation that had been established on their lands in the 1950s.[20] Having extended Hunguko's processing facilities, he left briefly to pursue his own coffee-processing ambitions by leasing another factory from an earlier, renowned Asaro rural capitalist: Sinake Giregire. But in 1995 he was called on again to manage the Hunguko factory. As his friend Moroho put it:

> Mondave was heavily influenced by what Fred Leahy said, and he [FL] passed on all his ideas and business to him only. And Mondave has become big now. … He is a big man, he is a farmer now (Moroho, interview 8 January 1995, Kasena).

In 1995 Mondave was living with his wife and five children and a varying number of relatives in Goroka. He was not only a large coffee grower himself, employing many labourers, but also the largest single shareholder in Hunguko Coffee, manager of two coffee-processing factories, and a budding real estate speculator. The kaukau had been for Mondave a way to accumulate initial capital, as it had in fact been for many expatriate coffee planters two decades earlier. He managed to do this not only by utilizing his own considerable business acumen, but by constantly enlisting others to assist him in his own projects. In turn, of course, he became himself enrolled in other people's programmes, most notably Fred's. In this sense, he is the *actor* writ large, defining his own agenda and methods to a substantial extent, rather than simply a 'big peasant' acting out a predetermined script. However, although tangential to the kaukau story, recent events in Mondave's life illustrate once again the social and cultural limits within which an actor such as Mondave must manoeuvre.

Voices of dissent and jealousy in his 'adopted' village of Roka, where he had his first large coffee garden and house, gradually became more strident, especially after his change of residence to Goroka. As he is not born into the Onguponizuho clan, there were those who claimed that he should return the land and the house to its 'proper' owners. This he did in early 1995, having ample evidence of the destructiveness of such disputes, if they are allowed to develop, from the hostilities across the Asaro River at Foinda. When I interviewed him, he was in the process of establishing a new base in his 'true' natal village of Nizemuso. Although he wanted to continue living in Goroka, if not move to Australia (where he has travelled), he well realized the importance of maintaining and cultivating the ties to his ancestral clan if he wanted to maintain his other substantial holdings. He expressed his sentiments thus: '*Graun em i – olsem yu save, em i fri land. Dispela em i bagarapim olgeta samting*' ('Land – you know, it is free. This destroys everything'). One cannot help but marvel at the ironies which so often accompany the use of that word – free. If what is meant is 'the absence of property rights', this is patently not the case. But, yes, the absence of well-defined (and probably more importantly, well-respected) *private* property rights has upset many a plan.

❧ Megi Okoropi

Another name frequently mentioned in discussions about the origin of the kaukau trade to Lae is that of Megi Okoropi from Kasena. A few years junior to Mondave, he has followed closely in his footsteps, although he has been less expansive and more localized in his business ventures. His formal education was likewise cut short, in his case by accident: Megi broke his leg when playing rugby, had to quit school and never went beyond Grade 6. The consensus in Lunube was that he had got where he is now through sheer hard work, and had not relied much on a particular patron. But when I started tracing the history of Megi's social network, Fred Leahy appeared yet again. When still young and unmarried, Megi also worked as a coffee buyer for Foinda. He travelled widely in the Eastern Highlands and made a handsome profit. He maintained that he had been among the most successful of the buyers.

In the mid-1970s he got the idea of growing kaukau on a large scale on a block belonging to his father. Although centrally located beside the main Kasena *hauslain*, the land was mostly in a *kunai* grass fallow (*Imperata cylindrica*) at the time. Megi set about clearing the site himself. He then went to Fred Leahy and asked him to buy fencing wire. Fred was not too keen at first, perhaps after having been burnt several times before by similar requests. After Megi approached him the second time, he came and had a look, then 'gave' him the wire. Megi next secured the use of a bulldozer for clearing tree stumps and bamboo roots, and finally asked Fred for a tractor. Reluctantly this was granted, but against a promise of payment for both the tractor and the bulldozer. Megi said he had at last realized that Fred's reluctance was due to others overhearing their conversations. He therefore waited until he could approach him alone, and then things went smoothly. A personal relationship was seen as the key to success.

Megi planted kaukau, and in due course harvested and sold it in Goroka market. The returns, K2,000, enabled him to pay off his debt to Fred Leahy and to buy a small second-hand utility truck. The next time he planted he applied some fertilizer and got a very good yield, selling again in Goroka. The third lot he sold in Lae, having purchased a larger truck in the meantime. He then sold in Lae several times.

The achievements of Mondave, Megi, and other initiators did not go unnoticed. As one of my interlocutors put it: 'We were heartened by this and we all went!' (Monika, interview 28 March 1995, Kasena). Not only other growers from Lunube, but also from other areas in the Asaro Valley followed suit. As a result, the trickle of kaukau down to Lae eventually became a flood. This coincided with the sealing of the Okuk Highway through the Eastern Highlands and Morobe Provinces, which was completed in 1984, resulting in much reduced travel time and less wear and tear on trucks. In the mid-1980s the market in Lae was just about saturated. As for Megi, he lost interest in kaukau after a while and decided to plant coffee, which now furnishes the family with a comfortable income. He no longer sells kaukau, although his wife continues to sell in Lae every now and then.

It is noticeable in these stories that with the large-scale cultivation and marketing of kaukau in the 1970s, the crop was back in the realm of 'male' commodities. This was 'farming':

> The kaukau ... it is women's work, we usually say. Many men think that kaukau is not something of value. But it is more valuable than coffee now. I should know! (Mondave, interview 18 June 1995, Goroka).

It suddenly became all right for men like Mondave and Megi to do work which traditionally was done by women. In my conversations with them, both men emphasized that they themselves had toiled in the gardens and sold in the markets – something more or less unheard of when growing for one's own subsistence and selling smaller quantities at the local markets of Asaro and Goroka. It must be noted that both of them could call on a female labour force – their wives and female relatives – to assist. But the point is that the large-scale commoditization of kaukau entailed a redefinition of entrenched gender roles. The changes reveal a pragmatic culture, which has a reasonably easy-going attitude to 'tradition'.

❧ Transportation to Lae

For many growers wanting to sell at the Lae market, the major constraint was transportation. They were dependent upon those few fellow villagers who had vehicles, and had to pay substantial amounts of money for hiring them. Such was the case for Moroho Kukuwo, who became one of the most energetic marketers. He told me how once he had to fork out K150 for getting his load of kaukau down to Lae. This prompted him to look for alternatives:

> I paid K150 to hire my brother's vehicle and I was furious, and I went and asked for transport down at the SP Brewery ... Huge truck, you know ...
> I asked, and he said: 'You pay the driver 10 or 5 kina, and you can transport your kaukau' (Moroho, interview 8 January 1995, Kasena).

Still not entirely satisfied, he asked at the large transport company and subsidiary of Collins & Leahy, East–West Transport, the headquarters of which are in Goroka. He and his wife Nesime relished telling me about the success they had, as the following unedited part of the interview testifies:

> MOROHO: I asked another white man, Dan Leahy, I went and asked him ...
> NESIME: *Masta* Kevin.

THE TRAVELLING TUBER: KAUKAU AND ITS COMMODITIZATION

MOROHO: Yeah. *Masta* Kevin ...

NESIME: Dan's clerk ...

MOROHO: Yeah. Important white man.

KARL: All right, yes?

MOROHO: We now got friendly with him ... this white man, and ...

NESIME: He asked us: 'Where are you from?' That's what he said, and Moroho said: 'I am from Asaro.'

MOROHO: He asked me ...

NESIME: He said that, and the white man then said: 'We will remain friends until we die.' That is what he said to him.

MOROHO: He said that, and many times I brought kaukau there for free transport ... in the trucks, his huge trucks, to Lae. And everybody here in the village and elsewhere [asked]: 'What is it that you are doing, when you take your kaukau to the trucking company?'

KARL: Ah, you did not tell them?

MOROHO: No, I did not tell them.

NESIME: He did not tell the others! He alone used to take his kaukau ...

MOROHO: In Kevin's big trucks.

(Moroho and Nesime, interview 8 January 1995, Kasena)

The truthfulness of this account, and of Moroho's claim to have been the first to enlist the trucking company, is beside the point;[21] the extract is nevertheless telling. While Moroho and Nesime have obviously condensed somewhat the process of establishing a friendship, it is noticeable that they portray the relationship with the transport company manager as a very personal one. Success is seen as depending on how well one can get others enmeshed into one's own social network, preferably creating a lasting relationship that must be actively nurtured. Later in the interview they told me how they had attempted to cement the friendship with gifts of fresh vegetables and *bilums*.

On the other hand, Dan Leahy – the ultimate boss of the transport company – told me that the company itself had come up with this arrangement in order to help the growers in general. Except in the coffee season, trucks which bring general supplies up to the highlands from Lae have to return with empty containers. Thus there was ample scope for backloading fresh produce down to Lae.[22] The growers/sellers themselves were supposed to take a PMV to Lae and receive the produce at an agreed point.

This was thus an indirect subsidy, which served to hide the 'real' transport costs, at least for a while. As the 1980s proceeded, more and more growers were taking advantage of this new mode of transport, either for free or by paying the driver some 'pocket money'. Not only East–West Transport, but other transport companies running large articulated rigs on the Okuk Highway participated. This finally became so popular with the growers as to cause considerable headaches for the companies. Many growers allege that the last straw was when a man got himself locked up in one of the containers with his kaukau, in order to save on the PMV fare. According to this story, when the container was finally opened, the hapless fellow was rather dazed – even unconscious, according to some versions – because of the lack of fresh air, and together with his *lain* (relatives) subsequently sued the company. Just as success is personalized, so is failure perceived as resulting simply from the irresponsible actions of other individuals, rather than any inherent structural limitations of the process.

East–West Transport staff on the other hand maintained that the operation had simply become unmanageable. Frequently nobody would turn up in Lae to take delivery of the produce at the agreed place, resulting in damage or theft, for which the company was then held responsible. 'They are just totally unreliable!' exclaimed an expatriate manager. Most of the large companies have now forbidden their drivers to pick up produce along the road, although the rule is not always heeded. On the other hand, growers can of course come in and ask for their cargo to be transported to Lae like any other freight. This they occasionally do, as a manager for Pagini Transport – the other large freight company – told me: 'Sometimes a PMV comes in here with people hanging all over and a load of vegetables'. But for the growers' point of view this is altogether more complicated, as well as being prohibitively expensive: they are now charged at the rate of K22 per cubic metre.

Other truckers have come to the rescue. Many small-scale transport businesses are now run by Papua New Guinean nationals, either based in towns or even in rural villages such as Kasena. These usually have a contract with a wholesaler or retailer for carrying sundry goods up to the various highland centres, utilizing smaller trucks (6–10 tonnes). These days most of the kaukau and other fresh foods is transported to Lae from Asaro Station or other places on such vehicles, for a set fee of K2 per bag of produce. The sellers most often jump aboard together with their bags, which makes for an uncomfortable but cheap journey. More detailed descriptions of such operations are provided in the next chapter.

THE TRAVELLING TUBER: KAUKAU AND ITS COMMODITIZATION

... then we take Port Moresby: The kaukau goes to sea

Especially following the sealing of the Okuk Highway from Lae to Goroka, the growers from Lunube and elsewhere became a common sight in the market in Lae. As more got into it, such enterprise lost some of its attractiveness, which prompted the highland growers to look further afield. A road from the Ramu Valley over the mountains to Madang was completed in the early 1980s, which opened a new marketing possibility, although not a particularly attractive one, given the small population of Madang and the slow, unsealed, and somewhat unreliable road. Port Moresby was considered a more attractive option. Again a few individuals can take the credit for having *opim rot* (opened the way).

Moroho and Nesime again

When I asked people in the Asaro Valley which villages first started taking kaukau to Port Moresby, the Lunube tribal area was most often mentioned. And – lo and behold – in discussions with the Lunube people themselves, the name of Moroho Kukuwo cropped up yet again. His was the first trial shipment, completed as early as 1981. While selling in Lae, he had got the idea from a conversation with a man who knew a bit about the workings of the shipping companies. Moroho telephoned his *pikinini* (child) in Port Moresby; a young man named Kiff, whom he had looked after in his youth, and who now was working in the capital. He agreed to receive Moroho's six bags of kaukau at the wharf. The enterprise proved that it was technically possible to get produce by sea to Port Moresby without it getting totally spoiled, but it cannot be said that Moroho benefited in financial terms in the process:

> Three bags he gave to my sister. And Kiff himself sold three bags. But these two did not send me the money, they spent it. The two spent it, Kiff and that sister (Moroho, interview 8 January 1995, Kasena).

In his account of this allegedly first sale, we already have a pointer to a crucial feature in the social construction of the current market: even one's closest relatives are not to be trusted with money.[23] Moreover, it is relatively difficult to move cash around other than carrying it personally. The result is that even when the produce is destined for Port Moresby, the growers themselves prefer to go there and sell it rather than enlist relatives living there, or simply let specialized traders do the job. Trust is indeed a scarce resource in Papua New Guinean economic life. Contracts are difficult to enforce and transaction costs are correspondingly high. Intermediaries of any kind have not gained a permanent foothold in the market. Any commission or price differential between the grower and the retailer is perceived as a rip-off. Moroho and Nesime have since taken their kaukau to Port Moresby three times. In each case, one (or both) of them has flown to the capital and completed the *bisnis*.

❧ *Mande Sirifave: an important node in the network*

The next and crucial step in the development of the Port Moresby kaukau trade was taken in 1987–88 by two men who knew of Moroho's exploits. These were Mande Sirifave, another dogged entrepreneur, and Ralph Yanderepo, a Salvation Army pastor. Both are from the Lunube village of Openga. Both now reside in Port Moresby, but in the late 1980s Ralph was living at home in Openga.

Mande is in his forties. He joined the Papua New Guinea Defence Force in 1974, and went to the University in Technology in Lae to study engineering. In 1983 he shifted his career from the army to business, when he took over a tradestore at East Boroko, one of Port Moresby's suburbs. The store was part of the *Stret Pasin Stoa* scheme, which aimed at getting indigenous Papua New Guineans into activities formerly dominated by expatriates (Cole 1987). Mande had observed how his Goroka *wantok*, Pepe Gotoha, found his fortune through this scheme (see Finney 1993: 49–51). Mande's business was a typical Papua New Guinean tradestore of the urban variety, selling a range of imported foodstuffs and household needs to a clientele of middle- and low-income people. The store faced a small corner market and large informal settlements were not far away. Mande himself lived with his wife Margaret (from Asaro) and children above the shop. They usually had some young men from Lunube in their employ as shop assistants or security guards, and their house and the courtyard at the back of it subsequently became a base for numerous sellers from Lunube.

In 1987 Mande teamed up with his cousin Ralph, who had invested in a second-hand tractor at a government auction, and who also owned a small utility truck. They prepared a large garden in Openga specifically with the Port Moresby market in view. Ralph told me how he had had to overcome the misgivings of shipping line staff, who did not want to carry the produce from Lae to Port Moresby unless the consigners themselves took full responsibility for what might happen to it. But in 1988, as the kaukau matured, Ralph sent a weekly consignment of ten bags off from Lae to Port Moresby, where Mande received it and handed it over to his wife, who sold it in Gordons Market. Mande said that Port Moresby marketgoers had been a bit sceptical at first, but eventually they had learnt to appreciate those wayfaring tubers.

This was to all intents and purposes a successful exercise, which other Asaro Valley growers soon started to emulate. As for Mande himself, his reputation was greatly enhanced at home in Lunube through this venture, as well as because of his Port Moresby *bisnis*. When he went back to Openga for a visit in 1991, following his mother's death, he was greeted with exhortations to go into politics. The Lunube people, it was reasoned, had produced quite a few well-educated and successful men, but had not yet managed to get 'their own' *memba* into national Parliament. Two candidates from other Lunube clans had already come forward for the elections to be held in 1992, and there was talk of the third. Mande succumbed to the pressure from his own clansmen (his own interpretation) and decided to stand as an independent candidate.

And politics is perhaps the ultimate *bisnis* in the highlands. Mande had to finance the largesse which is inevitable for a political campaign. He was rather short of money at the time, and again he looked to kaukau. This time he planted a tract large enough to yield 10 shipments of 20 bags each. He shipped his own Dyna truck over to Lae and thence to Lunube, and moved temporarily up to Lunube himself to do much of the hard work – and to woo the voters. He told me how he had sometimes packed a load in the evening, had driven down to Lae during the night, unloaded the kaukau at the wharf, and driven immediately back up to Asaro again to campaign as best he could on the following day!

However, some of the produce did not make it to Moresby unscathed. Some rotted before reaching the consumers. In all he got K6,000 out of this sale, all of which he says went to buy food, beer, and other 'politically correct' items to distribute among his supporters. The campaign cost him K8,000 and he did not win the seat.

Enough of politics for the time being. What should be acknowledged is that Mande is the person who perhaps can be credited above anyone else for opening up the Port Moresby market for highland kaukau. In the late 1980s and early 1990s, first the Lunube people, and then others from the Asaro Valley, started to appear in the capital's marketplaces in increasing numbers. Many of the new arrivals were their relatives, close or distant. They stayed with Mande and Margaret, who helped them transporting the produce from wharf to market, and assisted them in general terms to find their feet in a big city which few of them had previously visited. In 1994–95 I observed highlanders selling kaukau in all the large markets and most smaller marketplaces of Port Moresby. A new 'real market' had been created.

For the Gamizuho people, an additional factor contributed to the rapid expansion of plantings and trips to Port Moresby in the early 1990s. This was intergroup warfare. Squabbles over land had resulted in an all-out war in 1990–91 between the Onguponi tribe and its supporters and Gamizuho and their Lunube've allies. Several lives were lost on both sides, and considerable property destroyed. This greatly increased the need for money, to pay compensation and to reward allies for their support. For this purpose, I was told that in 1991–92 Kasena people planted much larger kaukau gardens than before, and eventually held a large redistribution ceremony to discharge their obligations.

CONCLUSION

By now it should be amply clear that long-distance trading by growers has come about through a combination of factors. I have emphasized the agency of several central figures, by somewhat selectively sketching those aspects of their life histories that are most relevant to the 'cultural biography' of the kaukau itself. At the same time, links with the social universe of which these individuals are a part have never been far from the surface. Neither have the structural processes of economic integration, which have transformed the highlands in the postwar era, presenting opportunities as well as constraints for actors. The accompanying growth of urban populations, and the emergence of a transport system, are central to the story.

The highlands kaukau, before starting out on its road to commoditization, was not a major item of long-distance trade, which prior to Australian colonial rule had involved mostly the means of production (stone axes) and 'luxuries' of various sorts (e.g. shells and ornaments, salt). Kaukau was cultivated mostly by women. The crop itself was not burdened by a complex set of cultural meanings as some other 'symbolically supercharged'[24] staples in the highlands and elsewhere in Papua New Guinea (although it was closely linked to the production of pigs, which were and are highly symbolically significant). On the other hand, it was not at all culturally coded as utterly worthless and thus unexchangeable, like Kopytoff (1986: 74) reports for manioc (cassava) in an African context, for instance. While it thus had a somewhat mundane identity in the culture, there was also 'high ideological value ... given to staple foodstuffs and their exchange' (Maclean 1989: 79). This made possible the ready transmutation of kaukau into a commodity following 'first contact', but it may also have contributed to it keeping its place as an important subsistence item among those who commoditized it.

Even if kaukau was not traded out of the highlands in any quantity until quite recently, its commoditization in the Asaro Valley came about in a 'Polanyian' manner, through the developing relationships between the local people and the incoming strangers. Trading did not emerge 'locally' in the sense of it having developed within the village communities themselves, following the introduction of money. According to neoclassical theories, which build on a universal model of the human actor and of the market, the latter course might have been expected. A vigorous town and village market for the staple eventually developed, but only after mission stations, government institutions, and plantations had been buying kaukau for a number of years.

Those who started selling kaukau were almost exclusively male, as were those who later initiated the trade out of the highlands. Many have used kaukau to accumulate initial capital, which has been channelled into various other ventures, most notably coffee. Also here, the cultural imprint on actors' behaviour is unmistakable. The pressures on men in highlands cultures to demonstrate their worth through fighting, gift exchange, politics, and latterly, *bisnis*, was and is relentless. Ploeg is right, but only partially so, when he says that 'Undertaking bisnis is for many Papua New Guineans a try-out, a way of finding out if they really understand the workings of the Western economic system, imposed upon them' (1985b: 373). It is equally possible to say that highlanders have hijacked the ideal of business for monetary gain, using *bisnis* as much to accumulate 'cultural' or 'symbolic' capital (Bourdieu 1977) as economic capital. But then, purely 'economic' business may well be a fiction, even in Western society.

NOTES

1 A much earlier introduction, at approximately 1,200 years before present, was tentatively proposed by Golson, but he later abandoned this hypothesis in favour of the more widely held view that the crop has been in the region no more than 400 years (see Golson 1977), and possibly for a somewhat shorter period (Bourke 1985: 90). Only a few writers, such as Gorecki (1986) and Haberle (1993), have kept open the possibility of an early arrival in their interpretations of the region's prehistory.

2   Bayliss-Smith thinks this may in fact be ancient practice, related to intensive yam cultivation. Remains of such tillage, up to 2,500 years old, have been found in swamp sediments (Bayliss-Smith 1996: 517).

3   The energy content of a 100 g portion is 477 kJ for boiled tubers, and 590 kJ for baked ones (Woolfe 1992: 124). A 100 g portion of boiled rice contains 135 kJ. A thorough review of chemical and nutritional research is found in Woolfe (1992).

4   Tests have shown that kaukau can been stored effectively for 40–50 days at least using simple methods . This is not practised in Papua New Guinea.

5   Not all Papua New Guineans are as enthusiastic, however. The 1973 Papua vs New Guinea Rugby League game 'led to three days of rioting in Port Moresby. The fighting erupted in the crowd during the second half when a Papuan woman disparagingly referred to New Guineans as "kaukau eaters"' (Dorney 1990: 157).

6   Notably Jim Leahy, the same who introduced Goroka people to the wonderful world of the tradestore (see Chapter 4). See Finney 1973: 42–45.

7   Rice – delivered cheaply by ship – had in fact long been the staple for labourers on coastal plantations, see Chapter 4, note 21.

8   In the novel *The Stolen Land* (Downs 1970), the author (former District Commissioner and later planter, Ian Downs) fantasizes about possible political developments in Papua New Guinea in the 1970s. His main character – and political activist – is a Papua New Guinean truck driver who works for an Australian planter. The mobility afforded by the truck is the key to his political success. The story also emphasizes the local importance of the plantations and the planters – although Downs, who was one of the architects of the idea of 'partnership', was never one to underestimate his own importance, judging from his other writings.

9   Daniel Leahy Jr, who took the reins of the trading firm Collins & Leahy from his uncle Jim.

10 Smallholder coffee plantings had increased dramatically in the 1960s, whereas world market prices had declined and selling the crop had become harder. Thus the Administration was persuaded in 1967 by the Highlands Farmers and Settlers' Organization (an interest group of expatriate plantation owners) to direct its extension service towards 'accelerating land use away from coffee and into alternative crops' (McKillop 1976: 25; see also Gerritsen 1979).

11 This account is distilled from interviews with Fred Leahy, Raisis Gorondawe, Sailas Atopare, Mondave Wobo, Sinake Giregire, and numerous people in Lunube and elsewhere.

12 One from each Census Division within the area: Upper Asaro, Lower Asaro, and Watabung.

13 These flats (see Map 3), between the Asaro River and its tributary, the Lembina, were neither densely settled nor cultivated in former times, being borderlands

between Lunube, Kofena, Onguponi, and Amaizuho tribes. In the 1970s several *hauslains* were in place, and gardens were gradually replacing the *kunai* and *pitpit*. Many of the AWRDC-assisted projects were located there.

14 Among these are: Gai Duwabane from Kofena (died in 1994, then sitting MP for Daulo Open), Paul Bayango from Kofena (coffee, see p. 169), Mondave Wobo from Lunube (currently coffee, see below), Raisis Gorondawe from Kofena (coffee), Sowa Gunia from Koreipa (at the time of fieldwork, MP for Daulo Open), David Mehuwo from Asaro (member of the Provincial Assembly, coffee grower) and Sailas Atopare from Kabiufa (former MP and now prominent coffee grower and Goroka businessman). Ethnographers have noted that age groups were traditionally very important in male interaction (Read 1951; Newman 1965), as evidenced by the Dano term *ambo*. It used to refer to a group of men who had been through initiation ceremonies together, but now parallels the Tok Pisin term *poroman*. The *ambo* or *poroman* I mentioned have certainly made their mark in the area, although some of their later interactions have unfortunately been of the 'this-town-ain't-big-enough-for-both-of-us' variety.

15 Fred Leahy stayed on for a while, but left for Australia in 1989 because of health problems. In 1995, when I interviewed him, he had returned to Papua New Guinea and was managing another coffee factory at Banz in the Western Highlands Province.

16 Tribal tensions in the densely settled Kofena valley in fact date back to pre-contact times, and the pattern of landholdings and claims is extremely complicated in the area (see Howlett 1962: 127–130).

17 A qualification is necessary: some products, such as sago and yam in certain systems, are in fact stored over periods of some months. Also I have mentioned that trading between people in adjacent ecological zones is common, but this is usually a local phenomenon.

18 Formerly part of DAL, but now under the FPDC (see Chapter 5).

19 The devaluation of the kina by more than 20 per cent in September and October 1994 made kaukau somewhat more competitive than it was in the 1970s and 1980s.

20 This plantation is discussed further in Chapter 8.

21 Several others claimed to have pioneered this strategy.

22 In 1991 it was estimated that the freight trucked out of the highlands amounted to only 20 per cent of the tonnage moved in the opposite direction (Asian Development Bank 1991: 40).

23 Not that any permanent hard feelings were created by Kiff's failure to deliver the money. While loyalty to one's relatives is supremely strong in highlands culture, nobody really trusts others to care for one's material belongings anyway, and in that sense Moroho simply got what he bargained for. Kiff remains a valued individual in his social network.

24 The expression is Kopytoff's, who offers the example of bread in East European peasant culture (Kopytoff 1986: 74). The best example of a symbolically supercharged staple in Papua New Guinea is probably the yam (*Dioscorea* spp.). Elaborate ceremonial display and exchange complexes have been constructed around yam in the Trobriand Islands and the Sepik region, where *D. alata* tubers are grown to such lengths that they become inedible (Bryant J. Allen, pers. comm., 1996; see also Lea 1969).

7

Economic dimensions, daily practice, and social networks in the long-distance trade

> *I was surprised of how many wantoks and people from nearby my village I saw loading their kaukau into the ... dry containers at the wharf ... To be honest, I never have seen so much kaukau at one place before (Romco with Gebesmair 1992: 2).*

THE RISE OF THE LONG-DISTANCE KAUKAU TRADE was linked in no small part to the agency of a few enterprising individuals, whose life stories have been traced. I now step sideways from these personal stories, to consider the current state of the trade. The emphasis is on the most recent – and organizationally complex – addition to the scene, namely the shipments to Port Moresby. The quantities shipped vary considerably, both seasonally as well as from one year to the next, and understanding these fluctuations is not straightforward. Considerable differences also set long-distance marketing apart from the more established local marketing, in economic and social terms. It is the wide price differentials between the Eastern Highlands and coastal (especially Port Moresby) markets which make selling on the coast an attractive option for growers in the first place. The observer is also struck by a quite different gender balance in the two types of markets.

Everyday practices in the long-distance trade are then described, by following the people with their produce down the road, and outlining the structuring of space and time thus created. The logistics of the trade and the social networks of sellers are examined in some detail. Logistically kaukau sellers, collaborating with other actors, have come up with novel additions to Papua New Guinea's somewhat rudimentary transport systems.

As selling on the coast involves staying at the point of sale for some days at least, they have also made creative use of their kinsmen or other contacts in town. The cultivation of social networks is therefore important, and here again local culture makes its mark.

THE CURRENT EXTENT OF THE KAUKAU TRADE

Accurate data on the total quantity of produce descending from Kassam Pass on the back of the numerous trucks are not available. A full-blown traffic survey was beyond my resources during fieldwork. It is possible, however, to rank these destinations by order of their importance for the highland kaukau sellers. On the basis of observations of growers' movements, and a visual assessment of the markets in Lae, it seems that this city is the single biggest kaukau market for Asaro Valley growers (beyond the Asaro–Goroka area itself), with somewhat smaller quantities being taken all the way to Port Moresby. Lae has now become very much a part of the activity space of villagers of the Upper Asaro. Constant traffic of PMV buses and trucks carries people and produce down the Okuk Highway and up again. Transport costs are reasonably low, which means that taking quite small quantities is easy enough. It is also easy for most villagers to arrange a stay in Lae. The city moreover has a high proportion of people from traditionally 'kaukau-eating' cultures. It is therefore no wonder that scores of highlander kaukau sellers can be found in marketplaces in Lae at any one time, frequently 30–40 of them in the main market alone.[1]

Madang on the other hand is not often visited by Asaro Valley sellers. The traffic, especially truck traffic, is much less frequent, and fares and freight costs are considerably higher. Those highland sellers who go there are mostly from the eastern part of the Eastern Highlands. Shipments to other markets are sporadic, but they do occur.

This leaves only the capital. Data on kaukau (and other produce) shipped from Lae to Port Moresby have been systematically collected since mid-year 1992, when staff of the Fresh Produce Development Company noticed these important developments (Figure 13). The FPDC has since published shipping figures for each week in its monthly newsletter, compiled from freight documents supplied by the shipping company, Consort Express Lines. These documents distinguish between consignments of kaukau, potato, ('English') cabbage, and carrot, but the residual category of 'Others (unknown)' in all likelihood includes some kaukau as part of mixed

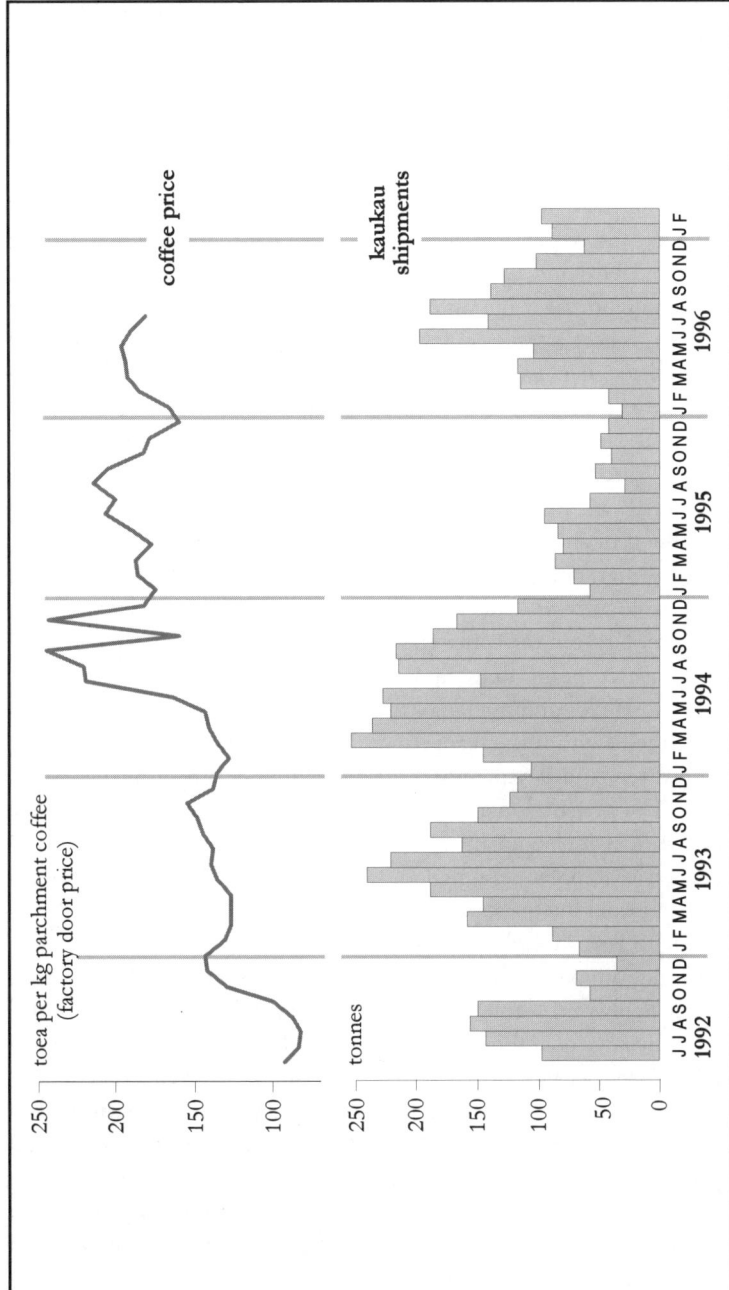

Figure 13: Monthly shipments of kaukau from Lae to Port Moresby, and prices received by coffee growers

consignments. Kaukau and potato are the two crops shipped in largest quantities, each usually accounting for more than a third of all produce.[2] Carrot and cabbage together make up less than 5 per cent of the freight on average. This means that about 25 per cent of every shipment is unspecified. Additional suspicion of underreporting is added because of the methods used in the collation of the data.[3]

The data nevertheless give a fairly good indication of the temporal development, and of the large fluctuations of the trade. Seasonality is marked. In 1992 to 1994, and again in 1996, definite mid-year peaks appeared, with largest quantities being shipped in the period from June to September. These peaks reflect a spate of new plantings which had taken place six to eight months earlier. Two influences are likely to have produced this. The first relates to climate, notably rainfall. Whereas seasonal variation in rainfall is generally low in the highlands, a *taim bilong san* (drier period) occurs at mid-year throughout the northern part of the Eastern Highlands, from which virtually all the kaukau comes. New gardens are not planted if there is a likelihood of an extended dry period. As the months from October to March are wetter, new plantings are better undertaken at this time.

The seasonality of kaukau shipments may also have something to do with the link between the coffee economy and the kaukau trade. These two forms of cash cropping draw upon the same pool of labour: that of the growers' households and migrant settlers. Coffee picking is a laborious task which, at the height of the main harvesting season (which usually starts in May and extends into September), demands most of the available labour resources. The preparation and planting of large-scale, commercial kaukau gardens are likewise labour-intensive, and often involve hired workers. It is therefore easier to organise in periods when coffee activities are minimal.

Non-seasonal fluctuations are also remarkable. By 1992 the producer-seller trade to Port Moresby was well established, with about 100 tonnes of kaukau being shipped each month. It appears, however, that 1994 (when I started my fieldwork) was indeed 'the year of the kaukau'. For most of that year relatively large quantities were being shipped to Port Moresby, around or over 200 tonnes per month.[4] This has not been repeated since. The following year, 1995, shows a different picture altogether. For the whole year, monthly quantities stayed well below 100 tonnes per month and the mid-year peak period was hardly discernible. This of course begs the question whether the long-distance trade, to Port Moresby at least, was proving yet another bubble in the highlands economy, like the cattle boom before it. What happened?

Again it is reasonable to look to coffee for an explanation, this time the price of that commodity (Figure 13). Orthodox economic theory would suggest that growers, when deciding to plant kaukau, considered to some extent the opportunity cost of labour. Coffee prices increased substantially in mid-1994 after several rather lean years in that *bisnis*. This could have contributed to the drop in kaukau shipments in 1995, as growers lost interest in kaukau and diverted labour back to coffee. It seems possible that the high coffee price throughout late 1994 and most of 1995 resulted in reduced planting of kaukau and thus kept shipments down.

As 1995 and 1996 progressed, coffee prices remained fairly high. In spite of this, the Port Moresby kaukau trade bounced back in 1996, rising to similar levels as in 1993. Hence, I conclude that while growers are obviously sensitive to changes in the relative returns to labour for these two cash crops, the linkages between them are not by any means mechanical. It is appropriate, therefore, to be wary of interpretations which see the rise of the kaukau trade as a direct and simple response to the vagaries of the world coffee market. As we have already seen, the emergence of the Port Moresby trade was a culmination of a long process of commoditization and indigenous agency in markets.

PRICES AND RETURNS

Broad trends in time and space

Since 1971, staff of provincial Departments of Primary Industry (DPIs) have collected weekly data on retail prices of selected crops in some major urban markets of Papua New Guinea, for the National Statistical Office (NSO). These data are used in the calculation of the Consumer Price Index (CPI). Among the markets covered are Goroka, Lae, and Port Moresby, in all of which the Asaro Valley growers sell their kaukau.[5] Some gaps exist in the temporal coverage and caution is needed in interpretation. Nevertheless, the series gives reasonably good indications of the price differentials between the three towns and the long- and short-term fluctuations that have occurred (Figure 14).

An examination of the series reveals consistently higher prices in Port Moresby than in the other centres, frequently three times the Goroka price, for instance. Lae prices on the other hand seem to be generally very close to those of Goroka, although the Lae data are admittedly very patchy. For

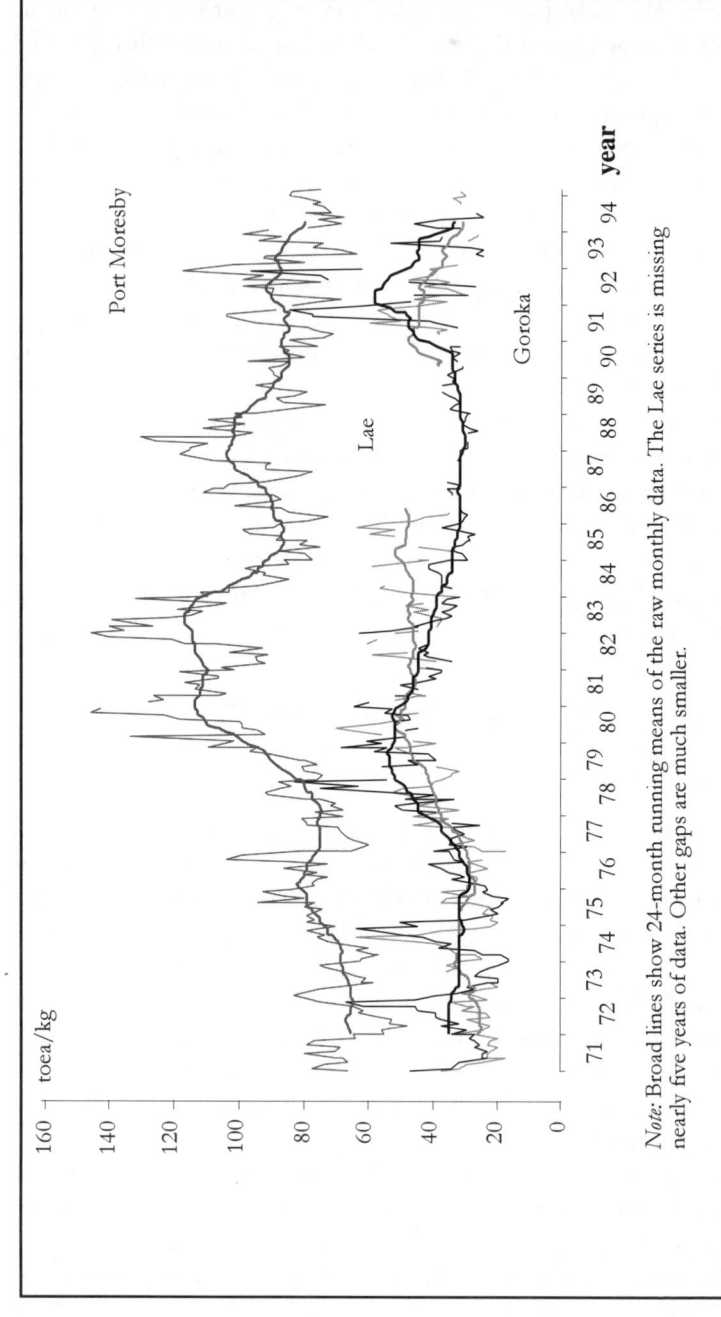

Figure 14: Kaukau retail prices in three urban areas, 1971–95, in constant 1995 currency

Goroka, there have been shorter periods of greatly increased prices, sometimes surpassing the Port Moresby prices. The peaks at the beginning of the time period are associated with occasional food shortages or *taim hangre*, which have complex causes (Bourke 1988). For the extraordinary, but short-lived price jumps of the early 1990s in Goroka (which drag the smoothed line upwards) I have no explanation, other than possible data collection problems.

When the series are smoothed to reveal broader trends, it appears that prices were edging upwards until about 1980 in all centres. They then stabilized for some four years in Port Moresby and somewhat longer in Lae, but were slowly falling in Goroka for most of the 1980s. Port Moresby prices have always fluctuated widely, but the long-term trend through the late 1980s and early 1990s has been downwards. One is hard pressed, though, to discern any definite effect on retail price of the increased supply following the Eastern Highlanders' conquests in the Lae market in the 1980s and in Port Moresby in the early 1990s.

The large amount of 'noise' in the raw data is also suggestive of the lack of market integration, on which observers have repeatedly commented (e.g. Joughin and Kalit 1986: 6–10; Fereday 1993: 18; Longmire 1994). Apart from difficult and expensive transport, which probably largely accounts for the lack of integration, information on prices and the state of the markets in general does not travel particularly well between the cities and the producing areas. The practice of selling a varying volume of produce for a set price makes comparisons between different markets more difficult than if prices were decided per unit of weight. Moreover, communication is hampered by limited education and to some extent by cultural differences, although near-universal adoption of Tok Pisin as a *lingua franca* has partially helped to overcome the fragmentation. Supply and demand are not easily coordinated in such circumstances: the 'market signals', which the universal model of the market takes for granted, are faint or scrambled. As a result, the 'invisible hand' is somewhat lacking in fine motor skills.

Prices in local and coastal markets in 1995

While the CPI data are indicative of the broad pattern of price differentials, a more detailed picture of the situation as it was during fieldwork will now be sketched. Numerous surveys were undertaken in various local and coastal markets. These were not full-blown market surveys of the type blueprinted by Epstein (1982), but more limited ones. For the whole market, data on number, sex, and origin of sellers were elicited, as well as type of produce sold. The kaukau sections of the markets would then be examined further, with some heaps weighed to obtain the local price, and questions asked about quantities brought to the market.[6] Each market was visited at least twice during the fieldwork period.

A rather unsurprising pattern emerges from these data (Figure 15). As the distance from the Asaro Valley – the heartland of the commercial kaukau growing area – increases, the produce becomes progressively more expensive. The variation in price also increases, which is to be expected given that the sales are made by volume and not weight.

In Kasena village itself, women sell only small quantities of kaukau, often harvested from gardens that are being retilled for the next planting, long after the main harvest has taken place.[7] Such tubers are generally not of good quality and many heaps consist mainly of small and broken ones. The end consumers are not only humans: in many instances the buyer has his or her hungry pigs to feed. All this is reflected in the price, which was only about 10–12 t/kg when I did my surveys, and did not vary much.

In the roadside markets the produce is of better quality and the price is twice that of the village, but lower than in town. Some Goroka residents told me that they occasionally went to Asaro or the other roadside markets to do their weekly kaukau shopping, realizing that prices are generally markedly lower in the roadside markets and the quality excellent.

Prices at the main Goroka market are frequently around or just above the 30 t/kg mark, and the heap size is more variable than in the small roadside markets. Sellers stated that, in deciding on the appropriate quantity for each heap (kaukau is sold mostly in K1 or K2 lots), they do indeed factor in the extra costs of selling in Goroka, namely transport costs and the gate fee. At the end of the day, the returns to the sellers per unit of produce are about the same. This is a well-supplied, balanced market, although there are seasonal variations in supply and, as we have seen, occasional serious shortages. At the other major town market in the Eastern Highlands, Kainantu, prices are somewhat lower, reflecting perhaps the much smaller demand than in Goroka.[8]

Of course, if the growers were to view the world in strictly economic terms, the net return when transport and other costs have been taken into account would be of more importance to them than selling prices alone. Very few of the growers/sellers do such calculations explicitly. In fact many have only a very elementary grasp of arithmetic. It appears that they

ECONOMIC DIMENSIONS, DAILY PRACTICE, AND SOCIAL NETWORKS

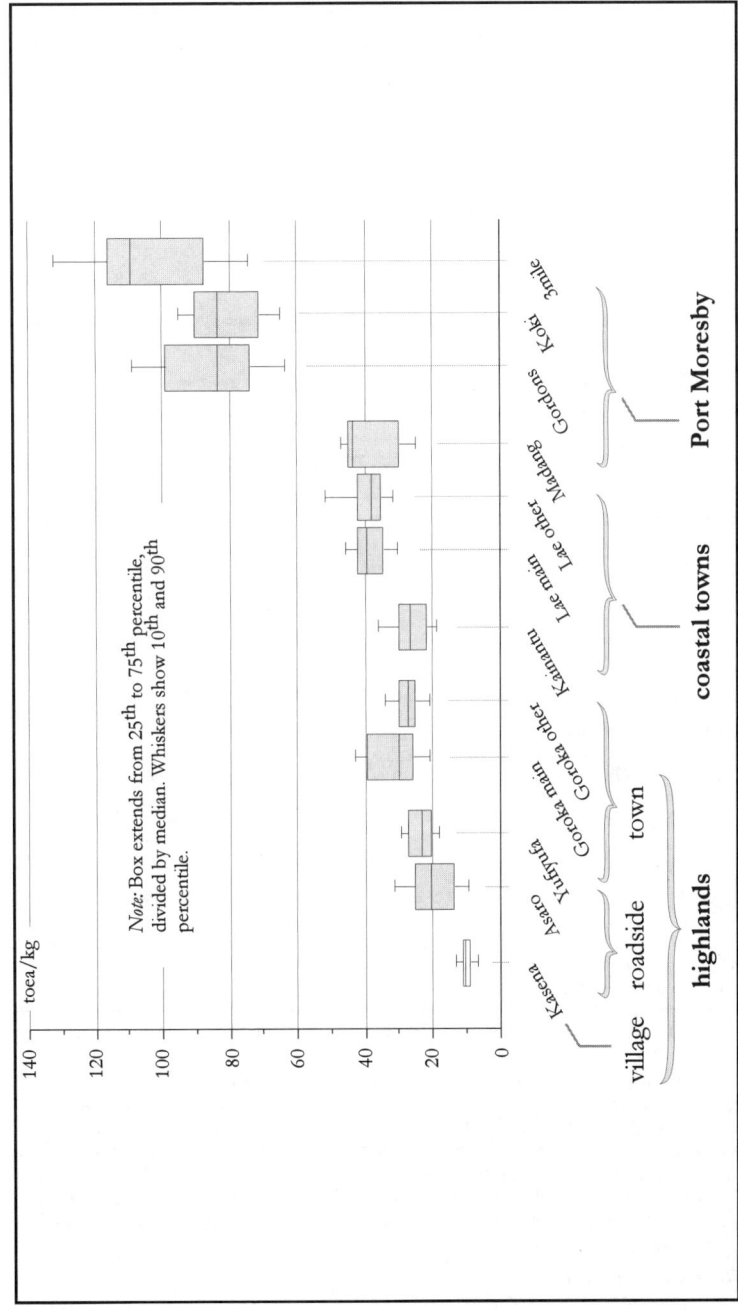

Figure 15: Kaukau prices in various marketplaces, 1995

nevertheless have a good sense of the differing returns from the various markets. To illustrate this, I have calculated likely net returns from 'typical' selling trips to four different markets in 1995 (see Table 6). While small quantities (two bags or less) are often sold locally – In the Asaro or Goroka markets – sellers try to take no less than five to ten bags when going to Lae, and 20 bags or more to Port Moresby.

In addition to the direct transport and marketing costs involved, going to Lae or Port Moresby involves staying there for some days at least, which needless to say also incurs costs. These costs are hard to ascertain however, and widely variable, depending on the access people have to *wantoks* and

Table 6: Returns from sales trips from Kasena to four different markets

	Asaro	Goroka	Lae	P. Moresby
Bags/bilums brought to market	1 bilum	1 1/2 bags	10 bags	25 bags
Quantity sold	30 kg	60 kg	750 kg	1,875 kg
Market price per kilogram*	23t	32t	39t	87t
Gross return	6.90	K19.20	K292.50	K1,631.25
COSTS†				
Road transp. (seller and produce)	0	K2.00	K41.00	K128.50
Sea transport (produce)	n.a.	n.a.	n.a.	K112.50
Air transport (seller)	n.a.	n.a.	n.a.	K132.00
Market fees	n.a.	K1.00	K20.00	K28.00
Total costs	0	K3.00	K61.00	K401.00
Costs per kilogram	0	5t	8t	21t
Net return	K6.90	K16.20	K231.50	K1,230.25
Net return per kilogram	23t	27t	31t	66t

Notes: (*) Average price in these markets during the fieldwork period (November 1994–July 1995).
(†) Road transport costs to Lae are calculated on a per-bag basis, whereas shipping costs are determined by weight. Market fees are K2 per bag of kaukau in Lae, but in Gordons Market (Port Moresby) sellers are charged K2 per day. The airfare is a 50 per cent discount ticket GKA–POM–GKA, which most of the sellers use. I have assumed a selling period of two weeks in Port Moresby. The cost of living in either city is not taken into account, nor is the opportunity cost of labour for the seller. Usually neither is seen as critical when growers decide where to sell.
n.a. = not applicable
Source: Fieldwork data.

friends in the city. I have excluded these from the table, but if fully costed, they would lower the net returns further. So too would damage to the produce during transport and storage (dehydration, rot), which is sometimes a significant problem for the Port Moresby sellers especially, forcing them to discard some of their produce.[9]

When looking to the coastal city markets of Lae and Madang, we notice that the price moves up a notch. Again, the price increase reflects travel and marketing costs rather neatly.[10] Returns to sellers are somewhat higher, but not dramatically so, than from sales in Goroka or at Asaro. Many Lae sellers now choose to stay in paid accommodation in Lae, rather than stay with *wantoks*, as will be discussed later. This is not reflected in Table 6, and would probably bring the returns on a par with Goroka.

But it is also obvious from all of this data that the big money is in Port Moresby. The price jump does much more than simply reflect travel costs. There is no question that Port Moresby is undersupplied with kaukau. For the growers, journeying all the way to the capital can make good sense in economic terms.

GENDER DIVISIONS

Male sellers are few and far between in the local markets in the highlands. Those who do sell there are mostly either older men offering crops that are traditionally gendered as 'male', such as bananas or sugarcane, or landless

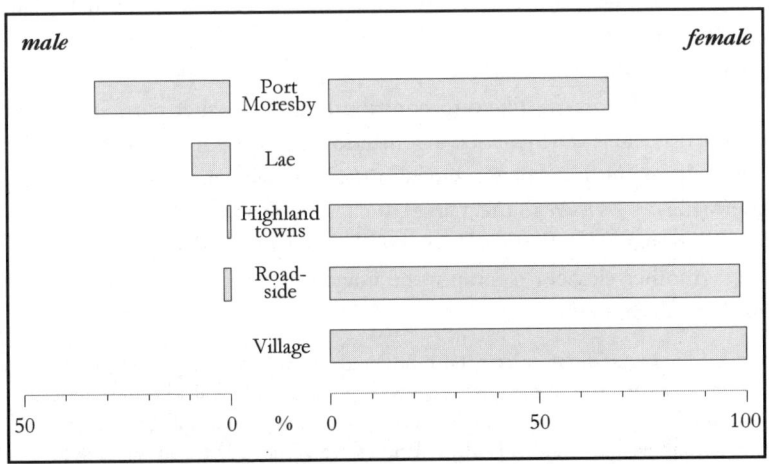

Figure 16: Gender division of kaukau sellers in different types of markets

migrants like the Simbu settlers at Asaro, who peddle tobacco or *buai* in the market there. Kaukau is almost never sold by men in the highland markets, whether in town or in the villages (Figure 16). Women, traditionally the pillars of subsistence production, originally came into the kaukau trade from the subsistence angle, and they are the ones who now supply these markets with staples.

Not unexpectedly, when I asked why this sharp gender division of labour persisted, neither men nor women offered any detailed explanations, beyond a vague notion of honour or abilities: *'Ating ... ol i sem long maket, o kain olsem'* ('I suppose ... they are ashamed of selling in the market, or something like that'), responded Monika, a Kasena woman in her early forties, about why men did not sell. This was echoed by numerous others. Monika also opined that men were generally not knowledgeable when it came to assembling the bundles or heaps for sale – they would invariably put too much in each heap and hence bring home less money than women. *'Meri fit long salim kaikai'* ('Women are good at selling food') was her simple final assessment.

Such (post-hoc?) rationalizations about the situation in the local markets sit uneasily with the less clear-cut division of labour in the markets of Lae and Port Moresby. One of the major differences in the social construction of local selling compared with long-distance marketing is that men do indeed participate in the latter (see Plate 6). As we saw in Chapter 6, the instigators of the trade were male 'entrepreneurs'. Women have, however, followed closely in their footsteps, and now there are more female than male kaukau sellers in Port Moresby, even if the balance is much more even there than in the other markets.

Several factors are likely to contribute to the higher participation of men here. One is the increased organizational complexity of the enterprise. Not only selling is involved, but also dealings with numerous extra-local intermediaries *en route* to the market, such as truckers and shipping line staff. Such 'international relations'[11] have traditionally been the responsibility of men. Another element is simply the novelty value and the excitement of visiting a distant city:

> Like going to distant places, both husband and wife must have a chance to go on such a trip. If the husband always goes, the wife will be really angry. And if it is always the wife, the husband will get angry. Like, if the wife goes during the first round of kaukau planting, when they plant again she should stay and the husband go instead (Esta, interview 15 April 1995, Kofika).

Plate 6: Saina at the main market in Lae, preparing his kaukau for sale. Other sellers from Lunube in the background. Compare the gender of sellers with Plates 4 and 5.

In most of the households I examined, this had in fact been the outcome. Third, several of my interviewees mentioned the much-publicized *raskol* problem of Port Moresby (see Levantis 1997), which deters some women from going there. Probably the most significant factor, however, relates to the association, from the start of the trade, of large-scale commercial kaukau growing with *bisnis*. Whereas the amount of money brought home from a day at the local market is often dismissed by the men as insignificant, stories are constantly told of the allegedly spectacular amounts of money made by the instigators of the Port Moresby trade. Some of these stories are exaggerations, but others are to a large extent true.

Maybe, then, the question could be put differently: why do women, whose activity space has traditionally been rather restricted, undertake these journeys at all? Again I refer to Monika, who stated that, apart from men's inherent lack of market savvy, many women have misgivings about what their husbands might get up to in their absence in the city, amongst temptations such as alcohol and prostitutes. Judging from my conversations with men, such fear is not groundless in some cases.

But it is also significant that in the generally well-supplied Lae market, the profits that are to be made are by no means extravagant any more, if they in fact ever were (see Figure 14). Men are therefore simply not as interested in participating there as they were initially. Port Moresby, however, still has that Midas-touch to a certain extent. If the kaukau price were to come down, it is likely that it too would be left chiefly to women.

Indeed, some previous observers have concluded that women came to predominate in food marketing largely by default (Jackson and Kolta 1974: 12–13; Overfield 1995). Economic opportunities such as coffee, which yield higher returns to labour, have opened up for men, leaving women behind in the race for cash income. It would be wrong to suggest that all coffee income automatically remains in the hands of men: its distribution is subject to negotiation, where women admittedly are in a much weaker position. The outcome differs considerably from household to household. By contrast, women generally do not share the rather small amounts of money they earn by selling in local markets, but use much of it more or less immediately for daily household needs. Selling in the coastal markets presents a different picture. In so far as it does bring in substantial amounts of money, it is one of the more favourable developments for many rural women, giving them a measure of economic power hitherto denied. The tables are turned when it comes to negotiating the share of income.

ON THE ROAD: SPACE, TIME, AND ACTORS

How, then, does this newly emerged 'real market' function? If the economic and social characteristics outlined above are among its major structural features, how are these reflected in the daily practices of those who take part? We are here concerned here with the *durée* of the daily, and how it meshes with spatial practices of the actors concerned to create a distinctive time-geography in the kaukau trade.

The long-distance trade requires substantial organization and forethought on the part of the growers/sellers. For newcomers, getting everything right can be daunting, but for the old hands in the *bisnis* the trips have become routine. After some years of experimenting, a system has emerged in the

ECONOMIC DIMENSIONS, DAILY PRACTICE, AND SOCIAL NETWORKS

1990s which, by and large, works in spite of glaring inefficiencies. I shall now trace what happens to people and produce as they travel from the gardens of Kasena first down the Okuk Highway to Lae, and then on to Port Moresby.

From village to highway

The large kaukau gardens of Kasena village are located in two main areas, neither adjoining the road. The first transport problem to be solved, as a garden is being harvested, is to get the produce to a point which is accessible to a vehicle. For the most part, this task literally falls on the shoulders (or foreheads) of the women. Long the carriers of most things in highland society, they have continued to act as such into the commoditized present.

If the quantities are substantial, the owner of the garden mobilizes several women, close relatives, or members of the family, to load the freshly harvested kaukau into *bilums* or bags and then trudge along the often slippery, muddy path to the village or the roadhead. Men, particularly younger male relatives, may also participate, especially if the owner and prospective seller is male (Plate 7). At times, the larger growers hire labour to both harvest the garden and transport the produce the first step.[12]

Plate 7: Carriers on the way from garden to roadhead. Streams have cut deep gullies into the level surface of the alluvial fan on which most gardens are located.

At the other end, the produce is unloaded into a large heap. Leaves are put on top to shield the tubers from the rays of the sun. The next step is to stuff it into the sacks in which it will be transported. These sacks are sold in the agricultural supply stores of Goroka and Asaro. Large copra bags made of hessian are preferred, but the smaller coffee bags and nylon stockfeed bags are also used. While the large bags become extremely unwieldy when full, the practice of charging transport fees according to the number of bags encourages the growers to stuff them as full as they can.

The preparation of the bags for transport is almost always done by men. To do this properly (i.e. to get the maximum quantity of kaukau in) is a tricky task, as each and every tuber needs to be carefully placed.[13] Often two men work together on one bag to speed up the process, with one sifting through the heap to find tubers of the shape best suited at the moment, the other arranging them in the bag. Finally, with the tubers invariably protruding from the opening, they are covered with leaves and the bag is sewn up, either with nylon thread or with *busrop* (strong vines traditionally used for building and other tasks).

The next step is to get the bags to the highway – a distance of some 7 kilometres from Kasena. For this purpose, village utilities or trucks in varying condition are used. Most clans have one or more vehicle owners in their ranks, and these are enlisted. If the owner is part of the grower's extended family, the transport may be done for free, but in most cases some payment is demanded, at least to cover the fuel costs.

The use of a vehicle is seldom secured beforehand. Sometimes people have difficulty in finding transport when they are ready to take to the road. Vehicle owners generally get going early in the morning, taking a trip to town and coming back in the late afternoon. Kaukau growers often wait until the morning after the harvest to get transport.

The slowness of traffic in the middle of the day is exacerbated in the wet season, when some vehicle owners avoid going as far as Kasena because of the difficult road conditions. There are times when only four-wheel drives can make it all the way. Another obstacle is the sorry state of many of the small bridges. Parts of the bridge decking have often rotted away[14] and not been replaced, except that enterprising villagers sometimes make them momentarily passable – for a fee – by bridging the ominous gaps with logs or pieces of Marsden matting. All this adds up to considerable 'friction', which makes moving the produce the short distance down to Asaro more arduous and costly than it would be if the rural transport infrastructure were maintained to adequate standards.

During the course of a week, some produce is taken down the road on most days, but Thursday afternoons are the liveliest. This reflects the shipping schedules, as the weekly Port Moresby-bound freighter leaves Lae on Friday evenings. The growers who have set their sights on the Port Moresby market, time their harvest so that they can be at the wharf in Lae early on Friday morning.

The Okuk Highway: worlds of truckers and traders

On a Thursday afternoon, single loads of kaukau (ranging in size from 3 or 4 to over 30 bags) can be seen awaiting transport at various points by the roadside between Goroka and Asaro, but certain important transit locations have emerged. Foremost amongst these is the junction at Asaro, opposite the local market. In the early afternoon the first growers come down from the villages, unload their sacks, and start the waiting game. Late in the afternoon trucks start arriving. Most of these are equipped with iron 'gates' and covered by canvas (Plate 8), protecting the cargo from the elements. A single truck can load the produce of two or three sellers, depending on the number of bags. The *boskru* and the sellers of the bags together lift them aboard and arrange them, while the driver looks on or remains in the truck's cab. The

Plate 8: Lae-bound truck loading kaukau.

kaukau seller pays the driver. The charge is K2 per bag from Asaro to Lae. This can add up to substantial amounts of money as more sellers are taken aboard.

When the cargo is in place, it is the turn of the accompanying sellers. They pay their K5 fare, which is half the usual PMV fare down to Lae. A limited number of male acquaintances or relatives of the truckers get to ride in the cab, but others – be they men, women, or children – clamber aboard over the bags and take their place under the canvas, huddled in the darkness in front of the load, just behind the cab. The rear gate is then closed, the whole outfit somewhat resembling a moving gaol cell. But it would be a bit of an overstatement, however, to say that these people are prisoners of commoditization.

The first leg of the journey, or to Goroka, is short. Arriving in the town at dusk, the driver fills up with diesel. Most of the tattered 2-kina notes just claimed from the kaukau people swiftly find their way into the service station's till. Driver and *boskru* might also stop at a *kaibar* in town for dinner, whereas the growers are most likely to dine on a piece of cooked kaukau from their *bilum*. The final stop is usually at a cluster of shops on the southern edge of the town, where *buai* is sold, to stock up on this essential accompaniment on the long and tiring drive through the night.

Many drivers say they prefer making the trip at night. It is cooler and the traffic on the highway is only sporadic. Also, the pedestrians who line the edge of the road during the day are mostly absent. Some drivers coming from the west told me that they tried to get through the Chuave and Watabung areas in daylight, as these are notorious for frequent robberies of highway travellers. Such robberies also sometimes occur in certain places east of Goroka, but during the time of my fieldwork, police had dealt with some of the offenders in the usual subtle manner – by burning down the *hauslains* from which they were known to come. Hence, at this time it was considered safe to travel east from Goroka in the dark.

The hilly terrain makes for a slow drive through the Eastern Highlands Province in the heavily laden trucks. The darkness of the nocturnal landscape is punctuated by flickering hurricane lamps and the occasional bright electric light in homes, stores, and clubs. Electrification of the rural areas has followed the route already laid out by the road builders, as has economic development in general.

A few enterprising *kaibar*-owners have started catering for the highway truckers and other creatures of the night. Halfway between Goroka and Kainantu, one such establishment is perched on the roadside in a small building, its name curiously referring to an altogether more significant entity in the world economy: *California Trading*, open 24 hours. Another is located just east of Kainantu. But the most recent addition is down in the Markham Valley, namely the new Umi market.

This remarkable addition to the economic and social life of the upper Markham was established after the collapse of the Umi bridge in 1994. During the day it is a sleepy spot. A few sellers sit there in the shade in brand new shelters, offering peanuts (in bulk), coconuts, or *buai* to passing travellers. At night, however, the Umi market comes alive. A new group of sellers arrives, many of them settlers who were relocated here after a landslide destroyed their home village in the Finisterre Range, others coming from the neighbouring villages of Mutzing and Zumin. They set up their offerings, which include not only local produce, but also cooked meals and coffee, in the new market sheds. As the night progresses, truckers heading in both directions pull up.[15] They eat, drink, and socialize for a while.

Some truckers on the way to Lae park here and get a few hours' sleep before continuing towards the city. Those who do not choose to sleep at Umi arrive in Lae in the early hours of the morning. From Umi to Lae is 2 to 3 hours' drive on a fast road, although a police roadblock just out of Lae may slow things down somewhat. Vehicles coming from the highlands are frequently searched for marijuana, weapons, and wanted criminals.

Clear of all hindrances, the trucks head towards the centre of town. The city of Lae also looks different at night. Numerous trucks and PMV buses are parked in the centre, their drivers, *boskru*, and sometimes passengers sleeping as best they can in their vehicles or simply on the sidewalk. Lae, in fact, is notorious for strained relations between its numerous highlander residents and visitors, and those of coastal origin. The police station opposite presumably adds a degree of security for the sleeping drivers, most of whom are highlanders. There is also safety in numbers here: always someone is awake, small groups of men walking the streets, exploring the city centre.

Small-scale trucking businesses

It is clear from the description so far that the owners of small trucking businesses and their employees have become essential actors in the kaukau trade. Most, but not all, are highlanders, with many enterprises based in Simbu or Western Highlands Provinces, as well as in the Eastern Highlands. When the large transport companies (which were involved in the 1980s when the trade started) abandoned the kaukau growers (see Chapter 6), these small operators entered the scene. Without them, it is doubtful that the initial wave of trading out of the highlands would have been sustained and expanded. The opposite is also true: many truck operations are themselves kept afloat partly with the help of the vegetable cargo. We need a clearer picture of these operations and those who have shaped them.

Automotive vehicles have long had a symbolic association with progress and personal achievement in the highlands of Papua New Guinea, as they do also in many other parts of the world. Ownership and operation of vehicles are seen as a marker of success. This is not surprising, as vehicles were for a long time owned and operated by expatriates only. In the late 1950s and early 1960s, however, local clan groups started buying and running their own vehicles. Or running them into the ground, which happened not infrequently. In fact, a patrol officer in the late 1960s bemoaned the infatuation of the people of the Asaro with the motorcar:

> Every group has one or two vehicles and skeletons of disused ones are everywhere ... While group pride transcends national pride and while money is 'for comforts' vehicle purchase will increase, forming perhaps an integral part of the culture of the people to the damnation of development (Alder 1969: 2–3).

At this time, ownership of vehicles was almost invariably on group basis. This has since changed. Many of those whom I interviewed commented that communal ownership had repeatedly led to disputes and had proved unworkable. Most small trucks and PMVs are now owned by individuals or families, who have accumulated money for their purchase through extensive coffee growing and other *bisnis* ventures. Many prominent personalities in national and local politics are involved. There are also those who have ploughed their earnings from waged jobs in the government sector into such projects, which make them more visible in their local villages. One such man is Leslie Gasa.

❧ Leslie Gasa: an owner of a highway truck

Now in his late thirties, Leslie hails from Kenemba village in Lunube, but was in 1995 living with his wife and children in nearby Anengu village, in the foothills of the Bismarck Range. His 10-ton truck is one of those which frequently pick up kaukau bound for Lae. The story of his 'entrepreneurship' resembles that of many other small-scale businessmen in the area. Actually, here we have a team, as his wife is no less involved in the running of the business.

Leslie's main occupation is teaching. He graduated from teacher's college in 1981 and spent the next 13 years teaching at various primary schools in the Eastern Highlands Province. In 1994 he managed to get himself posted to Anengu Community School, as he wanted to be close to his home village. He had gradually, since 1988, been building up a small trucking and PMV business back home. When teaching at schools not too far away, he would come home on weekends and carry passengers between Kenemba and Goroka on his utility, although he did not have a PMV licence.

In 1990 Leslie and his wife bought an old truck for use on the highway, and started transporting coffee to Lae for the large coffee export firm, ANGCO. Kaukau soon came to be used as a stopgap cargo, but Leslie stated that his truck had been the first of these smaller trucks to do so: 'So one day there is no coffee, and I started carrying kaukau bags down to Lae' (Leslie, interview 29 May 1995). He also explained how the current figure of K2 for a bag of produce was arrived at. ANGCO had paid him K1.86 per bag of green-bean coffee transported from Goroka to Lae. Leslie had reasoned that charging K3 would be reasonable for the much heavier kaukau bags, but this proved more than growers were willing to pay, and it was not long before the price had stabilized at K2. If his story is correct, he was thus instrumental in shaping the current transport arrangements in the kaukau trade.

Finally, he secured a contract with a highlands wholesaler to bring cargo up from Lae, and the enterprise was on a firmer footing. They have since renewed the truck, and bought a new 15-seater bus which they run as a PMV. They employ drivers from their home village, but getting reliable and responsible drivers has been somewhat difficult. The drivers are paid a fortnightly wage, plus a commission if Leslie thinks they have done a particularly good job. The *boskru* are also on the payroll. In 1995 the business was for the first time renting a building in Goroka and employing a mechanic for servicing the vehicles. Written on the doors of the vehicles is the name of the registered company, 'E&M TRANSPORT'. E stands for Eric and M stands for Michael – the couple's two sons. The ideal of a 'small family business' seems to have taken firm hold.

But not only is the trucking business becoming more complex. Leslie and his wife have also been experimenting with other forms of small-scale enterprise. When I interviewed him, they had just sent out a group of men to a couple of remote locations to buy 'cherry' coffee, which they would then process, dry, and resell. Occasionally the wife had herself planted kaukau or other produce for sale on the coast, and had also established chicken projects in the village.

She had also been trying to get her husband to give up teaching and become a 'full-time' businessman, as their various small projects were getting more demanding. Leslie himself agreed – but foresaw that they would then have to move to Goroka to avoid the redistributive pressures to which a village-based entrepreneur is constantly subjected:

> Well, *wantoks* coming in ... who push our nose into contributing money, money goes left and right ... Village life is a bit hard, because, you know what: you might hear a knock in the morning, and then he's gone. Lunch, somebody comes and knocks at the door. People like us, we have truck here. Not ... well-off businesspeople, but ... (Leslie, interview 29 May 1995, Anengu).

There is a close similarity here with the story of Mondave Wobo (Chapter 6). Leslie too must walk a thin line between individualist economic ventures at least partly designed to enhance his reputation in the village, and collective demands arising inevitably from that reputation. This applies to many other small-scale truck owners who carry kaukau down the highway. The turnover of vehicles and operators is considerable.

❧ Driving for a living

Like the owners of motor vehicles, their crews – drivers and *boskru* – enjoy favourable social standing in the highlands. Especially in former times, these were seen as glamorous jobs. Their holders were well-travelled cosmopolitans in otherwise circumscribed local societies. With increased familiarity some of this glory has faded, but driving is still an attractive option for many young highland males.[16] Most truck drivers are recruited from the villages, graduating from small utilities needing only a basic driving licence, to the highway trucks.

Life on the road can be quite hectic. For instance, one trucker I spoke to, whose business had a contract with a highlands retail chain, was supposed to make three return trips to Lae during the course of a week. As the trip takes a minimum of 5 to 6 hours each way (Goroka–Lae, Lae–Goroka), such a schedule calls for long working hours.

The pain is alleviated somewhat by the pleasure of having money to spend. Most of the drivers insist that the kaukau money they are paid by the growers is used straight away for meeting daily running costs and maintenance, and that the truck owners expect them to hand over whatever might be left. Accounting is nonexistent, however, and many vehicles are

ECONOMIC DIMENSIONS, DAILY PRACTICE, AND SOCIAL NETWORKS

not particularly well looked after (see Vignette 4). Understandably, many crews use part of the money for their own maintenance: to buy food, *buai*, tobacco, or other pleasures on the road. Constant chewing of betel nut, with its stimulating properties, makes the driving bearable, as a driver told me: *'Sapos mi kaikai buai, ai bilong mi i no inap raun, mi no inap slip. Em olsem PK bilong Papua New Guinea!'* ('As long as I chew *buai*, I do not feel dizzy, I don't fall asleep. It's like Papua New Guinea's chewing gum!')

Vignette 4: A truck's life

The state of the truck – a Mitsubishi – leaves something to be desired. It is probably about four years old, perhaps more though. It has a big bullbar in front, and the load area is surrounded by iron pipes, covered by canvas. Two spare tyres are there, but these – and the other tyres – are almost bald. The windscreen and side windows are surrounded by wire mesh, to prevent stones from breaking the windows presumably, maybe raskols too. I imagine it is distracting for the driver, but many trucks and Landcruisers are thus outfitted ...

I found myself casting a glance frequently at the dashboard. A red light was flashing, and seemed to glow more or less continuously at times. I thought of the sad story Kaunsil Gumineve had told me not long ago. His Toyota Stout had ended its working life at Kassam Pass, as a reckless *brata* of his who was driving it did not heed the warning lights. At last I couldn't help but mention this to the driver, who had seemed totally oblivious. 'Yes,' he said, 'it is the oil pressure warning lamp. It has been like this for a few days now. The oil must be getting sticky. I must check it sometime'

(Fieldnotes from trip to Lae, 5–7 April 1995)

Once when I was at the wharf in Lae at dawn after a night on the road, an articulated rig from a large transport company pulled up. Its driver told me that his company had a contract with Kutubu Joint Venture, the large oil project in the Southern Highlands, bringing equipment and provisions up from Lae. When driving through Mount Hagen the night before he had been waved down by a potato trader and asked to take a large quantity of potatoes to Lae. This he did, without his employer's knowledge, and charged K100 for the service. Needless to say, all of that money went into his own pocket. 'I make big money for the company – they get K5,000 for each trip', he reasoned. At the wharf in Lae he used some of the money to hire three young men, who sat there waiting for the shipping line's depot to open, to unload his truck. They got K2 each, for approximately half an hour's work. Still a nice sum left.

There is an interesting blurring of boundaries between 'formal' and 'informal' actors here. The potato trader is a professional wholesaler from the Western Highlands. The big rig is very much part and parcel of the formal economy. The eventual destination of the potatoes is the formal retail market of Port Moresby. Yet the produce actually gets moving in a most informal manner, with resourceful actors lubricating the creaky wheels of the formal economy. Development planners in Papua New Guinea have hitherto mostly ignored the possibilities of such moonlighting as a partial solution to the thorny problem of transport.

The voyage to Port Moresby

As the 'rose-fingered Dawn' finally assumes its reign and the people of Lae wake up to the busyness of yet another Friday, the dazed kaukau growers line up at the door of the warehouse of Consort Express Lines. They have stacked their bags into old containers which have been cut in half and stand beside the warehouse. It opens at eight o'clock. A forklift operator then starts picking up these weighing containers one by one. They are brought into the warehouse and put on a large weighing device. Growers wait anxiously as a worker reads the weight off the digital display. The figure is passed on to a clerk, sitting at a table beside the door. He works out the freight charge on his calculator and tells the grower. Usually the charges turn out to be more than the growers had expected. Sometimes too much (see Vignette 5). But pay they must, at the office at the end of the building, before any kaukau goes to sea.

Financing of a sales trip to Port Moresby can be a difficult hurdle. In order to undertake such a trip successfully, the grower has to have a minimum fund of K400 to draw upon for expenses along the way, as all transport has to be paid up front. This is a substantial amount of cash by any measure. If any capital has been saved from a previous trip, it might be used to finance the next one, or more likely, money from recent coffee sales may be channelled this way. The growers frequently have to borrow most or all of this money from relatives in the village or in town.

But back to Consort Express Lines in Lae. Upon entering the shipping company's office, one immediately senses that this is one of these locales where people of very different lifeworlds meet and interact. More than elsewhere

ECONOMIC DIMENSIONS, DAILY PRACTICE, AND SOCIAL NETWORKS

> **Vignette 5**: Nasty surprises
>
> We were early and had to wait for two hours before the bags were taken by a forklift and put on the scales. The bags were a lot heavier than expected. The man said that Saina would have to pay about K150 in freight charges. This amount of money Saina did not have in his pocket, and neither did I. He had expected to pay K100 at most. He therefore removed four of the bags, and had the remaining 17 re-weighed. That came out as 1,639 kg, or K99. This amount Saina paid.
>
> When looking back, I think we were all a bit sleepy this morning, Saina, the Consort worker, and myself. The first time, the guy with the calculator probably forgot to subtract the weight of the cut-up container into which we had stuffed Saina's bags for the forklift to take to the scale. If there are between 90 and 100 kg of kaukau in each copra bag (I had weighed the kaukau being stuffed into one bag while at Saina's village, and it was no less than 100 kg!), the total freight should not have cost more than K120 …
>
> We therefore walked to the market and started selling kaukau from the two bags Saina had left there. In the afternoon he had enough money to pay for shipment of the four bags which were left. We then stayed at the market until the following day, and finished selling. That afternoon we took a PMV back up to Goroka.
>
> (Fieldnotes from trip to Lae, 5–7 April 1995)

on the way from garden to market, here is an 'interface' situation, where the knowledge and power of modern business practices meets the kaukau grower head on. The main floorspace is occupied by clerks behind desks, male and female, busily doing their sums and moving pieces of paper from one tray to the other. At the back the managers – many of whom are expatriates – reside in separate glass-fronted cubicles, equipped with the phones and fax machines and high-backed executive chairs which are necessary for men of their status.

The customer, be it a kaukau grower or some other person, is kept thoroughly separated from all this. Just inside the front door, a customers' desk, a small calculator attached to it with a sturdy metal bracket, demarcates a space of some 5 or 6 square metres. Sturdy iron bars from desk to ceiling complete the separation. Their primary justification is of course the security they provide against intruders, as robberies are a persistent problem in Lae. Yet their effect is one of reinforcing the distance between the 'business' world and the grower's world, each of which remains a bit of a mystery to the other.

Numerous posters in Tok Pisin and English make the ground rules clear: No payment means no shipment. No credit given. No responsibility taken for what happens to unchilled produce at sea. No chewing of *buai* allowed on the premises.

After paying up, the growers receive their bills of lading. No PMV routes take in the main wharf in Lae, so people have to walk a kilometre to the main market or 3.5 km to Eriku, which is the point of departure for highlands-bound PMVs. Most return to the village, as their precious produce will not reach Port Moresby until the following week. Some bring smaller quantities of kaukau or other items to sell at the main market in Lae as well, and many call at the market anyway, as some of their neighbours and friends are bound to be found there. People may stay in Lae overnight with relatives. They then catch a PMV up to Goroka, paying K10 this time, admittedly for an altogether more comfortable trip than on the truck down.

The weekend is over and it is time to leave for Port Moresby. The growers head to Goroka again, to catch the Air Niugini flight, the ticket for which they have bought some days earlier. The flight is a short hop of nearly an hour. At Jackson's airport they are greeted by friends or relatives, whom they have managed to call beforehand from the always-crowded payphones outside the post office in Goroka. Alternatively, they may have to take a PMV into town. For some – although this number is rapidly diminishing as more and more people have made similar sojourns before – this is their first experience of a city which in Papua New Guinean terms is a true metropolis.

The ship leaves Lae on Friday evenings, arriving in Port Moresby on the following Tuesday. On Wednesday morning the containers are opened up for the owners of the cargo to reclaim it. By then, an army of highlanders, men and women, has gathered at the wharf. They include not only growers, but also other market sellers, of whom we shall hear more later. An identification card, costing K4 or so, is needed in order to get access to the port area.

Simultaneously a procession of light trucks enters through the boom gates of the wharf area. The growers enter into negotiation for these trucks to transport their kaukau and other produce to the market. Again, the problem of transport has been solved wholly informally and, it appears, in a well-functioning manner. Truck operators, both local Papuans and highlander migrants, have entered the scene in much the same way as on the highway. For them, the weekly influx of highlander sellers is a welcome one. Generally the charge is K2 for each bag from the wharf to the destination, which in most cases means approximately 10 km up to Gordons Market, the largest municipal marketplace in the capital. Compared with the same charge for the 320 km from Asaro to Lae, this appears a bit steep, and many growers try to get the truckers to lower their charges, sometimes successfully. But this is *Mosbi*, where things tend to be expensive anyway.

A shipping line employee emerges, clutching a bunch of papers. As the containers are opened, the names on these papers are matched with names of people present, and the names which had been scrawled on the bags at the wharf in Lae. The trucks are reversed into place and the growers start man-handling their produce once more.

At Gordons Market the shelters are arranged in a triangular pattern. As in Lae, few kaukau sellers sit inside the sheds, partly because their produce is so bulky, and partly because it is not as perishable as much of the other produce sold at the market. Perhaps the outsider status of the kaukau sellers also has something to do with it. In any case, the bags are stacked up at the back of the shelters and the sellers assume their place in the open space adjoining the walkways. One by one the bags are opened and their contents arranged as usual.

It usually takes 1–3 weeks to finish the selling in Port Moresby. Storage is a problem for the sellers, as they have no option but leave their still unsold produce in bags outdoors, day and night. The kaukau deteriorates quickly in the hot climate. Also, although the marketplace is locked up at night, produce that is left there is occasionally stolen. It is thus desirable to sell as quickly as possible. Towards the end, sometimes the sellers lower the price (i.e. enlarge the heaps) substantially in order to speed up the sale of the last remaining produce.

STAYING IN TOWN: *WANTOKS* AND *PASINDIA*

A crucial feature in the social construction of the long-distance kaukau market is the reliance of the growers on their relatives and friends – their *wantoks* – for accommodation and other assistance during their sales trips. It is hardly an exaggeration to state that without the '*wantok* system', the trade would not have developed. Urban migrants are duty-bound to house and feed their visiting *wantoks*, just as they themselves can expect similar treatment if or when they visit their home villages, ever the 'ambivalent townsmen' (Levine and Levine 1979). Ties of kinship linking urbanites and villagers also frequently involve reciprocal exchange of money or food (see Chapter 3). Yet, although such reciprocity with no questions asked is the ideologically preferred state of relations, it can put a strain on all concerned.

❧ 'They were so happy to see me'

Kondagule (see Chapter 3) described to me in vivid colours her own experience on her first sales trip, emphasizing at every step the importance of reciprocity. She went with her husband Gumineve to Port Moresby around 1990, selling some 28 bags of kaukau. They were among the pioneers from Kasena village. They were privileged in that their daughter and son-in-law, both of whom are educated and employed, were able to do much of the organizing. They had bought a ticket for the parents for an evening flight from Nadzab (Lae), and the approach to Port Moresby left a deep impression on Kondagule:

> 'Aiiyaaaa!' We saw the lights. 'Aiiyaaaa! So that is Moresby! Moresby is really different! Aiiyaaaa!' We got lower and we looked in all directions ... 'Nothing but lights, lights, lights! Aiiyaaaa! Moresby, which people have told us about, excellent town!' Then we landed at 7-mile (Kondagule, interview 1 January 1995).

They had a number of relatives in Port Moresby, but communications had been limited and nobody was there to meet them at the airport at night. After wondering for a while what to do, they accepted an offer from a Simbu man to drive them for K10 to the suburb of Erima, where some *wantoks* lived: *'I no Goroka na mitupela i kam nating! Mosbi ya, na poketmani i stap.'* ('This wasn't Goroka, where we would arrive empty-handed! This was Moresby, and we had pocket-money.')

The Erima relatives, while happy to see them, were not the ones she had banked on for assistance. They took them out to a true *brata* who lived with his family in a settlement on the outskirts of the city. There they received a very warm welcome. They presented food which they had brought with them on the plane:

> Kaukau, sugarcane, and cabbage, pigmeat which we had stuffed in bamboo[17] as best we could ... I gave this to the *wantoks*. And they were really happy. And they cried: 'Ooo, you have come from the village, and ...' They were happy and cried for me ... (Kondagule, interview 1 January 1995, Kasena).

Importantly for the task that lay ahead, the *brata* worked for the City Council, running errands all over town. He could thus help out with transport from the wharf, although the smallish car he had control of could only carry two bags at a time! Kondagule sold at Gordons while her husband sold at the smaller Waigani market. The latter, incidentally, is frequented by people from the Morata settlements, where many highlanders live.

After a photo of the couple appeared in one of Port Moresby's newspapers, they were inundated by *wantoks*, who brought them small gifts as deemed appropriate: *'Smuk paket, muruk, skon, dring – Fanta, Mirinda, pis; kain kain samting bilong stua ol i kam kapsaitim long mitupela.'* ('Cigarettes, tobacco, scones, drink – Fanta, Mirinda, fish; they gave us plenty of store goods.') The high point came just before their departure, when a feast was held in their honour:

> My brother said: 'You crossed the sea to come here. I deeply appreciate that.' He then killed a huge pig! He put 100 kina on top of that. They wanted to give us 100 kina! Now, the relatives came in droves, and they put 20 kina, 30 kina, 10 kina, 20 kina, on and on ... 350 in all! ... They held a big party ... And the two of us bought them beer (Kondagule, interview 1 January 1995, Kasena).

It is easy to see how such extravaganzas, while pleasant, may be difficult to sustain in the long term.[18] For urban dwellers, visitors may indeed constitute a real economic burden. Highlander migrants in the cities are mostly in low-paid, unskilled jobs – those who do have formal employment that is. Few belong to Papua New Guinea's budding middle class, let alone the country's affluent elite. Visitors can, and sometimes do, strain the resources of these urban households to breaking point. The hefty increases in the prices of imported foods during the mid-1990s have certainly not made life any easier for these households. This was increasingly felt by the visitors, as comments made by Esta, a woman in her early twenties, show:

> Suppose you yourself had a house, it would be all right. When you stay with relatives and so on, you know, some are unhappy ... They are tired of visitors from the highlands, who come and stay with them ... Some, like your brothers and sisters who live there, and you stay with them, you don't have to worry about that. But if you stay with more distant relatives, they ... it's a bit awkward. Like, you use their house and so on ... it's ... you must buy food too, and things like that (Esta, interview 15 April 1995, Kofika).

In Lae at least, an alternative exists which is used by a growing number of highland travellers, indicating that they well realize the unsustainability in the long run of the reliance on *wantoks*. This is a hostel, *Haus Pasindia*, which is run by the Salvation Army at Eriku. It provides rather basic accommodation in a large communal hall for a modest K2 per night. In the evening, tired *pasindia* (travellers) – kaukau sellers and others – turn up one by one, finding a space for themselves on the bare floor. They can sleep there knowing that mosquitoes and undesirables are kept at a distance by the screened windows and security guards, respectively. No similar low-cost alternatives exist in Port Moresby.

❧ Wantoks in excess: Frida and Ben

Frida and Ben Sirifave, of Openga village in Lunube, are in their thirties. Ben graduated from Aiyura National High School in 1983 and soon after found work with the Post and Telecommunication Corporation (PTC) in Port Moresby, where they subsequently married and lived for some ten years.[19] Frida proudly told me that after they married she had never been totally dependent on her husband for money; she used to sell cooked rice during the lunch hour at certain office buildings, and developed a modest base of regular customers. When they got their *fotnait* (wages), she would wait for her payment at the gate. Her earnings she used mostly for daily household expenses.

Moreover, Ben and Frida maintained close contact with their place of origin. After the initial success of Ben's brother Mande, they occasionally went to Openga and planted kaukau for sale in Port Moresby. Frida told me that on the 1991 election day, she had voted early in her Daulo electorate, taken the plane to Moresby, and done some excellent trade in the market – as most other kaukau sellers had been absent. Soon after the election, however, they came in droves.

But although her story illustrates yet another aspect of the construction of rural–urban links, this was a digression. We are concerned now with the experience of urban dwellers. And here Frida has a lot to tell:

> In 1990, only a few went down to Moresby. In 1991 they poured into my house. 1992 I had a bellyful of it ... You know, power bill – lots of people using the water and the water bill went up – they stayed inside and had the lights on, they sat watching TV ... Those who came, they liked the TV ... And the people used to come and finish the money, which made us embarrassed, and when we wasted money in this way ... in one day we would waste 30 kina to buy coconuts, greens, chicken ... It's the way we do things in Papua New Guinea! [Laughs] (Frida, interview 15 February 1995, Openga)

Frida emphasizes what is for her the wastefulness of traditional hospitality gone mad in an urban setting. In her anglicized Tok Pisin, she repeatedly uses the negative expression *westim mani* (waste money) instead of more neutral (or even positive, given the cultural emphasis on reciprocity) *spendim mani* (spend money). Her way out of the situation? To move back to the village.

I said: 'If we stay on, will they continue to come with their kaukau? ... I don't care. We ... live off your [Ben's] income only now. We must move to the village.' And – I told my husband: 'When you read the newspaper, you must look for work – at home. We cannot stay there without a job, it would not be good if I did not have soap or something. We must check that ... that newspaper, the job ads. You apply for a job and then we can go (Frida, interview 15 February 1995, Openga).

Eventually Ben managed to get himself transferred to PTC in Goroka. They made the move in 1993, shipping their utility truck around to Lae, loaded with most of their material possessions – including the TV set. Even more importantly, when they themselves caught the flight to Goroka, they brought with them the foundations for the further accumulation of capital (and prestige), namely 5 piglets they had bought at a piggery close to Port Moresby. These provided the basis for a small piggery of their own, which now provides them with added income.

THE EMERGENCE OF SPECIALIZED MARKET TRADERS

Long-distance trading is a time-consuming activity for the growers, and demands considerable resources and organization on their part. Moreover, the hospitality of their *wantoks* in town, while genuine, is not inexhaustible. In terms of institutional economics, here is a market with substantial transaction costs. It is easy to see how these costs might be lowered by bulking and/or intermediary traders.

I did not come across bulk *buying* in the village itself. Sometimes, however, growers with relatively small quantities entrust their bags to someone else (usually a close relative) who is planning a marketing trip, who then sells on their behalf. This is more common among women than men.

On the other hand, intermediary traders are found in Goroka, albeit only in an embryonic form. During my fieldwork I came across two people in the town who bought kaukau in bulk and sent to town markets in the New Guinea islands. This was a man of New Ireland origin, who had his own business, and a woman from the Western Highlands, who held a managerial job with a large local firm. They did not advertise their activities, and indeed they had not been doing this for long, nor were they doing it on any regular basis as yet. Both had started buying from a particular village with which they had previous relations, but word had got out and they both told me that they were now frequently approached by growers from all over the valley. They shipped occasional containers of kaukau over to Kavieng and

Plate 9: Urban market traders attempting to buy kaukau in bulk from Eastern Highlands growers at the wharf in Port Moresby. These women are migrants from Tari, Southern Highlands Province.

Lorengau, where they had *wantoks* who sold it. As these markets were of limited size, they were careful not to send too much at a time.

A different form of intermediary trading is found in Port Moresby. As the highland growers receive their kaukau from the containers on the wharf in Port Moresby, they are approached by urban dwellers, who want to buy a few bags for reselling in the marketplaces (Plate 9). Some growers, particularly those with large consignments, are willing to part with a limited number of bags in this way, but often the price put up by growers is not compatible with what the retail marketers are willing to pay.

In fact, such retail trading seems to be better established in the case of potatoes than kaukau.[20] Some commercial highlands potato 'exporters' now dispose of much of their shipments by doing the rounds in the suburban markets of Port Moresby and selling bags directly to specialized market traders. During my fieldwork in Port Moresby, I mainly encountered migrants from Goilala (Central Province) and the Southern Highlands for whom this was their major source of livelihood.

The emergence of these traders may be one symptom of a wider change towards 'informalization' in Port Moresby's economic life, which some recent observers have also noted (Keichi Kumagai, pers. comm., 1996; Ila Temu, pers. comm., 1996). The 'informal sector', long in evidence in neighbouring Indonesian and other Southeast Asian cities, may finally be taking hold, in spite of a politico-economic climate in Papua New Guinea that has until now discouraged rather than assisted it.

CONCLUSION

I have in this chapter described the reality of the present-day, long-distance kaukau trade and market from several different angles. First, in quantitative terms long-distance trading is now a substantial activity, with 100 tonnes frequently shipped to Port Moresby per month, and at least similar quantities taken from the highlands to Lae. Shipments to Port Moresby show marked year-to-year and seasonal fluctuations, pointing both to an interrelationship with the production regime of coffee, the other major cash crop, and to the operation of other factors.

The specialization of the Asaro growers in kaukau is striking. The large urban markets of Papua New Guinea seem not, however, to be developing into anything like the 'webbed producer-seller markets', based on a realization of comparative advantage, which Epstein envisaged some time ago (Epstein 1982). From an economic viewpoint it is clearly premature to talk about a country-wide integrated market for this commodity. The Port Moresby market is especially isolated, whereas there is a semblance of integration between the markets in Goroka and Lae. Information about supply, demand, and price does not, however, travel well between even these two markets, which are reasonably close in terms of time and cost of travel, if not in absolute distance. Expectation of growers when they board the truck at Asaro is often much higher than the actual amounts they get after having sat in the market for days.

Inflated expectations or not, an examination of prices and costs reveals that long-distance trading of producer-sellers is economically sound. It does not, however, (with the partial exception of Port Moresby) bring any extraordinary rewards above what could be gained by selling in Goroka itself. There are obviously limits to the size of the local market in Goroka, but those few intermediary traders that exist, who ship kaukau out from Goroka to other markets pay comparable prices.

To reiterate a point made repeatedly already: it is abundantly clear that the form which the market has taken has at least as much to do with social and cultural factors as with economic logic. Like any other market, the kaukau market is made up not only of sellers and buyers (the latter have not been discussed specifically), but of a *network of actors*. A detailed examination of daily practice on the kaukau trail identified several of these. The market works, because in a somewhat peculiar way it links together growers, trucking entrepreneurs and drivers, and not least, the town-dwelling relatives of the growers. By travelling outside the Asaro Valley, the growers leave their daily space of action, but in a sense they do not leave their village or kin group. The dilemma is that while the channelling of social interaction through *wantok* relations has made the trade possible, it also puts a very real strain on those urban *wantoks* whose hospitality is relied upon.

There are signs that many growers are now realizing these social limits to their enterprise, as well as its economic limitations: the costs involved in making lengthy journeys to Lae and Port Moresby. It is possible that the future will see increased use made of intermediary traders. At present, such traders are few and far between, and their share in the total quantity of kaukau sold is very small.

NOTES

1 Kaukau sellers from villages close to Lae are usually somewhat fewer, and these bring much smaller quantities, along with a variety of other lowlands produce. Potato, cabbage, carrot, and various other vegetables are also brought by highlanders to this marketplace, which on the whole offers a better selection of produce than many, if not most, other markets in the country.

2 Much of the potato, however, is shipped by a few firms (specialized large-scale growers and/or wholesalers) but not individuals, and is destined for the supermarkets.

3 Freight charges were long calculated on the basis of the number of bags. Some people told me how they had cheated on the shipping company by not giving the correct number. Moreover, the FPDC calculated the total quantity on the basis of average weight per bag, which was also conservatively estimated as 56

ECONOMIC DIMENSIONS, DAILY PRACTICE, AND SOCIAL NETWORKS

kg for kaukau. In my experience, the average would be closer to 80 kg, and I once weighed as much as 100 kg being stuffed into a large copra bag. In 1995 a proper weighing facility had been set up at Consort's base in Lae and freight charges were calculated by weight.

4   The lower figure for July 1994 has 'natural causes': the bridge over the Umi River in the Markham Valley collapsed on July 13 (Nalu and Palme 1994), cutting the highlands off from Lae. A temporary crossing for motor vehicles was not established until some weeks later. In the meantime, some highlands traffic was diverted to Madang, but that road is unsuitable for heavy transport. Some high-value cargo was either airlifted from the coast directly to the highlands or, in the case of mining equipment, taken over the Umi by helicopters. Other, including bags of kaukau and other fresh produce – and human travellers – were carried across the muddy waters of the Umi by local porters for a set fee – K5 for a bag and K2 for a person. The episode had little permanent impact, other than leading to the construction of marketing facilities on the eastern side of the river, where trade in coastal produce has since thrived.

5   Also included in the CPI data collection are Madang and Rabaul, which are not significant outlets for Asaro growers, although they are sometimes found selling there (notably in Madang). These data have been analysed in more detail by Spencer and Heywood (1983) and Joughin and Kalit (1986, 1987), and the analysis of the latter was extended to 1991 by Fereday (1993).

6   Some market women reacted negatively to my requests for permission to weigh their heaps, seeing me perhaps as yet another male, and a *waitman* to boot, intruding on their lives. But suspicion most often evaporated when they saw me rearranging as best I could the heaps of other sellers after weighing them.

7   Among the sellers are migrant settler women who work in the large gardens of the landowning locals. Often such labourers are allowed to harvest those remaining tubers for own consumption or for sale, when retilling a large garden.

8   Kainantu is the only market surveyed that is not supplied at least in part by sellers from the Asaro Valley. Kaukau in Kainantu comes from the immediate vicinity, and from villages near the Kainantu–Okapa road (see Map 10).

9   From conversations with sellers in Port Moresby it was estimated that discards of kaukau were seldom in excess of 5 per cent in the case of kaukau sellers, even if the produce is shipped in ambient temperatures from Lae to Port Moresby. This is a much more acute problem for more perishable vegetables of course, although these are now shipped mostly in cooler containers.

10 It must be noted, however, that the long-term view (Figure 14) shows that prices in the Lae market have often been no higher than in Goroka.

11 In the precolonial order, where (larger) polities did not exist, any long-distance interaction was truly comparable to international relations.

12 The use of hired labour for gardening tasks is discussed further in Chapter 8.

13 I have weighed as much as 100 kg stuffed into a single copra bag, but the average seems to be about 80 kg. The white stockfeed bags weigh at least 60–70 kg fully stuffed.

14 Or been removed: I was told that bridge timber in good condition was excellent material for shotgun stocks, and home-made shotguns are commonly used in fighting in the area.

15 I have counted up to 30 trucks parked at Umi at one time.

16 Women are absent from commercial driving – in fact from most driving in the highlands, although some urban women have driving licences.

17 Traditional cooking method in parts of the highlands: bamboo tubes stuffed with food are cooked in hot coals. Now used mainly in feasting in the Asaro Valley.

18 Possibly some customary payment was involved in the particular show of generosity I described, although Kondagule did not indicate that.

19 It is appropriate to establish some connections here: Mathew, one of Ben's older brothers, is married to Frida's sister Wewi. The sisters hail from the village of Kofena, on the western side of the Asaro River. Mathew, Wewi, and their children were part of the core group of households during my fieldwork, although I did not trace their genealogy and social networks in Chapter 3. Another older brother of Ben is Mande, who was identified in Chapter 6 as one of the instigators of the Port Moresby kaukau trade.

20 *Buai* is however the crop around which the most complex system of intermediary trading has emerged. It is notable that much of *buai* retailing is in the hands of 'outsiders'. In Port Moresby, highlander assembly traders buy *buai* off Mekeo people outside the city, and resell to (also mostly highlander) retail traders at Tokarara Market. In and around Goroka, it is settlers from Simbu who do most of the *buai* trading.

8

Locality, land, and labour: processes of production in Lunube

Later we will have problems. Down on the flats, land will be a problem. Before [around 1970], when I walked to the school at Omborda, it was all kunai *and* pitpit *on the way. I think that ... in ten years, we will have land problems (George, interview 7 February 1995, Kasena).*

SO FAR I HAVE FOCUSED on the social construction of the fresh food markets in which the people of the Asaro Valley participate. The long-distance kaukau trade is the most distinctive of these markets, and a prime example of an imperfect yet somehow functional exchange system which is deeply embedded in social life. It involves the construction and nurturing of social networks which extend into places far removed from the daily space of action of the growers of the crop.

In this chapter attention is shifted from the trading to the production side. While not attempting a full-scale ecological analysis, I describe the local physical environment which forms the material basis of the various market gardening activities, and the management of this environment by the growers. The changes in settlements and agroecological characteristics that have occurred since 'contact' are discussed, as well as how local people perceive and interpret these changes. Land management is a complex process, where many and sometimes conflicting objectives come into play. An issue that looms large is the long-term sustainability of current processes, especially given an increasing population. As the quote above suggests, people in Lunube are now questioning with some trepidation what the future holds.

Not long after I finished fieldwork, in 1997, Papua New Guinea experienced its worst drought in many decades (Allen and Bourke 1997a, 1997b).

Needless to say, this had wide implications for agricultural production, both for subsistence and for market, but this year of hardship was followed by a year of favourable weather patterns and bountiful harvests. The drought seems to have caused no fundamental changes in the social systems or the management of physical resources.

ENVIRONMENT AND VILLAGE LOCATIONS

The vigour of production in the Upper Asaro, in all its forms, is to a large extent based on an exceptionally favourable environment.[1] The soils are fertile and easily worked. Daytime temperature maxima are usually 23–29°C and nightly minima 11–18°C. Annual rainfall is in the vicinity of 2,000 mm, with a drier period of three to four months around mid-year, although seasonality is less marked in the Upper Asaro Valley than in Goroka and Bena Bena.

The territory of the Lunube clans extends over several ecological zones, shaped mainly by altitude and landforms (Map 11). Each household manages several plots of land, making use of different ecological conditions.

Ecological conditions

The floor of the Asaro Valley consists of alluvial and colluvial terraces, incised by numerous streams. The lowest part of the Lunube territory at its southern border lies at 1600 m above sea level. From there, gently sloping, dissected alluvial fans[2] (see Löffler 1977: 105–108), extend towards the north and northeast. It is on these fans that the most intensive cultivation occurs. The soils are dark, rich in organic matter and quite fertile.[3] Those patches that are not gardened assume a fallow vegetation of *kunai* (*Imperata cylindrica*) and other short grasses. *Kunai* is valued as thatch for the round houses traditional to the region – but rectangular houses with roofs and sometimes walls of *kapa* (corrugated iron) have made inroads here as elsewhere in Papua New Guinea, the *haus kapa* being a potent symbol of wealth and modernization.

Rivers and streams have cut numerous steep incisions into the fan surfaces. Many pig houses are located in these gullies, as such land is used mainly for the foraging of pigs. Because the topsoil has been eroded, the lower soil strata have been exposed. Such soil is reddish in colour, rather infertile, and not suitable for gardening. However, coffee has been planted in some of the gullies and incisions.

LOCALITY, LAND, AND LABOUR

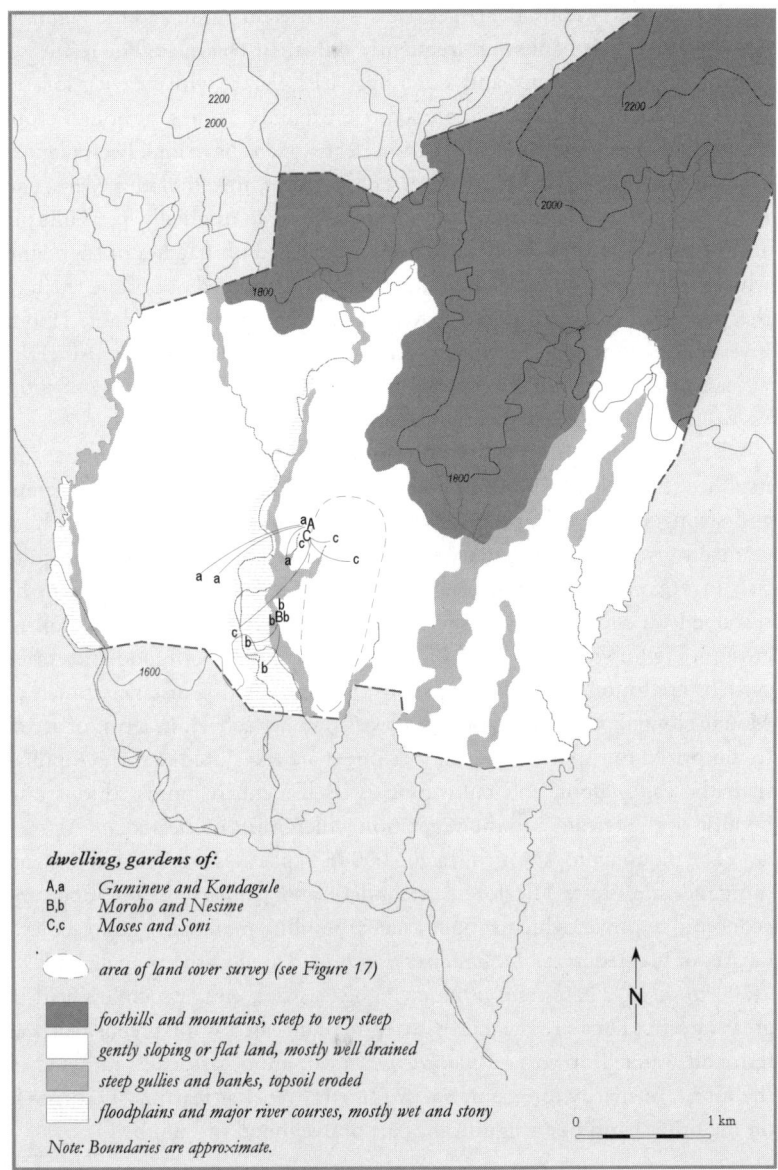

Map 11: Land types in the Lunube territory

During heavy rains, the larger rivers – such as the Asaro and the Lembina – often burst their banks and frequently shift their channels. The result is a narrow floodplain, stony and waterlogged in places, with heavier soils of light grey colour. Again, such areas are left mainly to pigs, although crops such as bananas, sugarcane, and various leafy greens have long been planted there in some places. In recent times, coffee groves, mixed food gardens, and more permanent settlements (often by families who originally had built pig and/or garden houses there) have been established on patches of such land which have been stable for some time and are considered out of the reach of the river. Coffee growing and gardening here require considerable labour investment in drainage, as well as fencing to keep the pigs away. Also, the wettest areas are a valuable source of *pitpit* – soft cane grass (*Phragmites karka*) which is used extensively for building.

The transition from valley bottom to mountain occurs at about 1,750 m above sea level. The foothills up to 2,000 m are vegetated with a different and stronger kind of cane grass (*Miscanthus floridulus*), and scrub, which gradually gives way to secondary and primary forest. The forest soils are quite rich in organic matter, but long fallows are needed if gardening is to be sustained on such land without exhaustion of fertility and loss of soil to erosion. Pig foraging is the main form of land use, but both food and coffee gardens are found in the lower part of the foothills (for instance, much of Mount Hunguko (1,901 m above sea level(is under coffee). In terms of access to motorized transport, however, these areas are less suited to cash cropping than the valley floor, and cultivation is itself a much more arduous task because of the terrain and the vegetation which must be cleared.

The mountaintops, which reach 3,000 m in places, are covered in primary montane rainforest. The forest, secondary and primary, is an important economic resource, which supplies many building materials (rattan, poles). Groves of planted *karuka* (*Pandanus jiulianettii*) are located at an altitude of 2,200 m or so. These trees produce highly seasonal nuts which are held in great esteem. They are owned by extended families. 'Wild' greens, such as fern and water dropwort (*Oenanthe javanica*), are occasionally gathered in the forest, primarily for use in *mumus* (earth ovens) at feasting. Hunting is on the other hand not a significant part of livelihood in Lunube.

Settlement history and land use changes

One of the remarkable features of post-contact change in the Asaro Valley, as in fact in many other parts of the highlands (see Grossman 1984: 41–46;

LOCALITY, LAND, AND LABOUR

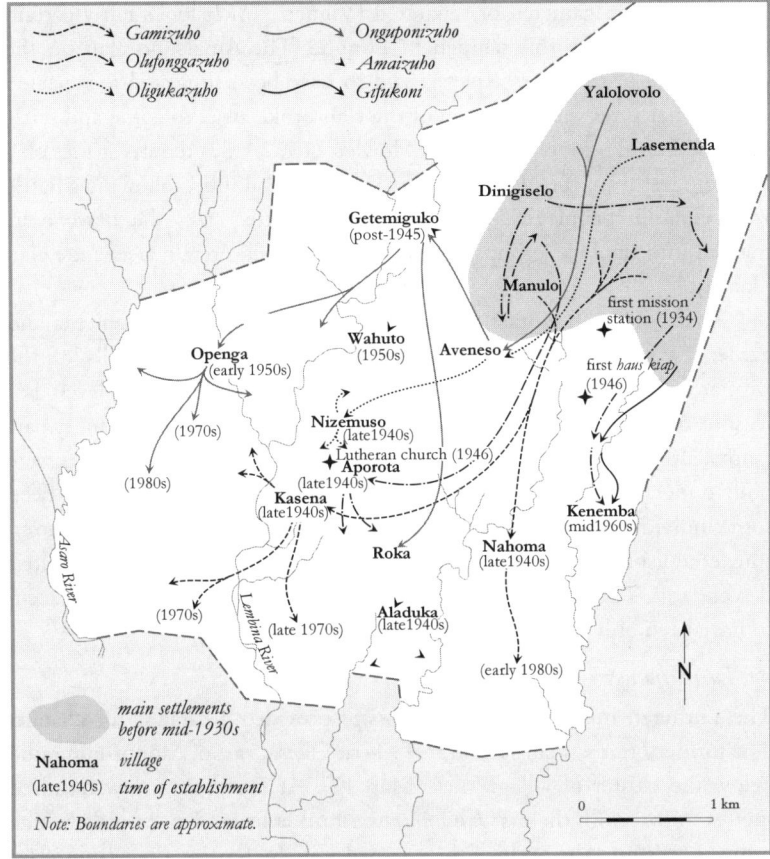

Map 12: Movement of Lunube groups since about 1930

Bourke 1992), is the relocation of settlements and corresponding reorganization of land use. Evidence was collected of these changes from numerous older people in Lunube. Although memories of the exact situation at and just before contact have faded somewhat, there is good agreement on most previous settlement locations (Map 12).

❧ Settlement in precolonial times

In the middle of this century (see Newman 1962: 26–28), and presumably in pre-contact times, social organization in the Upper Asaro was quite fluid. Tribal confederations and clans split up and reorganized, and subclan settlements were amalgamated or separated (Vignette 6). It looks fairly certain that the 1920s saw this happen in Lunube. The Amaizuho clan on the western side of the Asaro River is said to have been subjected to repeated raids at that time, and a portion of the clan broke away to come and settle with the Lunube people. Likewise, Howlett (1962: 182) reports stories of 'a few' refugees from the Notofona tribe settling in Lunube, following a battle with Gahuku people in the 1920s. In the latter case, the newcomers merged into the local groups, whereas the Amaizuho retain a separate clan identity.

At the time of contact in the early 1930s, the main settlements and gardens were located on the ridges and spurs in the foothills of the Bismarck Range, at an altitude of 1,900–2,200 m above sea level. For reasons of security, the *kunai*-covered valley bottom was for the most part empty, although during relatively peaceful periods some small hamlets were built under Mount Hunguko. Also, throughout there seem to have been some individuals who occasionally made their gardens in the valley bottom, thus establishing and maintaining the basis for subsequent claims of their descendants. The boundaries between tribal areas in the valley bottom seem to have been only loosely defined, however.

Early changes

The Lutheran missionaries and the *kiaps* provided a catalyst for change. The former built a small station in 1934 at Okesa, east of Mount Hunguko below the cluster of village sites (Map 12). At Gambaro a few hundred metres to the south the first *haus kiap* was built a little later – a place which pulled locals into the orbit of the colonial state by hosting the all-powerful *kiaps* on their intermittent patrols. Both initiated some movement downwards, although by no means a wholesale movement of villages.

According to my informants, the decisive stimulus to relocation was the cessation of warfare, which radically altered the conditions of landholding and settlement. During the early years of contact, some men managed to appropriate sizeable portions of the 'no man's land' on the flats, or consolidate claims to such land based on ancestral deeds, by virtue of their aggressive personality coupled with partial pacification. Much of this land was only later brought into production (see K.E. Read 1952, for the Lower Asaro).

Gumineve's father, Gimbe (see Chapter 3), was one of these men. He acquired large tracts of land at Hanabako, not far from the southern edge of the tribal territory, as well as west of the Lembina River. He took no less

LOCALITY, LAND, AND LABOUR

Vignette 6: Oral accounts of the origins of the Gamizuho people

Accounts of the origins of the various social groups in Lunube vary, and in all probability well and truly mix oral history and myth. Nevertheless they point to important continuities from past to present, concerned as they are with political splits and alliances.

The tribal groupings of the Upper Asaro share a common story of their emergence as political units. This story, which the Gururumba told Newman in about 1960 (Newman 1965: 30–31), was still being recounted in Lunube in the mid-1990s. It tells of an original large village in the valley bottom not far from present-day Asaro, whose members subsisted mostly on wild mushrooms and other foods they gathered or hunted in the bush. A minor quarrel over some highly prized mushrooms escalated into fighting, which led to the splitting up of the village into separate units. The groups moved up into the hills and became the tribes of the present. One such was the Lunube've – the people of Lunube.

As for the Gamizuho clan specifically, its name is said to manifest their origin in a faraway place: Kami, which is a tribal grouping close to Goroka. Why they left is uncertain, but on the way they stayed for some time with the Kofika people, who now live in the centre of the Asaro Valley not far from the Asaroka mission station. They then left for Lunube following a large earthquake. A subclan of the Gamizuho is still named Gohikezuho, recalling the association with the Kofika clans. It is even stated that the Gohikezuho could invoke claims to Kofika land if need be.

Upon moving to Lunube, a portion of the Gamizuho clan settled on the ridge to the northeast of Mt Hunguko, where the winds still blow stronger than elsewhere. Here they grew yams. When the wind rustled the yam leaves, their neighbours would admire how much yam they had planted. Hence this became the Ambilisezuho subclan (Dano: *Ambilise* – a variety of yam).

Another group settled closer to the Lunube've people who had lived there previously, and became the Lunubezuho subclan.

This oral history establishes the Gamizuho as the 'junior partners' to the 'original' Lunube've. Traditionally, tribal confederations such as the Lunube've-Gamizuho almost always consisted of such politically and territorially cohesive pairs (see Newman 1965: 33), whose strength was unequal. The story highlights the importance of identifying and maintaining links to allied groups, and importantly, to land. The myth of the mushroom also situates ongoing tribal rivalry and enmities firmly in the past.

than nine wives[4] and allocated separate blocks of the land to each. Such strategic deployment of female labour was common among traditional big-men,[5] and enabled them to activate and maintain usufruct rights to large areas, which otherwise would have been up for grabs at a patrilineage or subclan level. It is these lands which Gumineve and other descendants of Gimbe still cultivate. Some have established sizeable coffee plantings, whereas others, like Gumineve, have extensive *kaukau* market gardens.

During the Pacific War the people of the region witnessed Japanese air attacks, notably on the mission station at Asaroka and the Administration facilities at Bena Bena. A young Lunube man was killed in the latter, bringing home the terror of modern warfare. Some clans decided to retreat higher up into the forested zone, where they would be harder to spot. Others stayed put. The mission retreated from Okesa to the main station at Asaroka.

~ *The* hauslain: *a symbol of development*

Soon after the end of the Pacific War, the Australian 'modernization offensive' (Seib 1994) was launched. Tribal warfare was largely suppressed, and with it disappeared the necessity for easy defence as the prime criterion of village sites. Hamlets were moved from the foothills downwards, first to the upper reaches of the valleys, and then still further down. The *haus kiap* was moved to present-day Nahoma. Religious conversion got under way seriously, and a Lutheran church was built under the Hunguko Mountain in 1946. The large villages of Kasena were established in the vicinity, the site chosen by Gosi, the first *luluai* appointed by the Administration. Hence, the location of Kasena enjoyed the blessings of Christ and *kiap* alike in an attempt to centralize the Lunube population, making spiritual and political surveillance easier.

In other words, the immediate postwar years mark the start of the *hauslain* period, with the building in the late 1940s or early 1950s of the linear villages of Nahoma, Aporota, Kasena, Nizemuso, and Openga, and in the 1960s, Kenemba. An increasing proportion of the fertile and well-drained flats was converted from *kunai* to gardens.[6] Likewise, the new cash crop, coffee, was exclusively grown down on the flats during its early adoption period in the 1950s. The *kiap* roads, most of which were also built in the 1950s, cemented the centrality of the new settlements in a world that had been radically and irreversibly altered, not only in a political and religious sense, but also in an economic and spatial sense.

The heyday of the *hauslains* came in the 1960s and early 1970s, when zealous local councillors[7] attempted to make them into model villages. The *hauslains* were fenced to keep pigs out, latrines were dug, flowers were planted: a local emulation of the perceived hallmarks of development. Kasena, for instance, became well known in the district for its neatness.

❧ Recent changes

These model *hauslains* did not age well, however. Many are now rather haphazard-looking conglomerations, and some *hauslains* such as Aporota have all but disappeared. A forlorn cattle grid is all that remains of the allegedly pig-proof fence at Roka, and the pigs large and small now share the residential area with humans. Many older locals lament these developments and trace their beginnings to the relaxation of control over alcohol in the late 1960s. This, together with the gradual disappearance of the institution of the men's house since early mission days, is said to have led to the declining mores of the younger generation, and a deterioration of village life in general. 'In the olden days,' a middle-aged friend of mine frequently mused, 'when the men's houses still existed, and all boys had to go though initiation, the men were strong and clever. And they were fat.' Nostalgia is rampant in Lunube.

Another important factor in the decline of the *hauslains,* however, has been the general trend for extended families to move on to their own landholdings within the clan territory and establish small hamlets there. In some instances this has been done in order to better look after the coffee groves and prevent theft. Many also state that they simply grew tired of the inevitable rowdiness of a large *hauslain*. As a result, although the large villages remain in existence, settlement in Lunube is now scattered throughout the flats, mirroring a change in the use of land. A major issue now facing the Lunube people is one of the continued sustainability of ever more intensive agriculture on this prime agricultural land, which is already among the most intensively used pieces of land in the country (Bourke *et al.* 1994a).

Of the Lunube households introduced in Chapter 3, Gumineve and Moses reside with their families in the main *hauslain* (Kasena). Both also have a house adjacent to their gardens west of the Lembina River, where they sometimes stay overnight. Moroho and Nesime have built a *haus kapa* (house with tin roof) at the main village, but have nevertheless chosen to move the family out to their other *haus kunai* (bush-material house), where only the pigs resided previously. This is located close to their garden and to the dwellings of their closest relatives. Likewise, during the time of fieldwork, Saina was building a new house at his major food garden, a stone's throw away from his father, brothers, and sisters.

THE MANAGEMENT OF PHYSICAL RESOURCES

Recent commentators have implied that the term 'subsistence' is a hollow rhetorical device when used to describe present-day economic circumstances (see Chapter 2). It gives an impression of autonomy while disguising the real subsumption of household-based producers under capital. I find this a rather too strong assertion. While the distinction between subsistence and commodity production has become blurred following the widespread commoditization of crops old and new, this does not mean that subsistence is a thing of the past. Production for use is a central part of people's daily lives in Lunube, alongside with production for exchange.

Food gardening

It is not my intention here to describe subsistence crops and gardening methods in great detail, as such a description is available elsewhere (Bourke *et al.* 1994a, 1994b; see also Howlett 1962). It is appropriate, though, to highlight the main parameters. Gardening is based on a grass fallow cycle (when long fallows are used at all). Fallow vegetation is cut or remnants of previous crops uprooted, the material dried and burnt, and the soil tilled completely with spades. Crops are planted in rectangular beds, separated by shallow drainage ditches or tracks. Each garden contains a multitude of crops and intercropping is practised extensively, although the beds contain different constellations of crops at any one time. Harvesting is done by hand or using that ancient and simple implement, the digging stick (Plate 10).

❧ Crops and planning of gardens

The three contrasting examples below serve to highlight the complexity of the current physical organization of production. I present a listing of the crops grown by these households – which we met in Chapter 3 – and a map of their major food gardens.

As we have seen, Gumineve and Kondagule have long engaged in market gardening, on their own and in cooperation with their daughter and son-in-law, Nellynne and Rex. They currently manage some four plots of land (Map 11, Table 7), all formerly part of Gimbe's large estate. It is noticeable that their coffee holdings are not as substantial as such a history would suggest, but it should be recalled from Chapter 3 that some years ago they transferred their major coffee garden to a town-dwelling relative, but received less benefits than they had expected. At the time of my stay, they had become worried about their lack of good coffee plantings, and sometimes indicated that they would try and have the ownership returned to them, or at least some better compensation paid. Rex and Gumineve had also em-

Plate 10: Woman harvesting marketable kaukau tubers. This is the first harvest, and undeveloped tubers will be left in the ground. The cultivar is *Wanmun*, which is popular with coastal consumers.

barked on the rehabilitation of the remaining coffee garden (numbered 3 in Table 7).

In contrast to the limited and badly maintained coffee groves, their main food garden at Hanabako (numbered 1 in Table 7, see also Map 13) is a substantial piece of land, extending from the edge of the Lembina floodplain up to the drier flatland. It is large enough for them to have a continuing supply of kaukau and other crops for consumption and marketing. There is access for vehicles at the western corner of the garden, but sometimes produce is also carried up the wet and muddy path across the Lembina River and up to Kasena. A part of the garden is preserved for a variety of tree crops and greens for home consumption, including several

Table 7: Plots managed by Gumineve and Kondagule

Number of garden and major features	Main crops	Minor crops	Also grown
1 Main food garden at Hanabako, W of Lembina River. E part of garden wet, drained by 50cm deep ditches. W part lies higher, well drained. Part of the land is unfenced, used for pigs. 66 coffee trees.	kaukau potato peanut	maize cassava banana sugarcane coffee	pumpkin marita taro (*Xanth.*) ginger gohuno pineapple salat pitpit bean kapiak
2 Currently fallowed block, ca. 150 m W of main garden. Has not been cultivated for at least 7 years.	–	–	–
3 Main coffee garden, located at the main Kasena *Hauslain*, at the back of family house. Not well kept, but in rehabilitation. 388 coffee trees.	coffee	taro (*Xanth.*) banana	
4 Unfenced patch, some damage by pigs.	coffee	marita	

Source: Fieldwork.

'traditional' species which are no longer commonly planted. This is also, incidentally, a place for small family gatherings and feasts, away from the eyes of fellow villagers.

Moroho and Nesime's gardens are located in three different micro-environments (Map 11, Table 8). First, the main garden (1) and the small household garden (3) are on the tongue of flat alluvial terrace on which the Kasena village stands. Second, the steep slope adjacent to the house has been planted with coffee mainly (2). A separate garden (4) for banana, sugarcane, and greens is maintained on the wetter riverbank, as is a large coffee garden (5). In all, the household has over 1,300 coffee trees. This is a substantial number, although not all coffee plots had been well maintained in recent years and many trees were not yielding particularly well during the 1995 coffee season.

A closer look at their major food garden (Map 14) reveals that, like other households, they juggle 'subsistence' and 'commercial' plantings. It is noticeable however that carrot and potato, both of which are grown mostly for sale, feature prominently. As we have seen, Moroho has been an instrumental figure in commercial food gardening in Kasena. The original garden, which as a

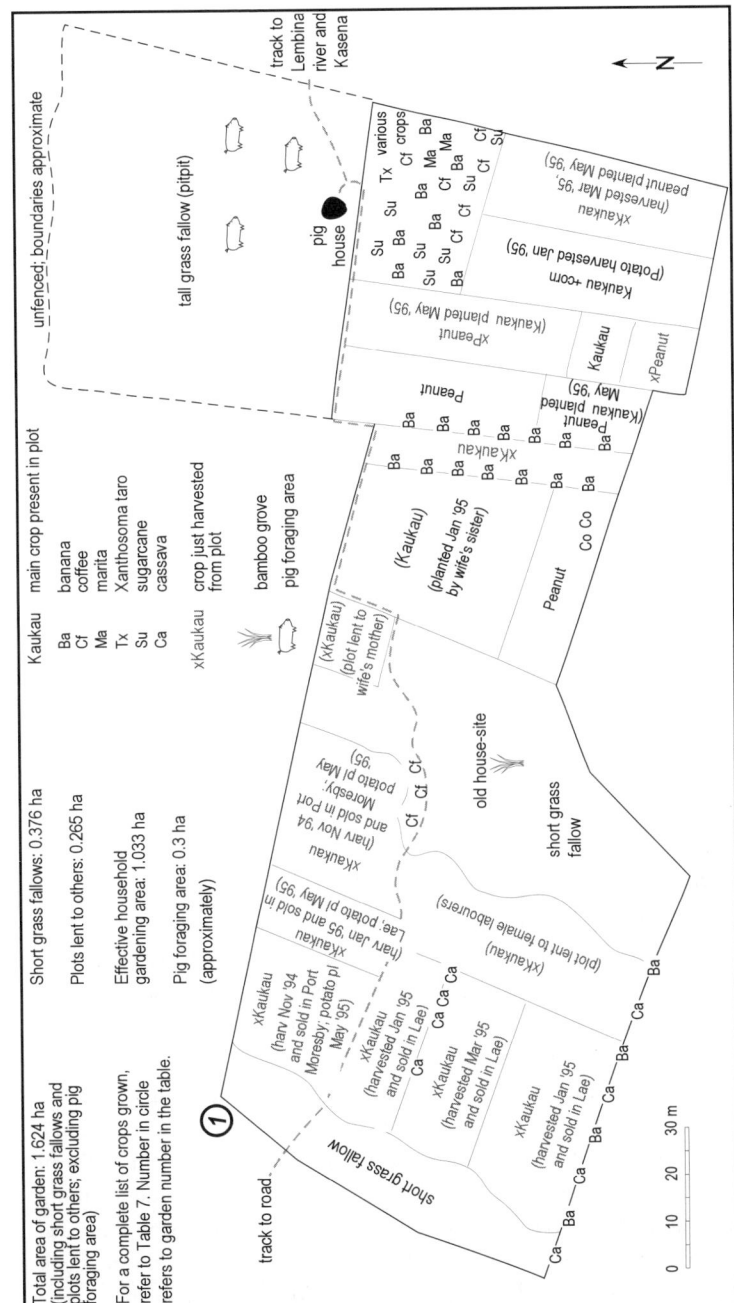

Map 13: Main food garden of Gumineve and Kondagule

Table 8: Plots managed by Moroho and Nesime

Number of garden and major features	Main crops	Minor crops	Also grown
1 Not far from family's house, S of main Kasena *hauslain*. Has been intensively cultivated for some 20 years. Parts lent out to Moroho's parents and sister. 527 coffee trees, partly intercropped with kaukau.	kaukau (9) coffee carrot peanut potato winged bean	yam spring onion cassava banana maize sugar-cane (2) taro (*Xanth.*)	ginger bean pumpkin taro (*Coloc.*) kapiak soybean
2 On steep slope immediately SW of house. Some damage by pigs. 252 coffee trees.	coffee	banana marita	kapiak gohuno vise makise
3 Very small household garden. 17 coffee trees.	coffee	taro (*Xanth.*) banana (2)	choko
4 Main coffee garden, close to Lembina River, banks eroded during floods. Trees unkempt; great damage by pigs. Previous garden land, coffee planted in part by Moroho some 20 years ago, in part by his father earlier. 532 coffee trees.	coffee	–	–
5 Close to river, soils wetter than in garden no.1.	banana (4)	sugarcane	lavoso sakave

Source: Fieldwork.

young man he had surveyed and registered (see Chapter 6), is to the left of the track which divides the block. The eastern part of the garden was until about ten years ago held by another family, which had not used it for a long time. Moroho and Nesime started clearing the fallow vegetation of *kunai*, and a village court case ensued. The matter was settled by their paying a token fine, but the plot remained theirs.

The household of Moses and Soni is somewhat unusual in that the land which is their main physical resource was acquired by the wife, from her father Gumuli. Their food gardens cover only about 6,500 sq m, but adjacent to the main garden (2 on Map 15) are two smaller areas over which Gumuli has claim, and which Soni and Moses could take into cultivation if needed. These plots are currently covered in *pitpit*. They are close to the river and would require substantial drainage if they were to be gardened.

LOCALITY, LAND, AND LABOUR

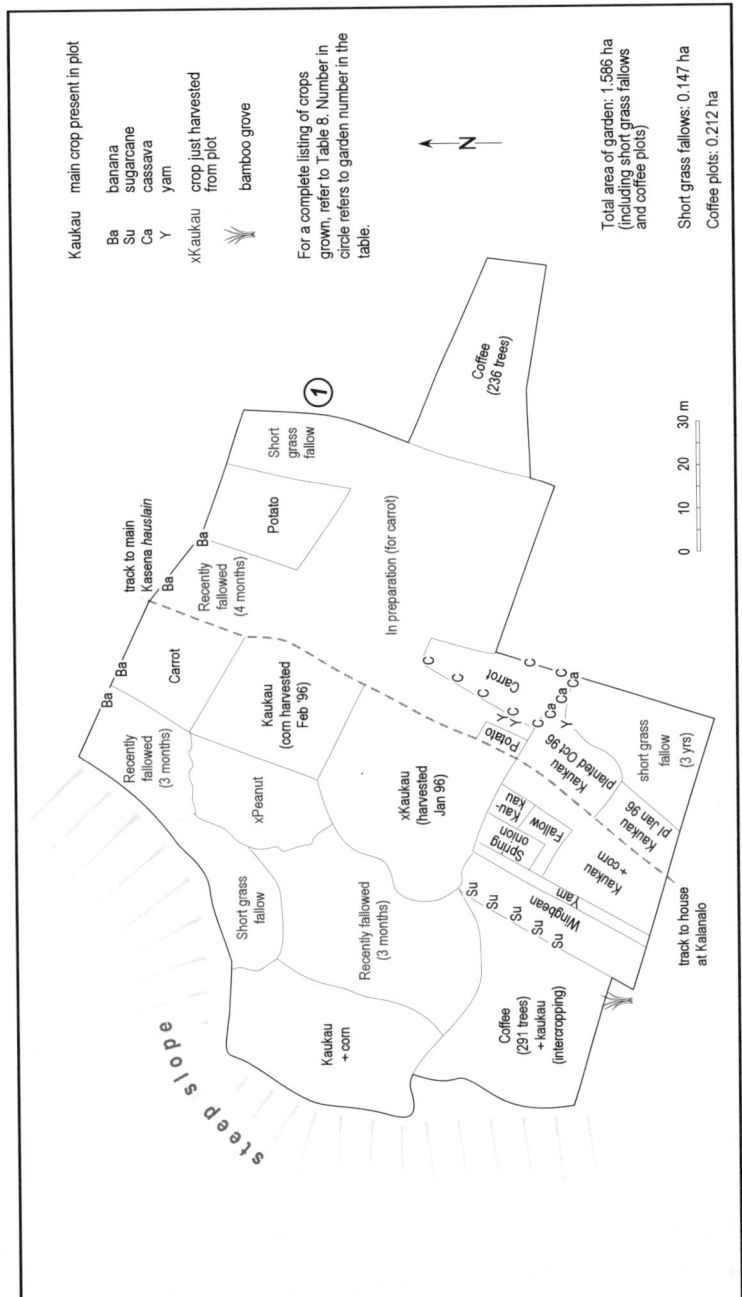

Map 14: Main food garden of Moroho and Nesime

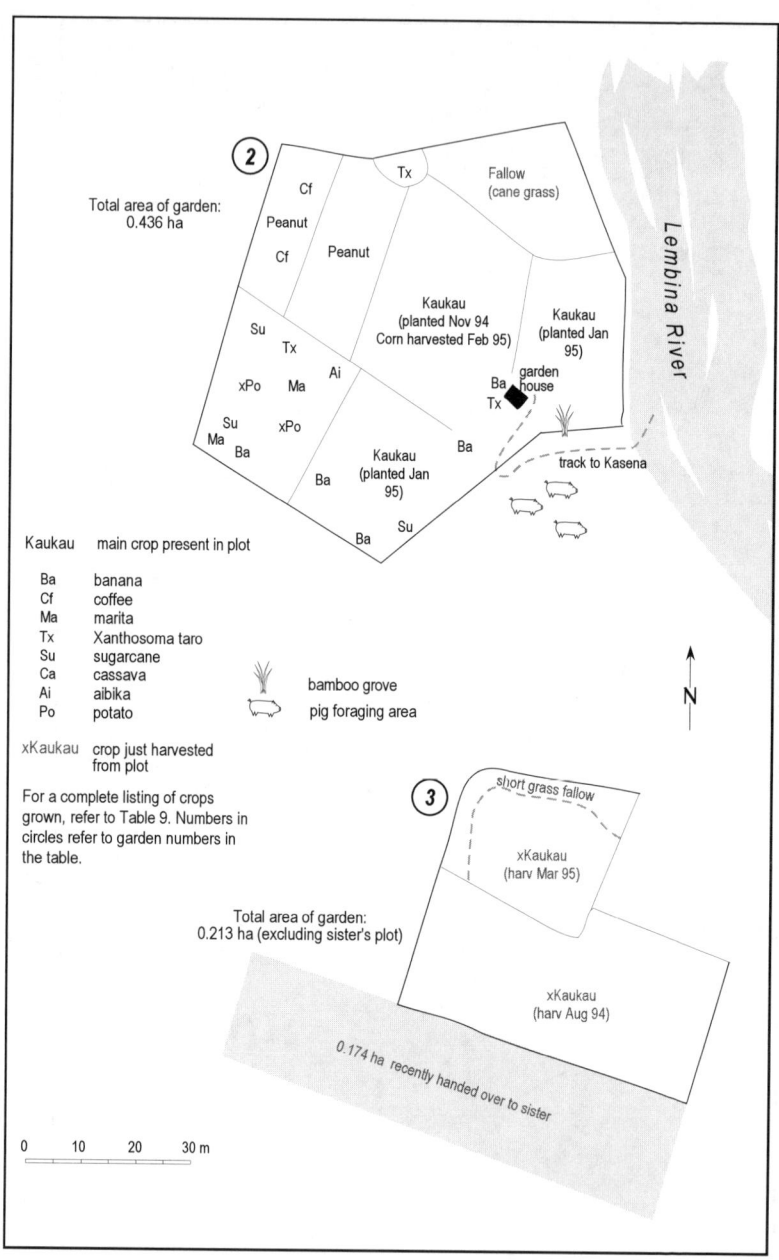

Map 15: Main food garden of Soni and Moses

Table 9: Plots managed by Moses and Soni

Number of garden and major features	Main crops	Minor crops	Also grown
1 At the back of house in the main *hauslain*. Household waste and coffee husk thrown into the coffee. Some pig damage. 282 coffee trees.	coffee	taro (*Coloc.*) banana (3) sugarcane tobacco	daka kapiak avocado pawpaw lemon guava
2 The main food garden, W of the Lembina River, 15 min. walk from home. Close to river; some erosion of banks during floods. Pigs kept nearby. Garden house.	kaukau (3)	potato taro (*Xanth.*) sugarcane (2) banana (3) maize peanut coffee marita	aibika taro (*Coloc.*) kapiak tobacco choko pitpit yam pumpkin cucumber avocado ginger cassava amba spring onion
3 Good land. Gardening for sale and home consumption. 10 min. walk from home. At start of fieldwork the garden had just been harvested of kaukau for sale, and was then gradually being dug up (remaining kaukau used for home consumption of humans and pigs) and then partly replanted in April 1995.	carrot kaukau		
4 Coffee trees unpruned; garden unweeded and damaged by pigs. 126 trees.	coffee		

Source: Fieldwork.

These examples confirm that, notwithstanding the commoditization of many crops, 'agrodiversity' is still very much in evidence. Given the intermixture of subsistence and commodity production, it is inevitable that decisions about commercial planting are linked to planting for household consumption. This is most notable in the case of Moses and Soni, whose gardens are limited in extent. Their commercial growing, while ongoing, tends to be on a small scale. Gumineve and Kondagule, on the other hand, have ample land and few mouths to feed. Together with their daughter and son-in-law, they tend to plan a large part of their gardening activities with market selling in view.

Coffee

It is of course coffee which has been the single most important post-contact addition to the repertoire of crops in Lunube. It takes up substantial portions of land, and just as importantly, has partially altered the relationship between people and land, and brought new pressures to bear upon tenurial arrangements and land management. We can usefully distinguish between 'plantation' and 'smallholder' coffee, although some of the small-holder coffee growers are not so small any more.

❧ *Plantation*

I have already mentioned Hunguko Coffee in passing several times. This enterprise, consisting of a plantation and coffee factory, has long been central to economic life in the area. One of the first coffee plantations in the Upper Asaro Valley, it was established in the early 1950s as Roka Coffee Estates, by an Australian named 'Sno' Macfarlan. He had worked for the Administration in Goroka, but resigned to try his hand at private enterprise, first as a trader in Goroka, and then as a coffee planter. The land was bought from the local clans after extended negotiations:

> I spent five days with the Lunapeve [sic] people acquiring this land, by custom ... each sub-clan had to have their say, each outdoing the other. Finally on the fifth day it was all settled, and to my surprise they also gave me timber rights to the land up in the tree line of the mountain (Macfarlan, quoted in Sinclair 1995: 114).

One can surmise from this account that the Lunube were quite eager to have a *waitman* in their midst, and did not at this time value highly the land they were 'selling'; a block of the *kunai*-covered alluvial fan towards the south of their territory. Macfarlan soon had over 100 acres (40 ha) of coffee, and assumed a similar place in Lunube social and economic life as did other planters. He became an employer of local and migrant labour, a buyer of smallholder coffee, as well as of fresh food for the labour line, and a general source of innovation and advice regarding Western ways and development. For example, when Gumuli (see Chapter 3) made history by becoming the first Kasena man to obtain a coffee pulper, it was through *masta Sino*.

At independence, the Gouna Development Corporation took over Roka Coffee Estates, making it the first expatriate-owned plantation to pass into national ownership. Gouna was formed in the 1970s and quickly became one of the largest firms in the region. It drew on a wide membership of villagers around Goroka, but prominent 'rural capitalist' Hari Gotoha was the *primus motor* (Donaldson and Good 1978: 15). While formed by national business interests, the corporation was clearly not perceived as a 'local' company by the Lunube people. Coffee theft and sabotage became endemic. In the end the Lunube formed their own company, which bought out Gouna. One of my interviewees reminisced: *'Mipela bagarapim Gouna nogut tru, na mipela yet kisim bek kopi!'* ('We wrecked Gouna good and proper, and got the coffee back for ourselves!')[8]

Macfarlan's former residence on the plantation is now the office of Hunguko Coffee Pty Ltd. Its list of shareholdings numbers 355 persons, 281 of these from the various Lunube clans, and 74 from villages outside Lunube. This indicates a wide public participation, although the five largest shareholders command about 30 per cent of all shares (and Mondave Wobo alone 14 per cent), and there is clearly some resentment of such concentration a of economic power. The shareholders are overwhelmingly, but not exclusively, male.

The company employs up to 22 people full-time during the coffee season, most of whom are from the Lunube clans. Also it hires 50–60 contract workers for pruning, spraying, and other maintenance of the plantation outside the picking season. Also large numbers of pickers are hired from day to day when needed. Pickers are paid 75t for a full drum of cherry coffee (15 kg). Most of these are migrants (although some local villagers also enlist for picking), whereas those overseeing their work are invariably from the local clans (Plate 11).

The coffee plantation and factory is thus a very significant player in the local economy. Contrary to most other plantations in the valley, this one has managed to make the transition into local ownership and local management without too much factional squabbling, except for the Gouna interlude. However, the expectations of the shareholding villagers for returns on their investment are very high, and it does not take much for suspicions to arise. The 7 per cent *winmoni* (dividend) paid by the company at the end of 1994 was disappointing to many shareholders, who looked to high coffee prices at the time. The company had obtained a large bank loan a few years previously, when a 'green bean' factory was built.[9] The bank had therefore insisted on managerial input from a coffee export company in Goroka, run by expatriates. This contributed to a suspicion of a rip-off amongst many

Plate 11: *Taim bilong kopi:* Overseer weighing coffee from pickers at the Hunguko Coffee plantation.

Lunube people. As always in such circumstances, the issue of the plantation land originally being bought for trinkets and *tamioks* (axes) was brought up. Although the company managed to defuse the anger, the situation at Hunguko Coffee shows how any large-scale private economic enterprise in the Upper Asaro Valley is a delicate balancing act. Conflicting interests, social demands, and lack of trust can easily become overwhelming.

Moroho and Nesime both hold shares in Hunguko: Moroho to the tune of K935, Nesime K300. They received a *winmoni* of K65 and K21, respectively, in December 1994. Gumineve and Kondagule also held small shares in the company, although Kondagule decided to sell her stock after receiving a meagre K7 dividend. Although the investments do not contribute significant amounts of money to the livelihood of these households, compared with their other activities, their direct involvement in capitalist production of this kind does not sit easily with their location as 'simple commodity producers' within a class-analytic theoretical framework.

❧ *Smallholder coffee*

In the overall scheme of things, however, it is the smallholders' own coffee which is most significant. The crop was promoted extensively by DASF in the 1950s. A coffee nursery was for instance set up at Asaro, and later also at Aporota, in Lunube. It was the same group of prominent men who had acquired much of the good land in the valley bottom, who took the lead in coffee. As occurred elsewhere in the highlands (see Brookfield 1968), the first coffee grove in Kasena was a semi-communal affair, where each man 'owned' one line of trees, but this soon gave way to separate plots on individual family land.

In Lunube, coffee was first planted at the very back of the *hauslains*, and much of the land closest to the dwellings is now occupied by coffee gardens. It only occupies approximately 15 per cent of the area, which arguably is the best piece of land in Lunube (see Map 11, Figure 17). Coffee gardens are now also found much further from the main *hauslain*. For example, much land adjacent to the Lembina River is planted with coffee. The soil there is considered too heavy and wet for kaukau, but given some drainage, quite suitable for coffee. It can therefore hardly be argued that it has displaced food gardens away from settlements, or to marginal land, although it has added to pressures on land in general.

The cash crop has in fact contributed to another, quite beneficial change in land use: a major tree-planting effort which has certainly changed the complexion of the Asaro Valley. The accounts of K. E. Read (1965), Howlett (1962: 25), and Newman (1962) from the 1950s portray the valley bottom as an expanse of grassland, with *kunai* and *Themeda* species featuring prominently. Coffee changed all that. During the 1950s coffee boom, trees (mainly *yar,* or *Casuarina oligodon*) were widely planted to provide shade for the coffee. Eucalypts and other introduced species were also planted in some villages. Apart from the larger continuous kaukau gardens, the fans of Lunube have taken on a heavily wooded appearance. The planted trees provide firewood, building timber, and fencing posts. Women, for example, are partly relieved of the task of collecting firewood on the forested slopes.

Of the 11 households with which I had most interaction during fieldwork, all but one have coffee. The extent of plantings varies widely, and averages may hide more than they illuminate. At the lower end of the scale are those with only 200–300 trees, whereas the largest have ten times that number. There is also a handful of households with coffee holdings well beyond these figures.

Maintenance of the coffee groves is likewise very varied. Some of the larger growers adhere to a strict schedule of pruning and weeding, but most others do not. Major weeding is done with a *busnaip* (machete), but herbicides are also used. Perhaps eight out of every ten coffee growers use chemical weedkillers at least occasionally. Gramoxone[10] is the brand most often seen, but Roundup is also used by some. The latter is longer-acting but also more expensive. The vehicle owners in the village sometimes mix Gramoxone and sump oil – in the rare event that they change the oil – and this is said to be very effective. The ownership of knapsack sprayers is often on an extended family or patrilineage basis.

Chemical fertilizer is on the other hand seldom applied to coffee, but those coffee gardens that are close to dwellings usually receive the household garbage. Although plastic bags and empty tins may have limited value for enriching the soil, peelings and other food scraps are undoubtedly beneficial. They also make coffee gardens a popular target of scavenging pigs, who do considerable damage at times.

Most work related to a coffee garden is undertaken by members of the household that owns it. Men do much, but not all, of the weeding and pruning, but when it comes to picking the coffee, women and children do a lot of the work.[11] It is also common for the larger coffee growers to hire extra pickers – mainly migrant settlers – who are remunerated with 5t for every kg they pick.

In each of the Lunube clans, one or more individuals are found, who have taken 'smallholder coffee' a step further. In Kasena, Megi Okoropi is the best example. He and his wife now own over 9,000 coffee trees, planted in the same block of land where Megi started his entrepreneurial career as a large-scale kaukau grower (see Chapter 6). The coffee development was financed by loans from the Agricultural Bank, while the National Plantation Management Agency provides managerial assistance. A group of Lufa migrants works for him on a permanent basis, and a varying number of labourers are called upon for picking and other special tasks. He and his wife have also built a new kit house in the middle of his garden, surrounded by the round houses of other family members. Megi has, however, neither assumed an important political status in the village, nor set himself apart from his fellow villagers, but continues to participate in village affairs on much the same level as anyone else.

Attempts at collective management of smallholder coffee have failed, although this has often been seen by planners as a key to more efficient production and higher returns. The Gamizuho set up one such enterprise in the late 1980s, when Ron Ganarafo, a local man with university business education, formed a *bisnis grup* (business group) together with several other clansmen. Concrete vats were built for 'wet' processing. Many growers delegated to him the management of their coffee plots and processing of their coffee. The group dissolved after only two years. The plot owners took back their coffee, as they considered the returns too low and suspected embezzlement by the manager. The processing plant is now overgrown. Ron, however, now lives in Goroka, where he was the CEO of the Coffee Industry Corporation during the time of my fieldwork, and had in addition acquired substantial coffee holdings of his own in Kasena.

The emergence of large coffee growers is linked to a radical change in the relations between people and land. In what amounts to *de facto* privatization of land, coffee blocks small and large are now frequently bought and sold by individuals within the villages. This is discussed further later in the chapter.

Pig husbandry

Analyzing data from the Gamizuho people of Kasena (discussed further below), I estimate that the pig population of Lunube is close to one pig per person (0.95 is the average for the households about which I have reliable data). This is in line with previous findings from the Asaro Valley (Howlett 1962: 208; Moulik 1973: 53–57),[12] as well as from various other parts of the highlands (summarized in Bourke 1988: 17–19).

Pigs are not tethered, but roam free in the villages and those areas not gardened. The contiguous gardening area to the east and south of the main Kasena *hauslain* is collectively fenced off. Most other gardens are individually fenced. In spite of these efforts, pigs often get into gardens, where they can do great damage. If the pig owner is different from the garden owner, a village court case usually results, with the owner of the offending pig having to pay compensation (some tens of kina usually) for the damage. The amount is decided with reference to the crops damaged, with higher compensation awarded for crops destined for sale, such as potato or carrot.

Sometimes the pigs are brought into old gardens, tethered there and allowed to forage. This brings a limited amount of manure to the garden, helps to break up the soil, and the pigs clear the plot of old kaukau.

It was suggested to me by an Australian observer that pigs were becoming a serious cause of soil erosion. Because the space available for them to roam was shrinking, and now largely confined to slopes, their foraging and trampling had triggered runoff and resulted in the bare strips of soil widely seen in the district. It is likely that this is at least partly true, but I did not investigate the issue specifically. It should be noted, however, that several older people remarked that more pigs had been kept previously. Gumineve said that the expansion of gardening had limited the possibilities for pig foraging, and suggested moreover that as more kaukau was now being sold, pigs mostly got *pipia* (rubbish, worthless) kaukau and were not as well fed as before.

Caring for pigs is a task of women, although many men do take some part. The animals are given a ration of (boiled or *mumu*ed) kaukau tubers daily, the owner buying kaukau if none is available from her or his own garden. Kaukau leaves or other succulent greenery is occasionally fed to pigs also. They are housed at night and let out early in the morning. Pig husbandry is a time-consuming activity, especially for those whose pig houses are located in the foothills.

Apart from the obvious ecological centrality of pigs, they are still a vitally important part of economic and social life in the Asaro Valley. The arrival of monetary exchange has not wiped out the previously vibrant gift economy, but meshed with it, as the following comment makes clear:

> Money and pigs are absolutely equal. Pigs do not make money less important. And money does not make pigs less important. The two are equal. If there were big troubles, and we compensated with money only, the other side would not be satisfied. If we handed over pigs as well as money, they would be happy. And the worries would be over (Lukas, interview 7 January 1995, Kofena).

Hence, as well as being a frequent cause of minor quarrels within or between villages, pigs are a necessary part of settlement in major disputes that arise. Other, more positive social relationships are also mediated by pig exchange. For example, pigs make up a part of brideprice and subsequent reciprocal exchange between clans allied through marriage (e.g. *nuspes* and *beksaitbun*, see Chapter 1), pork is the major ingredient in mortuary payments (Plate 12), and pigs are occasionally killed and distributed within a subclan, patrilineage, or extended family to mark important events of the group. Also, clans reward their allies with a generous bestowal of pigs after periods of warfare. In fact, in 1995 many told me that pig numbers were still somewhat lower than they would be under 'usual' circumstances, resulting from partic-

LOCALITY, LAND, AND LABOUR

Plate 12: Man handing out pork at a mortuary exchange ceremony in Kasena.

ularly large pig kills in 1991–92, when the Gamizuho acknowledged the help of many Lunube've clans in their recent fighting with the Onguponi.

Like elsewhere in the highlands, decisions regarding such strategic disposal of pigs are very much in the male domain. Pigs are never distributed live. They are killed, and usually butchered and cooked in a *mumu* before being given to the receiving individual or group. The exception is *nuspes*-ceremonies, where freshly killed pigs are handed over to the receiving clan.

Gumineve and Kondagule have a pig house close to their main garden, from where the pigs forage in a large tract of *pitpit*-covered land (Map 13). They had eight pigs when I started observing their operation. A pig was killed in early December 1994 for a small family feast, but two piglets born in January added to the herd. Moroho and Nesime also kept eight pigs in

1995, six adults and two piglets. They said this was somewhat fewer than usual. In fact, in December 1994 Moroho contributed K50 towards buying a large pig. Five households then pooled their resources for a K250 pig, which was bought at a government-run piggery in Bihute, the occasion being a large food exchange ceremony embarked upon by the Gamizuho following the death of a wealthy local man.

There are places in the Eastern Highlands where new religious taboos, notably those of Seventh Day Adventists (SDAs), have clashed with the tradition of pigkeeping, but not here. The SDAs of Lunube are not that numerous, and even they are pragmatic enough to keep some pigs for exchange – if not for own consumption. For example, Saina and Dinamo are SDAs, but had six pigs. The animals are housed together with those of Saina's father, in a gully away from the main settlement of Aladuka.

Changes with commoditization of food crops

One must be careful not to assume that a static subsistence regime must have existed in the Asaro before the arrival of the market economy. On the contrary, change in the choice of crops and methods used was in all likelihood common, as the 'biography' of the kaukau has in fact shown. Since the 1930s, growers have held on to much, but not all, of their precolonial array of subsistence crops, and have shown no hesitation in adopting new ones in the post-contact period. Some of the new crops (spring onion, bean) have become common consumption items, whereas others are grown primarily for sale (potato, carrot). Certain formerly quite important crops, such as yam and taro, have faded into relative insignificance. Some reduction has also occurred in the number of cultivars of older crops, as discussed below in the case of kaukau. However, the overall picture is of a cultivation system that maintains a considerable degree of 'agrodiversity' (Brookfield 1996).

That said, cash-cropping of coffee and the large-scale commoditization of kaukau have been involved in a major change in gardening practices in a relatively short space of time. The general tendency has been towards an intensification of land use, in tandem with the continuing changes in settlement location described above. We will now look at the most important aspects of these changes.

❧ Intensity, fallows, and crop rotations

Use of the gently sloping fan surfaces, where most commercial kaukau gardens are located, has been intensified to the point that fallow periods are now

LOCALITY, LAND, AND LABOUR

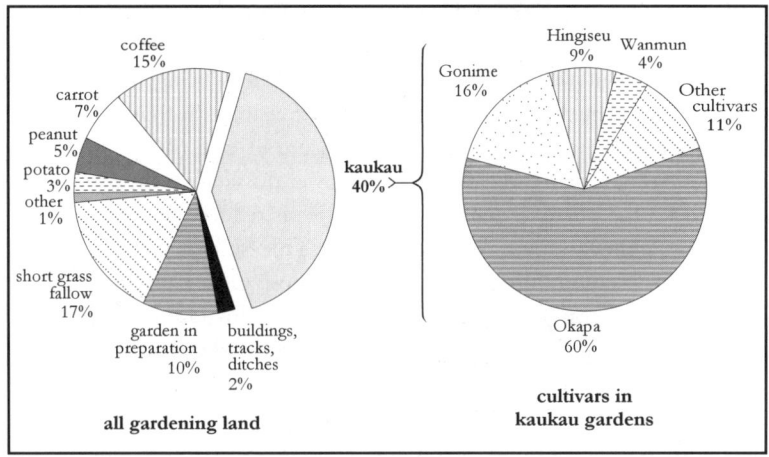

Figure 17: Land cover on the fan east of the main *hauslain* at Kasena

very short (less than a year) or non-existent on much of such land. Thus a land cover survey of the most intensively used garden land in Lunube (Map 11, see also Plate 1) carried out in June 1995 revealed that only 17 per cent of the land was under short-grass fallow at the time (Figure 17, left).[13] When a garden has been harvested, various herbaceous weeds quickly take over, but grasses need at least a year to become the main fallow vegetation. In short, gardeners in Lunube are well on the way towards making a radical change from shifting cultivation to site-stable agriculture.

No less than 40 per cent of the surveyed area was under kaukau, at various stages of its approximately 6-month cultivation cycle. However, this certainly does not imply that the cultivation system is veering towards a monoculture of kaukau. Kaukau gardens in the early stage are generally interplanted with other crops, most notably maize, but cassava may be planted on the edges of the beds, and scattered plantings of green leafy vegetables are usually present. Maize, which grows to maturity in 3–4 months, partly acts as a marker of the kaukau's stage of development, and the timing of garden maintenance. Likewise, the survey results obscure the intercropping that takes place in coffee groves. Bananas are extensively planted in many coffee gardens, but also *Xanthosoma* (or Chinese) taro and various greens. Bananas are also planted at the boundaries of landholdings, together with the traditional boundary-marking plant, *tanget* (*Cordyline fructicosa*).

Intercropping of coffee and kaukau does occur, although it is not particularly common. This is seldom done to any extent in a well-maintained coffee garden, but when a neglected coffee garden is being rehabilitated, kaukau is sometimes planted underneath the coffee trees. Such intercropping is also sometimes used as a temporary measure in case of land shortage. Gardeners recognize that the practice may lower the yield of the coffee trees unless either the planting density of the coffee is reduced or some kind of fertilizer is applied, but usually neither of these measures is taken.

Legume rotation with peanut is used almost universally to maintain soil fertility. It is common to plant kaukau two to three times in a garden, with very short 'resting' periods between main harvest and replanting, and then to plant peanut. Bean and the 'traditional' winged bean are used to a much lesser extent for the same purpose, but the latter is grown more for its eating qualities than to replenish the soil. Other crop rotations, for example potato or carrot in the wake of kaukau, are generally considered beneficial, even if these species do not have the nitrogen-fixing capacity of the legumes.

Accounts of older villagers confirm the supposition that the elimination of the fallow period in this location is for the most part a recent development. Twenty years ago there was still much left of the short-grass fallow vegetation, although gardens had been made on the *gelenda* east of Kasena village since its postwar establishment, and sporadic gardening had taken place for much longer. Today it is getting difficult to obtain *kunai* for thatching, to the extent that even that previously ubiquitous resource is metamorphosing into a commodity.

Admittedly, one reason for the scarcity of *kunai* is another ecological change, which according to local informants is quite recent. This is the establishment of *kaugras* or *maygras* (*Melinis minutiflora*) at the expense of *kunai* and *Themeda*. In April–May much of the remaining grassland of the Asaro Valley takes on the distinctive reddish hue of the flowering *kaugras*. Its Tok Pisin name translates literally as 'cow grass', which indicates an association with the cattle development projects of the 1960s and 1970s (Henty 1969: 124).[14] There are differing opinions of the desirability of *kaugras* as a fallow vegetation, but the majority of respondents did not think highly of it.

✥ *Kaukau plantings and cultivars*

One very conspicuous change following large-scale commoditization of kaukau has occurred in the balance of varieties grown. Cultivars of *Ipomoea batatas* are especially numerous in Papua New Guinea (see Chapter 6), and in the highlands a single grower has traditionally planted a large number of varieties in her gardens. Through their long occupation of their territory, gardeners in Lunube have built up an impressive stock of experiential knowledge about the cultivation of subsistence crops, not least kaukau. Taking account of soils, drainage, and climate they, as other farmers the world over, are practitioners of what van der Ploeg (1989) aptly calls *art de la localité*. In addition, new 'scientific' knowledge has become available to some extent,[15] as has 'indigenous' knowledge from other localities.

In Lunube I identified some 33 cultivars, which incidentally corresponds to an average given by Bourke (1982b: 47) in his summary of previous research findings in various locations. When mapping the extent of their planting, however, it became clear that only a handful are now grown in any quantities (Figure 17, right).

Foremost is a variety popularly called *Okapa*. This is a recent introduction to Lunube, and has probably not been grown there for more than two decades. Its name suggests an introduction from the Okapa district, but the accuracy of that is hard to ascertain. *Okapa* is considered high-yielding and not particularly fussy about soils, although it prefers well-drained sites – such as the *gelenda* flatlands with which Lunube is so well endowed.[16] What explains its present overwhelming dominance, however, is its popularity in lowland markets: *'ol i guria long baim'* ('they are really keen on buying it'), a grinning grower told me. Coastal consumers seem to be more enthusiastic about the variety than the Asaro Valley growers themselves, many of whom consider its eating qualities inferior to those of some older varieties.

Another recently introduced cultivar, *Wanmun*, enjoys a similar reputation of marketability. It has not, however, reached the same popularity as *Okapa*, partly because growers have found out that it requires quite fertile soils.[17] *Gonime* (or Konime), an old favourite of local growers and consumers, retains a substantial share. Other 'old' cultivars – *tumbuna kaukau* – are planted in much smaller quantities, mostly to provide a bit of variety for the well-honed tastebuds of the grower and the members of her family.

The shift towards marketable kaukau cultivars has thus been very definite. Other 'traditional' food crops, such as starchy bananas and taro, have undergone a somewhat similar process of simplification. Old varieties have disappeared and only a few are now cultivated extensively. Yet it would be an overstatement to conclude that a dramatic loss of varietal diversity has as yet occurred, following commoditization. While people tell stories of numerous varieties that have *ranawe pinis* (disappeared), improved communications and increased travels have made it easier for growers to obtain new cultivars

HARVESTING DEVELOPMENT

and try them out, and there are no signs that such experimentation is about to cease.

✤ Labour

We have already seen how long-distance trade of kaukau has partially altered the division of labour in marketing (Chapter 7). The same applies to some extent in gardening: traditional patterns have been partially changed. The gender division of labour in subsistence production was rather sharp in the past. When a garden was made out of fallowed land, men were responsible for cutting the fallow vegetation, whether it was short or tall grass. They also dug the drainage ditches which separate the planting beds. The grass was allowed to dry before it was burned, the burning being a task of women. Women and men sometimes cooperated in the tilling of the soil, especially in a new garden. When replanting in the same garden, women did most of the clearing and tilling.

This gender division of labour still holds for some tasks, but one should avoid drawing the boundaries too sharply. Women still do the bulk of the planting work as well as subsequent weeding and *stretim lip* (arranging the leaves so that the mounds receive sunlight, assisting in tuber development), which is done two or three times during the growing period. I did, though, see men performing these tasks also (Plate 13), which would have been un-

Plate 13: Man tending kaukau garden. Note intercropping with maize.

heard of some years ago if earlier accounts are to be believed. Women whom I asked specifically about this, stated that most men did contribute to general garden work. Finally, the harvest itself is usually done by women, although women and men often cooperate in the post-harvest handling.

For other commercial food crops, such as carrot or potato, the input of men is more marked. They prepare beds for planting, plant and weed, at least to the same extent as women. There is a slight incongruity here with the views aired by one of my interviewees, a man who stated that the planting and care of 'small things' such as peanuts or greens was best left to the women, while men took care of 'large things' such as bananas or sugarcane. Yet carrot seeds are very small things indeed, and the tending of carrot gardens subsequent to sowing is quite labour-intensive. It is, of course, the association of these new crops with entrepreneurship – with proper *bisnis* – which attracts male attention and male labour.

When large kaukau gardens are prepared and planted specifically for sale, extra-household labour is more often than not involved. If the job is not too large, the assistance of the garden owner's close female relatives is enlisted. They are not specifically remunerated, except perhaps with a generous meal at the end of the day, but can expect the favour to be returned later. For larger jobs, gangs of labourers are sometimes hired. These may be groups of male or female youths, with or without church associations, wanting to raise some money for themselves or for some collective endeavour. More frequently, the Lunube kaukau growers look to the landless Lufa migrants who reside in their midst. These are hired either for the day or for extended periods, often a fortnight. The remuneration is a modest K2–5 per day, or alternatively K20–30 per fortnight.

In fact, such use of extra-household labour is so widespread among kaukau growers that it is doubtful that the trade would have grown to its current proportions, had the migrants not been there. The three households whose gardening activities we looked at earlier in the chapter have all made use of this pool of labourers. Moroho and Nesime call on them for particular day jobs. The same can be said for Soni and Moses, although during Moses' pregnancy in 1995 they hired workers for extended periods for larger tasks.

Gumineve and Kondagule provide a particularly interesting example of the complications that sometimes arise when mobilizing labour. When I moved to Kasena late in 1994, their household was a lot larger than it later became (see Chapter 3). Lembinave, a male relative of the wife, was living

Plate 14: Tractor tilling land for kaukau.

permanently with them, providing much-needed male labour during the frequent absences of Gumineve due to Council politics. The 'sister' of Kondagule, Gahevena, was then also living with the couple, together with her five daughters. Hers was a troubled family. After her husband was killed in 1990 in the fighting with the Onguponi, disagreements between Gahevena and her firstborn son had made it impossible for her to stay in their former family house at Kalanalo. She had therefore been invited to stay in the large house of Gumineve and Kondagule, together with her daughters. The two oldest ones had in fact married, but left their violent husbands and were back in the home village, or sometimes staying with Nellynne and Rex at Aiyura, minding house and children. In any case, in 1994 this seemed to work out reasonably well for all concerned. Gahevena and her daughters worked in their patrons' large gardens, and planted a part for themselves. They carried the produce to market in Lae. In short, they were involved in the whole set of household activities.

All that was to change following an accident in late January 1995. The second-youngest of the daughters, playing in the windowless house at midday using a kerosene-filled fish tin for light, inadvertently set fire to the house. Kondagule and Gumineve lost all their household possessions, which were substantial by comparison with those of other households. So did Gahevena, but she and her daughters were squarely blamed for the incident. 'Trouble seems to follow these women,' many male villagers brooded. 'They laugh too much; the older daughters' husbands did after all get rid of them.' The women retreated to the pig house for some days, then moved out to settle with another household of relatives.

This left Kondagule and Gumineve seriously short of labour. After a while they activated another 'patron–client' relationship, this time with a young Lufa couple. The wife had worked for them before. From then on she worked for them more or less permanently, comparing herself to an adopted daughter. Sometimes she called in two other Lufa women as well, her own relatives. Monetary payments were made for their labour, albeit irregularly, depending not least on whether money was forthcoming from Nellynne and Rex, who had a large say in the overall organization of work. Importantly, the patronage was cemented by allowing the Lufa women to use a part of the garden land (Map 14). There they grew their own food, mostly kaukau, occasionally having enough surplus to sell in Goroka or even Lae.

Eventually however, when the emotional heat of the housefire incident had dissipated somewhat, Gahevena's unofficial banishment faded away. On invitation from Kondagule, she came back to help in the couple's gardens. When a kaukau garden was harvested in late May, Gahevena and the Lufa women were all there. Interestingly, the harvest proved smaller than Gumineve had anticipated, and he started to suspect that the Lufa women had stolen some of the kaukau.

The whole episode thus identifies the two most vulnerable groups in the Lunube community: (a) unmarried, widowed, or divorced women who have to depend on others for access to land resources and other necessities of daily life, and (b) the migrants. The standing of the migrant groups is tenuous indeed. Most migrants continue to have contact with their villages of origin, where they can claim access to land if they wish to return. However, this prospect does not seem particularly appealing to those who have lived for most of their lives in the much more economically 'developed' Asaro Valley. From an outsider's perspective, they are in a sense Lunube's rural proletariat, having nothing to offer but their own labour power – indispensable yet utterly marginal.

ᨠ *Material and mechanical inputs*

Food crop gardeners have not taken to the use of chemical inputs in any significant way. Exceptions are found among some of the larger kaukau growers, who do use chemical herbicides instead of weeding by hand, and in the cultivation of some 'introduced' vegetables which require fertilizer or other chemical inputs. Carrot is generally grown without the use of fertilizer, whereas potato growers commonly use chicken manure from various small chicken projects which have now become a common feature of the village economy.

Mechanization of soil tillage, which was also initiated during the period, has not been sustained. Tractors are few and far between. In Lunube only one tractor is operational (Plate 14), and that one is greatly underutilized. Its owner uses it for rotavating[18] and harrowing his own gardens, as well as his next-of-kin's (without payment, except a contribution for fuel), but others are dissuaded by the hefty K50 fee which he demands for a day's work.

The story is similar for other areas. Technology has not caught on in the same way as some expatriate observers in the 1960s and 1970s anticipated. It still has a hold though on the imagination of the 'progressive': in the early 1990s the Eastern Highlands Provincial Government attempted to come to the rescue by buying tractors and entrusting them to the care of the various members of the Provincial Assembly. One such is located at Asaro, intended to serve the Lower Asaro constituency, which includes Lunube. Growers can hire it and its driver – one of the politician's own security guards – for K30 minimum. Very few do so. Not only is the fee a deterrent, but so is the association with highly factionalized provincial politics. Cheap labour of locals and migrants is more attractive.

One altogether more successful technical innovation is fence nets in order to keep the pigs out of the gardens. 'Traditional', bush-material fences are virtually absent in Lunube, but these are common in many other parts of the highlands.[19] As we saw in Chapter 6, this innovation was pushed during the rural development efforts of the 1970s, when Fred Leahy, for example, supplied his young clients with fence nets for their projects. Its adoption has had substantial labour-saving effects, albeit in a highly gendered way, as men are wholly responsible for fencing work.

QUESTIONS OF SUSTAINABILITY

The picture emerging of local processes of production in the economy of Lunube is one of considerable vibrancy. Here we have a busy place indeed. We must now ask whether the continuation of these processes, let alone their intensification, can be sustained in the long run. An examination of sustainability has to start with the sheer numbers of human population.

✤ Population pressure

Bourke et al. (1994b) estimated the population density in the most intensive agricultural system in the Eastern Highlands Province, which included most of the Lunube area, as 157 persons per sq km. It should be noted that the figure is based on the 1980 census, and a corresponding figure for the mid-1990s would be substantially higher. Moreover, as the calculations are based on mapping on the scale of 1:500,000, they include of necessity a fair amount of generalization, and ample scope remains for local variation. Yet this gives a good indication of the population density relative to other areas in the country. According to the LMP database, the area has the highest density found in any agricultural system on the mainland of Papua New Guinea, although parts of other highlands provinces come close. Higher densities are only found on a few small offshore islands.

My own calculation of population density in Lunube, using a fairly generous definition of land used for agriculture (including much of the foothills which are not much gardened now), indicates an overall population density in the vicinity of 200 persons/sq km (Table 9). The figure for the Gamizuho of Kasena, who have practically all their gardens in the valley bottom, is higher still, or just over 300 persons per sq km, which is extremely high by Papua New Guinea standards.[20]

It is obvious, from these numbers and from the previous discussion of settlement expansion, that the increase in population over the past few decades has been substantial. But how fast is the population growing? The best estimates available are from the Papua New Guinea Institute of Medical Research in Goroka, which during the 1980s undertook a detailed survey of a sample of the Asaro Valley population (Coakley et al. 1993). The region as a whole had a natural population increase of 2.1 per cent per annum, but a substantial urban–rural divide was evident, with the urban population of Goroka growing much faster by virtue of high birth rates and low death rates. By contrast, the rural population of the Upper Asaro (where one Lunube clan was included) had lower birth rates and higher death rates, resulting in natural increase of 'only' 1.63 per cent (see Table 10 below). While much lower than the national average according to the 1990 census figures, this is still considerable growth, reflecting a population doubling time of just over 40 years.

Hence, concurrent with the changes in settlement location and the advent of two different forms of cash cropping on top of subsistence production, population increase has played a major role in the recent land-use changes

Table 10: Population, land, and basic demographic parameters

a. Gamizuho and others residing on Kasena land (1995)*	
Area of settlements, coffee, food gardening and fallow land	2.4 km²
Population according to fieldwork survey	731
Population density	305 persons/ km²
b. All Lunube clans and settlements (1995)	
Area of settlements, coffee, food gardening, and fallow land	14.8 km²
Population projected from 1990 Census†	2,755
Population density	186 persons/ km²
c. Asaro Census Division (1980s):	
Crude birth rate	29
Crude death rate	13
Natural increase	1.63%
Infant mortality rate	94

Notes: (*) The Gamizuho clan resides in two separate areas, centred on the villages of Kasena and Nahoma, respectively (see Map 3). I enumerated the total population of the Kasena-Gamizuho plus others (migrants) residing on their land. The land effectively used by this population was delimited on an aerial photograph. The Nahoma-Gamizuho are not included.

(†) Calculated by taking the census figures for all Lunube clans in 1990 and projecting to 1995, assuming a growth rate of 1.63 per cent p.a. (see below). Note the comments in footnote 8, regarding the reliability of the 1990 census in Eastern Highlands Province.

Sources: Fieldwork; NSO (n.d.); Coakley *et al.* (1993).

in the Upper Asaro, where intensification is leading to site-stable cultivation. An important question is whether these fertile, albeit limited areas of good agricultural land are showing any signs of strain, and if not, for how long the soils can withstand the continually increasing pressure.

❧ Environment: intensification and land degradation

During the fieldwork period yields from several kaukau gardens were estimated roughly as these were being harvested for sale, by counting the number of kaukau bags and multiplying by the average bag weight, and pacing the garden for size. The outcome was an average yield of 13.8 t/ha. Compared with previous research results (summarized in Bourke 1985: 99), this is similar to many other highland locations. Although considerably higher yields have been noted, much lower figures are also reported from the highlands.

In fact, since my figure is based on the first and main harvest only, the 'true yield' over the span of a full year of progressive harvesting is likely to be substantially higher. The first harvest is done six months after planting. Marketable tubers are then dug up, but smaller ones are left to develop further. These are then either gradually harvested for consumption at home, or a complete secondary harvest is undertaken approximately two months after the first one. The second harvest also yields a marketable quantity, albeit much smaller than the first. Finally, upon replanting the garden, all the remaining tubers are collected and used for human food or pig feed.

These limited data do not, therefore, provide any stark evidence of soil exhaustion, in spite of fallows having been all but eliminated. When questioning growers themselves about the fertility of their soils and whether they had noticed a change, mixed answers were received. Some did not consider soil exhaustion a critical issue. Others were definitely concerned, and pointed to pockets of land close to the main Kasena *hauslain* (parts of the area for which the land use is shown in Figure 17), which have been particularly intensively cultivated for as much as 20 years. In fact, this may play a part in the popularity of *Okapa* kaukau. It was stated that this cultivar yielded relatively well in 'old' gardens, compared with varieties such as *Wanmun* or *Hagen*, which were best planted in a garden just out of fallow.

Nesime, for example, had noticed some loss of yields in the western half of the garden (beds west of the track, see Map 14), which have been under more or less continuous cultivation for at least 25 years. The eastern part, says Nesime, is still very fertile, but she realizes the strain put on the soil with such intensive use, and tries to rest different parts of the whole garden for a year or two occasionally.

Similar concerns are evident elsewhere in the densely populated valley. Lukas Kifilo of Kofena told me, for example: *'Graun em lapun, olpela. Olpela tru.'* ('The soil is old, worn out. Really worn out.') He also commented that, in the more hilly Kofena territory, erosion was becoming a problem. During the rainy season the fertile black soil was being washed down from exposed gardens.

Legume rotation had long been practised to some extent using the traditional winged bean (*Psophocarpus tetragonolobus*), but peanut was widely adopted as a rotation crop with kaukau in the 1950s, when the valley bottom had become the main area of gardening. Its use is now almost universal, and it has undoubtedly helped in preventing the system to lapse into unsustainability.

The technique of composting, which has been used in the western parts of the central highlands to great effect (see e.g. Waddell 1972; Wohlt 1978; Sillitoe 1996), has not caught on in the Asaro, although I did talk to one grower who did practise it. He had learnt the method as a farmer trainee, and had incorporated it into his otherwise typical Asaro cultivation methods. Composting is a labour-intensive process, however, and this works against its popular adoption.

Although an ecological breaking point has thus not been reached, many local people are aware of the imminent dangers of continuing population increase concurrent with expanded market gardening. But they point to a buffer that still exists. This consists of the foothills which their parents or grandparents abandoned some 50 years ago. The old garden sites are now mostly overgrown with tall cane grass and woody regrowth, but a handful of older people continued to live and make their gardens up on the mountain after the bulk of the population moved downwards. Many 'lowlanders' have also maintained their pig houses on the old clan grounds. Talk is now frequently heard about taking the hillsides into cultivation on a large scale once more. Some new gardens are already being made. Yet this buffer is also of limited extent and, under prevailing technology, the land requires more frequent and longer fallowing in order to maintain fertility and prevent erosion than the more auspicious valley bottom. Environmental sustainability of gardening in both these agro-ecological zones could be threatened in the long run, unless radical innovations are put in place.

❧ *Society: land disputes and individualization*

Another question regarding continued intensification of land use relates to the capacity of the social system to maintain order, or conversely, prevent disintegration. Even a large-scale recultivation of the previously abandoned foothills and mountainsides can hardly be a solution for the long term. The marginal location of such land, in a monetized economy based increasingly on commodity production and easy access to transportation, means that it is doubtful whether young people, who are establishing households on their own, would be content with it. In all likelihood, tussles over land on the densely settled flats will increase, but such contests are already an endemic feature of life in the Lunube villages (see Vignette 7).

The two main cash crops, coffee and kaukau, relate differently to land tenure, in part because of a differing sense of permanence of the crops. There has long been considerable flexibility in the allocation of land for

Vignette 7: *'Ol i no wanbel'* ('They have not reached agreement')

The task of Amoko Auwo is not an easy one. Since 1964 he has been the *kiap bilong graun* in Lunube – the government-appointed land mediator. Whenever there is a dispute over ownership or use of land, which happens not infrequently, his advice is sought. Unfortunately, his records were not complete enough to enable me to assess whether land disputes and/or land sales have increased in frequency or severity during the recent decade or two. However, in 1990, for which the data are fairly reliable, Amoko held nearly 70 mediation meetings in Lunube. Because of his skills at resolving land conflicts, he is also sometimes called upon to sort out troubles far away from Lunube.

Often the disputes arise because someone has started to make a garden on fallowed and unfenced land to which someone else has a claim. Amoko listens to both sides of the story, and endeavours to find out who has a stronger historical link to the plot. Sometimes it is difficult to ascertain ownership, and he ends up dividing the plot between the claimants and planting *tanget* on the new borders. If there is a genuine case of intrusion, the offender either returns the land, or is allowed to continue using it after paying a fine to the rightful owner. Amoko registers the incidents in his small notebook, or on a piece of paper which he keeps in the book. Most often the ink is blue. He records the date, place, names of those involved, and then adds a tersely worded comment about the outcome of the case:

17 AUGUST 1992
PLES: GETEYA
BUNDI GIMISEVE VS. MOTE SINEKOMITI
GIVIM LONG BG NA OL I WANBEL.
(MS hands land over to BG and the two have reached agreement).

But sometimes things are not so smooth:

OL I NO WANBEL. BAI HARIM GEN BIHAIN.
(They have not reached agreement. Will hold another meeting later.)

If no agreement is reached after six attempts at mediation, the case is referred to the Land Court in Goroka. There is also the occasional incident involving physical violence, which has warranted the use of *red* ink:

I BIN PAIT LONG GRAUN. OL I NO WANBEL.
(They have fought over the land. They have not reached agreement.)

Amoko has also facilitated many peaceful transactions which are, to all intents and purposes, private sales of land. The buyers are mostly the larger coffee growers, who are enlarging or consolidating their holdings; the sellers often older men with few sons to pass on their lands to. The land mediator then works out a price according to a valuation provided by his superiors. For a coffee bush of average quality the buyer pays K4, for a badly maintained plant K3, but up to K12 for an exceptionally vigorous one.

food gardens. While leading *bigmen* were considered the 'owners' of most land, usufruct rights to land for cropping could be activated by relatives or others in need, without jeopardizing the 'ownership'. Coffee, being a perennial tree crop which needs continual care, introduced a certain fixity into the system. It has played a part in the relocation of many family compounds from the main *hauslains* out to plots owned by the household head, which may be seen as a symptom of individualization of land tenure. Ownership of economic trees had long been on an individual basis, but in the precolonial economy such trees were largely limited to the pandanus species, *karuka* and *marita*. The difference may explain why disputes over coffee land are viewed altogether more seriously than those over food gardening land.

The whole issue of privatization is highly ironic. In the national context, numerous outside observers and consultants have for a long time seen the continuance of 'customary' land ownership as an impediment to the mobilization of land for development (Shand 1966: 101; AIDAB 1993: 106–107; Economic Insights Pty Ltd 1994: 45). However, any real or perceived move by the state to further the individualization of landholding has invariably met with strong popular resistance.[21] When individuals or companies *have* obtained legal titles to land through available avenues of tenure conversion (as for example in the case of some large coffee growers and plantations), village people have often made it abundantly clear that they do not consider 'traditional' clan rights thus rendered null and void (see Zorn 1992). There are few coffee plantations in the Asaro Valley, for instance, that are not subject to some dispute over land ownership. The state has proved incapable of providing security for 'legal' owners. In contrast with this, local pragmatism has allowed for *de facto*, if not *de jure*, privatisation of land.[22] A blanket legislative approach would be doomed to failure, as the very legitimacy of the state to intervene in these matters is contested.[23]

The problem of land is not easily solved. It is unrealistic to presume that current fragmentation into ever smaller family plots can continue *ad infinitum*, or to expect that the problems will continue to be solved in the manner described above. The demands placed upon these plots are heavy. They must furnish not only subsistence food for the occupants, but also for their pigs, which remain central to the social universe of the Lunube. The land is also the source of cash, used to fulfil the modest everyday consumption needs of villagers, as well as to maintain and amplify the circulation of gifts.

CONCLUSION

Circumstances in Kasena village, and Lunube as a whole, provide an insight into the many parallel processes set in train by the commoditization of rural society, but they also point to the place-specific nature of the outcomes of these processes. The advent of colonial rule and the world economy radically changed the premises of settlement and of land use. New villages came into being, which were seen as models for 'development', although subsequent reorganization suggests that the model has not been universally successful. Most importantly, the people got firmly hooked on capitalism and 'the market' with the help of coffee. The emergence of the urban kaukau market has added a new dimension to their market participation, and has led to considerable intensification of production.

But the area also differs from many other rural societies in developing countries. Lunube people have in fact done rather well in the last 50 years or so. In a sense, they have much more power over their own lives than peasants in some other countries or even other Papua New Guineans. They have several possibilities for earning income, and pursue these possibilities with considerable enthusiasm. They are free to dispose of their income as they see fit, instead of being subjected to heavy rents or taxes by landlords or the state. Importantly, their subsistence production has not been decimated through the process of commoditization. Theirs is still a diverse and seemingly robust agricultural system, where the knowledge about crops and environments accumulated by previous generations continues to have a place.

Yet there is reason for some concern regarding the long-term sustainability of the current regime of production. Gardening of the intensity I observed in 1994–95 has only been undertaken for perhaps 20 years in the pockets of land where intensification first took place. Now most of the flat, accessible, and easily worked valley bottom is under more or less steady cultivation, with long fallowing of plots becoming rare. The pressure will increase markedly in the next decade or so, and the outcome in environmental terms remains to be seen.

The issue of social sustainability is no less important. It relates to the link between people and environment, and touches the very heart of Lunube social organization and social order. Commoditization of land and individualization of tenure is already happening, although the market so created functions through semi-customary institutional arrangements, rather than fully-fledged individual titles formally backed by legislation and power of the state. Once again, we have ended up with a 'real market' with its own specific features.

NOTES

1 The Papua New Guinea Resource Information System (PNGRIS) contains much information on the physical environment, which has been used to some extent in the description that follows. The delineation of Resource Mapping Units (RMUs), which are the central analytical units of the system, was, however, done at the scale of 1:500,000, which is too coarse for detailed local information.

2 Dano: *gelenda*. See Dano–English glossary in Appendix 1b for more local terms for land forms and soils, and Appendix 2 for a list of botanical terms.

3 Possibly dystrandepts – moderately weathered ash soils with thick black topsoils – according to PNGRIS.

4 Only four of these remained with Gimbe and had children with him.

5 See p. 159, regarding one man's use of female labour for market gardening. Gimbe, however, was man of tradition, and did not himself make a leap wholeheartedly into the market economy – although he planted coffee in the 1950s.

6 To the eyes of Fred Leahy, who came to the area in the early 1960s (see Chapter 6), most land in the valley bottom was 'empty' well into the 60s (Fred Leahy, interview 20 June 1995, Banz).

7 The Asaro LGC was established in the early 1960s, and extended in the mid-1960s to include the Watabung region.

8 Good (1986: 59–64) interprets this (and many similar incidents) as evidence of popular revolt against an emergent class of rural capitalists. The Lunube themselves stress that they saw the 'foreign' (i.e. extra-tribal) control of the plantation as the main problem, not accumulation as such.

9 The final step in processing of the coffee bean before roasting it. The parchment and 'silverskin' surrounding the bean is removed. Most Papua New Guinean coffee is exported as green bean.

10 This is a multipurpose chemical: I was told that Gramoxone was sometimes used to poison arrowtips in times of fighting.

11 In fact, Overfield's Bena Bena study showed that women's overall contribution to coffee work was substantially higher than men's (Overfield 1995).

12 Howlett (1962: 208) reports no fewer than 2.8 pigs per person in Makiroka village (close to Goroka), which seems exceptionally high, but her figure for Fondiwe'i village (west of Lunube) is 1.0.

13 Bourke *et al.* use the term 'short fallow' for periods of less than one year between harvest and replanting, but 'short grass' fallow vegetation in their classification refers to the clearing of grasses less than 1.5 m in height after a 'long fallow', i.e. a fallow period of more than one year.

14 The upper Asaro never had many of these projects, which were more numerous in the less densely-settled grasslands towards the east of Goroka and around Kainantu. *Melinis minutiflora*, or 'molasses grass' (Henty 1969: 124) is very widespread in the Kainantu area.

15 However, arguments of agricultural scientists and extension workers for growing certain varieties have fallen on deaf ears, to the extent that during my fieldwork period the Highlands Agricultural Experiment Station at Aiyura was planning to do a survey in order to find out why 'scientific knowledge' had not been successful in the never-ending varietal selection process (Robert Lutulele, pers. comm., 2 February 1995).

16 I should mention that people in the Lufa District explained to me that they were unable to participate in the kaukau marketing boom to the same extent as the Asaro people, as the varieties that sold best on the coast did not grow well in their more mountainous environment.

17 The survey summarized in Figure 17 was done on the most intensively cultivated piece of land in Kasena (Map 11). Based on a visual assessment, *Wanmun* plantings are proportionally larger in other gardening areas, where long fallows (>1 year) are still used.

18 I was surprised to find such an expensive piece of machinery as this not-so-old rotavator attached to a rather tired-looking tractor. It turned out that the rotavator had been 'left behind' by the Salvation Army when it abandoned its school and farm at Omborda following the fighting between the Gamizuho and the Onguponi over its land.

19 And in the 'bushier' parts of the upper Asaro Valley, such as Keremu–Anengu to the north of Lunube.

20 Similar densities were found in parts of Simbu Province more than two decades ago (Howlett et al. 1977: 24), in a much less favourable environment. The Simbu have long migrated to towns and other provinces in large numbers, whereas outmigration from the Asaro Valley is not nearly as great. Indeed, many Simbu have settled in the Asaro.

21 In 1995 there was widespread unrest in the country, not least in the highlands provinces, over a World Bank proposal to register all customary land, as part of the Bank's Structural Adjustment Programme for Papua New Guinea. This was seen as the first step towards the privatization of land ownership.

22 Somewhat similar processes are reported from other Pacific Islands in a volume edited by Ward and Kingdon (1995).

23 An intriguing example of the limited capacity of state powers in matters of land is provided by one of its own institutions, the village court. A small but sturdy weatherboard house was erected in the mid-1970s for the village court in Lunube, in what was then the Aporota *hauslain*. The owner of the plot on which it was built has long since taken it back, dissatisfied with the state's unwillingness to pay him compensation beyond that originally agreed upon.

9

Harvesting development through the market? Actors, theory, and practice

> The two extremes, local and global, are much less interesting than the intermediary arrangements that we are calling networks ... The words 'local' and 'global' offer points of view on networks that are by nature neither local nor global, but are more or less long and more or less connected (Latour 1993: 122).

THE CONSTRUCTION OF EMBEDDED MARKETS

MARKETS ARE PERVASIVE ECONOMIC INSTITUTIONS in people's lives the world over, as commoditization has reached almost every corner of the globe. More than half a century ago, Polanyi suggested that this process amounted to a 'great transformation', through which economic life became 'disembedded' from the social. Yet, as Granovetter suggests, such a divorce is forever an unfinished project:

> [E]conomic institutions do not emerge automatically in response to economic needs. Rather, they are constructed by individuals whose action is both facilitated and constrained by the structure and resources available in the social networks in which they are embedded (Granovetter 1991: 78).

In short, *all* markets are 'embedded'. This apparently simple announcement opens up a rich tapestry of local diversity which begs investigation, and which also has practical implications. An investigation of markets and commoditization can be undertaken in a variety of ways: indeed, a tale such as that of an embedded market will never be adequately told from a singular 'Archimedean' vantage point.

At the beginning of this book it was argued that a universalist approach was not helpful for understanding actually existing markets, be it the universalism of modernization theory and neoclassical orthodoxy, which takes 'the market' more or less as a given, or the universalism of Marxist political economy, which overemphasizes economic determination and class. Instead, a close look at *social agency* in the creation of markets was advocated, taking into account the changing meanings accorded to things being exchanged, the perpetual contests of power, and the braiding of social networks, which feature in the process.

Such a 'social constructivist' position has informed this study of rural transformation in Papua New Guinea. In the preceding chapters I traced the emergence and characteristics of several types of fresh food markets, in which the people of the Asaro Valley have energetically participated in recent years. The micro-situations encountered in daily life were highlighted, in order to reveal the 'emergent' quality of the fledgling market structures. Reference was also made to supra-local connections and processes. A national picture was presented of the milieu under which food marketing operates, and emphasis placed on the construction of social networks, which extend well beyond village and region.

Where does this leave us, then, in terms of an understanding of the processes of market integration and rural transformation? Does the emphasis on social agency point the way to better theorization of markets? In this regard, the issue of scale – spatial and social – is central.

ON ACTORS, STRUCTURES, AND NETWORKS

Social theory has long oscillated between two poles, accentuating either local particularism or global universalities. Drawn-out wars have been waged over whether to assign explanatory privilege to agency or structure (Gregory 1994b). This has been reflected in thinking about development. There was a time in rural development studies when explanations were sought in the macro-structures of the capitalist world economy. Local specificities were all but forgotten. Poststructural/postmodern writings have lately tipped the balance quite markedly towards agency, variability, transformation, and change, rather than the seeming solidity of structure. Development theorists and practitioners – with geographers, anthropologists, and rural sociologists among the most prominent voices in that cacophonic choir – have been busily 'rediscovering diversity' (Booth 1992: 4–12) at various scales, but not least locally.

The distance – if not downright hostility (see Brass 1995) – between those who privilege agency *vis-à-vis* structure, or between the local and global poles of enquiry, is unfortunate to put it mildly. An appreciation of micro-level diversity should not lead to an abandonment of concern with patterns and processes occurring on a larger scale, and vice versa. In fact, these different perspectives complement each other. Globalization of economic activity is all too obvious, but it is given meaning through human experience, which always remains local. And global economic forces are hardly ever experienced locally in a passive manner: they are frequently resisted, subverted, or coopted, according to locally defined agendas. Local actors are knowledgeable about their own social situation, and capable of influencing the course of events, albeit to a differing degree. This is the gist of the actor-oriented approach which was outlined in Chapter 2 and referred to in subsequent interpretation.

Many examples are found, on the pages of this book, of such struggles and disjunctures of meaning. The Gamizuho and their neighbours have embraced 'the market' but they have done so on their own terms. They have created their own 'real' and thoroughly embedded markets, which are not solely economic, but also no less social. Their makers use the markets to assert their individuality and social standing, to test the limits of their power, and to make statements about their own place in the world.

The wholesale depots of Goroka and vicinity aptly illustrate this point. These are precarious institutions, despite a long-standing official effort to secure their place in the national food market against the spectre of global competition. Much of their instability results from the disjunctures of power evident in their everyday operation. The produce growers have a feeling that their efforts are not reflected in the prices they receive, and are resentful of the subordinate position in which they find themselves when entering the depot. And most do have other alternatives. The commercial growing of vegetables is but one of many options open, and often there are other projects to take up if market gardening does not bring the intended results. If nothing works, no great harm is done. One did at least try.

By contrast, the open marketplaces, rural and urban, are locales of greater importance to the rural producers-cum-sellers, who have themselves negotiated their character and meaning as more powerful, knowledgeable actors. These are not merely places to buy and sell; they are inextricably embedded in social life in general, as meeting places of a highly heterogeneous population. Almost all food crops are sold by women in the local markets, which are therefore important loci of a gender struggle in a patriarchal society.

HARVESTING DEVELOPMENT THROUGH THE MARKET?

The marketing of highlands kaukau in the coastal towns, which received most attention in the study, is the most recent and in many ways the most thoroughly homespun addition to the cash-earning repertoire of the people of the Asaro Valley. As with other types of markets, participation in the long-distance kaukau trade is meaningful not only in the economic sense for the Gamizuho and their neighbours. It also carries meanings of movement, of personal achievement, and of being in touch with relatives and with an exciting urban world. It furnishes a 'space to manoeuvre', which they relish, although the structuring of the market around producer-sellers and their reluctance to delegate the retail sales to other intermediaries sets limits to economic efficiency.

It has been charged that, when translated into empirical study, the theoretical prominence given to social actors in this approach leads *de facto* to a lack of attention to the structural context of action – in other words, it is seen as coming perilously close to voluntarism. This is linked to the fact that actor studies tend to be 'micro' in both the social and spatial sense, dealing with face-to-face interaction in a particular locality and thus running the risk of ethnographic particularism. It has been argued that even if (and perhaps precisely *because*) the concept of *space-for-manoeuvre* (and how this space is constructed by actors) lies at the centre of the actor argument, attention must be paid to constraints upon action, that emerge at the regional or national level, and/or over longer periods of time (Booth 1994a: 17–18). Political economic analysis must therefore be reconstructed, according to this view, but in a form shorn of its previous essentialist heavy-handedness.

For this purpose, new theoretical directions and concepts have been advocated in recent years by several scholars dealing with rural transformation (see the volumes edited by Schuurman (1993) and Booth (1994b). In particular, the regulation theory first formulated by French political economists has translated into new approaches in political economy, for looking at the integration of agricultural producers with the nation state and global markets, using concepts such as 'food regimes' or 'agro-food complexes' (Friedmann and McMichael 1989; McMichael 1994). The way forward for the politico-economic analysis of agrarian development is posited as being via a comparative study of the historical trajectories of such regimes, at the national and supra-national scale (Buttel and McMichael 1994; Mouzelis 1994).

I have reservations about the 'food regime' approach, and about regulation theory in general, for several reasons. The stress on 'modes of social regulation' as a way of securing the reproduction of the capitalist system contains definite echoes of macrostructural and functionalist political economy (Martin 1994: 32). Accordingly, these approaches are more inclined to emphasize the importance of state power, of legislatory frameworks, and of global markets, instead of agency.[1] In many contexts, these need not be the most important aspects to look at if we want to understand processes of market integration and their outcomes. In Papua New Guinea it is true that the state has a long history of involvement in the creation of markets. The institutional form which these markets have taken, however, owes much more to local actors than to structures put in place by the state. In this particular context at least, an emphasis on actors makes much more sense for understanding the workings of markets. In short, we are still stuck with approaches that cling to quite different social and spatial scales of analysis, lend themselves better to use in some contexts than others, and that remain largely unconnected.

It may sound absurd to suggest that the fresh produce sellers from Lunube can teach us anything much about other, global, and seemingly infinitely more complex, market systems. Yet the extremes of the rural marketplace and the global commodity market are both in the last instance created by face-to-face interactions (Schrader 1996: 18). This is not to say that the biggest of pictures can be understood fully by analysing only such microtransactions and aggregating them,[2] but it alerts us to the flux – the 'emergent' quality – which is inherent in all market structures (Long 1989a: 228; Long and van der Ploeg 1994: 81). Such structures are made, and continually changed, by market actors. They all consist of networks of interactions, although some are a lot longer than others, and some are altogether less stable than others.

And here again we discern traces of actor-network theory, which was briefly introduced in Chapter 2. It involves 'following a commodity' (Busch and Juska 1997) or thing through its twisted route in time and space, noting at every turn which persons, institutions, or other things influence its trajectory, and how these actors define one another through their interactions. As a metaphor, 'network' differs from 'structure' in that nothing is guaranteed; its links and nodes are not given at the outset, but negotiated through a process of translation:

> (I)nstead of starting from universal laws – social or natural – and to take local contingencies as so many queer particularities that should be either eliminated or protected, [actor-network theory] starts from irreducible, incommensurable, unconnected localities, which then, at a great price, sometimes end into provisionally commensurable connections (Latour 1997).

HARVESTING DEVELOPMENT THROUGH THE MARKET?

Making connections is what the people of Lunube are doing all the time, and indeed these connections are made at a great price. 'Translation', in the social and cultural context which is Papua New Guinea, is fraught with difficulties. Some of these difficulties stem from the sheer physical geography of the country. Others derive from a weak state, which has not been able to maintain, let alone extend, a fairly rudimentary infrastructure, or guarantee its citizens that they can move about securely. Others still have to do with cultural and social features, firmly sedimented in the *habitus* of the highlander sellers, such as a pervasive lack of trust. It takes considerable ingenuity to overcome these difficulties.

The stories told in the preceding chapters show ample evidence of such ingenuity. A successful kaukau trader has to enlist in his or her project the power of other family members and fellow villagers, both to secure access to land, and, in the literal sense, their muscle power; of large brown hessian bags originally made for copra; of trucks with diesel engines which smoke ominously when ascending the hills; of drivers, and *buai* to keep them driving; of *wantoks* in town; of world-weary 2-kina notes, to name only a few entities in this network. And this works, somehow, for the time being. These stories have also, however, shown the limitations and the instability of the market networks so created.

What is exciting about actor-network theory is that it offers a much more relaxed set of concepts to work with than have previous approaches. One of the roles of 'theory', and not the least significant one, should in my view be to generate new ways of telling real-world stories, and here it does rather well. Bruno Latour, for instance, proposes a new, and delightfully earthy, set of metaphors to replace the ones that social scientists have long been so fond of:

> [S]ocieties cannot be described without recognizing them as having a fibrous, thread-like, wiry, stringy, ropy, capillary character that is never captured by the notions of levels, layers, territories, spheres, categories, structure, systems (Latour 1997).

Perhaps I should add 'tuberous' to his list?

ON THEORY, PRACTICE, AND ELEPHANTS

Still I have made precious few direct suggestions as to how the volatile market structures which are in the making in Papua New Guinea might be made more durable, robust, and beneficial to those people, both rural and urban, who increasingly depend on them. I am, after all, uneasy about the arrogant assumption of an exclusive access to (one-dimensional) truth, which tends to lurk in prescriptive advice. During fieldwork I dreaded the inevitable questions by food growers, agricultural specialists, or town planners, about *what should be done*. The people of the developing world have seen many a stranger arrive on their scene with a grandiose proclamation as to what is to be done to improve their lives; many an immaculately conceived theory to be put to the test. Yet the results have been chequered, to say the least, and there is now in both academic circles and in society at large a profound disillusionment, it seems, about the possibilities of turning development theory into practice. The very ideas of 'development' and 'progress', on which the whole enterprise rests, have been severely punctured of late (Sachs 1992; Latouche 1993; Escobar 1995; Rahnema and Bawtree 1997).

I have considerable sympathy with the postmodern critics of the development project. I find it not difficult to agree with the charge that much development activity is governed by hard-nosed donor interest rather than altruistic motives,[3] and that the hordes of consultants which keep the 'development tourism' industry going are, at least to some extent, seeking their own instant gratification rather than lasting betterment of the lot of the poor and disadvantaged.[4]

That notwithstanding, I have to stick my neck out and say that I am intensely uncomfortable with abandoning the notion of progress, for several reasons. Postmodern social science, if taken to an extreme, results in a 'careless espousal of relativistic and nihilistic positions' and 'the critique of a prioristic notions of progress' is frequently extended 'to cover all general enquiries about progress' (Booth 1992: 16; see also Kiely 1999). In addition, the notion of progress is of course firmly ingrained in my own cultural baggage. This is something that I am well aware of, which I could not and would not wish to escape from. Nonetheless, I remain deeply suspicious of the one-dimensional economism which continues to dominate much Western development discourse. Finally, my hesitancy about joining the anti-development chorus is caused by my experience of the lifeworld of the Lunube people. I do not think that my good friends in Kasena would be impressed if I told them that they should instantly forget their own visions of the future as something better and brighter than the present. That their own expectations are sometimes inflated well beyond any real and immediate possibilities, given the state of their country (not least, the state of the State) and its place in the world, is quite another matter. That their ideas of the meaning of 'development' and 'progress' may well be different from my own (see Dahl and Rabo 1992) is also another matter.

So we are stuck with this compelling yet slippery idea, and thus with development practice. I find myself in agreement with Michael Edwards, when he states that a separation between theory and practice 'can lead only to research which is irrelevant and practice which is deficient' (1994: 289). The merit of an actor-oriented or actor-network approach to the study of development should be judged in no small part by whether it can point the way to better practice. This is manifestly not to say that its proponents should be expected to produce yet another ready-made, fill-in-the-blanks form for development 'projects', designed to enable the technicians of intervention to rein in the unruly social reality of the world outside. Rather, I argue that such an approach has the potential to make practice more responsive to local environments, social processes, power structures, and cultural specificities, by refusing to privilege either the universal and purely economic model of the market, or the teleology which attributes just about anything that happens anywhere to the despotism of global capitalism. An actor-oriented or actor-network approach has a significant voice to contribute to the 'multivocality' (Martin 1994) which is so vital to development studies and development practice.

A genuine attention to the practical implications of local diversity entails that we 'allow actors to *teach us* the causes of the success or failure' (Murdoch 1995: 753, original emphasis), without fixing these causes at the outset in a grand theory of some kind. Some networks are more stable than others, and only by 'following the network ... builders in action' (Murdoch 1995: 753) can we start to appreciate how stability gets created or how chaos takes over. And here the Lunube actors may have something to teach project planners and practitioners.

The establishment of institutional conditions in support of formal wholesale trading in vegetables and fruit in Papua New Guinea has been a popular problem for development agencies to tackle. Unfortunately, an *a priori* assumption of a clear-cut separation between 'commercial' and 'subsistence' growers seems to have characterized much previous policy and planning work, which has directed extension activities and other development efforts.[5] Contrary to this assumption, building a socially and economically sustainable formal marketing chain in this context depends on recognizing the close linkages between the demands of subsistence and commodity production, and the interlocking of productive activities *in toto* with the social and cultural constructions of what constitutes meaningful agency. Instead of aiming forever at 'the commercial farmer', development policy and projects to do with wholesale trading must find a way of constructing this market in such a way that small and/or erratic suppliers have a place. This would mean trying to narrow the knowledge/power gap between traders and growers, and making the depot a less intimidating place for the latter.

The marketplaces have received less official attention, at least in recent years, except as sources of revenue. In Goroka, considerable sums of money are collected from sellers in the form of gate fees. Very little seems to be reinvested in maintaining, let alone in upgrading, the market facilities. Considerable scope exists for improvement in this regard, but there is little point in conjuring up plans and rules and physical infrastructure if it is done from the top down. The end-users – buyers as well as sellers – have repeatedly shown their capacity for subverting agendas from the outside, however well-intentioned these may be. The participation of women, in particular, is essential if such plans are to have any meaning at all.

While the long-distance kaukau market seems to have become firmly established, and it now contributes substantially to rural incomes in the Asaro Valley, it is not by any means 'perfect'. Price information is limited, it travels rather badly from, say, Port Moresby to Kasena, and accurate price comparisons are next to impossible for the growers. The practice of kaukau growers themselves to travel to the market in order to sell their produce adds substantially to transportation costs. Growers increasingly realize the limitations of their enterprise, but whether specialized traders will establish themselves to greater extent than at present is unclear. Smoothing the 'translation' process in this network would require a long-term, patient approach. It would entail mundane things like making sure that roads are passable; that telephones are accessible and in working order; that money can be transferred from one place to another without excessive difficulties; that places are found where tired travellers can stay overnight without having to rely on *wantoks*. Nothing particularly heroic and large-scale here, but this is, I think, what the network builders in this particular case are trying to teach us.

. . .

It was in June 1997. Finally, long after leaving the fields of the Upper Asaro for the libraries of Canberra, I unearthed something that could have relieved some of my anxieties during fieldwork. A slim volume, recently published by a respected international organization, outlining a simple approach to developing markets, step-by-step. It included snippets of theory about how markets work in space, in the form of Christaller's famous hexagons. It went on to tell the development worker in considerable detail what is to be done: which surveys must be completed, how to prepare a master plan for the marketplace, the principles of market stall design. It contained numerous informative photographs of existing markets, in places as diverse as Kathmandu, Mexico City, London, the shores of Lake Victoria. It also contained many splendidly elegant architectural plans for marketplaces large and small. It even included, in an appendix, 'Model Market Regulations' in no fewer than 96 numbered paragraphs, into which the designer of the market only has to insert the names of relevant local authorities, etc. in a few places.

Had I been in possession of this book during my fieldwork, I could have flicked it open in an authoritative and self-confident manner whenever needed, and pointed to, say, page 79 and said, 'well, that's the way they do it in Brno. It should work here in Goroka. Get all this physical and legal infrastructure in place, add people and stir, and I guarantee that you will have a perfect market before you can even turn around and say "income elasticity"'. Would it have worked? Probably not. Maybe it was just as well I did not have that book. There are enough developmental elephants of the white kind in Papua New Guinea already, in all shapes and sizes: large and small, ugly and beautiful.

I am not mocking this particular publication, which bears the stamp of a genuinely concerned author, with a great deal of experience and practical know-how to his credit. But somehow I reckon that the way people think, act, and *construct through their daily dealings the space within which they act*, differs quite a bit from one place to another. These days it is of course routinely asserted that a thorough understanding of the diversity of local circumstances is central to successful development interventions, including those that deal with the marketing of food. Yet the point is equally routinely ignored, and it seems no exaggeration to say that many development projects continue to founder by clinging to a global, universal conception of 'the market' instead of allowing for the existence of a multitude of 'real markets', as shifting networks of only ever partially commensurable localities.

Hence, I shall end with a plea to all those concerned with 'the market', whether as theorists or planners or sellers or buyers, in whatever setting it may be, that they never forget to 'hold in propinquity the lovely, smelly mess of life' (Inglis 1993: 239). The market consists of spaces and places which are part of the identity and everyday worlds of its makers, and which are subject to ceaseless refashioning by the actors taking part at any given time. Possibilities do exist for harvesting meaningful development through increased market integration, but the realization of those possibilities has much to do with acknowledging and harnessing the messiness, imperfections, and odours of embedded markets.

NOTES

1. It has been argued, however, that the French regulationists themselves were concerned not only with the state, but with local modes of regulation, 'involving local-level networks, institutions, practices and meanings which solidify and stabilise a particular regime of accumulation' (Coombes and Campbell 1996: 12). See also Tickell and Peck (1992), and Moran *et al.* (1996).
2. As, for example, Collins (1981) would have it.
3. Mega-sized construction projects – bridges, powerstations and the like – have been especially popular in international development aid. Is it cynical to point to similarities with the extravagant pig-killing ceremonies of Lunube? Who gains most, donor or receiver?
4. Or, as Michael Edwards caustically remarked: 'Development has become a spectator sport, with a vast array of experts and others looking into the "fishbowl" of the Third World from the safety and comfort of their armchairs' (quoted in Booth 1994a: 24).
5. For example, in a consultant's report on these matters it is stated that 'Commercial farming is a totally different practice to the traditional subsistence gardener [sic]' (Lincoln International 1994: 11).

Glossary

TOK PISIN–ENGLISH TERMS

beksaitbun	customary payment by husband's kin to wife's kin
bigman	leader
bilum	string bag
bisnis	business, occupation
bosboi	overseer
boskru	truck or PMV driver's assistant
brata	1. brother, 2. cousin, 3. friend, mate
buai	betel nut
daka	betel pepper
didiman	agricultural extension officer
fotnait	wages
gavman	government, state
haiwe	highway truck
haus kaikai	food bar, restaurant
haus kapa	house with roof made of corrugated iron
haus kunai	thatched house
haus sik	health centre, hospital
hausboi	male domestic worker
hauslain	village or part of village, hamlet
kaibar	food bar
kaikai	food
kambang	powdered lime
kampani	company, firm
kapa	corrugated iron
kaukau	sweet potato
kaunsil	1. local government council; 2. councillor
kavivi	a variety of betel nut grown in the highlands
kiap	1. government official; 2. district officer (pre-1975)
kopimasin	coffee pulper
kumu	leafy green vegetables
kunai	1. sword grass; 2. grassland in general
lain	1. kin group, clan; 2. group of people
luluai	government-appointed village chief (pre-1975)
maket	market
maket raun	mobile market

277

masta	expatriate
memba	member of: 1. parliament; 2. provincial assembly
meri	woman
Mosbi	Port Moresby
mumu	earth oven, cooking pit
nuspes	customary payment by husband's kin to wife's kin
pasindia	1. traveller; 2. free-loader
pikinini	child
pitpit	cane grass
poroman	1. friend; 2. age mate
raskol	criminal
simen	concrete
singsing	song and dance
taim bilong kofi	coffee season or 'flush'
taim bilong ren	wet season
taim bilong san	dry season
tambu	1. coiled shell money; 2. in-laws; 3. forbidden
tanget	plant used for marking land ownership
tinpis	tinned mackerel
trak	truck
tumbuna stori	stories of the ancestors
waitman	expatriate
wantok	1. someone from the same area, 2. friend
wok fama	farmers' work
wok meri	women's work

DANO–ENGLISH TERMS

ambo	1. age mate; 2. friend
gelenda	flat land, dry
golo	mountain
gomoso	flat land, wet
gonobu	black
gulehe	red
menihe	kunai grass
misubo	soil
vilize	steep land

List of botanical terms

English	Tok Pisin	Dano	Scientific name
amaranthus	(kumu)		*Amaranthus* spp.
avocado	bata		*Persea americana* Mill.
banana	banana	gizese	*Musa* spp.
bean	bin	ovi	*Phaseolus vulgaris* L
cabbage	kebis		*Brassica oleracea* var. *capitata* L
carrot	kerot		*Daucus carota* L
cassava	tapiok	mangala	*Manihot esculenta* Crantz
Chinese taro	taro kongkong	koko	*Xanthosoma sagittifolium* (L) Schott
choko	sioko	silesile	*Sechium edule* (Jacq.) Swartz
coconut	kokonas		*Cocos nucifera* L.
corn	kon	kire	*Zea mays* L
cucumber	kukamba	gamu	*Cucumis sativus* L
ginger	kawawar	ekimbe	*Zingiber officinale* Rosc.
lemon	muli		*Citrus limon (L.)* Burm. f.
onion	anian		*Allium cepa* var. *cepa*
orange	swit muli		*Citrus sinensis* (L.) Osbeck
pandanus	karuka	anese	*Pandanus jiulianetti* Martelli
pandanus	marita	loso	*Pandanus conoideus* Lamarck
pawpaw	popo	kusikusi	*Carica papaya* L
pea		asiasiovi	*Pisum sativum* L
peanut	pinat	galip	*Arachis hypogea* L
potato	patete		*Solanum tuberosum* L
pumpkin	pamken	oruga	*Cucurbita moschata* Duch ez Poir
rungia	(kumu)	amba	*Rungia klossii* S. Moore
sago	saksak		*Metroxylon sagu* Rottb.
sugarcane	suga	avoso	*Saccharum officinarum* L
sweet potato	kaukau	govi	*Ipomoea batatas* (L) Lam.

English	Tok Pisin	Dano	Scientific name
taro	taro tru	masa	*Colocasia esculenta* (L) Schott
watercress	wara kebis	karakaras	*Nasturtium officinale* R. Br.
water dropwort	(kumu)	gindelehalize	*Oenanthe javanica* DC
wingbean	asbin	avise (bean)	*Psophocarpus tetragonolobus* (L) DC
yam	yam	gasa	*Dioscorea* spp.
	aibika	ihese	*Hibiscus manihot* L
	hailans pitpit	gondoni	*Setaria palmifolia* (Koenig) Stapf
	kapiak	embehe	*Ficus dammaropsis* Diels
	karuka	anese	*Pandanus jiulianetti* Martelli
	kumu mosan	gohuno	*Ficus copiosa* Steud.
	salat		*Laportea interrupta* (L) Chew
	wel karuka	anese handene	*Pandanus brosimos* Merrill & Perry
	(kumu)	sakave	*Nasturtium schlechteri* OE Schultz

Source of scientific names: French, B. R. 1978: *Food Plants of Papua New Guinea: A Compendium.* Sheffield, Tas.: B. R. French

References

Abarientos, E. P. and A. S. Flores (1992) 'Rice production: prospects for increasing food production, employment and improving nutrition in Papua New Guinea.' In Levett, Earland, and Heywood (1992), pp. 148–153.

Acheson, J. M. (ed.) (1994) *Anthropology and Institutional Economics*. Lanham and London: University Press of America.

AIDAB (1993) *The Papua New Guinea Economy: Prospects for Sectoral Development and Broad Based Growth*. Canberra: Australian International Development Assistance Bureau.

Alder, C. K. (1969) 'Goroka Patrol Report No. 8 of 1969/70.' Goroka: Department of District Administration. (Unpublished report.)

Aldous, T. (1976) 'Storage of sweet potato tubers.' In Wilson and Bourke (1976), pp. 229–236.

Alexander, J. and P. Alexander (1995) 'Commodification and consumption in a Central Borneo community.' *Bijdragen tot de Taal-, Land en Volkenkunde* 151(2), pp. 179–193.

Allen, B. J. (1976) 'Information flow and innovation diffusion in the East Sepik, Papua New Guinea.' Canberra: Department of Human Geography, Australian National University. (Unpublished PhD dissertation.)

—— (1982) 'Subsistence agriculture: three case studies.' In B. Carrad, D. A. M. Lea and K. K. Talyaga (eds), *Enga: Foundations for Development*. Armidale: Department of Geography, University of New England, pp. 93–127.

—— (1993) 'Issues for the sustainability of agriculture systems in Papua New Guinea, 1990–2015.' *Issues in Papua New Guinea Agriculture*. Canberra: Australian International Development Assistance Bureau, pp. 1–23.

—— (1996) 'Land management: Papua New Guinea's dilemma.' *The Asia–Pacific Magazine* 1(1), April, pp. 36–42.

—— and R. M. Bourke (1997a) *Report of an Assessment of the Impacts of Frost and Drought in Papua New Guinea*. http://www.ausaid.gov.au/publications/pdf/pngdroughtrep.pdf. Port Moresby: Australian Agency for International Development.

—————— with others (1997b) *Report of an Assessment of the Impacts of Frost and Drought in Papua New Guinea – Phase 2*. http://www.ausaid.gov.au/publications/pdf/pngdroughtrep2.pdf. Port Moresby: Department of Provincial and Local Government Affairs.

Allen, B. J. and R. Crittenden (1987) 'Degradation and a pre-capitalist political economy: the case of the New Guinea highlands.' In Blaikie and Brookfield (eds) (1997), pp. 145–165.

Amarshi, A., K. Good, and R. Mortimer (1979) *Development and Dependency: The Political Economy of Papua New Guinea*. Melbourne: Oxford University Press.

Apffel Marglin, F. and S. A. Marglin (eds) (1990) *Dominating Knowledge: Development, Culture, and Resistance.* Oxford: Clarendon Press.

Appadurai, A. (1986a) 'Introduction: commodities and the politics of value.' In Appadurai (ed.) (1986b), pp. 3–63.

—— (ed.) (1986b) *The Social Life of Things: Commodities in Cultural Perspective.* Cambridge: Cambridge University Press.

—— (1997) *Modernity at Large: Cultural Dimensions of Globalization.* Delhi: Oxford University Press.

Arce, A. and T. K. Marsden (1993) 'The social construction of international food: a new research agenda.' *Economic Geography* 69(3), pp. 293–311.

Asian Development Bank (1991) *Papua New Guinea Road Transport Sector Profile.* Asian Development Bank.

Atkinson, G. and H. Lewis (1992) 'Recent and future trends in the marketing of fresh fruit and vegetables in Papua New Guinea.' In Levett, Earland, and Heywood (1992), pp. 232–239.

Avalos, B. (1995) 'Women and development.' *Pacific Economic Bulletin* 10(1), pp. 73–83.

Bai, B. (1992) 'Policy options for food production.' In Levett, Earland, and Heywood (1992), pp. 10–14.

Bakker, M. L. (1996) *The Provincial Populations of Papua New Guinea: Profiles Based on 1990 Census Data.* Port Moresby: UNFPA, ILO, and National Planning Office.

Bank of Papua New Guinea (1996) *Quarterly Economic Bulletin* 24(1).

Bannister, T. (1982) 'Farmer training in food production: an overview.' In Bourke and Kesavan (eds) (1982), Vol. 3, pp. 519–522.

Banuri, T. (1990a) 'Development and the politics of knowledge: a critical interpretation of the social role of modernization theories in the development of the Third World.' In Apffel Marglin and Marglin (1990), pp. 29–72.

—— (1990b) 'Modernization and its discontents: a cultural perspective on the theories of development.' In Apffel Marglin and Marglin (1990), pp. 73–101.

Barber, B. (1995) 'All economies are "embedded": the career of a concept, and beyond.' *Social Research* 62(2), pp. 387–413.

Barnes, T. (1988) 'Rationality and relativism in economic geography: an interpretive review of the homo economicus assumption.' *Progress in Human Geography* 12(4), pp. 473–496.

—— and E. Sheppard (1992) 'Is there a place for the rational actor? A geographical critique of the rational choice paradigm.' *Economic Geography* 68(1), pp. 1–21.

Baulch, B. (1987) *An Assessment of the Impact of Import Restrictions on Introduced Vegetables in Five Urban Centres in Papua New Guinea.* Port Moresby: Department of Agriculture and Livestock. (Technical Report 87/15, July 1987.)

Bayliss-Smith, T. P. (1996) 'People–plant interactions in the New Guinea Highlands: agricultural hearthland or horticultural backwater?' In D. R. Harris (ed.), *The Origins and Spread of Agriculture and Pastoralism in Eurasia.* London: UCL Press, pp. 499–523.

Benton, J. (1987) 'A decade of change in the Lake Titicaca region.' In Momsen and Townsend (eds) (1987), pp. 215–221.

Bernstein, H. (1981) 'Concepts for the analysis of contemporary peasantries.' In R. E. Galli (ed.), *The Political Economy of Rural Development: Peasants, International Capital, and the State.* Albany: State University of New York Press, pp. 3–24.

—— and B. K. Campbell (eds) (1985) *Contradictions of Accumulation in Africa.* Beverly Hills: Sage Publications.

REFERENCES

Berthoud, G. (1992) 'Market.' In Sachs (ed.) (1992), pp. 70–87.
Blaikie, P. (1985) *The Political Economy of Soil Erosion in Developing Countries*. London: Longman.
—— and H. Brookfield (eds) (1987) *Land Degradation and Society*. London: Methuen.
Bleeker, P. (1983) *Soils of Papua New Guinea*. Canberra: Commonwealth Scientific Industrial Research Organization and Australian National University Press.
Bohannan, P. and L. Bohannan (1968) *Tiv Economy*. Evanston: Northwestern University Press.
Booth, D. (1992) 'Social development research: an agenda for the 1990s.' *European Journal of Development Research* 4(1), pp. 1–39.
—— (1994a) 'Rethinking social development: an overview.' In Booth (1994b), pp. 3–34.
—— (ed.) (1994b) *Rethinking Social Development: Theory, Research and Practice*. Harlow: Longman Scientific & Technical.
Bourdieu, P. (1977) *Outline of a Theory of Practice*. Cambridge: Cambridge University Press.
Bourke, R. M. (1982a) 'Growing sweet potato for sale in the highlands.' *Harvest* 8(2), pp. 47–58.
—— (1982b) 'Sweet potato in Papua New Guinea.' In Villareal and Griggs (eds) (1982), pp. 45–57.
—— (1985) 'Sweet potato *(Ipomoea batatas)* production and research in Papua New Guinea.' *Papua New Guinea Journal of Agriculture, Forestry and Fisheries* 33(3–4), pp. 89–108.
—— (1986) 'Periodic markets in Papua New Guinea.' *Pacific Viewpoint* 27(1), pp. 69–76.
—— (1988) '*Taim hangre*: variation in subsistence food supply in the Papua New Guinea highlands.' Canberra: Department of Human Geography, Australian National University. (Unpublished PhD dissertation.)
—— (1992) 'Fifty years of agricultural change in a New Guinea highland village.' In Levett, Earland, and Heywood (1992), pp. 26–53.
—— and V. Kesavan (eds) (1982) *Proceedings from the Second Papua New Guinea Food Crops Conference*. Goroka: Department of Primary Industry (3 volumes).
——, B. Carrad, and P. Heywood (1981) *Papua New Guinea's Food Problems: Time for Action*. Port Moresby: Department of Primary Industry.
——, B. J. Allen, G. S. Humphreys, C. Ballard, R. Grau, and R. L. Hide (1991) 'The composted mounds of the Papua New Guinea Highlands.' Canberra, Department of Human Geography, Australian National University. (Unpublished conference paper.)
——, B. J. Allen, and R. L. Hide (1994a) *Notes on Smallholder Agriculture, Eastern Highlands Province, Papua New Guinea*. Canberra: Australian International Development Assistance Bureau.
——, B. J. Allen, R. L. Hide, D. Fritsch, R. Grau, P. Hobsbawm, E. Lowes, and D. Stannard (1994b) *Eastern Highlands Province: Text Summaries, Maps, Code Lists and Village Identification*. Canberra: Department of Human Geography, Research School of Pacific and Asian Studies, Australian National University.
Bowman, R. G. (1946) 'Army farms and agricultural development in the Southwest Pacific.' *Geographical Review* 36(3), pp. 420–446.
Box, L. (1986) 'Commoditization and the social organization of crop reproduction: conceptualization and cases.' In Long, van der Ploeg, Curtin and Box (eds) (1986), pp. 100–116.
Boyd, D. J. (1985) 'The commercialisation of ritual in the Eastern Highlands of Papua New Guinea.' *Man (New Series)* 20, pp. 325–340.

Brass, T. (1995) 'Old conservatism in "new" clothes.' *Journal of Peasant Studies* 22(3), pp. 516–540.
Braudel, F. (1981) *Civilization and Capitalism, 15th–18th Century. Vol. I – The Structures of Everyday Life: The Limits of the Possible*. London: Collins.
—— (1982) *Civilization and Capitalism, 15th–18th Century. Vol. II – The Wheels of Commerce*. London: Collins.
Brohman, J. (1995a) 'Universalism, Eurocentrism, and ideological bias in development studies: from modernisation to neoliberalism.' *Third World Quarterly* 16(1), pp. 121–140.
—— (1995b) 'Economism and critical silences in development studies: a theoretical critique of neoliberalism.' *Third World Quarterly* 16(2), pp. 297–318.
Bromley, R. J., R. Symanski, and C. M. Good (1975) 'The rationale of periodic markets.' *Annals of the Association of American Geographers* 65(4), pp. 530–537.
Brookfield, H. C. (1968) 'The money that grows on trees: the consequences of an innovation within a man–environment system.' *Australian Geographical Studies* 6(2), pp. 97–119.
—— (ed.) (1969) *Pacific Market-places*. Canberra: Australian National University Press.
—— (1972) 'Intensification and disintensification in Pacific agriculture: a theoretical approach.' *Pacific Viewpoint* 13(1), pp. 30–48.
—— (1984) 'Intensification revisited.' *Pacific Viewpoint* 25(1), pp. 15–44.
—— (1996) 'Meanings of "agrodiversity".' *PLEC News and Views* 7, pp. 13–15.
—— and J. P. White (1968) 'Revolution or evolution in the prehistory of the New Guinea highlands: a seminar report.' *Ethnology* VII(1), pp. 43–52.
Brown, J. K. (1970) 'Goroka Patrol Report No. 31 of 1969/70.' Goroka: Department of District Administration. (Unpublished report.)
Bryant, R. L. (1992) 'Political ecology: an emerging research agenda in Third-World studies.' *Political Geography* 11(1), pp. 12–36.
Busch, L. and A. Juska (1997) 'Beyond political economy; actor networks and the globalization of agriculture.' *Review of International Political Economy* 4(4), pp. 688–708.
Buttel, F. H. and P. McMichael (1994) 'Reconsidering the explanandum and scope of development studies: toward a comparative sociology of state–economy relations.' In Booth (1994b), pp. 42–61.
Calcinai, B. L. and R. M. Bourke (1982) 'Institutional food production and consumption in Eastern Highlands and Enga provinces.' In Bourke and Kesavan (eds) (1982), pp. 184–190.
Callon, M. (1986) 'Some elements of a sociology of translation: domestication of the scallops and the fishermen of St Brieuc Bay.' In J. Law (ed.), *Power, Action and Belief: A New Sociology of Knowledge?* London, Boston and Henley: Routledge & Kegan Paul, pp. 196–233.
Carrier, J. G. (1992) 'The gift in theory and practice in Melanesia: a note on the centrality of gift exchange.' *Ethnology* 31(2), pp. 185–193.
—— (ed.) (1997) *Meanings of the Market: The Free Market in Western Culture*. Oxford: Berg.
Chayanov, A. V. (1966) *The Theory of Peasant Economy*. Homewood: Richard D. Irwin.
Chevalier, J. (1983) 'There is nothing simple about simple commodity production.' *Journal of Peasant Studies* 10(4), pp. 153–186.
Christie, M. (1980) *Changing Consumer Behaviour in Papua New Guinea: Its Social and Ecological Implications*. Canberra: Centre for Resource and Environmental Studies and UNESCO/UNEP.

REFERENCES

Clarke, W. C. (1971) *Place and People: An Ecology of a New Guinea Community.* Canberra: Australian National University Press.

—— (1977) 'A change of subsistence staple in prehistoric New Guinea.' In C. L. A. Leakey (ed.), *Proceedings of the Third Symposium of the International Society for Tropical Root Crops.* Ibadan, pp. 159–163.

Coakley, K., D. Lehmann, D. Smith, I. Riley, P. Howard, H. Gratten, H. Siwi, A. Poli, G. Saleu, M. Kakazo, J. Taime, S. Lupiwa, M. Kajoi, K. Zarike, C. Coakley, S. Tulloch, T. Smith, and M. Alpers (1993) *The Asaro Valley Surveillance Unit of the Papua New Guinea Institute of Medical Research: Methodology, Demography and Mortality.* Goroka: Papua New Guinea Institute of Medical Research.

Cole, R. (1987) 'Stori bilong stret pasin stoa.' *Pacific Economic Bulletin* 2(2), pp. 31–34.

Collins, R. (1981) 'Micro-translation as a theory-building strategy.' In K. Knorr-Cetina and A. V. Cicourel (eds), *Advances in Social Theory and Methodology: Toward an Integration of Micro- and Macro-sociologies.* Boston, London and Henley: Routledge & Kegan Paul, pp. 81–108.

Connell, J. (1979) 'The emergence of peasantry in Papua New Guinea.' *Peasant Studies* 8(2), pp. 103–137.

—— (1982) 'Development and dependency: divergent approaches to the political economy of Papua New Guinea.' In R. J. May and H. Nelson (eds), *Melanesia: Beyond Diversity* (Vol. II). Canberra: Research School of Pacific Studies, Australian National University, pp. 501–527.

—— and J. Lea (1994) 'Cities of parts, cities apart? Changing places in modern Melanesia.' *The Contemporary Pacific* 6(2), pp. 267–309.

Cook, A. (1994a) 'Mines and mining projects in Papua New Guinea.' In Economic Insights Pty Ltd (1994), pp. 195–210.

—— (1994b) 'Oil and gas in Papua New Guinea.' In Economic Insights Pty Ltd (1994), pp. 211–244.

Coombes, B. and H. Campbell (1996) 'Pluriactivity in (and beyond?) a regulationist crisis.' *New Zealand Geographer* 52(2), pp. 11–17.

Corrigan, B. (1949) 'Goroka Patrol Report No. 5 of 1948/49.' Goroka: Department of District Administration. (Unpublished report.)

Crespi, F. (1992) *Social Action and Power.* Oxford: Blackwell.

Crocombe, R. G., W. J. Oostermeyer, J. Gray, and J. Langmore (1967) *Papuan Entrepreneurs.* Port Moresby: Australian National University.

Crotty, T. M. (1970) 'History of road development in the Territory of Papua and New Guinea.' *Search* 1(5), pp. 239–243.

Dahl, G. and A. Rabo (1992) *Kam-ap or Take-off: Local Notions of Development.* Stockholm: Department of Social Anthropology, Stockholm University.

DAL (1990–92) *Reports on the Food Crop Market Survey 1988.* Port Moresby: Rural Statistics Section, Department of Agriculture and Livestock. (Separate reports for Alotau, Koki, Lae, Madang, Mt Hagen, and Rabaul Markets.)

Davis, J. (1996) 'An anthropologist's view of exchange.' *Oxford Development Studies* 24(1), pp. 47–60.

Department of the Eastern Highlands (1980) 'Draft Five-Year Development Plan 1980–1984.' Goroka: Department of the Eastern Highlands, Office of Agriculture. (Draft report.)

Dever, K. J. and A. L. Voigt (1976) 'Vegetable production methods at the Kabiufa Adventist High School gardens.' In Wilson and Bourke (1976), pp. 205–210.

Dickerson-Putman, J. (1986) 'Finding a road in the modern world: the differential effects of culture change and development on the men and women of an Eastern

Highlands Papua New Guinean community.' Department of Anthropology, Bryn Mawr College. (Unpublished PhD dissertation.)

Dilley, R. (1992a) 'Contesting markets: a general introduction to market ideology, imagery and discourse.' In Dilley (1992b), pp. 1–34.

—— (ed.) (1992b) *Contesting Markets: Analyses of Ideology, Discourse and Practice.* Edinburgh: Edinburgh University Press.

Donaldson, M. and K. Good (1978) *Class and Politics in the Eastern Highlands of Papua New Guinea.* Port Moresby: University of Papua New Guinea and Department of Primary Industry. (History of Agriculture Working Paper No. 9.)

———— (1988) *Articulated agricultural development: Traditional and capitalist agricultures in Papua New Guinea.* Aldershot: Avebury.

Donne, C. W. S. (1965) 'Goroka Supplementary Patrol Report No. 13 of 1964/65.' Goroka: Department of District Administration. (Unpublished report.)

Dorney, S. (1990) *Papua New Guinea: People, Politics and History since 1975.* Sydney: Random House.

Dowa, P. (1995) 'Squatter houses go up in flames.' *Post-Courier*, April 28–30, pp. 1–2.

Downs, I. (1970) *The Stolen Land.* Milton: Jacaranda Press.

—— (1986) *The Last Mountain: A Life in Papua New Guinea.* St Lucia: University of Queensland Press.

Duncan, J. S. (1985) 'Individual action and political power: a structuration perspective.' In R. J. Johnston (ed.), *The Future of Geography.* London: Methuen, pp. 174–189.

Duncan, R. and I. Temu (1995) 'Papua New Guinea: longer term developments and recent economic problems.' *Asian–Pacific Economic Literature* 9(2), pp. 36–54.

Dwyer, P. D. and M. Minnegal (1998) 'Waiting for company: ethos and environment among the Kubo of Papua New Guinea.' *Journal of the Anthropological Institute* 4, pp. 23–42.

Eastern Highlands Provincial Government (1994) *Nokondi One: Five Year Development Plan 1994–1998.* Goroka: Eastern Highlands Provincial Government.

Economic Insights Pty Ltd (1994) *Papua New Guinea: The Role of Government in Economic Development.* Canberra: Australian International Development Assistance Bureau.

Edwards, M. (1994) 'Rethinking social development: the search for "relevance".' In Booth (1994b), pp. 279–297.

Eggertsson, T. (1990) *Economic Behavior and Institutions.* Cambridge: Cambridge University Press.

Ennew, J., P. Hirst, and K. Tribe (1977) '"Peasantry" as an economic category.' *Journal of Peasant Studies* 4(4), pp. 295–322.

Epstein, T. S. (1968) *Capitalism, Primitive and Modern – Some Aspects of Tolai Economic Growth.* Canberra: Australian National University Press.

—— (1982) *Urban Food Marketing and Third World Rural Development – The Structure of Producer–seller Markets.* London and Canberra: Croom Helm.

Escobar, A. (1995) *Encountering Development.* Princeton: Princeton University Press.

Etzioni, A. and P. R. Lawrence (eds) (1991) *Socio-Economics: Toward a New Synthesis.* New York and London: M. E. Sharpe.

Evers, H.-D. (1994) 'The trader's dilemma: a theory of the social transformation of markets and society.' In Evers and Schrader (1994), pp. 7–14.

—— (1995a) *The Changing Culture of Markets.* Bielefeld: Universität Bielefeld, Fakultät für Soziologie, Forschungsschwerpunkt Entwicklungssoziologie. (Working Paper No. 239.)

REFERENCES

—— (1995b) *Globale Märkte und soziale Transformation* [Global Markets and Social Transformation]. Bielefeld: Universität Bielefeld, Fakultät für Soziologie, Forschungsschwerpunkt Entwicklungssoziologie. (Working Paper No. 234.)

—— and G. Schlee (1995) *Die Strukturierung sozialer Welten: Zur Konstruktion von Differenz in den Handlungsfeldern Markt und Staat* [The Structuration of Social Worlds: Of the Construction of Difference in the Arenas of Market and State]. Bielefeld: Universität Bielefeld, Fakultät für Soziologie, Forschungsschwerpunkt Entwicklungssoziologie. (Working Paper No. 231.)

—— and H. Schrader (eds) (1994) *The Moral Economy of Trade: Ethnicity and Developing Markets*. London: Routledge.

Ewing, A. C. (1951) 'Goroka Patrol Report No. 4 of 1943/44.' Goroka: Department of District Administration. (Unpublished report.)

Fahey, S. (1986) 'Rural differentiation in Papua New Guinea.' *Pacific Viewpoint* 27(2), pp. 144–164.

Fairbairn, T. I. J. (ed.) (1988) *Island Entrepreneurs: Problems and Performances in the Pacific*. Honolulu: East–West Center.

Fallon, J. (1992) *The Papua New Guinean Economy: Prospects for Recovery, Reform and Sustained Growth*. Canberra: Australian International Development Assistance Bureau.

Feil, D. K. (1984) *Ways of Exchange: the Enga Tee of Papua New Guinea*. St Lucia: University of Queensland Press.

—— (1987) *The Evolution of Highland Papua New Guinea Societies*. Cambridge: Cambridge University Press.

Fereday, N. (1993) *The Changing Cost of Food and its Implications for Food Policy in Papua New Guinea*. Port Moresby: Department of Agriculture and Livestock. (Policy Working Paper No. 3.)

Ferguson, J. (1992) 'The cultural topography of wealth: commodity paths and the structure of property in rural Lesotho.' *American Anthropologist* 94, pp. 55–73.

Finch, J. (1997) 'From proletarian to entrepreneur to big man: the story of Noya'. *Oceania* 68(2), pp. 123–133.

Finney, B. R. (1970) '"Partnership" in developing the New Guinea Highlands, 1948–1968.' *Journal of Pacific History* 5, pp. 117–134.

—— (1973) *Big-men and Business: Entrepreneurship and Economic Growth in the New Guinea Highlands*. Canberra: Australian National University Press.

—— (1987) *Business Development in the Highlands of Papua New Guinea*. Honolulu: Pacific Islands Development Program, East–West Center.

—— (1993) 'From the stone age to the age of corporate takeovers.' In Lockwood, Harding, and Wallace (eds) (1993), pp. 102–116.

——, U. Mikave, and A. Sabumei (1974) 'Pearl shell in Goroka: from valuables to chicken feed.' *Yagl–Ambu* 1(4), pp. 342–349.

Fintrac Consultants Asia (n.d.) Agricultural Marketing Support Services Project – TA No. 694 – PNG – Draft Final Report. Singapore: Fintrac Consultants Asia Pte Ltd. (Draft of report prepared for DPI Papua New Guinea and Asian Development Bank.)

Fitzpatrick, P. (1980) *Law and State in Papua New Guinea*. London: Academic Press.

Forbes, D. K. (1975) 'Trends in vegetable marketing in Port Moresby.' *Pacific Bulletin* (1), pp. 17–21.

Foster, R. J. (1999) 'The commercial construction of "new nations".' *Journal of Material Culture* 4(3), pp. 263–282.

FPDC (1994) 'Survey of Women Sellers in the Mt Hagen Market, December 1993–January 1994.' Mt Hagen: Fresh Produce Development Company. (Unpublished paper, March 1994.)

French, B. R. (1978) *Food Plants of Papua New Guinea: A Compendium.* Sheffield, Tas.: B. R. French.
Fresh Produce News (1992) 'Golden opportunities for Engan farmers', 25 Jan., pp. 1–2.
Friedmann, H. (1980) 'Household production and the national economy: concepts for the analysis of agrarian formations.' *Journal of Peasant Studies* 7(2), pp. 158–184.
—— (1986) 'Patriarchal commodity production.' *Social Analysis* 20, pp. 47–55.
—— and P. McMichael (1989) 'Agriculture and the state system: the rise and decline of national agricultures, 1870 to the present.' *Sociologia Ruralis* 29(2), pp. 93–117.
Ganarafo, R. G. (1974) 'M's trade store: a small highlands business.' *Yagl–Ambu* 1(2), pp. 149–153.
Garnaut, R. (1995) 'Monetary stability or more devaluation?' *Pacific Economic Bulletin* 10(1), pp. 19–23.
Gelber, M. G. (1986) *Gender and Society in the New Guinea Highlands: An Anthropological Perspective on Antagonism toward Women.* Boulder, CO, and London: Westview Press.
Gerritsen, R. (1979) 'Groups, classes and peasant politics in Ghana and Papua New Guinea.' Canberra: Australian National University. (Unpublished PhD dissertation.)
—— (1981) 'Aspects of the political evolution of rural Papua New Guinea: towards a political economy of the terminal peasantry.' In R. Gerritsen, R. J. May, and M. A. H. B. Walter (eds), *Road Belong Development: Cargo Cults, Community Groups and Self-help Movements in Papua New Guinea.* Canberra: Department of Political and Social Change, Research School of Pacific Studies, Australian National University, pp. 1–60.
Gewertz, D. B. and F. K. Errington (1999) *Emerging Class in Papua New Guinea: the Telling of Difference.* Cambridge: Cambridge University Press.
Gibbon, P. and M. Neocosmos (1985) 'Some problems in the political economy of "African socialism".' In Bernstein and Campbell (eds) (1985).
Gibson, J. (1993) *Rice Self-sufficiency and the Terms of Trade: Why Rice is a Good Thing to Import.* Canberra: Research School of Pacific Studies, Australian National University.
—— (1994) 'Rice import substitution and employment in Papua New Guinea.' *Pacific Economic Bulletin* 9(1), pp. 46–52.
—— (1995) *Food Consumption and Food Policy in Papua New Guinea.* Port Moresby: Institute of National Affairs.
Giddens, A. (1979) *Central Problems in Social Theory: Action, Structure and Contradiction in Social Analysis.* London: Macmillan.
—— (1984) *The Constitution of Society: Outline of the Theory of Structuration.* Berkeley: University of California Press.
Golson, J. (1977) 'The making of the New Guinea highlands.' In J. H. Winslow (ed.), *The Melanesian Environment.* Canberra: Australian National University Press, pp. 45–56.
Good, K. (1986) *Papua New Guinea: A False Economy.* London: Anti-Slavery Society.
—— and M. Donaldson (1977) *The Development of Rural Capitalism in Papua New Guinea: Coffee Production in the Eastern Highlands.* Port Moresby: Department of History, University of Papua New Guinea. (History of Agriculture Discussion Paper No. 29.)
Goodman, D. (1999) 'Agro-food studies in the "age of ecology": nature, corporeality, bio-politics.' *Sociologia Ruralis* 39(1), pp. 17–37.

REFERENCES

Gorecki, P. P. (1986) 'Human occupation and agricultural development in the Papua New Guinea highlands.' *Mountain Research and Development* 6(2), pp. 159–166.

Gorogo, G. D. (1976) 'Review of the operations of the Fresh Food Project in the Central District.' In Wilson and Bourke (1976), pp. 287–293.

Gould, P. and G. Olsson (eds) (1982) *A Search for Common Ground*. London: Pion.

Granovetter, M. (1985) 'Economic action and social structure: the problem of embeddedness.' *American Journal of Sociology* 91(3), pp. 481–510.

—— (1991) 'The social construction of economic institutions.' In Etzioni and Lawrence (eds) (1991), pp. 75–81.

—— (1992) 'The nature of economic relations.' In Ortiz and Lees (eds) (1992), pp. 21–37.

Grau, R. and T. Smith (1992) 'Dietary patterns at the district level in Papua New Guinea, 1982/83.' *Papua New Guinea National Nutrition Policy Workshop*. Port Moresby: Institute of National Affairs, pp. 222–236.

Gregory, C. A. (1979) 'The emergence of commodity production in Papua New Guinea.' *Journal of Contemporary Asia* 9(4), pp. 389–409.

—— (1982) *Gifts and Commodities*. London: Academic Press.

Gregory, D. (1982) 'Solid geometry: notes on the recovery of spatial structure.' In Gould and Olsson (eds) (1982), pp. 187–219.

—— (1994a) *Geographical Imaginations*. Oxford: Blackwell.

—— (1994b) 'Social theory and human geography.' In Gregory, Martin, and Smith (eds) (1994a), pp. 78–109.

——, R. Martin, and G. Smith (eds) (1994a) *Human Geography: Society, Space and Social Science*. Basingstoke and London: Macmillan.

——, R. Martin, and G. Smith (1994b) 'Introduction: human geography, social change and social science.' In Gregory, Martin, and Smith (eds) (1994a), pp. 1–18.

Gregson, N. (1987) 'Structuration theory: some thoughts on the possibilities for empirical research.' *Environment and Planning D: Society and Space* 5(1), pp. 73–91.

Grey, M. (1993) 'Agriculture: problems and prospects.' In AIDAB (1993), pp. 85–123.

Grossman, L. S. (1983) 'Cattle, rural economic differentiation, and articulation in the highlands of Papua New Guinea.' *American Ethnologist* 10(1), pp. 59–76.

—— (1984) *Peasants, Subsistence Ecology, and Development in the Highlands of Papua New Guinea*. Princeton: Princeton University Press.

—— (1987) 'Subsistence production, autonomy and development.' *Australian Geographer* 18(2), pp. 170–176.

Groube, L., J. Chappell, J. Muke, and D. Price (1986) 'A 40,000 year-old human occupation site at Huon Peninsula, Papua New Guinea.' *Nature* 324, pp. 453–455.

Gudeman, S. and A. Rivera (1990) *Conversations in Colombia – The Domestic Economy in Life and Text*. Cambridge and New York: Cambridge University Press.

Gupta, D. (1995) 'Current economic trends.' *Pacific Economic Bulletin* 10(1), pp. 3–13.

Haberle, S. (1993) 'Late Quaternary environmental history of the Tari Basin, Papua New Guinea.' Canberra: Department of Biogeography and Geomorphology, Australian National University. (Unpublished PhD dissertation.)

—— (1994) 'Anthropogenic indicators in pollen diagrams: problems and prospects for late Quaternary palynology in Papua New Guinea.' In J. G. Hather (ed.),

Tropical Archaeobotany: Applications and New Developments. London and New York: Routledge, pp. 172–201.

Habermas, J. (1985a) *Theorie des kommunikativen Handelns. Band 1: Handlungsrationalität und gesellschaftliche Rationalisierung.* Frankfurt am Main: Suhrkamp Verlag.

—— (1985b) *Theorie des kommunikativen Handelns. Band 2: Zur Kritik der funktionalistischen Vernunft.* Frankfurt am Main: Suhrkamp Verlag.

Hägerstrand, T. (1984) 'Presence and absence: a look at conceptual choices and bodily necessities.' *Regional Studies* 18(5), pp. 373–380.

Halperin, R. H. (1988) *Economies across Cultures: Towards a Comparative Science of the Economy.* Basingstoke: Macmillan Press.

—— (1994) *Cultural Economies Past and Present.* Austin: University of Texas Press.

Harris, G. T. (1978) *Urban Food Supplies in Papua New Guinea, with Particular Reference to Port Moresby.* Port Moresby: Economics Department, University of Papua New Guinea. (Discussion Paper No. 35.)

Harrison, M. (1977) 'The peasant economy in the work of A. V. Chayanov.' *Journal of Peasant Studies* 4(4), pp. 323–336.

—— (1979) 'Chayanov and the Marxists.' *Journal of Peasant Studies* 7(1), pp. 86–100.

Harriss, B. (1989) 'Commercialisation, distribution and consumption: Rural–urban grain and resource transfers in peasant society.' In Potter and Unwin (eds) (1989), pp. 204–232.

Harriss, J., J. Hunter, and C. M. Lewis (eds) (1995) *The New Institutional Economics and Third World Development.* London & New York: Routledge.

Hart, G. (1992) 'Imagined unities: constructions of "the household" in economic theory.' In Ortiz and Lees (eds) (1992), pp. 111–129.

Hasluck, P. (1976) *A Time for Building: Australian Administration in Papua and New Guinea, 1951–1963.* Melbourne: Melbourne University Press.

Hayfield, S. (1992) 'Some thoughts on vegetable production and marketing.' *Fresh Produce News,* 29 May 1992, pp. 8–9.

Hays, S. (1994) 'Structure and agency and the sticky problem of culture.' *Sociological Theory* 12(1), pp. 57–72.

Healey, C. (1990) *Maring Hunters and Traders: Production and Exchange in the Papua New Guinea Highlands.* Berkeley: University of California Press.

Healy, P. (1954) 'Goroka Patrol Report No. 10 of 1954/55.' Goroka: Department of District Administration. (Unpublished report.)

Henty, E. E. (1969) *A Manual of the Grasses of New Guinea.* Lae: Division of Botany, Department of Forests.

Heywood, P. (1982) 'Population, food supply and nutrition.' In *Population of Papua New Guinea.* New York and Noumea: United Nations and South Pacific Commission, pp. 203–212.

—— and R. L. Hide (1994) 'Nutritional effects of export-crop production in Papua New Guinea: a review of the evidence.' *Food and Nutrition Bulletin* 15(3), pp. 233–249.

Hide, R. L. (1993) 'Women and market trade.' (Unpublished manuscript.)

Hindess, B. (1988) *Choice, Rationality, and Social Theory.* London: Unwin Hyman.

Hirsch, E. (1990) 'From bones to betelnuts: processes of ritual transformation and the development of "national culture" in Papua New Guinea.' *Man* 25(1), pp. 18–34.

Holzknecht, H. and K. K. Kalit (1995) 'Forest resources: what hope for the future?' *Pacific Economic Bulletin* 10(1), pp. 95–100.

REFERENCES

Howlett, D. R. (1962) 'A decade of change in the Goroka Valley, New Guinea: land use and development in the 1950s.' Australian National University. (Unpublished PhD dissertation.)

—— (1973) 'Terminal development: from tribalism to peasantry.' In H. C. Brookfield (ed.), *The Pacific in Transition. Geographical Perspectives on Adaptation and Change.* London: Edward Arnold, pp. 249–273.

—— (1980) 'When is a peasant not a peasant? Rural proletarianization in Papua New Guinea.' In J. N. Jennings and G. J. R. Linge (eds), *Of Time and Place: Essays in Honour of OHK Spate.* Canberra: Australian National University Press, pp. 193–210.

——, R. Hide, E. Young, J. with Arba, H. Bi, and B. Kaman (1977) *Simbu: Long Wanem Rot?* [Simbu: Which way?] Port Moresby: Nesenel Plening Ofis.

Hughes, I. (1971) 'Recent Neolithic trade in New Guinea: the ecological basis of traffic in goods among stone-age subsistence farmers.' Canberra: Department of Geography, Australian National University. (Unpublished PhD dissertation.)

—— (1977) *New Guinea Stone Age Trade: The Geography and Ecology of Traffic in the Interior.* Canberra: The Australian National University.

Hydén, G. (1980) *Beyond Ujamaa in Tanzania: Underdevelopment and an Uncaptured Peasantry.* London: Heinemann.

Inglis, F. (1993) *Cultural Studies.* Oxford and Cambridge: Blackwell.

Jackman, H. (1977) 'Some thoughts on entrepreneurship in Papua New Guinea.' *Australian Outlook* 31(1), pp. 24–37.

Jackson, R. T. (ed.) (1976a) *An Introduction to the Urban Geography of Papua New Guinea.* Port Moresby: Department of Geography, University of Papua New Guinea.

—— (1976b) 'Lae.' In Jackson (1976a), pp. 274–304.

—— (1976c) 'The impact of the introduction of markets: a case study from the highlands of Papua New Guinea.' *Savanna* 5(2), pp. 175–183.

—— (1977) 'The growth, nature and future prospects of informal settlements in Papua New Guinea.' *Pacific Viewpoint* 18(1), pp. 22–42.

—— (1979) *Industrialisation in Papua New Guinea: A Social or Economic Investment?* Rotterdam: IGU Commission on Industrial Systems and Economisch Geografisch Instituut, Erasmus Universiteit Rotterdam.

—— and K. Kolta (1974) *A Survey of Marketing in the Mount Hagen Area.* Port Moresby: Department of Geography, University of Papua New Guinea.

Joughin, J. and K. Kalit (1986) *The Changing Cost of Food in Papua New Guinea – An Analysis of Prices in Five Urban Markets.* Port Moresby: Department of Primary Industry. (Technical Report 86/4, December 1986)

—— (1987) *Falling Prices in the 1980's: Another Look at the Changing Cost of Food in Papua New Guinea.* Port Moresby: Department of Agriculture and Livestock. (Technical Report 87/13, July 1987.)

—— (1988) 'Food prices in Papua New Guinea – a guide to the changing urban diet.' *Papua New Guinea Medical Journal* 31(2), pp. 133–140.

Kahn, M. and L. Sexton (1988) 'The fresh and the canned: food choices in the Pacific.' *Food and Foodways* 3(1), pp. 1–18.

Kaitilla, S. (1999) 'Invisible real estate agents and urban housing development on customary land in Papua New Guinea.' *Environment and Urbanization* 11(1), pp. 267–275.

Kautsky, K. (1988) *The Agrarian Question.* London: Zwan Publications.

Kaynak, E. (ed.) (1986) *World Food Marketing Systems.* London: Butterworths.

Keil, D. E. (1977) 'Markets in Melanesia? A comparison of traditional economic transactions in New Guinea with African markets.' *Journal of Anthropological Research* 33(3), pp. 258–276.

Kent, J. W. (1957) 'Goroka Patrol Report No. 8 of 1956/57.' Goroka: Department of District Administration. (Unpublished report.)

Kepui, T. B. (1986) 'Food security in Papua New Guinea.' Port Moresby: Department of Primary Industry. (Unpublished report, November 1986.)

Kiely, R. (1999) 'The last refuge of the noble savage? A critical assessment of post-development theory.' *European Journal of Development Studies* 11(1), pp. 30–55.

Kiff, U. (1976) 'Gardening at Kasena.' *Oral History* 4(2), pp. 89–97.

King, D. (1992) 'Socio-economic differences between residential categories in Port Moresby: results of a University of Papua New Guinea urban household sample survey of Port Moresby, 1987.' *Yagl–Ambu* 16(3), pp. 1–16.

—— (1993) 'Urbanization in Papua New Guinea: trends from 1966 to 1990.' In T. Taufa and C. Bass (eds), *Population, Family Health and Development*. Port Moresby: University of Papua New Guinea Press, pp. 68–85.

—— and J. Diala (1988) *Socio-Economic Differentiation in Urban Areas of Papua New Guinea: Analysis of the 1980 Census*. Port Moresby: Department of Geography, University of Papua New Guinea.

Kopytoff, I. (1986) 'The cultural biography of things: commoditization as process.' In Appadurai (ed.) (1986b), pp. 64–91.

Kuimbakul, T. (1995) *Coffee Report No. 35*. Goroka: Industry Affairs Division, Papua New Guinea Coffee Industry Corporation (March 1995).

Kuman, C. E. P. (1987) 'Women and banking policy.' In Stratigos and Hughes (eds) (1987), pp. 89–95.

Latouche, S. (1993) *In the Wake of the Affluent Society: An Exporation of Post-Development*. London and New Jersey: Zed Books.

Latour, B. (1993) *We Have Never Been Modern*. Cambridge, MA: Harvard University Press.

—— (1997) 'On actor-network theory: a few clarifications.' *Actor Network Resource*. http://www.keele.ac.uk/depts/stt/stt/ant/latour.htm, Centre for Social Theory and Technology, Keele University. (Internet document, accessed May 1997.)

Lavoie, D. (ed.) (1990a) *Economics and Hermeneutics*. London and New York: Routledge.

—— (1990b) 'Introduction.' In Lavoie (1990a), pp. 1–15.

Law, J. (1994) *Organizing Modernity*. Oxford: Blackwell.

—— (1997) 'Traduction/Trahison – Notes on ANT.' *Actor Network Resource*. http://www.comp.lancs.ac.uk/sociology/stslaw2.html, Department of Sociology, Lancaster University. (Internet document, accessed April 2000.)

Lea, D. (1969) 'Some non-nutritive functions of food in New Guinea.' In F. Gale and G. H. Lawton (eds), *Settlement and Encounter: Geographical Studies Presented to Sir Grenfell Price*. Melbourne: Oxford University Press, pp. 173–184.

Lederman, R. (1986) *What Gifts Engender: Social Relations and Politics in Mendi, Highland Papua New Guinea*. Cambridge and New York: Cambridge University Press.

Lenin, V. I. (1956) *The Development of Capitalism in Russia: The Process of the Formation of a Home Market for Large-scale Industry*. Moscow: Foreign Languages Publishing House.

Levantis, T. (1997) 'Urban unemployent in Papua New Guinea – it's criminal'. *Pacific Economic Bulletin* 12(2), pp. 73–84.

—— and J. Livernois (1998) 'Taking a piece of the pie: Papua New Guinea's log exports and optimal taxation.' *Pacific Economic Bulletin* 13(2), pp. 99–116.

REFERENCES

Levett, M. P. (1992) 'Urban gardening in Port Moresby: a survey of the suburb of Gerehu.' *Yagl–Ambu* 16(3), pp. 47–68.

—— and M. Uvano (1992) 'Urban gardening in Port Moresby: a survey of the suburbs of Morata and Waigani.' *Yagl–Ambu* 16(3), pp. 69–91.

——, J. Earland, and P. Heywood (eds) (1992) *Changes in Food and Nutrition in Papua New Guinea: Proceedings of the First Papua New Guinea Food and Nutrition Conference*. Port Moresby: University of Papua New Guinea Press and Department of Agriculture and Livestock.

Levine, H. B. and M. W. Levine (1979) *Urbanization in Papua New Guinea: A Study of Ambivalent Townsmen*. Cambridge: Cambridge University Press.

Lewis, M. (1992) *Wagering the Land: Ritual, Capital and Environmental Degradation in the Cordillera of Northern Luzon, 1900–1986*. Berkeley: University of California Press.

Lewis Jr, D. E. (1988) 'Gustatory subversion and the evolution of nutritional dependency in Kiribati.' *Food and Foodways* 3(1), pp. 79–98.

Lincoln International (1994) *PNG: Project Design for Phase 2 of the Fresh Produce Development Company Project*. (Draft Report, July 1994.)

Lipton, M. (1977) *Why Poor People Stay Poor: A Study of Urban Bias in World Development*. Cambridge, MA: Harvard University Press.

Lockie, S. and S. Kitto (2000) 'Beyond the farm gate: production–consumption networks and agri-food research.' *Sociologia Ruralis* 40(1), pp. 3–19.

Lockwood, V. S., T. G. Harding, and B. J. Wallace (eds) (1993) *Contemporary Pacific Societies: Studies in Development and Change*. Englewood Cliffs: Prentice Hall.

Löffler, E. (1977) *Geomorphology of Papua New Guinea*. Canberra: Commonwealth Scientific and Industrial Research Organization.

Long, A. (1992) 'Goods, knowledge and beer: the methodological significance of situational analysis and discourse.' In Long and Long (eds) (1992), pp. 147–170.

Long, N. (1986) 'Commoditization: thesis and antithesis.' In Long, van der Ploeg, Curtin and Box (eds) (1986), pp. 8–23.

—— (1989a) 'Conclusion: theoretical reflections on actor, structure and interface.' In N. Long (ed.) (1989b), pp. 221–243.

—— (ed.) (1989b) *Encounters at the Interface: A Perspective on Social Discontinuities in Rural Development*. Wageningen: Landbouwuniversiteit Wageningen.

—— (1992) 'From paradigm lost to paradigm regained? The case for an actor-oriented sociology of development.' In Long and Long (1992), pp. 16–43.

—— (1996) 'Globalization and localization: new challenges to rural research.' In H. L. Moore (ed.), *The Future of Anthropological Knowledge*. London and New York: Routledge, pp. 16–43.

—— and A. Long (eds) (1992) *Battlefields of Knowledge: The Interlocking of Theory and Practice in Social Research and Development*. London: Routledge.

—— and J. D. van der Ploeg (1994) 'Heterogeneity, actor and structure: towards a reconstitution of the concept of structure.' In Booth (ed.) (1994b), pp. 62–89.

—— and M. Villarreal (1993) 'Exploring development interfaces: from the transfer of knowledge to the transformation of meaning.' In F. J. Schuurman (ed.) (1993), pp. 140–168.

——, J. D. van der Ploeg, C. Curtin, and L. Box (eds) (1986) *The Commoditization Debate: Labour Process, Strategy and Social Network*. Wageningen: Agricultural University Wageningen.

Longmire, J. (1994) 'Marketing systems for agriculture: diagnosing problems and price and market analysis for Papua New Guinea.' *Papua New Guinea Journal of Agriculture, Forestry and Fisheries* 37(1), pp. 117–132.

Lubasz, H. (1992) 'Adam Smith and the invisible hand – of the market?' In Dilley (1992b), pp. 37–56.
Maclean, N. L. (1989) 'The commoditization of food: an analysis of a Maring market.' *Canberra Anthropology* 12(1–2), pp. 74–98.
MACMIN 2000: *Crater Mountain Project.* http://www.macmin.com.au/Crater.html. MACMIN N.L. (Internet document, accessed April 2000.)
MacWilliam, S. (1988) 'Smallholdings, land law and the politics of land tenure in Papua New Guinea.' *Journal of Peasant Studies* 16(1), pp. 77–109.
—— (1996) '"Just like working for the dole": rural households, export crops and state subsidies in Papua New Guinea.' *Journal of Peasant Studies* 23(4), pp. 40–78.
Mahoney, C. (1980) 'Marketing patterns in Port Moresby and Lae.' In R. Jackson, J. Odongo, and P. Batho (eds), *Urbanization and its Problems in Papua New Guinea – Proceedings of the 1979 Waigani Seminar.* Port Moresby: University of Papua New Guinea, pp. 195–207.
Malinowski, B. (1922) *Argonauts of the Western Pacific.* London: Routledge.
Mann, S. A. and J. M. Dickinson (1978) 'Obstacles to the development of capitalist agriculture.' *Journal of Peasant Studies* 5(4), pp. 466–481.
Marsden, T. (2000) 'Food matters and the matter of food: towards a new food governance?' *Sociologia Ruralis* 40(1), pp. 20–29.
—— and A. Arce (1995) 'Constructing quality: emerging food networks in the rural transition.' *Environment and Planning A* 27, pp. 1261–1279.
Martin, R. (1994) 'Economic theory and human geography.' In Gregory, Martin, and Smith (eds) (1994a), pp. 21–51.
Marx, K. (1960) 'Der Achtzehnte Brumaire des Louis Bonaparte' [The Eighteenth Brumaire of Louis Bonaparte]. *Karl Marx – Politische Schriften* (Erster Band). Stuttgart: Cotta-Verlag, pp. 268–387.
May, R. J. (ed.) (1984) *Social Stratification in Papua New Guinea.* Canberra: Department of Political and Social Change, Research School of Pacific Studies, Australian National University.
McCall, M. (1987) 'Carrying heavier burdens but carrying less weight: some implications of villagization for women in Tanzania.' In Momsen and Townsend (eds) (1987), pp. 192–214.
McCloskey, D. N. (1990) 'Storytelling in economics.' In Lavoie (ed.) (1990a), pp. 61–75.
McKillop, R. F. (1966) 'Changing farming systems in the Goroka Valley, Eastern Highlands District.' *DASF Newsletter* 8(2), pp. 52–56.
—— (1975) 'Catching the didiman.' *Administration for Development* 3, pp. 14–21.
—— (1976) 'A history of agricultural extension in Papua New Guinea.' In G. Dick and B. McKillop (eds), *A Brief History of Agricultural Extension and Education in Papua New Guinea.* Port Moresby: Department of Primary Industry, pp. 4–44.
McMichael, P. (ed.) (1994) *The Global Restructuring of Agro-food Systems.* Ithaca: Cornell University Press.
Miller, B. (1992) 'Collective action and rational choice: place, community, and the limits to individual self-interest.' *Economic Geography* 68(1), pp. 22–42.
Millett, J. (1990) *Private Sector Development in Papua New Guinea.* Port Moresby: Institute of National Affairs.
Mingione, E. (1991) *Fragmented Societies: A Sociology of Economic Life beyond the Market Paradigm.* Oxford and Cambridge, MA: Basil Blackwell.
Modjeska, C. N. (1977) 'Production among the Duna: aspects of agricultural intensification in Central New Guinea.' Canberra: Australian National University. (Unpublished PhD dissertation.)

REFERENCES

Mollok, B. (1989) 'The evolution and growth of Goroka Council from 1963 to 1984.' *Yagl–Ambu* 15(3), pp. 4–17.

Momsen, J. H. and J. Townsend (eds) (1987) *Geography of Gender in the Third World*. London: Hutchinson.

Moran, W., G. Blunden, M. Workman, and A. Bradly (1996) 'Family farmers, real regulation, and the experience of food regimes.' *Journal of Rural Studies* 12(3), pp. 245–258.

Morgan, R. (1992) 'Vegetable production in Telefomin District.' *Fresh Produce News*, 17 April 1992, pp. 2–5.

Moulik, T. K. (1973) *Money, Motivation and Cash Cropping*. Port Moresby: The Australian National University.

Mouzelis, N. (1994) 'The state in late development: historical and comparative perspectives.' In Booth (ed.) (1994b), pp. 126–151.

Munster, P. (1985) *A Short History of Goroka*. Goroka: Papua New Guinea Centennial Committee.

—— (1986) 'A history of contact and change in the Goroka Valley, Central Highlands of New Guinea, 1934–1949' (2 vols). School of Social Sciences, Deakin University. (Unpublished PhD dissertation.)

Murdoch, J. (1995) 'Actor-networks and the evolution of economic forms: combining description and explanation in theories of regulation, flexible specialization, and networks.' *Environment and Planning A* 27(5), pp. 731–757.

—— and T. Marsden (1995) 'The spatialization of politics: local and national actor-spaces in environmental conflict.' *Transactions of the Institute of British Geographers (New Series)* 20, pp. 368–380.

Nalu, M. and R. Palme (1994) 'Bridge crash cuts Lae link highway.' *Post-Courier*, 14 July 1994, pp. 1–2.

National (1995) 'Plea to shift national departments to Arona,' 10 March, p. 7.

Nederveen Pieterse, J. (1995) 'The cultural turn in development: questions of power.' *European Journal of Development Research* 7(1), pp. 176–192.

Nelson, H. (1976) *Black, White and Gold: Goldmining in Papua New Guinea 1878–1930*. Canberra: Australian National University Press.

Neuendorf, A. K. and A. J. Taylor (1977) 'The churches and language policy.' In S. A. Wurm (ed.), *New Guinea Languages and Language Study. Vol. 3: Language, Culture, Society, and the Modern World*. Canberra: Department of Linguistics, Research School of Pacific Studies, Australian National University, pp. 413–428.

Newman, P. L. (1962) 'Supernaturalism and ritual among the Gururumba.' Department of Anthropology, University of Washington. (Unpublished PhD dissertation)

—— (1965) *Knowing the Gururumba*. New York: Holt, Rinehart & Winston.

Nicholls, D. (1973) 'The Lowa Marketing Co-operative Ltd of Goroka.' *Harvest* 2(4), pp. 129–133.

—— (1975) 'The Lowa Marketing Co-operative Limited of Goroka.' In M. W. Ward (ed.), *Change and Development in Rural Melanesia – Papers Delivered at the Fifth Waigani Seminar 1971*. Canberra: University of Papua New Guinea and Research School of Pacific Studies, Australian National University, pp. 173–188.

NSO (1994a) *Report on the 1990 Population and Housing Census in Eastern Highlands Province*. Port Moresby: National Statistical Office.

—— (1994b) *Report on the 1990 Population and Housing Census in Papua New Guinea*. Port Moresby: National Statistical Office.

—— (n.d.) *1990 National Population Census. Final Figures, Census Unit Populations: Eastern Highlands Province*. Port Moresby: National Statistical Office.

Olsen, M. E. and M. N. Marger (eds) (1993) *Power in Modern Societies*. Boulder, CO, and Oxford: Westview Press.

Oram, N. D. (1976) 'Port Moresby.' In Jackson (1976a), pp. 140–172.
Ortiz, S. and S. Lees (eds) (1992), *Understanding Economic Process.* Lanham: Society for Economic Anthropology.
Overfield, D. (1995) 'The economics of social subordination: gender relations and market failure in the highlands of Papua New Guinea.' Leeds: School of Geography, University of Leeds. (Unpublished PhD dissertation.)
Papua New Guinea (1989) *Report of the Commission of Inquiry into Aspects of the Forest Industry (Commissioner Thomas E. Barnett).* Port Moresby: Department of the Prime Minister. (Final report.)
Pile, S. (1993) 'Human agency and human geography revisited: a critique of "new models" of the self.' *Transactions of the Institute of British Geographers* 18, pp. 122–139.
Ploeg, A. (1985a) 'Food imports into Papua New Guinea.' *Bijdragen tot de Taal-, Land- en Volkenkunde* 141(2–3), pp. 303–322.
—— (1985b) 'Little landlessness, but …' In G. N. Appell (ed.), *Modernization and the Emergence of a Landless Peasantry – Essays on the Integration of Peripheries to Socioeconomic Centers.* Williamsburg: Department of Anthropology, College of William and Mary, pp. 371–399.
PNG Forest Authority (1996) *The National Forest Plan for Papua New Guinea.* Port Moresby: The Papua New Guinea Forest Authority.
Polanyi, K. (1944) *The Great Transformation.* New York and Toronto: Rinehart & Co.
—— (1957) 'The economy as instituted process.' In K. Polanyi, C. M. Arensberg, and H. W. Pearson (eds), *Trade and Market in the Early Empires: Economies in History and Theory.* New York: Free Press, pp. 243–270.
Post-Courier (1984a) 'Land owners want royalties.' 16 Feb., p. 9.
—— (1984b) 'Foinda plantation is taken over.' 12 Sept., p. 30.
Potter, R. B. and T. Unwin (eds) (1989), *The Geography of Urban–Rural Interaction in Developing Countries.* London and New York: Routledge.
Pred, A. (1977) 'The choreography of existence: comments on Hägerstrand's time-geography and its usefulness.' *Economic Geography* 53(2), pp. 207–221.
—— (1982) 'Social reproduction and the time-geography of everyday life.' In P. Gould and G. Olsson (eds), *A Search for Common Ground.* London: Pion, pp. 157–186.
—— (1983) 'Structuration and place: on the becoming of sense of place and structure of feeling.' *Journal of the Theory of Social Behaviour* 13(1), pp. 45–68.
—— (1984) 'Place as historically contingent process: structuration and the time-geography of becoming places.' *Annals of the Association of American Geographers* 74(2), pp. 279–297.
Radford, R. (1987) *Highlanders and Foreigners in the Upper Ramu: The Kainantu Area 1919–1942.* Melbourne: Melbourne University Press.
Rahnema, M. and V. Bawtree (eds) (1997) *The Post-Development Reader.* London: Zed Books.
Rappaport, R. A. (1968) *Pigs for the Ancestors: Ritual Ecology of a New Guinea People.* New Haven: Yale University Press.
Read, D. (1969) 'Goroka Patrol Report No. 1 of 1969/70.' Goroka: Department of District Administration. (Unpublished report.)
Read, K. E. (1951) 'The Gahuku–Gama of the Central Highlands.' *South Pacific* 5(8), pp. 154–164.
—— (1952) 'Land in the Central Highlands.' *South Pacific* 6(7), pp. 440–449, 465.
—— (1954) 'Cultures of the Central Highlands, New Guinea.' *Southwestern Journal of Anthropology* 10(1), pp. 1–43.

REFERENCES

—— (1965) *The High Valley*. New York: Scribner.
Reilly, B. (1999) 'Party politics in Papua New Guinea: a deviant case?' *Pacific Affairs* 72(2), pp. 225–246.
Roa, J. R., H. A.-Francisco, A. M. del Mundo, E. D. Garzon, and R. P. Mula (1991) 'Marketing sweet potatoes in the Philippines.' In *Sweet Potato Cultures of Asia and South Pacific – Proceedings of the 2nd Annual UPWARD International Conference*. Los Banos: UPWARD, pp. 317–360.
Romco, M. with E. Gebesmair (1992) 'A story from a successful highlands kaukau trader.' *Fresh Produce News*, 26 June 1992, pp. 1–3.
Rondinelli, D. A. and H. Evans (1983) 'Integrated regional development planning: linking urban centres and rural areas in Bolivia.' *World Development* 11(1), pp. 31–53.
—— and K. Ruddle (1978) *Urbanization and Rural Development: A Spatial Policy for Equitable Growth*. New York: Praeger Publishers.
Rose, C. (1987) 'The problem of reference and geographic structuration.' *Environment and Planning D: Society and Space* 5(1), pp. 93–106.
Rumint, C. (1987) 'Women, banking and business.' In Stratigos and Hughes (eds) (1987), pp. 96–99.
Sachs, W. (ed.) (1992) *The Development Dictionary: A Guide to Knowledge as Power*. London: Zed Books.
Sahlins, M. D. (1972) *Stone Age Economics*. Chicago: Aldine–Atherton.
Salisbury, R. F. (1962) *From Stone to Steel: Economic Consequences of a Technological Change in New Guinea*. Melbourne: Melbourne University Press.
Schiel, T. (1994) 'The trader's dilemma: the perspective of the *longue durée*.' In Evers and Schrader (eds) (1994), pp. 15–26.
Schindler, A. J. (1952) 'Land use by natives of Aiyura Village, Central Highlands, New Guinea.' *South Pacific* 6(2), pp. 302–307.
Schrader, H. (1994a) 'The discussion of trade in social science.' In Evers and Schrader (eds) (1994), pp. 27–47.
—— (1994b) *Zum Verhältnis von Markt und Moral in westlichen und nichtwestlichen Gesellschaften* [On the Relationship between Market and Morality in Western and non-Western Societies]. Bielefeld: Universität Bielefeld, Fakultät für Soziologie, Forschungsschwerpunkt Entwicklungs-soziologie. (Working Paper No. 217.)
—— (1995) *Zur Relevanz von Polanyis Konzept der Einbettung der Wirtschaft in die Gesellschaft* [On the Relevance of Polanyi's Concept of Embeddedness of the Economy in Society]. Bielefeld: Universität Bielefeld, Fakultät für Soziologie, Forschungsschwerpunkt Entwiklungs-soziologie. (Working Paper No. 219.)
—— (1996) *Globalisation, (de)civilisation and morality*. Bielefeld: Universität Bielefeld, Fakultät für Soziologie, Forschungsschwerpunkt Entwiklungs-soziologie. (Working Paper No. 242.)
Schuurman, F. J. (ed.) (1993) *Beyond the Impasse: New Directions in Development Theory*. London and New Jersey: Zed Books.
Scott, J. C. (1976) *The Moral Economy of the Peasant: Rebellion and Subsistence in Southeast Asia*. New Haven and London: Yale University Press.
—— (1985) *Weapons of the Weak: Everyday Forms of Peasant Resistance*. New Haven and London: Yale University Press.
Scott, K. J. and G. A. Atkinson (1989) *Transport of Vegetables in Papua New Guinea*. Canberra: Australian Centre for International Agricultural Research.
Seib, R. (1994) *Papua–Neuguinea Zwischen Isolierter Stammesgesellschaft und Weltwirtschaftlicher Integration* [Papua New Guinea between Isolated Tribal Society and Integration into the World Economy]. Hamburg: Institut für Asienkunde.

Sexton, L. (1986) *Mothers of Money, Daughters of Coffee: The Wok Meri Movement.* Ann Arbor: UMI Research Press.

—— (1993) 'Pigs, pearlshells, and "women's work": Collective response to change in highland Papua New Guinea.' In Lockwood, Harding, and Wallace (eds) (1993), pp. 117–135.

Shand, R. T. (1966) 'Trade prospects for the rural sector.' In E. K. Fisk (ed.), *New Guinea on the Threshold: Aspects of Social, Political and Economic Development.* Canberra: Australian National University Press, pp. 80–102.

—— and W. Straatmans (1974) *Transition from Subsistence: Cash Crop Development in Papua New Guinea.* Port Moresby and Canberra: Australian National University.

Sillitoe, P. (1996): *A Place against Time: Land and Environment in the Papua New Guinea Highlands.* Amsterdam: Harwood Academic Publishers.

Simonsen, K. (1991) 'Towards an understanding of the contextuality of mode of life.' *Environment and Planning D: Society and Space* 9(4), pp. 417–431.

Sinclair, J. (1995) *The Money Tree: Coffee in Papua New Guinea.* Bathurst: Crawford House Publishing.

Skeldon, R. (1982) 'Recent urban growth in Papua New Guinea.' In *Population of Papua New Guinea.* New York and Noumea: United Nations and South Pacific Commission, pp. 101–116.

—— (1987) 'Some methodological aspects of census enumeration in Papua New Guinea.' In T. M. McDevitt (ed.), *The Survey under Difficult Conditions: Population Data Collection and Analysis in Papua New Guinea.* New Haven: Human Relations Area Files, pp. 29–43.

Slater, D. (1992) 'Theories of development and politics of the post-modern – exploring a border zone.' *Development and Change* 23(3), pp. 283–319.

Smith, A. (1900) *An Inquiry into the Nature and Causes of the Wealth of Nations (Book I).* Melbourne, Sydney and Adelaide: E. W. Cole.

Smith, C. A. (1976) 'Regional economic systems: linking geographical models and socioeconomic problems.' In C. A. Smith (ed.), *Regional Analysis – Vol. 1: Economic Systems.* New York: Academic Press, pp. 3–63.

Smith, R. H. T. (ed.) (1978) *Marketplace Trade – Periodic Markets, Hawkers, and Traders in Africa, Asia and Latin America.* Vancouver: Centre for Transportation Studies, University of British Columbia.

Sorenson, E. R. and D. C. Gajdusek (1969) 'Nutrition in the Kuru region – I. Gardening, food handling, and diet of the Fore people.' *Acta Tropica* 26(4), pp. 281–345.

South Pacific Economic and Social Database (1995) 'Statistical annex.' *Pacific Economic Bulletin* 10(1), pp. 101–138.

Spate, O. H. K., C. S. Belshaw, and T. W. Swan (1953) 'Some problems of development in Papua New Guinea.' Canberra: Australian National University. (Report of a Working Committee of the Australian National University.)

Spencer, T. and P. Heywood (1983) 'Staple foods in Papua New Guinea: their relative supply in urban areas.' *Food and Nutrition Bulletin* 5(3), pp. 40–46.

Spiro, H. M. (1987) 'Women farmers and traders in Oyo state, Nigeria – a case study of their changing roles.' In Momsen and Townsend (eds) (1987), pp. 173–191.

Standish, W. (1984) 'Big men and small: Simbu politics in the 1970s.' In J. May (ed.) (1984), pp. 256–295.

—— (1992) 'Simbu paths to power: political change and cultural continuity in the Papua New Guinea highlands.' Canberra: Department of Political and Social Change, Australian National University. (Unpublished PhD dissertation.)

REFERENCES

Stapleton, G. (1997) *Plantation Cost of Production Survey 1995.* Goroka: Coffee Industry Corporation Ltd. (Coffee Discussion Paper No. 19.)

Storper, M. (1985) 'The spatial and temporal constitution of social action: a critical reading of Giddens.' *Environment and Planning D: Society and Space* 3, pp. 407–424.

Strathern, A. (1971) *The Rope of Moka: Big-men and Ceremonial Exchange in Mount Hagen, New Guinea.* Cambridge: Cambridge University Press.

Strathern, M. (1988) *The Gender of the Gift: Problems with Women and Problems with Society in Melanesia.* Berkeley, Los Angeles and London: University of California Press.

Stratigos, S. and P. J. Hughes (eds) (1987) *The Ethics of Development: Women as Unequal Partners in Development.* Port Moresby: University of Papua New Guinea Press.

Thomas, G. S. (1982) 'Review of the prospects for food processing in Papua New Guinea.' In Bourke and Kesavan (eds) (1982), Vol. 2, pp. 408–420.

Thomas, N. (1991) *Entangled Objects: Exchange, Material Culture, and Colonialism in the Pacific.* Cambridge, MA: Harvard University Press.

Thompson, H. (1986) 'Subsistence agriculture in Papua New Guinea.' *Journal of Rural Studies* 2(3), pp. 233–243.

—— (1987) 'Theorizing simple commodity production in Papua New Guinea.' *Journal of Contemporary Asia* 17(4), pp. 436–455.

—— (1993) 'Papua New Guinean rainforests: problems, solutions and questions.' *Sustainable Development* 1(1), pp. 64–71.

—— and S. MacWilliam (1992) *The Political Economy of Papua New Guinea: Critical Essays.* Manila: Journal of Contemporary Asia Publishers.

The Land Management Project (2000) http://rspas.anu.edu.au/lmp/, The Land Management Project, Research School of Pacific and Asian Studies, The Australian National University. (Internet document, accessed September 2000.)

Thrift, N. J. (1983) 'On the determination of social action in space and time.' *Environment and Planning D: Society and Space* 1(1), pp. 23–58.

—— (1993) 'The arts of the living, the beauty of the dead: anxieties of being in the work of Anthony Giddens.' *Progress in Human Geography* 17(1), pp. 111–121.

—— (1996) *Spatial Formations.* London, Thousand Oaks and New Delhi: Sage Publications.

Tickell, A. and J. Peck (1992) 'Accumulation, regulation and the geographies of post-Fordism: missing links in regulationist research.' *Progress in Human Geography* 16(2), pp. 190–218.

Times of Papua New Guinea (1990) 'Elcom says Arona demands absurd.' 7 June, p. 18.

Trenchard, E. (1987) 'Rural women's work in sub-Saharan Africa and the implications for nutrition.' In Momsen and Townsend (eds) (1987), pp. 153–172.

Turner, M. M. (1984) 'Problems of social class analysis in Papua New Guinea.' In May (ed.) (1984), pp. 55–62.

Unwin, T. (1989) 'Urban–rural interaction in developing countries: a theoretical perspective.' In Potter and Unwin (eds) (1989), pp. 11–32.

van der Ploeg, J. D. (1989) 'Knowledge systems, metaphor and interface: the case of potatoes in the Peruvian highlands.' In N. Long (ed.) (1984), pp. 145–164.

van Donge, J. K. (1992) 'Waluguru traders in Dar Es Salaam: an analysis of the social construction of economic life.' *African Affairs* 91(363), pp. 181–205.

Vandenberg, J. (1969) 'Goroka Patrol Report No. 13 of 1968/69.' Goroka: Department of District Administration. (Unpublished report.)

Vandergeest, P. (1988) 'Commercialization and commoditization: a dialogue between perspectives.' *Sociologia Ruralis* 28(1), pp. 7–29.

Verschoor, G. (1992) 'Identity, networks and space: new dimensions in the study of small-scale enterprise and commoditization.' In Long and Long (eds) (1992), pp. 171–188.

Villareal, R. L. and T. D. Griggs (eds) (1982) *Sweet Potato – Proceedings of the First International Symposium.* Tainan: Asian Vegetable Research and Development Center.

Villarreal, M. (1992) 'The poverty of practice: power, gender and intervention from an actor-oriented perspective.' In Long and Long (eds) (1992), pp. 247–267.

von Fleckenstein, F. (1975) 'Observations on coffee marketing in the Eastern Highlands.' *Yagl–Ambu* 2(2), pp. 116–132.

—— (1976) 'Sweet potato in the Goroka market, a Melanesian market?' In Wilson and Bourke (1976), pp. 351–364.

—— (1978) *Dooryard Food Gardens in Port Moresby: an Original Study of Morata together with a Comparison of Other Studies, Past and Present.* Port Moresby: Department of Economics, University of Papua New Guinea. (Occasional paper.)

Waddell, E. (1972) *The Mound Builders: Agricultural Practices, Environment, and Society in the Central Highlands of New Guinea.* Seattle and London: University of Washington Press.

Wagner, H. and H. Reiner (eds) (1987) *The Lutheran Church in Papua New Guinea: The First Hundred Years 1886–1996.* Adelaide: Lutheran Publishing House.

Walker, R. (1988) 'The geographical organization of production-systems.' *Environment and Planning D: Society and Space* 6(4), pp. 377–408.

Ward, R. G. (1974) 'The new New Guinea: constraints and opportunities.' *Australian Geographer* 12(6), pp. 497–509.

—— (1990) 'Contract labour recruitment from the highlands of Papua New Guinea, 1950–1974.' *International Migration Review* 24(2), pp. 273–296.

—— and E. Kingdon (eds) (1995) *Land, Custom and Practice in the South Pacific.* Cambridge: Cambridge University Press.

—— and M. W. Ward (1980) 'The rural–urban connection – A missing link in Melanesia.' *Malaysian Journal of Tropical Geography* 1, pp. 57–63.

——, N. Clark, D. Howlett, C. C. Kissling, and H. C. Weinand (1974a) *Growth Centres and Area Improvement in the Eastern Highlands District.* Canberra: Department of Human Geography, Research School of Pacific Studies, Australian National University. (Report to the Central Planning Office, Papua New Guinea, February 1974.)

——, D. Howlett, C. C. Kissling, and H. C. Weinand (1974b) *Maket Raun Pilot Project – Feasibility Study.* Canberra: Department of Human Geography, Research School of Pacific Studies, Australian National University. (Report to the Central Planning Office, Papua New Guinea, July 1974.)

Watson, J. B. (1965) 'The significance of a recent ecological change in the central highlands of New Guinea.' *Journal of the Polynesian Society* 74(4), pp. 438–450.

—— (1967) 'Horticultural traditions of the Eastern New Guinea highlands.' *Oceania* 38(2), pp. 81–98.

—— (1977) 'Pigs, fodder, and the Jones effect in postipomoean New Guinea.' *Ethnology* 16(1), pp. 57–70.

Watts, M. J. (1993) 'Development II: the privatization of everything?' *Progress in Human Geography* 18(3), pp. 371–384.

Williams, H. L. (1951) 'Goroka Patrol Report No. 7 of 1950/51.' Goroka: Department of District Administration. (Unpublished report.)

REFERENCES

Wilson, D. (1995) 'Excavating the dialectic of blindness and insight: Anthony Giddens' structuration theory.' *Political Geography* 14(3), pp. 309–318.

Wilson, K. and R. M. Bourke (eds) (1976) *1975 Papua New Guinea Food Crops Conference Proceedings*. Port Moresby: Department of Primary Industry.

Wohlt, P. B. (1978) 'Ecology, agriculture and social organization: the dynamics of group composition in the highlands of Papua New Guinea.' Department of Anthropology, University of Minnesota. (Unpublished PhD dissertation.)

Woolfe, J. A. (1992) *Sweet Potato: An Untapped Food Resource*. Cambridge: Cambridge University Press.

World Bank (1988) *Papua New Guinea Agricultural Assessment Review – Vol. II: Annexes*. The World Bank, Asia Regional Office. (Report, 18 February 1988.)

—— (1994) World Development Report. New York: Oxford University Press.

Yen, D. E. (1982) 'Sweet potato in historical perspective.' In Villareal and Griggs (eds) (1982), pp. 17–30.

—— (1991) 'The social impact of sweet potato introduction in Asia and the Pacific.' In *Sweet Potato Cultures of Asia and South Pacific – Proceedings of the 2nd Annual UPWARD International Conference*. Los Banos: UPWARD, pp. 18–27.

Zimmer-Tamakoshi, L. (1997) 'The last big man: development and men's discontents in the Papua New Guinea highlands'. *Oceania* 68(2), pp. 107–122.

Zinkel, C. (1970) 'I want to be a farmer.' *Journal of the Papua and New Guinea Society* 4(2), pp. 65–8.

Zorn, J. G. (1992) '*Graun bilong mipela*: local land courts and the changing customary law of Papua New Guinea.' *Pacific Studies* 15(2), pp. 1–38.

Index

accessibility, 103, 109–110, 111
actants, 50
action: as decision-making, 46; communicative, 47; portfolio model of, 46
actor-network theory, 19, 50, 270–271, 273
actor-oriented approach, 4–5, 17, 29–30, 34, 44–50, 49, 268, 273
actors, 3, 4, 5, 22, 174, 210, 220, 268; in PNG marketplaces, 140–148; non-human entities as, 50; rational 46, *52*; *see also* actor-oriented approach
adoption of children, 68, 76, 78
age groups, *185*
agency, *see* action
agency, see action
Agricultural Bank, 244
agrodiversity, 239, 248
agro-food complex, 269
aid, 82
air travel, 212, 214, 217
Aladuka, 73, 74, 248
alcohol, 105, 111, 145, 147, 200, 231, *see also* beer
Alele, 122, *150*
Amaizuho, 13, 73, *185*, 228
Ambilisezuho, 13, 55, 229
Anasi, 127
Anengu, 206, 207
ANGCO, 207
Aporota, 230, 231, 243, *265*
Areca catechu, see *buai*
Areca macrocalyx, see *kavivi*
army farms, 125
Arona Valley, *115*; climate, 224; Development Authority, 146

Asaro River, 12, *20*, *184*
Asaro, 9, 11, 145, 178; marketplace at, 145–147; kaukau prices at, 194–196; Simbu migrants in, 198
Asaro–Watabung: Local Government Council, 11, 59, 145, 167, 168, *264*; Rural Development Corporation (AWRDC), 166–169; Rural Development Trust (AWRDT), 167
Asaroka: Bible School, 56; Lutheran High School, 56, 68, 72; mission station, *79*, 126, 159, 229, 230
Associated Distributors Freezer,127, 132, 134–135, 136
autonomy of rural people, 39, 40, 232

bananas, 226, 249; and gender, 158, 197, 253; as gifts, 14, *158*; as a staple, 103, 104, 105, 155; starchy, 251
Baptist religion, 76
barter exchange, 23, *51*, 124, 159
bean, 248, 250
beer, 96, 100
Bena Bena, 38, 92, 142, 162, 163, 230, *264*; army farms in, 125; seasonality of rainfall, 224; tomato growing in, 129
Bena Bena River, *20*
Bena Development Corporation, 167
betel nut, see *buai*
bigman, 35, 37, 39, *52*, 55, 68, 150, 152; and polygamy, 228–229
big peasants, 35–37, 46, 148, 160, 166, 167, 174
Bihute, 248
birth rates, 257
Bougainville, 84, 155
bourgeoisie, 30

INDEX

buai, 33, 108, *116*; consumption of, 209; trading of, 61, 91, *117*, 141, 151, *222*;
Bukaua, 112
Bulolo, 96, 162
bureaucratization, 50
business groups, 75–76

cabbage, 189–190
cane grass, 226, 247, 260
carrot, 129, 131, 132,133, 135, 253, 256
cash crops, 105–108
cassava, 104, 249
Casuarina, 12, 156; *oligodon*, 243
Catholic Church, 124
cattle projects, 35, 37, 39, 43, 250
chicken projects, 111, *117*, 256
Chinese taro, see *Xanthosoma*
Chuave, 204
class analysis, *see* political economy, social differentiation
cocoa, 108
coconut, 104, 108, 112; in Goroka Market, 142
Coffee Industry Corporation, 94, 108, 245
coffee, 105, 107–108, 240–245; and big peasants, 35–37; and intercropping, 249, 250; and land use, 243; buyers, 173, 175, 207; labour demands, 190, 244; processing, 67, 173, 241, 245, *264*; regions where grown, 105, 107, *116*; smallholder, *184*, 243–245
coffee plantations: as early markets for kaukau, 160, 161; establishment of, 159, 160, 240, 242; ownership of, 241
Collins & Leahy, 92, 93, 94, 147, *150*, 176
Colocasia esculenta, see taro
commoditization, 3, 4, 5, 30–34, 41, 50; in rural PNG, 36, 38–39, 78
commodity stabilization funds, 39, 108
compensation, 182, 245, 246
composting, 156, 260
Consort Express Lines, 210–212, *221*
Consumer Price Index (CPI), 191–193, *221*
consumption, 33; *see also* food consumption

cooking methods, *222*
Cordyline fructicosa, 249, see also *tanget*
costs 196–197; *see also* transport costs
Crater Mountain, *115*
crime, 96, 136, 199, 204, 205, 211
crops: introduced, 8, 137, 190, 248; traditional, 8, 233–234, 248, 250, *see also individual crops*
cultural capital, 183
cultural ecology, 43

Daulo Pass, 142
Daulo, 42
death rates, 257
Department of Agriculture and Livestock (DAL), 124, 126, 138, 148, 163
Department of Agriculture, Stock and Fisheries (DASF), 162–165, 243
Department of Primary Industry (DPI), 63, 191
development corporations, 167
development theory, 267, 272–273
direct bulk selling, 118, 136–138
distance, effects on kaukau prices, 194
drought, 223

E&M Transport, 207
East–West Transport, 176–178
Eastern Highlands Capital Authority, 11, 143–144
Eastern Highlands Provincial Government, 256
ecology, 223, 224; *see also* cultural ecology; political ecology
economics, 4, 153; institutional, 28, *52*; neoclassical, 27, 30, 35, *52*, 183, 267
economy of affection, 25
Enga, 84
elections, 59, 76, 181, 216
Electoral Development Funds, 98
embeddedness, 25–30, *52*, 118, 123, 223, 266, 268
entrepreneurship, 35, 37, 172–172, 206–208
epistemology, 28
eucalyptus, 243
Evangelical Brothers' Church (EBC), 12, 67
exchange rates, *21*

303

fallows, 175, 224, 232, 249, 250, *264*; planting with *Casuarina*, 156
farmer training programme, 163–165, 172
feasting, 111, 247, *see also* gift exchange
fences, 256
fern, 226
fertilizer, 256
firewood, 243
fish: fresh, 101; tinned, 94, 111, *116*, 120
Foinda, 162, 167, 168, 173, 174, 175
Fondiwe'i, *264*
food bar, 132, 136, 137; *see also haus kaikai, kaibar*
food consumption: of expatriates, 119–120; meat, 111, *117*; rural, 110–111; urban, 100–102
food imports, 96, 121–122
Food Marketing Corporation, 121, 123, 126, 134, 166, 170
food regimes, 269
food shortages, 193; *see also* drought
Fore, *115*, *150*
forest: use value of, 226, 243
formal food market, 118, 148, see also wholesale trading
fostering, *see* adoption of children
freight charges, *see* costs, transport
Fresh Produce Development Company, 122–124, 134, *149*, 188, *220*
functionalism, 28, *52*
fundamentalist religion, 145, 146

Gambianggwi, 169
gambling, 39, 60, 67
Gamizuho, 9, 12, 13, 182, 229, 247, 257, 258, *265*
gate fees, 143–145, *see also* costs
gender, 40–43, 216, *221*; and commodity production, 41–42, 160, 176, 200; and gift exchange, 247; and marketplace selling, 141, 142, 143, 146, 197–200; and the formal market, 131; association of crops with, 158, 197; division of labour, 41–42, 158, *222*, 229, 246, 252–253, 256
gift economy, 246
gift exchange, 13–14; as part of everyday life, 15, *21*; *beksaitbun*, 14, 246; brideprice, 14, 246; *nuspes*, 14, *21*, 246, 247; post-funeral, 61, 246, 247, 248; use of money in, 14; *see also* reciprocity
Gifukoni, 13
globalization, 268
Gohikezuho, 13, 229
Goilala, 112, 219
gold, *see* mining
Gonobozuho, 13
Gordons Market, 98, 139, 180, 212–213
Goroka, 11, 92–95; history of, 92, 159; kaukau prices in, 191–197; marketing of *buai* in, *151*, *222*; settlements in, 92, 94; urban landscape of, 93–94; vegetable wholesalers in, 124–136
Goroka Local Government Council, 11, 141, 143–145
Goroka Market, 139, 141–145
Gouna Development Corporation, 167, 240–241
Government Fresh Food Project, 121
grading, 134
Gross Domestic Product, 83, 84
Gulehezuho, 13
Gururumba, 229

haus kaikai, 137; *see also* food bar, *kaibar*
hauslain, 12, 230–231
herbicide, 244, 255
hermeneutics, 8
Highlands Agricultural Experiment Station, 56, 165, *265*
Highlands Farmers' and Settlers' Organization, *184*
Highlands Highway, *see* Okuk Highway
Highlands Labour Scheme, 159
hired labour, 37, *221*, 253, 255
house types, 224, 231
Hoveku Farms, 127
Hunguko Coffee, 67, 173, 174, 240, 241–243

identity, 48
Imperata cylindrica, see *kunai*
import quotas, 121–122
import substitution, 120
indigenous knowledge, 251

INDEX

individualism, 61
informal food markets, 118, 138–148, 149; *see also* marketplaces
informal sector, 91, 219
intensification, 248–250, 256, 258–260
intercropping, 232, 249
interface, 50, 119, 134, 136, 211
Ipomoea batatas, see kaukau
Ipomoean revolution, 8, 155–157

Kabiufa Adventist High School, 127
kaibar, 204; *see also* food bar, *haus kaikai*
Kainantu, 127, *221*, 264; kaukau prices in, 194, 195
Kamaliki Vocational Training Centre, 163–164, 172
Kami, 229
Kanosa, 168–169
karuka, 226, 262
Kasena: description of village, 9, 12; establishment of village, 230; kaukau prices in, 194, 195; Lutheran church in, 230; social organization in, 12–15; tradestores in, 147, *152*; *see also* Lunube
kaukau, 5, 8, 23; and coffee production, 191; and land use, 249; and social change, 156; as staple, 104; cultivars, 156, 250–252, 259; cultural valuation of, 158, 182, *184*; early commoditization of, 158–165; in coffee gardens, 250; interregional trade in, 41–42, 171–183, 188–191; nutritional value of, 157, *184*; price competition with rice, 171, 172; processing of, 169–170; retail price of, 191–193; rural consumption of, 110; seasonality of commercial plantings, 190; shipments to Port Moresby, 189–191; storage of, 158, *184*; success of in the PNG highlands, 155–157; urban consumption of, 101; worldwide history of, 154; yields, 155, 258–259
Kavieng, 217
kavivi, *116*
Kenemba, 206, 230
Keremu–Anengu, *152*, *265*
kiap, 9, 12, 228
Kofena, 162, 168, *185*, 259; warfare at, 60, *80*, 169

Kofika, 229
Koki Market, 138, 139, *151*
Korofeigu, 163, 172
kunai, 175, *185*, *223*, 224, 228, 230, 236, 240, 243; scarcity of, 250
Kutubu, 84, 96, 209

Lae, 84, 95–97; ethnic tension in, 96–97; kaukau prices in, 191–193, 195–197; marketing of highlands *kaukau* in, 173, 175, 188; settlements in, 96–97
Lae Market, local suppliers, 112, *220*
Land Court, 261
land degradation, 43–44, 258; *see also* soil, erosion
land disputes, 44, 260–262
land management, 223, 232–240
Land Management Project, 16, 104, *116*, 257
land ownership, 38–40, 164, 245, 261, 262; marking of boundaries, 249
land shortage, 73–74, 260, 262
language: Dano, 11, *20*; English, 15; Gahuku–Gama, 11; Gimi, 15, 68; Kâte, 56, *79*; Tok Pisin, 15, 16, *19*, 193
leadership, 35
legume rotation, 250
Lembina River, 12, 226, 231, 233
Lindima, 169
local vs. global, 1, 17, 50, 267–268
logging, 86–88; environmental and social impacts of, 87–88; and exports, 25, 83, 87
Lorengau, 218
Lowa Census Division, *150*
Lowa Marketing Cooperative (LMC), 165–166, 168
Lufa, 265; *see also* Lunube, migrants in
Lunube, 12–13; clans residing in, 13; ecological conditions, 224–226; migrants in, 13, 15, 68, *221*, 244, 253, 254; settlement history of, 226–231; smallholder coffee growing in, 230; territory of, 9, 10, 12; Lunube, tobacco growing in, 168
Lunube've, 13, 229, 247
Lunubezuho, 13, 63, 229
Lutheran Church, 11, 12, 56, 67, 68, *79*, 92, 230; *see also* Christianity

305

Madang, 179, 188; kaukau prices in, 195, 197
maize, 249
maket raun, 140
Makiroka, *264*
malaria, 97
manufacturing, 96
marijuana, 205
marita, 262
market as network, 49–50, 220
market exchange: and morality, 25, 29; and politics, 25; as a universal principle, 27, *52*, 79, 119, 183, 273; in Melanesia, 24, *51*, 135
market integration, 193, 219
market surveys, 193–197
market trading, as a specialized activity, 217–219
marketplaces, 27, 138–148, 268, 274; fees, 196; history of in PNG, 138–140; roadside, 145–147, 194, 195; village, 147–148, 194, 195
Marketed Fruit and Vegetables Project, 122–124, 126
Markham Valley, 112, 125, 205
marxist analysis, 30–32, 35–37, 39
mechanization, 256
Mekeo, *222*
Melinis minutiflora, 250, *264*
men's house, 231
methodological individualism, 28, *52*
methodology, 8, 16
migrant labour, 40, *see also* Lunube, migrants in; hired labour
migration, *see* rural-urban migration
mining, 83–86, 95; *see also* Porgera
Miscanthus floridulus, 226, *see also* cane grass
missionaries, *115*, 124, 228
mode of economic integration, 26
mode of production, 2
mode of social regulation, 269
modernization, 2, *52*, 89, 160, 224, 230
Morobe Produce Marketing, 127
Morobe Provincial Government, 96
motor vehicles, 206, 208, *see also* transportation
Mount Hagen, 92, 139, 140
Mumeng, 112

Nahoma, 230, 258

namo cult, 56
National High School, 56, *80*
National Plantation Management Agency, 244
network, *see* actor-network theory, social networks
Nizemuso, 174, 230
nutrition, 110–111

Oenanthe javanica, *see* water dropwort
oil palm, 108
Okapa, *53*, *150*
Okuk Highway, 9, 84, 109, 122, 145, 178, 188; sealing of, 175; everyday life on, 203–205, 208–210
Oligokazuho, 13, 172
Olufonggazuho, 13
Omborda, *80*, 168, 223, *265*
Onguponi, *80*, 182, *185*, 247, 254, *265*
Onguponizuho, 13, *21*, 172, 174
Openga, 180, 181, 216, 230
opportunity cost of labour, 191, 196
Ovia, 56, 60

Pacific Fruits, 126–127
Pacific War, 124–125, 159, 230
pacification, 38, 228
Pagini Transport, 178
Pandanus jiulianetti, see *karuka*
Panguna, 84
Papua New Guinea Institute of Medical Research, 257
Papua New Guinea Resource Information System (PNGRIS), *264*
particularism, 267, 269
partnership, 160, 167, *184*
passion fruit, 125, 126
patriarchy, 32, 40–43, 268
Patrol Officer, *see* kiap
patron-client relationships, 60, 78, 254, 255
peace of the market, *51*
peanut, *116*, 125, 163, 164, 250, 253, 259
peasant studies, 30–32
petroleum, 84; *see also* mining
Phragmites karka, 226, *see also* cane grass
Phytophthora colocasiae, *see* taro blight
piggeries, 61, 217, 248
pigs: and soil erosion, 246; foraging areas of, 224, 226, 247; husbandry of,